JUVENILE JUSTICE

JUVENILE JUSTICE

THE ESSENTIALS

RICHARD LAWRENCE AND MARIO HESSE

St. Cloud State University

Los Angeles | London | New Delhi
Singapore | Washington DC

For information:

SAGE Publications, Inc.
2455 Teller Road
Thousand Oaks, California 91320
E-mail: order@sagepub.com

SAGE Publications India Pvt. Ltd.
B 1/I 1 Mohan Cooperative Industrial Area
Mathura Road, New Delhi 110 044
India

SAGE Publications Ltd.
1 Oliver's Yard
55 City Road
London EC1Y 1SP
United Kingdom

SAGE Publications Asia-Pacific
Pte. Ltd.
33 Pekin Street #02-01
Far East Square
Singapore 048763

Printed in the United States of America

Library of Congress Cataloging-in-Publication Data

Lawrence, Richard, 1944-
Juvenile justice: the essentials/Richard Lawrence, Mario Hesse.
    p. cm.
Includes bibliographical references and index.
ISBN 978-1-4129-7012-9 (pbk.)

 1. Juvenile justice, Administration of—United States. 2. Juvenile delinquents—United States. 3. Juvenile courts—United States. I. Hesse, Mario. II. Title.

HV9104.L335 2010
364.360973—dc22   2009016042

This book is printed on acid-free paper.

09   10   11   12   13   10   9   8   7   6   5   4   3   2   1

Acquisitions Editor:	Jerry Westby
Assistant Editor:	Eve Oettinger
Production Editor:	Brittany Bauhaus
Copy Editor:	Kristin Bergstad
Typesetter:	C&M Digitals (P) Ltd.
Proofreader:	Sue Irwin
Indexer:	Diggs Publication Services, Inc.
Cover Designer:	Gail Buschman
Marketing Manager:	Jennifer Reed Banando

Brief Contents

Detailed Contents

Preface

This textbook is intended to cover the essential topics in juvenile justice in a more brief and concise manner than the larger comprehensive texts on the subject. *Juvenile Justice: The Essentials* presents an overview of the major subject areas in juvenile justice and summarizes the latest research available. The book includes special features to engage the reader in thinking critically about the subjects, with practical examples of cases, juvenile justice in action, laws, policies, and programs in juvenile justice.

The focus of this book is juvenile *justice*, not juvenile *delinquency*. The two topics are integrally related but are not identical. "Delinquency" is a subject of criminology and sociology with a focus on theories and causes of juvenile offending. "Juvenile justice" is a subtopic of criminal justice with a focus on the responses of juvenile justice officials—police, courts, and corrections—to juvenile delinquency. Delinquency and justice are clearly related and overlap in coverage of topics. A study of juvenile justice must begin with an overview of the definitions, extent, and explanations of the causes of juvenile delinquency—topics that are covered in more depth in juvenile delinquency texts. Delinquency prevention and juvenile justice policies and programs are based on beliefs about what causes delinquency. Students and justice professionals must therefore have some understanding of the causes and "correlates" of delinquency. Writing a textbook on the "essentials" of juvenile justice requires some compromises, deciding how much to cover and what topics to cover. This text will *not* provide in-depth coverage and discussion of the theories and explanations of juvenile delinquency. We encourage instructors and students seeking more information on juvenile delinquency to turn to the numerous other textbooks devoted to that topic. Four of the first five chapters in this text do, however, provide an overview of delinquency, criminological theories, and "correlates" of delinquency. The remaining 10 chapters focus on the juvenile justice process. We have worked as practitioners and have done research in the juvenile justice field. We welcome you to join us as we explore the interesting and changing world of juvenile justice.

Organization of the Text

Chapter 1: Defining and Measuring Juvenile Delinquency presents information on how delinquency is defined and viewed according to public perceptions and definitions, criminological research and self-reported delinquent behavior, and judicial definitions of formally adjudicated juveniles. The chapter also provides an overview of the measures of delinquency, the strengths of each measure, and the resulting differences in estimating the extent and seriousness of juvenile offending.

Chapter 2: The History of Juvenile Justice is an overview of the history and development of juvenile justice in America, from the "child-saving" movement to the first juvenile court, federal and state legislative changes, and the changes and trends to adopt more features common to the adult criminal court and hold juvenile offenders more accountable for crimes.

Chapter 3: Causes of Delinquency: Rational Choice and Individual Explanations summarizes the causes of delinquency, ranging from classical and rational choice theories, to those that focus on individual explanations, including biogenetic, biochemical, and psychological explanations. In addition to an overview of the explanations, we provide examples, policies, and practices that are based on the "individual explanations," and conclude the chapter with implications for juvenile justice, laws, and policies.

Chapter 4: Sociological Explanations of Delinquency summarizes the most prominent criminological explanations for juvenile delinquency developed by sociologists, including social structure, subcultures, and social process; labeling and conflict theories; and the developmental, life-course, and integrated theories. In addition to an overview of the explanations, we discuss the relative strengths of each theory, and conclude the chapter with a discussion of how the theories apply to policies and practices in juvenile justice.

Chapter 5: Correlates and Causes of Delinquency discusses the factors that are associated with delinquency; how they are associated; and under what circumstances they may be a cause, a consequence, or simply "go along with" youths' involvement in delinquency. The chapter concludes with a discussion of prevention and intervention programs developed to reduce delinquency and the problems associated with juvenile offending.

Chapter 6: Police and Juveniles highlights the roles of police in preventing delinquency and responding to juvenile offending. We discuss police roles and responsibilities with juvenile offenders, with an emphasis on the community policing function, preventive efforts such as D.A.R.E. and School Resource Officers, issues relating to police discretion, and alternatives to police arrest and custody.

Chapter 7: Due Process and Juveniles' Rights summarizes the similarities and differences between juvenile offenders and adults facing criminal court prosecution. The chapter summarizes U.S. Supreme Court cases involving juveniles' due process rights, including police interrogation, legal counsel, use of preventive detention, standard of evidence for determining guilt, the process for waiver and transfer to criminal court, and statutory changes in juvenile laws.

Chapter 8: Juvenile Detention and Court Intake introduces the post-arrest court intake process for juvenile offenders, the detention decision for youth who pose a risk to the community; assessment of youth risks and needs; and the prosecutorial decision-making process that may result in a petition alleging delinquency, waiver to criminal court, or other nonadjudicatory alternatives.

Chapter 9: Transfer to Criminal Court examines developments in waiver and transfer, legislative changes resulting in statutory exclusion and prosecutorial discretion in many states, and the effects of the widespread practice of juvenile waiver decisions.

Chapter 10: The Juvenile Court Process examines changes in the juvenile court process and the developments that have brought juvenile offenders most of the same due process rights as adults in criminal court. We discuss juvenile court officials and their roles and responsibilities, the adjudication process, dispositional alternatives available to the juvenile court, and juvenile court trends and reforms.

Chapter 11: Juvenile Corrections: Institutional and Residential examines the history and developments of institutional and residential corrections programs for juveniles, the development of boot camps and similar "challenge incarceration" programs, alternative residential programs such as "wilderness camps," research on effectiveness of correctional programs, issues regarding disproportionate minority confinement (DMC), and trends in institutional and residential corrections for juveniles.

Chapter 12: Juvenile Probation and Community Corrections examines the history and development of probation and community corrections programs for juveniles, probation officer roles and responsibilities, correctional counseling and treatment versus control and accountability, probation alternatives and intermediate sanctions, aftercare supervision, the effectiveness of community corrections, and trends in community corrections programs for juveniles.

Chapter 13: Restorative Justice discusses the movement referred to as "balanced and restorative justice" that endeavors to place equal emphasis on the offender, the community, and the victim. The differences between traditional retributive justice and restorative justice are highlighted along with examples and applications of restorative justice, challenges in its implementation, and its effectiveness in meeting goals and objectives.

Chapter 14: The Future of Juvenile Justice summarizes the developments and changes in juvenile justice, factors affecting the future of juvenile justice, evidence that the "get-tough" approach may be waning, and offers perspectives for public health and comprehensive approaches to delinquency prevention that are intended to improve justice for juveniles in the 21st century.

Each chapter includes features that serve as pedagogical and teaching aids:

- Chapter Highlights
- "Case in Point": Scenarios and cases with discussion questions
- "Policy and Practice": Applications and examples with discussion questions

- Bulleted summary points at the end of each chapter
- Key Terms at the end of each chapter
- Discussion questions at the end of each chapter
- Web links and sources at the end of each chapter

Acknowledgments

I have studied and written about juvenile justice for the past 40 years. Nearly 10 of those years were as a juvenile probation officer and a research and training director in a metropolitan juvenile court. During these four decades I have had the privilege of working with and learning from many dedicated juvenile justice professionals, researchers, mentors, and colleagues. I am greatly indebted to many persons, including the late Richard Moreno, Chief Juvenile Probation Officer, and my friends and former colleagues in the Bexar County Juvenile Court in San Antonio. Rolando del Carmen and other professors at the Criminal Justice Center of Sam Houston State University taught me the law, theories, and research that helped me put into perspective and better understand what I experienced in juvenile court, in detention, and in the challenges of supervising juveniles on probation. My former professors at "Sam" and numerous alumni and colleagues continue to provide the kind of intellectual stimulation and continuing desire to "know the truth" and to express it in written, scholarly work. I am indebted to many criminology and criminal justice colleagues I have come to know through annual meetings of the American Society of Criminology and the Academy of Criminal Justice Sciences over the past 30 years. At the risk of omitting some, I want to acknowledge Craig Hemmens, Barry Feld, Peter Benekos, Alida Merlo, Joe Sanborn, Steve Lab, John Whitehead, Donna Bishop, and Frank Zimring among those scholars and writers in juvenile justice who have made exceptional contributions to expanding my own knowledge and insights. I am also grateful to Howard Snyder, Melissa Sickmund, and Charles Puzzanchera for their accessibility and willingness to answer questions about the measures and statistics on juvenile arrests, court cases, and juveniles in corrections.

Administrators and colleagues at St. Cloud State University have provided the kind of academic environment and support that have allowed me to engage in the countless extra hours over the past several years that have enabled me to put in writing what I have shared with students in the classroom. I am especially grateful to my colleague Mario Hesse for his contribution to this book. He provided cases, policies, and practices for many of the chapters, and helped bring to life many of the concepts and issues in juvenile justice.

Several reviewers read the initial chapter manuscripts and offered comments for improving the book. Their suggestions were invaluable in bringing attention to topics that had been inadvertently omitted or not sufficiently emphasized; topics that needed further definition and development; and related suggestions to help get student readers engaged, interested, and involved in the issues and challenges of juvenile justice. I acknowledge and appreciate the time and helpful comments of the reviewers noted below.

I am especially grateful to Jerry Westby, Executive Editor at Sage Publications, who initiated the idea for an "essential text" in Juvenile Justice and offered his encouragement and support during the project and enabled its completion. My thanks also to the excellent editorial staff at Sage Publications, including Eve Oettinger, Karen Ehrmann, Brittany Bauhaus, and Kristin Bergstad. To become an author who produces work that is worth reading requires some personal experience and observations in the field coupled with years of reading and research. Without the assistance of an excellent editorial staff, however, our work would never get into print. Throughout this project, the editorial staff of Sage Publications balanced their "demands for excellence" with excellent editorial support.

My wife Dorothy provides the kind of companionship, support, and balance that makes her the most important person in my life. Despite the interruptions to our relationship and time together that a project like this requires, she understands and supports my passion for reading and writing. No doubt her 34 years as an eighth-grade English teacher accounts for much of that patience. She had a role in molding and encouraging the intellectual and personal development of many young people. I have written this book in the hope that those who read it will some day, in some way, contribute to better justice and a brighter future for all juveniles.

—*Richard Lawrence*

St. Cloud, Minnesota

May, 2009

The authors and SAGE gratefully acknowledge the contributions of the following reviewers:

Lee Ayers, *South Oregon University*

Pierrette Ayotte, *Thomas College*

Earl Ballou, *Palo Alto College*

George Burruss, *Southern Illinois University*

Kimberly DeTardo-Bora, *Marshall University*

J. Price Foster, *University of Louisville*

Kristin Johnson, *University of Florida*

William Kelly, *Auburn University*

Don Peavy, *Canyon College*

Frances P. Reddington, *University of Central Missouri*

Bill Sanders, *California State University, Los Angeles*

Nelseta Walters, *University of Louisville*

Patrick Webb, *University of Houston–Downtown*

About the Authors

Richard Lawrence is Professor Emeritus of Criminal Justice at St. Cloud State University in Minnesota. He holds a PhD in Criminal Justice from Sam Houston State University, an MA in Psychology from St. Mary's University in San Antonio, and a BA in Psychology from Bethel University in St. Paul, Minnesota. He is the author of *School Crime and Juvenile Justice* (two editions); *Juvenile Justice: A Text-Reader* (with co-author Craig Hemmens); and more than 40 articles and chapters in academic journals and books.

Mario Hesse is an Associate Professor at St. Cloud State University. He earned his PhD in Criminal Justice from South Dakota State University, his MS from St. Cloud State University, and his BA from the University of Minnesota, Duluth.

Defining and Measuring Juvenile Delinquency

❖

CHAPTER HIGHLIGHTS

❖ The Extent and Seriousness of Juvenile Delinquency and Victimization
❖ Measures of Juvenile Offending and Victimization

Juvenile crime is a serious problem in the United States and most other nations. A majority of young people admit to engaging in some types of delinquent behavior, though only a small number of youth are ever apprehended by police officers, and even fewer are ever referred to a juvenile court. The majority of crimes committed by juveniles are offenses such as theft and shoplifting, vandalism, drug and alcohol use, disorderly conduct, and simple assaults that include hitting, kicking, and fights that do not result in serious injury. Many youth engage in behavior such as curfew violations, running away, disobeying parents, school truancy, and alcohol violations, referred to as status offenses because they apply only to juvenile-age youth and children, and are not punishable under a state penal code.

In this chapter we examine the range of deviant and delinquent behaviors that may bring children and youth to the attention of law enforcement officials and the juvenile court. The definition of juvenile delinquency varies according to statutory definitions of each state. Most states define a "juvenile" for jurisdictional purposes as a person between the ages of 10 to 18 years of age; although in some states 16- and 17-year-olds may be treated as adults when they have committed a crime. A "delinquent child" is defined generally as a child who has violated any state or local law; a federal law or law of another state; or who has escaped from confinement in a local or state correctional facility. Juveniles are subject to police intervention for a broader range of behaviors than are adults. Juvenile status offenses include alcohol violations (possession of), curfew violations, disobeying parents, running away, and school truancy. Status offenders may be stopped and questioned by police, and returned home to their parents, to school, or to the juvenile court intake officer (explained later in Chapter 8).

Most serious property and personal violent crimes are committed by adult offenders over the age of 18. Considerable attention is directed at delinquent behavior and juvenile offending, however, for at least two reasons. Juvenile-age youth commit a disproportionate number of crimes (compared with their proportion of the population); and delinquency prevention efforts are the first step in reducing crime and violence committed by adult offenders. Criminologists, social scientists, lawmakers, and policymakers have focused their efforts on examining the causes of juvenile crime, and on developing programs and public policies to prevent delinquency and correct juvenile offenders.

The Extent and Seriousness of Juvenile Delinquency and Victimization

Children and youth are victims of theft and violent crimes. Some juveniles are victims of abuse and neglect at the hands of their parents or other caregivers. The term "dependent and neglected children" describes those who are not provided with proper shelter, clothing, food, clean and safe living conditions, and medical needs. Child abuse ranges from verbal abuse to physical and sexual abuse. The extent of child victimization is reported by the National Child Abuse and Neglect Data System (NCANDS) (U.S. Department of Health and Human Services, 2007). Child victimization has been linked to problem behaviors, delinquency, and criminal behavior later in life. An understanding of victimization and juvenile delinquency is therefore important for a better understanding of the most appropriate juvenile justice system responses to these problems. Some highlights from *Juvenile Offenders and Victims: 2006 National Report* (Snyder & Sickmund, 2006) indicate the seriousness and extent of juvenile victimization in the United States:

- On average, between 1980 and 2002 about 2,000 juveniles were murdered annually in the United States.
- In 2002, on average, four juveniles were murdered daily in the United States.
- Children under 6 years of age who were victims of murder were most often killed by a parent.
- Nearly one million (906,000) children were victims of abuse or neglect in 2003, a rate of 12 victims per 1,000 children ages 0–17.

- As juveniles age, they are less likely to be victims of a violent crime by a family member.
- About two thirds of violent crimes with juvenile victims occur in a residence.
- Youth between ages 7 and 17 are about as likely to be victims of suicide as they are to be victims of homicide.
- About half of all violent crimes experienced by male and female students occurred in school or on the way to and from school.
- Many youth are subjected to inappropriate and potentially dangerous experiences on the Internet (Snyder & Sickmund, 2006, pp. 19–52).

Juvenile offending is often perceived to be extensive and serious, despite the fact that most serious property and violent crimes are committed by offenders over 18 years of age. Violent crimes committed by juveniles less than 18 years of age have actually declined in the past several years. Crimes committed by youth are newsworthy events that get a lot of attention from the news media. Violent crimes naturally are reported more often, and get a disproportionate amount of news coverage, so the public often gets a distorted view of the true extent of juvenile crime. Television, radio, and newspapers play an important role in society, informing the public about important events. Citizens depend on the media as a source of information. Most Americans' knowledge and opinions of crime and justice are based on what they see on television and read in the newspapers (Warr, 2000). Research studies have shown that television and the news media present a distorted and exaggerated view of the extent and seriousness of crime, and tend to portray racial minorities as responsible for the majority of crime (Surette, 1998; Dorfman & Schiraldi, 2001). The extensive national television and news media reporting of school shooting incidents presented the false impression that most schools are unsafe and violent places, and that children and youth are more at risk of victimization in schools than elsewhere (Lawrence & Mueller, 2003). In fact, only a small percentage of violent victimization and homicides involving juvenile victims occur in schools. Children and youth are at greater risk of victimization in their own homes and in other parts of their communities. Understanding the true extent and source of juvenile crime and victimization is the first step to responding effectively to the problem.

Homicide tends to receive the most attention in government and news media reports of deaths of children and youth. Deaths by homicide, however, are *not* the most common causes of deaths of children and young people. According to the Centers for Disease Control, the leading cause of death for children and youth is accidents and unintentional injury; homicide ranks fourth for children ages 5–9, fifth for youth ages 10–14, and second for youth and young adults ages 15–19. More youth aged 10–14 were victims of suicide (244) than homicide (202) in the United States in 2003 (Heron & Smith, 2007). The rank and frequency of leading causes of death for young people are reported in Table 1.1. It should be noted that one reason homicide ranks higher as a cause of death among children and youth is because they are less likely to die of "natural" health-related deaths than older people. Other reports have confirmed that suicide is a leading cause of death of young people. Snyder and Sickmund (2006) reported that between 1990 and 2001, suicide was more prevalent than homicide among white juveniles (p. 25). The statistical reports from the Centers for Disease Control and Prevention (2008b) note that

| Table 1.1 | 10 Leading Causes of Death, United States, 2003 (All Races, Both Sexes) |

	Age Groups		
Rank	5–9	10–14	15–19
1	Unintentional injury 1,096	Unintentional injury 1,522	Unintentional injury 6,755
2	Malignant neoplasms 516	Malignant neoplasms 560	Homicide 1,938
3	Congenital anomalies 180	Suicide 244	Suicide 1,487
4	Homicide 122	Congenital anomalies 206	Malignant neoplasms 690
5	Heart disease 104	Homicide 202	Heart disease 393

SOURCE: Adapted from Heron, M. P., & Smith, B. L. (2007). Deaths: Leading causes for 2003. *National Vital Statistics Reports, 55*(10), p. 17.

while homicide is one of the leading causes of death among children and youth, many deaths can be prevented through better education and supervision to prevent accidental deaths and through more comprehensive provision of mental health services for young people. Law enforcement and juvenile justice officials are focusing efforts on reducing the number of homicides and nonfatal victimization of juveniles.

Measures of Juvenile Offending and Victimization

The primary measures of juvenile crime are official measures by police, courts, and corrections; self-report measures; and victimization surveys. *Official crime statistics* are often considered the most accurate measures of crime and are the ones most often reported in the news media and by justice agencies. They are not a precise measure of the true extent of crime, however, because many crimes are not reported to police or other criminal justice agencies. The problem of unreported crime led criminologists to devise other unofficial methods of measuring crime. Self-report measures are confidential questionnaires administered to samples of youth who voluntarily report on their own involvement in delinquent activities, whether or not they were ever caught. Self-reports provide a more complete picture of juvenile delinquency, but are not completely error free since they depend on subjects' honesty and reliability of memory. Victimization surveys are a third measure of crime designed to supplement official statistics and self-report measures. The National Crime Victimization Survey (NCVS)

Most Serious Offense	2005 Juvenile Arrest Estimates	Percentage of Juvenile Arrests		Percentage Change	
		Female	Under Age 15	1996–2005	2001–2005
Drug abuse violations	191,800	17	16	–10	–7
Driving under influence	17,800	22	2	–4	–13
Liquor law violations	126,400	36	9	–20	–13
Drunkenness	15,900	24	12	–39	–21
Disorderly conduct	201,400	32	40	3	14
Curfew and loitering	140,800	30	28	–27	0
Runaways	109,000	58	35	–44	–16

SOURCE: Adapted from Snyder, 2007, p. 3.

Law enforcement agencies arrested an estimated 2.1 million juveniles in 2005. Juveniles (under 18 years of age) accounted for 12% of all violent crime arrests in 2005, including 5% of murders, 11% of forcible rapes, 15% of robberies, and 12% of aggravated assaults; and 26% of all property crime arrests in 2005 (Snyder, 2007, p. 1). The number of arrests of juveniles for murder has been declining since the peak year of 1993 when there were 3,790 juvenile arrests for murder; in 2005 there were 1,260 juvenile arrests for murder, about one third of the number in 1993. Of the estimated 1,650 juveniles murdered in 2005, 36% were under 5 years of age, 71% were male, 50% were white, and 50% were killed with a firearm (Snyder, 2007, p. 1). There was a slight increase (2%) in juvenile arrests for murder from 1,110 in 2004 to 1,260 in 2005. The juvenile arrest rate for simple assault increased slightly, and females accounted for 33% of those arrests (Snyder, 2007).

Juvenile arrests disproportionately involved minorities. The racial composition of the juvenile population in 2005 was 78% white, 17% black, 4% Asian/Pacific Islander, and 1% American Indian. Most Hispanics (an ethnic group, not a race) were classified as white. Of the juvenile arrests for violent crimes in 2005, 48% were white youth, 50% were black youth, and Asian youth and American Indian youth each made up 1%. For property crime arrests, the proportions were 67% white youth, 30% black youth, 2% Asian youth, and 1% American Indian youth. Black youth were overrepresented in juvenile arrests (Snyder, 2007, p. 9).

Self-Report Measures

Criminologists have used self-report studies such as the National Youth Survey to get a more accurate measure of the true extent of delinquency (Elliott, Huizinga, & Ageton, 1985). Self-report surveys provide a more comprehensive measure of delinquency than police reports, but they also have weaknesses. The samples used are relatively small and may not be representative of the population of juvenile offenders, so the results may underreport juvenile crime. Self-report studies are also vulnerable to response errors, as youth may overstate or underreport their offending behavior. Self-report measures do, however, offer an important supplement to official measures of delinquency and provide a more complete picture of the true extent of juvenile crime. Results of self-report measures show that delinquent behavior is spread more equally among youth of all social classes, and in fact white middle-class youth report involvement in offenses such as drug violations to a greater extent than lower-class and minority youths (Elliott, Huizinga, & Ageton, 1985; Agnew, 2001). Self-report measures are very important for their contribution to providing a more complete picture of delinquent behavior. Findings that some delinquent behavior is nearly universal among all youth regardless of social class or ethnic and racial group led to the development of additional research and theories to explain delinquent involvement of middle-class youth and females. Elliott (1994) has emphasized the importance of using and integrating both self-reports and official statistics to gain a more complete understanding of the extent and seriousness of juvenile delinquency. Self-reports are regularly used to supplement official records, especially for the kinds of delinquent activities that are less likely to be reported by police. The "Youth Risk Behavior Survey" is regularly administered to a representative sample of youth in the United States to assess the extent and seriousness of risky behaviors in which youth are involved (Centers for Disease Control, 2008a). This includes both victimization experiences (being threatened with a weapon or assaulted) and deviant or illegal behaviors (being in a fight, carrying a weapon, using drugs). The "Monitoring the Future" surveys administered regularly to high school students are a good example of the value of self-reports for assessing the extent of young peoples' drug and alcohol abuse and other delinquent behavior (Johnston, O'Malley, Bachman, & Schulenberg, 2008).

SOURCE: © Butch Martin/Getty Images.

Photo 1.1   Juvenile males are at risk of engaging in deviant and delinquent behavior.

SUMMARY

- Juveniles are involved in many crimes each year, both as perpetrators and as victims.
- Children and youth are subject to legal intervention for status offenses such as running away, school truancy, and curfew violations.
- Juvenile delinquency is defined according to the age of jurisdiction and varies among the states in the United States.
- Official measures of juvenile crime include those by police, the courts, and corrections agencies.
- Unofficial measures of juvenile crime include self-report and victim surveys, and provide a more complete description of the true extent of juvenile crime.

KEY TERMS

Status offenses	Unofficial measures of delinquency
Juvenile delinquency	Self-report measures
Official measures of delinquency	Victimization surveys

DISCUSSION QUESTIONS

1. What are the ages for juvenile jurisdiction in your state? For the states next to you and in your region? Scan various Web resources (below) and review the differences in age limits for defining *juveniles* among the states.

2. What are the types of "official" measures of delinquency? What are the "unofficial" measures of delinquency? Which measures—official or unofficial—are likely to report a higher number of crimes or delinquent acts? Explain why.

3. Think back to when you were a teenager between the ages of 13 and 18. Based on personal experience, observation, or reliable admissions, how many acts of crime and delinquency do you personally recall having been committed by your friends, acquaintances, siblings, and yourself?

4. Do the same as in Question 3, but for how many times someone, including yourself, was a victim of a crime.

5. For how many of the above (No. 3 or No. 4) acts of delinquency was a person stopped, questioned, or apprehended by police?

WEB RESOURCES

Juvenile offenders and victims: 2006 national report: http://ojjdp.ncjrs.gov/ojstatbb/nr2006/downloads/NR2006.pdf

Photo 2.1 Police officers take a young boy into custody in the late 19th century.

adult criminals. Some punishments were very severe. Youth who committed serious offenses could be subjected to prison sentences, whipping, and even the death penalty. During the 19th century, criminal codes applied to all persons, adults and children alike. No provisions were made to account for the age of offenders. Originally there were no separate laws or courts, and no special facilities for the care of children who were in trouble with the law.

A number of developments during the 19th century paved the way for a separate system of justice for juveniles. An increase in the birthrate and the influx of immigrants to America brought a new wave of growth to American cities. With this growth came an increase in the numbers of dependent and destitute children. Urban youth and children of immigrants were thought to be more prone to deviant and immoral behavior than other youth. Early reformers who were members of the Society for the Prevention of Pauperism expressed dissatisfaction with the practice of placing children in adult jails and workhouses. They called for institutions that would instruct delinquent youth in proper discipline and moral behavior (Mennel, 1973).

Houses of Refuge and Legal Doctrines

The doctrine of *parens patriae* provided the basis for official intervention in the lives of wayward youth. Parents were expected to supervise and control their children, but when it became apparent that parents were not properly controlling and disciplining their children, the State was given the authority to take over that responsibility. The Society for the Reformation of Juvenile Delinquents in New York advocated for the separation of juvenile and adult offenders (Krisberg, 2005, p. 27), and in 1825 the New York House of Refuge was established to take in dependent, neglected, and delinquent youths. Other houses of refuge in Boston and Philadelphia were soon established, and these were followed shortly thereafter by reform schools for vagrant and delinquent juveniles. State reform schools opened in Massachusetts in 1847, in New York in 1853, in Ohio in 1857; and the first State Industrial School for Girls was opened in Massachusetts in 1856 (Law Enforcement Assistance Administration [LEAA], 1976, p. 65).

The doctrine of *parens patriae* was first tested in the Pennsylvania Supreme Court case of *Ex parte Crouse* in 1838. The father of Mary Ann Crouse argued that his daughter was illegally incarcerated without a trial. The Court denied his claim, stating that the Bill of Rights did not apply to juveniles. The Court stated that when parents are found to be "incompetent" in their parental duties, the State has the right to intervene and provide the child with guidance and supervision. The *Crouse* ruling was based on what the Court believed was the best interests of the child and the entire community, with the assumed intentions that the State could provide the proper education and training for the child. As States intervened in more juvenile cases, especially ones involving minor misbehavior, the concept of *parens patriae* would later meet more legal challenges.

The early juvenile reform schools were intended for education and treatment, not for punishment; but hard work, strict regimentation, and whippings were common. Discriminatory treatment against African Americans, Mexican Americans, American Indians, and poor whites remained a problem in the schools. Sexual abuse and physical attacks by peers (and sometimes staff members) also was a problem. Institutional abuses against incarcerated juveniles came under increasing criticism by the last half of the 1800s. The practice of taking custody of troubled youths under the concept of *parens patriae* led many by the mid-1800s to question whether most youths benefited from the practice. There is evidence that the State was not in fact an effective or benevolent parent, and that there was a significant disparity between the promise and the practice of *parens patriae*. Pisciotta (1982) reviewed the *Ex parte Crouse* ruling and noted that subsequent legal decisions revealed that judges in the 19th century were committing minors to reformatories for noncriminal acts on the premise that the juvenile institutions would have a beneficial effect. In theory, reformatories were "schools" that provided parental discipline, education, religious instruction, and meaningful work for incarcerated youth. Pisciotta examined the records, annual reports, and daily journals of superintendents, and found a significant disparity between the theory and practice of juvenile incarceration. He noted that discipline in the juvenile reform schools was more brutal than parental, and inmate workers were exploited under an indenture or contract labor system. Institutional environments that had a corrupting influence on the residents, as evidenced by assaults, homosexual relations, and frequent escapes, marked the schools.

Critics of this extensive State intervention argued against intervention of youth over minor, noncriminal behavior, and claimed that reformatories were not providing the kind of parental care, education, or training that was promised under the *parens patriae* doctrine. In a legal challenge, the Illinois Supreme Court ruled that "we should not forget the rights which inhere both in parents and children. . . . The parent has the right to the care, custody, and assistance of his child" [*People v. Turner*, 55 I11.280 (1870)]. The Court ruled that the State should intervene only after violations of criminal law and only after following due process guidelines. The ruling actually did little to change the prevailing practices in most other states, however. It would take later court decisions to define clearly the rights of children and their parents in State intervention.

The "Child-Saving" Movement

The failure of the houses of refuge and early reform schools brought more interest in the welfare of troubled youth who were abandoned, orphaned, or forced to work under intolerable conditions. In the latter half of the 19th century, following the Civil War period, humanitarian concerns were directed toward troubled children and their treatment. A pivotal point in the development of the juvenile justice system in America was what became known as the "child-saving movement" (see LEAA, 1976; Faust & Brantingham, 1979). The child-savers were a group of reformers that included philanthropists, professionals, and middle-class citizens who expressed concerns about the welfare of children. They pushed for state intervention to save at-risk children through shelter care and educational programs. The result of this child-saving movement was to extend government intervention over youth behaviors that had previously been the responsibility of parents and families. The leading advocates in the child-saving movement believed that such youth problems as idleness, drinking, vagrancy, and delinquent behaviors threatened the moral fabric of society and must be controlled. If parents could not or would not control and properly supervise their own children, then the government should intervene. They pushed for legislation that would give courts jurisdiction over children who were incorrigible or runaways, as well as those who committed crimes.

The First Juvenile Court

A reform movement that led to the development of a separate court for juveniles marked the latter part of the 19th century, following the Civil War. Some states, including Massachusetts in 1874 and New York in 1892, had passed laws providing for separate trials for juveniles. The first juvenile court was established in Cook County (Chicago), Illinois, in 1899. The *parens patriae* doctrine was the legal basis for court jurisdiction over juveniles and was central to the juvenile court philosophy, because children who violated laws were not to be treated as criminals. Children were considered less mature and less aware of the consequences of their actions, so they were not to be held legally accountable for their behavior in the same manner as adults. Under the juvenile justice philosophy, youthful offenders were designated as delinquent rather than as criminal, and the primary purpose of the juvenile justice system was not punishment but rehabilitation (see Mennel, 1972, and Davis, 1980).

The juvenile courts sought to turn juvenile delinquents into productive citizens by focusing on treatment rather than punishment. The laws that established the juvenile courts clearly distinguished their purpose as different from the adult penal codes. A ruling by the Pennsylvania Supreme Court in the case of *Commonwealth v. Fisher* in 1905 supported the juvenile court's purpose, and illustrates how the court's role in training delinquent children superseded the rights of children and their parents:

The design is not punishment, nor the restraint imprisonment, any more than is the wholesome restraint which a parent exercises over his child. . . . Every statute which is designed to give protection, care, and training to children, as a parental duty, is but a recognition of the duty of the state, as the legitimate guardian and protector of children where other guardianship fails. No constitutional right is violated. [*Commonwealth v. Fisher*, 213 Pa. 48 (1905)]

The Pennsylvania Supreme Court thus supported the juvenile court's treatment objectives over the rights of the juvenile or the parents. For the next 50 years, juvenile courts continued the practice of legal interventions over a broad range of juvenile cases, from status offenses to criminal code violations. The focus on offenders' needs for supervision and rehabilitation more than on offenses committed had an impact on judicial procedures and decisions. Decisions of what cases would go to court was made by a juvenile court intake division, unlike criminal court where district attorneys made the decision. Juvenile court intake considered extralegal as well as legal factors in deciding how to handle cases, and had discretion to handle cases informally, diverting cases from court action.

Because the purpose of the juvenile court was for the protection and treatment of the child and not for punishment, the juvenile proceeding was more civil than criminal. The juvenile legal process was purportedly "in the best interests of the child," so the hearing was more informal, unlike the more formal, adversarial criminal court process. Advocates believed that children did not need the formal procedural rights common in criminal court, so they were denied many of the legal rights of adults, such as formal notice of the charges and the right to legal counsel. The juvenile reform efforts were also based on the growing optimism that application of the social sciences was more appropriate for handling juvenile offenders than the law. Delinquency was viewed more as a social problem and a breakdown of the family than a criminal problem. Thus, social workers, probation officers, and psychologists took the place of lawyers and prosecutors. They examined the background and social history of the child and the family environment to assess the child's needs, and then developed a treatment plan that was intended to change delinquent juveniles. Ferdinand (1991) noted that the juvenile court judge was expected to be more like a father figure than a legal jurist. The focus was on offenders and not offenses, on rehabilitation and not punishment, and this was to be accomplished through individualized justice for juvenile offenders. The development of the first juvenile court in Chicago was followed shortly by one in Denver, and by 1945 all states had juvenile courts (Ferdinand, 1991). For the first half-century after it was first developed, the juvenile court system went largely unchallenged in the manner in which juvenile cases were processed. Despite some differences among states and jurisdictions, there was general agreement on the goals and objectives of juvenile justice, and how it should be similar to, and distinct from, the criminal justice system.

Changes and Trends in Juvenile Justice

The history and development of the juvenile court and a separate system of justice for juveniles presents a picture of a benevolent, caring system that promoted the "best interests of the child." Children and youth were separated from adult offenders in a legal process that combined both civil and criminal law. Juvenile court dispositions consisted mainly of a year or less of probation supervision or short-term treatment in "houses of refuge" or "reform schools." The early juvenile court clearly distinguished its goals and purposes as different from the goals of punishment and deterrence for adult offenders. Overall, the juvenile court process was promoted as progressive, humanitarian, and an improvement on the older practice that failed to differentiate offenders by age.

Questioning the Child Savers

The view of the juvenile court as a benevolent, humanitarian development that promoted the "best interests of the child" has not been shared in agreement by everyone. Anthony Platt (1977) has portrayed the child-saving movement as simply a part of a larger social movement in the 19th century. The "child savers," according to Platt, were a group of middle- and upper-class Americans who were concerned about the growth of a lower-class population of immigrants and unruly children who were not properly supervised and disciplined by their parents. The child savers' primary concern was to discipline and train these youth to enter the labor force and support the growth of corporate capitalism in America. Others have joined Platt in questioning the benevolent and humanitarian motives of the juvenile court. Pisciotta (1982) noted that there was a significant disparity between the care promised to minors by juvenile court judges and the actual training and care provided for them in houses of refuge, reform schools, and through the system of contract labor. The care provided was often more abusive than parental, the contact labor system was more exploitation than training, leading Pisciotta to conclude that the State was not an effective parent under the doctrine of *parens patriae*. Krisberg (2005) noted that the child savers viewed the lower-class urban families as a potentially dangerous class that could threaten order and progress in America. He has questioned the benevolent image of the child-saving practices, noting that lower-class youth were "placed out" with rural families and required to do long hours of hard labor. Black youth were leased out to railroad, mining, and manufacturing companies with little regard for their age, similar to the convict lease system commonly done in adult prison programs. The exploitation of labor and inhumane living conditions raises questions about the benevolent and humanitarian goals of the early juvenile court.

Cycles of Juvenile Justice

Every generation has had the opinion that many young people behave badly, and are much worse than the previous generation (Hamparian, Schuster, Dinitz, & Conrad, 1978). Bernard (1992) noted that every generation for the past 200 years or more has held the belief that the current cohort of juvenile delinquents is the worst ever and commits more crime than other groups. Bernard referred to a "cycle of juvenile justice" as tougher laws were passed in response to the "juvenile crime wave" and the mistaken assumption that juveniles commit more crime because the laws are too lenient. The assumption that lenient juvenile justice policies encourage juveniles to "laugh at" the system and commit more crimes leads the public and lawmakers to demand more punitive policies, less leniency, and harsher punishments for juveniles. DiIulio perpetuated the belief that juvenile crime was getting worse when he predicted a juvenile crime wave based on projections of the Philadelphia Birth Cohort Study and the growth of the juvenile population (Bennett, DiIulio, & Walters, 1996). Assuming that the Philadelphia cohort from the 1960s was applicable to the nation in the 1990s, DiIulio and his associates predicted that a large group of what he called juvenile "superpredators" would dramatically drive up the violent crime rate. Juvenile crime experts including Snyder and Sickmund (2006) and Howell (2003) have noted the methodological and statistical errors that incorrectly led to the superpredator myth. In short, it is a mistake to use aggregate or group data to predict individual behavior and trends; and it is a mistake to assume that crime rates from one decade will remain constant through following decades. Juvenile violence in fact has been decreasing each year since the peak year of 1994 (Snyder & Sickmund, 2006). Despite the annual decrease in juvenile crime over the years, perceptions of a juvenile "crime wave" and lenient laws prompted a number of changes away from the original juvenile justice philosophy of treatment toward more severe sanctions and a punitive philosophy.

Legislative Changes and "Getting Tough"

Following the federal statutory guidelines and the U.S. Supreme Court decisions that occurred in the 1960s and 1970s, the pendulum began to swing toward law and order in the 1980s. In response to public perceptions that serious juvenile crime was increasing and that the system was too lenient with offenders, many state legislators responded by passing more punitive laws. Some laws removed juvenile offenders charged with violent crimes from the juvenile system; other laws required the juvenile justice system to be more like the criminal justice system, and to treat more serious juvenile offenders as criminals but in the juvenile court. The result has been to exclude offenders charged with certain offenses from juvenile court jurisdiction, or to have them face mandatory or automatic waiver to criminal court. In some states, concurrent jurisdiction provisions give prosecutors the discretion to file certain juvenile cases directly in criminal court rather than in juvenile court (Snyder & Sickmund, 2006).

The trend continued through the 1990s as state legislatures continued to pass more punitive laws in an effort to deal more harshly with juvenile crime. Five areas of change have emerged as states passed laws to crack down on juvenile crime. Most of the statutory changes involved expanding eligibility for criminal court processing, sentencing juvenile offenders to adult correctional supervision, and reducing confidentiality protections that have been customary for juvenile offenders. Between 1992 and 1997, all but three states changed laws in one or more of the following areas:

- Transfer provisions: Laws in 45 states made it easier to transfer juvenile offenders from the juvenile to the criminal justice system.
- Sentencing authority: Laws in 31 states gave criminal and juvenile courts expanded sentencing options.
- Confidentiality: Laws in 47 states modified or removed traditional juvenile court confidentiality provisions by making records and proceedings more open.
- Victims' rights: Laws in 22 states increased the role of victims of juvenile crime in the juvenile justice process.
- Correctional programming: As a result of new transfer and sentencing laws, adult and juvenile correctional administrators developed new programs (Snyder & Sickmund, 2006, pp. 96–97).

The changes in juvenile justice laws reflect the belief that leniency in juvenile court processing accounted for what many perceived to be dramatic increases in juvenile crime. The tougher laws are based on the assumption that juveniles who commit "adult-like" crimes are equally culpable as adult offenders. Lawmakers pushing for "get-tough" legislation used phrases such as "adult crime, adult time" to win approval for statutory changes to existing juvenile laws. The belief was that juveniles who commit crimes that would be punished as felony convictions if committed by adults should be prosecuted and punished like adult offenders. The tougher laws also were intended to send the message to serious or chronic juvenile offenders that they will be held more accountable. The movement away from rehabilitation and treatment and toward retribution and just deserts has occurred simultaneously in both the criminal and the juvenile justice systems. Garland (2001) has documented political and social changes over the past 30 years that have led to demands for more formal social controls of juvenile and adult offenders. The changes that led to more formal controls have been the rising crime rates, challenges to the welfare system, a growing concern for victims, a more diversified population, and a perceived inability of families and other social institutions to control their deviant members. Until the 1980s, criminal justice practitioners generally recognized what criminologists had identified as the causes of deviant behavior, including inequities in society and the social influences on the offender. Under the practice of indeterminate sentencing, the courts took into account the individual and social problems that likely influenced the offender's criminal behavior, and individualized sentences were based on the crime as well as the offender's treatment needs. That practice has given way to determinate sentencing and the belief that individuals of all ages choose to commit crimes and need to be held accountable for their actions. Despite the movement to "get tough" with juvenile offenders, there is evidence that the public has not entirely given up on the possibility of saving children. Research findings by Moon and her associates (Moon, Sundt, Cullen, & Wright, 2000) show that there is still public support for juvenile rehabilitation.

Juvenile justice experts have differing opinions on the results and consequences of the statutory changes in juvenile justice. Research evidence is mixed as to whether tougher laws are likely to have much effect on reducing juvenile crime. The laws have clearly resulted in more juvenile offenders being waived to criminal court prosecution and sentencing, and more juvenile offenders serving time in adult correctional facilities.

What is not clear is whether the tougher laws have any significant deterrent effect on juvenile offenders. We will discuss more of the changes and reforms in the juvenile court and changes in correctional processing in later chapters of the book.

The End of the Death Penalty for Juveniles

The death penalty for juveniles convicted of murder has been a controversial issue. The United States has until recently been one of few nations in the world and the only democratic, industrialized nation to allow the execution of juveniles convicted of murder (Cothern, 2000; Streib, 2005). From 1973 through 2004, a total of 228 juvenile death sentences were imposed; 22 (14%) resulted in execution, and 134 (86%) were reversed or commuted (Streib, 2005). The majority of those executions (13, or 59%) occurred in Texas. Juvenile death sentences have accounted for less than 3% of the nearly 7,000 total U.S. death sentences since 1973; and two thirds of those were imposed on 17-year-olds, while about one third were imposed on 15- and 16-year-old juveniles (Cothern, 2000). As of the end of the year 2005, a total of 20 states authorized the execution of juveniles (under 18 years), with 9 states specifying the minimum age at 16 or less, 5 states specified the minimum age at 17, and 6 states not specifying a minimum age (Snell, 2006). The number of states that allow the death penalty for juveniles under 18 has been declining for years, and most states with statutes authorizing the juvenile death penalty have neither imposed nor carried out the death sentence on a person convicted of murder as a juvenile (Death Penalty Information Center, 2007).

On March 1, 2005, the U.S. Supreme Court ruled in *Roper v. Simmons* (U.S. 125 S.Ct. 1183) that imposition of the death penalty on persons who were under age 18 at the time of their crimes was cruel and unusual punishment and therefore a violation of the Eighth and Fourteenth Amendments. The *Roper* decision is the third and final ruling on juveniles and the death penalty in the past 20 years. In 1988 the U.S. Supreme Court in *Thompson v. Oklahoma* (487 U.S. 815) held that execution of juvenile offenders under age 16 violated the Eighth Amendment against cruel and unusual punishment. The next year (1989) the Court held in *Stanford v. Kentucky* (492 U.S. 361) that the execution of juvenile offenders 16 and 17 years of age was *not* unconstitutional. Fifteen more years passed before the Supreme Court in *Roper* put an end to the execution of all juvenile offenders under 18 years of age. In a close 5–4 majority opinion, the Court drew upon an earlier decision in *Atkins v. Virginia* (536 U.S. 304) forbidding execution of the mentally retarded. In *Roper* the Court held that capital punishment must be limited to those offenders who commit "a narrow category of the most serious crimes" and whose extreme culpability makes them "the most deserving of execution" (*Atkins v. Virginia,* 536 U.S. at 319; and *Roper v. Simmons,* 125 S.Ct. at 1186).

The decision was based in part on the earlier *Thompson* decision and rested on what the Court recognized as three general differences between juveniles under 18 and adults, and why juvenile offenders cannot be classified among the "worst offenders." First, because juveniles are susceptible to immature and irresponsible behavior, "their irresponsible conduct is not as morally reprehensible as that of an adult" (*Roper v. Simmons,* 125 S.Ct. at 1186; and *Thompson v. Oklahoma,* 487 U.S. 815, at 835). Second, the Court reasoned that because juveniles still struggle to define their own identity means that "it is less supportable to conclude that even a heinous crime committed by a juvenile is evidence of irretrievably depraved character" (125 S.Ct. at 1186). Third, because the Court recognized juveniles' diminished culpability compared with adults over 18, then (similar to the mentally retarded, in *Atkins*) "neither of the two penological justifications for the death penalty—retribution and deterrence of capital crimes by prospective offenders . . . provides adequate justification for imposing that penalty on juveniles" (125 S.Ct. at 1186). In ruling against the death penalty for juvenile murderers, the Justices acknowledged that they could not deny or overlook the brutal crimes that too many juvenile offenders have committed. While the State may no longer execute those juveniles under 18 for murder, the Court added a reminder that "the State can exact forfeiture of some of the most basic liberties" (125 S.Ct. at 1197); that is, a life sentence in prison. The *Roper* decision will have an impact on 20 states, 9 of which had specified the minimum age for the death penalty at 16, 5 states at 17 years, and 6 states had no minimum age established. Of the 38 states that authorize capital punishment, 18 of the states and the federal judicial system had already specified 18 as the minimum age for execution (Snell, 2006).

The close 5–4 decision of the Supreme Court was not without controversy. In the majority opinion, Justice Kennedy noted the trend in the United States of moving consistently away from executing juveniles; and he noted the overwhelming international sentiment against executing persons under 18. In a dissenting opinion, Justice Sandra Day O'Connor protested that the majority had not demonstrated that there existed a sufficient national consensus against executing juveniles to conclude that the practice violated the Eighth Amendment; and she argued that the sentence should be available for imposing the death sentence on juveniles who commit the most heinous murders. In an opinion of the other three dissenters, Justice Scalia (who has expressed opposition to allowing international laws and legal decisions to influence American case law) objected to the majority's reliance on national consensus and trends in other states, arguing that is more within legislative policy making. Justice Scalia also argued that the majority opinion was based on a selective, incomplete reading of social scientists' conclusions regarding juveniles and the death penalty.

The substitute for the death penalty that the majority opinion suggested for juveniles who murder is also not without question and controversy. Life in prison without parole (LWOP) has been raised as an issue now that thousands of juveniles have been sentenced to life in prison, and the American Civil Liberties Union (ACLU) has recommended that the maximum prison sentence for juveniles should be 25 years (Benekos & Merlo, 2005). The practice of LWOP for juveniles in the United States also constitutes a violation of Article 37(a) of the United Nations Convention on the Rights of the Child, which holds that:

> the death penalty cannot be imposed for a crime committed by a person who . . . was under 18 years of age . . . [and] No child who was under the age of 18 . . . should be sentenced to life without the possibility of release or parole. (Committee on the Rights of the Child, 2007, pp. 21–22)

The meaning of "cruel and unusual" has changed considerably over the past years, and not too long ago (1989) the U.S. Supreme Court in *Stanford v. Kentucky* held that executing juveniles did not violate this standard. Considering the "evolving standards of decency," Benekos and Merlo (2005) suggest that life imprisonment for juveniles may well be the next issue to be confronted by the Court.

SUMMARY

The history and development of the juvenile court and justice process are highlighted by a number of points:

- Laws and legal procedures relating to juvenile offenders have a long history, dating back thousands of years.
- American juvenile justice was based on English Common law that dates back to the 11th and 12th centuries.
- The legal doctrines of *parens patriae* and *in loco parentis* enable the State to take custody of a child and to exercise parental authority, and to provide guidance, protection, and needed services to needy children.
- Before the development of the juvenile justice system in America, parents were expected to control and discipline their children; and juveniles who committed crimes were treated the same as adults.
- Houses of Refuge were developed in New York, Boston, and Philadelphia in the 1800s, and were the first step toward development of reform schools.
- The "child-saving movement" was begun by a group of concerned child reform advocates who pushed for State intervention to save at-risk children through shelter care and educational programs.
- The first juvenile court was established in Chicago (Cook County), Illinois, in 1899, to provide for separate trials for juveniles.
- The Juvenile Delinquency Prevention and Control Act of 1968 recommended that children charged with noncriminal (status) offenses be handled outside the court system.
- State and federal legislation has altered many of the original treatment goals, instituted more punitive measures, and excluded many serious or chronic youthful offenders from juvenile jurisdiction.
- The U.S. Supreme Court in *Roper v. Simmons* [125 S.Ct. 1183 (2005)] held that the death penalty for juveniles was unconstitutional.

KEY TERMS

Parens patriae

In loco parentis

Houses of Refuge

Reform schools

"Child savers"

Juvenile Justice and Delinquency Prevention Act

Thompson v. Oklahoma

Stanford v. Kentucky

Roper v. Simmons

DISCUSSION QUESTIONS

1. Based on your understanding of the earliest laws relating to juvenile offenders (Code of Hammurabi, Roman civil and canon law, Jewish and Moslem laws), discuss whether they are significantly different than today, or quite similar.

2. Do you believe the power and authority of a state under the doctrines of *parens patriae* and *in loco parentis* are too severe, or appropriate under most circumstances?

3. Give an example of how some laws and policies governing youthful offenders are, in the opinion of some persons, too invasive and punitive. Offer support for the ways in which the laws and policies are for the best interests of children and youth.

4. Do any of the provisions of the Juvenile Justice and Delinquency Prevention Act reflect the movement to "get tough" on juvenile offenders? What provisions seem to emphasize some of the original goals of juvenile justice?

5. Present an argument for the following positions: (a) federal and state legislative changes to juvenile justice are based on the latest research findings on deterrence and effective correctional approaches; or (b) are based more on perceptions of increases in juvenile crime and public and political demands for more punitive sanctions.

6. Summarize arguments for and against the death penalty for juveniles. Based on readings in this text and supporting documents, what do you believe are the strongest arguments for each position?

WEB RESOURCES

The following Web sites provide information and discussion on the history and development of the juvenile justice system:

American Bar Association Juvenile Justice Center, on the Juvenile Death Penalty: http://www.abanet.org/crimjust/juvjus/EvolvingStandards.pdf

Juvenile offenders and victims: 2006 national report: http://ojjdp.ncjrs.gov/ojstatbb/nr2006/downloads/NR2006.pdf

Youth law center, on juvenile justice: http://www.buildingblocksforyouth.org/issues/

Death Penalty Information Center: http://www.deathpenaltyinfo.org/

Bureau of Justice Statistics, on Capital Punishment: http://www.ojp.usdoj.gov/bjs/pub/pdf/cp05.pdf

Juvenile Death Penalty Facts and Figures: http://www.abanet.org/crimjust/juvjus/dparticles/factsheetfactsfigures.pdf

Convention on the Rights of the Child (United Nations): http://www.unhchr.ch/html/menu3/b/k2crc.htm

Causes of Delinquency

Rational Choice and Individual Explanations

J uvenile delinquency may be caused by a multitude of factors. The original, classical theory of crime held that it was simply a voluntary and rational choice. Other explanations have focused on the individual and include biological, genetic, and psychological causes. Social explanations place the causes of delinquency in the structure of society, cultural differences, and social processes. Still other theories explain delinquency as a function of societal reactions to deviance, or conflict between the dominant and less powerful groups in society. Most of us have an opinion about what causes delinquency. Popular opinions include poverty, unemployment, poor parenting, peer pressure, gangs, and drugs. Criminologists and social scientists have sought for years to better understand and explain the complex origins and etiology of crime and delinquency. Criminological theories are constantly being developed, tested, and revised based on research studies that support or question their accuracy. The criteria for theories that best explain delinquency causation among youth from a variety of backgrounds and social settings are that the theories be (a) clear and simple, (b) testable, (c) based on observations and research data, and (d) logically consistent.

The number and complexity of theories explaining delinquency can be overwhelming, as criminologists seem to be competing with each other for the most correct and comprehensive theoretical perspective. In reality, however, the number and variety of delinquency theories attests to the complexity of the problem, its variation among subcultures and social classes, and across gender, ethnic, and racial lines. No single theory can adequately explain all the reasons behind deviant behavior and delinquency of youth; but the predominant theories, when considered together, are able to explain most delinquent behavior. Several criminologists have developed integrated theories of crime that combine the best features of several theories.

Why Study Theories of Crime and Delinquency? Crime is a problem that affects society and the quality of life of every citizen. Thousands of persons are victimized each year, and many more who have not suffered actual victimization have a fear of crime, thus crime affects the everyday behavior of most citizens. In addition to the effects on individuals, crime costs local, state, and federal governments billions of dollars each year. A problem of this magnitude demands our utmost attempts to understand its origins and causes. Social scientists have spent years studying the varieties of criminal behavior and the factors that seem to underlie the problem. The study of crime theories is not simply an academic or intellectual exercise. Understanding the causes of crime is essential in order to make rational, informed responses to the problem of crime. Laws, policies, and delinquency prevention programs are based on beliefs about what causes the problem. Those who argue in favor of passing tougher laws to combat crime assume that offenders are acting rationally, and may be deterred by tougher laws and harsh punishment. Those, on the other hand, who argue for more rehabilitation and treatment programs assume that underlying psychological problems, alcohol, or substance abuse have led to juvenile offending. Still others who believe that unemployment, poverty, and related social problems are responsible for delinquency would direct resources and remedial programs in that direction. Most of the explanations and responses are valid and appropriate for certain at-risk and delinquent youth, under given circumstances and conditions. Yet to assume that one crime prevention strategy will work effectively for all offenders under all circumstances is naive and doomed to fail. As with any problem facing society, it is necessary to understand the origins and causes of delinquency in order to make policy decisions that are more realistically in line with the true nature of the problem. Of course, no single explanation can account for the variety of delinquent behaviors of youth; and most of the major theories of causation do offer sound explanations for delinquency that are based on empirical research. The best theories also offer recommendations to policymakers for the most appropriate programs and strategies for delinquency prevention.

Rational Choice Explanations

Classical theory, also called rational or choice theory, is based on the early writings of Cesare Beccaria (1738–1794) and Jeremy Bentham (1748–1832). Their primary concern was not so much to explain criminal behavior, but to develop a legal system by which the punishment would fit the crime. According to classical theory, crime is explained as a free will, voluntary choice. Persons commit crime simply because they made a rational decision to do so. It was assumed that because crime was a rational choice, criminal offenders could be deterred by punishment. Classical theory has thus been referred to as a utilitarian approach to crime. Explanations of crime as rational choice are popular and widely supported by law enforcement, law makers, and academic disciplines such as the economics of crime, political science, and law (see, e.g., Cornish & Clarke, 1986; Akers, 1990). This explanation assumes that crime results from a rational process in which offenders make decisions and choices, often planning their criminal activity so as to maximize the benefits and avoid the risks (see Cornish & Clarke, 1986, pp. 1–2). Lawrence Cohen and Marcus Felson (1979) developed a version of rational theory called routine activity theory to explain trends and cycles in the crime rate since the 1960s. They concluded that crime is closely related to the interaction of three variables associated with the "routine activities" of everyday life: the availability of suitable targets of crime; the absence of capable guardians; and the presence of motivated offenders. Thus, as more homes are unoccupied due to more persons employed (and fewer neighbors, family members, or relatives looking after them), they are more likely to be targeted by unemployed teens or young adults. The routine activity approach links delinquency to social changes that increase the opportunities for crime, and emphasizes the role the victim's lifestyle and behavior have in the crime process. Felson (1994) described how the growth and social changes in cities, neighborhoods, and schools have increased the likelihood of crime occurring.

Critics of rational choice theory question the degree to which criminal behavior is always a rational, free will process. Ronald Akers (1990) questioned whether offenders really make rational decisions to commit crime based on knowledge of the law and possible punishments; and whether their decision was made in the absence of any situational factors that tend to influence crime. Rational choice proponents do not always hold to a strict definition of rationality, but acknowledge that situational factors do affect individuals' choices; and efforts have been made to integrate rational choice theory with other explanations (see, e.g., Felson, 1986; Hirschi, 1986). Certainly many crimes reflect rational choices of persons, and this holds true especially for so-called white-collar crimes often committed by persons in workplace situations that pose relatively little risk of detection, conviction, or punishment. Much juvenile crime reflects rational choice, especially when youth perceive that their chances of being caught are low; and even if caught, many are well aware that the punishment for juvenile crime is often much less than for comparable crimes committed by adults.

CASE IN POINT 3.1

Vinnie and Routine Activities Theory

Vinnie often goes to Mr. and Mrs. Johnson's "Ma and Pop" convenience store to buy candy after school, but on this particular day, Vinnie decides to go to a not-so-familiar store to purchase his candy. Vinnie enters the store, notices that the only attendant is stocking soda in the back, and that there are no other patrons in the store. Vinnie sees a sign that reads "Shoplifters will be prosecuted to the fullest extent of the law" next to the display of chocolate bars he means to purchase. Vinnie knows the penalty for stealing, but he knows that he can probably get away with it due to the absent surveillance.

Discussion Questions

1. How does this case illustrate the three points of routine activity theory (available target, absence of surveillance, and a motivated perpetrator)?

2. Think of similar situations that you were in, and did not choose to steal. Why not? What was different? What was missing from the three requirements for crime as a "routine activity"?

Rational Choice and Punishment

The logical response to crime as rational behavior is tougher punishment as a deterrent. Deterrence theory holds that punishment has a *general* effect, discouraging the general public from engaging in criminal activity by striking fear in them with the threat of punishment. Specific deterrence discourages offenders from repeating their crimes by threatening to punish them more harshly the next time. Tougher laws and sanctions *are* effective as deterrents against crime: Most persons (including offenders), after all, *do* obey most of the laws most of the time. The effectiveness of punishment as a deterrent to crime, however, depends on three factors: certainty, speed, and severity. Offenders will be deterred from crime only if they believe they are likely to be caught, convicted, and punished. Furthermore, punishment is more effective if it is administered soon after the violation, and if it is sufficiently severe. The last requirement, severity, is the one that lawmakers rely on the most, and that is relatively easier to achieve than the first two in that it is accomplished through state and federal legislation in a matter of weeks or months. Tougher laws, however, are effective only when they are accompanied by a high probability of quick and certain enforcement. It is more difficult to increase the certainty of police arrest and court conviction than the severity of punishment. That requires additional funding for hiring more police to increase the certainty of arrest, and more judges and attorneys to process more cases through the courts. Supporting effective administration of justice in the face of limited budgets and resources is a difficult task that generates heated debate throughout the political process at all levels of government and among citizens.

CASE IN POINT 3.2

Deterrence: Aims and Effects

Specific deterrence, which, at times, is referred to as "special" and/or "individual" deterrence, focuses on the individual in question. The aim of these "specific" punishments is to discourage the criminal from future criminal acts by instilling an understanding of the consequences. For example, Vinnie has been arrested for a second drug possession violation, and has been sentenced to 6 months of rehabilitation in addition to traveling to local schools in his area to speak with students on the harm drugs cause.

General deterrence, which, at times, is referred to as "indirect" deterrence, focuses on general prevention of crime by making examples of specific deviants. The individual actor is not the focus of the attempt at behavioral change, but rather receives punishment in public view in order to deter other individuals from deviance in the future.

Discussion Questions

1. Why is Vinnie's sanction "specific"? What other types of "specific" deterrence examples can you provide based on your own history?

2. Think of examples of "general deterrence." For example, how might a posted speed limit reflect "general" deterrence?

Individual Explanations

Positivist theories comprise the second category of delinquency explanations. Positivists hold that behavior is determined, or caused, by factors over which individuals have little or no control. Positivist explanations originated in the 19th century with Cesare Lombroso, who was the first person credited with using the scientific method to study crime. Lombroso was an Italian physician who noted what he believed to be distinguishing physical characteristics of criminals in prison. Lombroso described certain characteristics—or "stigmata"—such as an irregularly shaped head and face, a large jaw, protruding ears, and receding chin. He linked such stigmata to "atavism," a lower stage of biological development, and believed these to be related to criminal tendencies. Lombroso's original findings have since been largely discounted, but the influence of his early work provided the incentive for subsequent criminologists to apply the scientific method to studying criminals.

Positivist theorists have developed explanations for delinquency based on *individual factors* such as heredity, intelligence, and psychological characteristics; on *social structures* within society; on *social processes* within groups of persons; and on *political and economic structures* of society. Proponents of positivist theories argue that much criminal behavior is not the result of rational choice, but stems from a variety of individual and social factors that influence delinquent behavior. In the remainder of this chapter we define and explain the theories based on individual factors. Sociological, social reaction, and conflict theories are discussed in Chapter 4.

Biological and Genetic Explanations

Following the initial work of Lombroso, others have posited biological causes of crime. In the 1930s, Earnest Hooton, an American anthropologist, compared physical measurements of 10,000 male prisoners with those of noncriminals and discovered some distinctive differences. The physical differences, such as ear shapes, eye colors, or hair distributions, had no clear connection to crime other than a statistical correlation, however. In the 1940s, William Sheldon, a physician, developed a system for classifying human physique types (endomorphy, mesomorphy, and ectomorphy) and found that these have some correlation with personality and temperament. Mesomorphs tend to be characterized by high activity levels, restlessness, aggressiveness, and tend to seek adventure and danger. Sheldon reported that male and female offenders tended to be mesomorphs.

Genetic influences on delinquency have been examined through studies of twins and adopted children. Glenn Walters (1992) analyzed 38 family, twin, and adoption studies on the gene–crime relationship and found that only the older, poorly designed studies claim to show a relationship. The newer (1975–1989) better-designed studies provide less support for the gene–crime hypothesis. Rather than viewing criminal behavior as a product of nature *or* nurture, it seems preferable to examine the relative contributions of genetic and environmental concerns (Walters, 1992, p. 608). David Rowe and D. Wayne Osgood (1984) viewed genetic factors as contributing to certain individual differences that in turn interact with specific sociological and environmental conditions that influence delinquent behavior.

IQ and Delinquency

The relationship between IQ and delinquency received much attention in the early part of this century. Henry Goddard (1920) found that some juveniles in training schools were what he called "feebleminded," and he created much debate when he concluded that half of all juvenile delinquents were mentally defective. Relatively few studies were published on the topic again until the 1960s and 1970s. D. J. West and D. P. Farrington (1973) conducted a longitudinal study of 411 English boys and found that those who later became criminals had lower IQ scores than those who did not become criminals, leading them to conclude that intelligence is a predictive factor of future delinquency. Lis Kirkegaard-Sorensen and Sarnoff Mednick (1977) conducted a similar longitudinal study of 311 Danish children. Results on intelligence tests supported the West and Farrington study: Adolescents who later committed criminal acts had a significantly lower tested intelligence than their more law-abiding peers (p. 271). Travis Hirschi and Michael Hindelang (1977) examined several research studies, including Hirschi's data from his California study; and Wolfgang and associates' (Wolfgang, Figlio, & Sellin, 1972) data from the Philadelphia studies. They concluded that IQ is more important than race or social class for predicting delinquency. The findings of these studies were supported by analyses of data on Danish students that demonstrated that low IQ is related to delinquent involvement independently of the effects of socioeconomic status (Moffitt, Gabrielli, Mednick, & Schulsinger, 1981, p. 155). The authors suggest that the IQ–delinquency relationship is likely explained in part by the lower verbal ability of children with low verbal IQ, who experience frustration and failure in school. The frustrating school experiences may contribute to delinquency by creating a negative attitude toward authority, by leading the failing student to seek rewards in less socially desirable settings, or by making the student more vulnerable to delinquent peer pressure when peers provide a source of self-esteem (Moffitt et al., 1981, p. 155). Wilson and Herrnstein (1985) believe there is clear evidence for an association between intelligence and crime. A student who is struggling academically in the classroom may feel justified in engaging in theft, violence, and other illegal behavior outside school. School failure increases students' feelings of unfairness and in turn increases their chances of delinquent involvement. Failure in school also predicts a likelihood of failure in the workplace. Young people who fail in school also find it hard to get jobs, and are more likely to yield to the tempting rewards of criminal behavior.

Others have questioned the IQ–delinquency relationship. Rosenbaum (1976) argued that the practice of curriculum tracking may depress IQ of students placed in the lower tracks; and Simons (1978) suggested that IQ can change in response to environmental factors and is therefore unstable over time. Scott Menard and Barbara Morse (1984) believe that school practices of tracking that tend to generate failure may affect IQ itself and confound the relationship between IQ and academic performance. They concluded from an analysis of longitudinal data of San Diego high school students that the correlation of IQ with delinquency is not because IQ has a causal effect on delinquent behavior. Rather, it is one of many individual characteristics that schools tend to select for differential treatment among students.

Proponents of the IQ–delinquency hypothesis nevertheless insist that there is ample evidence to support a statistically significant relationship. Robert Gordon (1987) compared delinquency prevalence rates and concluded that the higher arrest rates and court appearance rates of minority males are best explained by differences in IQ—and not by geographical location, city size, or socioeconomic status. Gordon concludes that because there are differences in IQ between black and white students before they enter school, and the differences remain throughout schooling, we should seriously consider race differences in IQ when confronting the crime problem (Gordon, 1987, pp. 91–92). Wilson and Herrnstein (1985) suggest that intelligence makes a difference in the types of crimes committed by offenders, in that more intelligent offenders tend to commit crimes that have a lower risk of arrest and prosecution, and that involve preparation and planning. Less intelligent offenders, on the other hand, are more likely to commit crimes with an immediate payoff or gratification—generally, crimes of violence that are acted on impulsively (pp. 166–167). Empirical evidence from research studies does indicate that there is a relationship between intelligence and types of crimes committed by delinquents. Anthony Walsh (1987) analyzed IQ and offense data from the files of male delinquents and concluded that those with lower IQs commit impulsive and spontaneous crimes that offer instant gratification, while more intelligent offenders are more "future-oriented" as they tend to commit crimes that require planning and offer deferred gratification, but that also lead to more valuable pay-offs (pp. 288–289). Longitudinal research provides additional evidence of a relationship between early intelligence scores and later involvement in delinquent behavior. Paul Lipsitt, Sephen Buka, and Lewis Lipsitt (1990) analyzed data of 3,164 children involved in the Brown University cohort of the National Collaborative Perinatal Project. Children who scored lower on IQ tests at ages 4 and 7 had a significantly higher risk of later delinquent involvement. Their findings suggest that children with lower IQs who are identified as disruptive and with behavior problems at an early age may be helped to avoid further delinquent behavior in adolescence if they receive early intervention from school counselors and family therapists (see Lipsitt et al., 1990, p. 207).

Table 3.1	Biosocial Explanations of Delinquency	
	Explanation	**Strength**
Genetic	Delinquent traits and predispositions are inherited; deviance, criminality of parents may predict children's deviance.	Explains why only a small percentage of youth in high-crime areas become delinquent; and why some youth in low-crime areas do become delinquent.
Biochemical	Delinquency is a function of diet, vitamin intake, hormonal imbalance, food allergies, or toxic chemicals.	Shows how chemicals and the environment interact with personal traits to influence behavior.
Neurological	Delinquents often have brain impairments, learning disabilities, attention deficit hyperactive disorder, and brain dysfunctions that are related to deviance.	Explains irrational violent behavior and delinquency; shows how personal traits interact with the environment to influence behavior.

Learning Disabilities and Delinquency

Juvenile justice practitioners have noticed that delinquent youth seem unable to learn effectively in normal classroom settings. The idea that learning disabilities (LDs) may be a cause of delinquency originally stemmed from anecdotal evidence of persons who worked with delinquent populations. Learning disabilities refer not to lower intelligence, but to difficulties in the use of spoken or written language and in the ability to focus and attend to verbal tasks. According to the National Advisory Committee on Handicapped Children in 1975, children with special learning disabilities have a disorder in the psychological process involved in understanding or using spoken or written languages. The LD may involve a problem of listening, thinking, talking, reading, writing, spelling, or arithmetic. Conditions may include brain injury, minimal brain dysfunction, dyslexia, or aphasia (Podboy & Mallory, 1978). Learning disabilities do *not* include visual or hearing handicaps, mental retardation, or emotional disturbance. Research has established a link between low academic achievement and delinquency (see Maguin & Loeber, 1996); but that is not the same as a delinquency–LD connection, which has come under question because of methodological concerns.

Many researchers claim to have research evidence supporting a relationship between learning disabilities and juvenile delinquency. Several explanations have been offered for the apparent link between learning disabilities and delinquency (Post, 1981; Malmgren, Abbott, & Hawkins, 1999). One is the *susceptibility rationale,* which suggests that due to neurological and intellectual impairment along with impulsiveness and hyperactivity, LD (learning disabled) children are less receptive to social cues and may not learn from experience as well as other youth. Their learning disability leads to uncontrollable antisocial behavior, and they develop negative self-images as they are then grouped with children who perceive delinquent behavior as part of their expected roles. The second is the *school failure* explanation, that youth with learning disabilities experience academic failure and may be labeled by teachers and other students as school failures. In spite of how hard they try, LD children are faced with failure each day in the school setting. The daily experience of failure and frustration leads such children to withdraw and not participate in class work. They may attempt to gain recognition by acting out in the classroom. Learning disabled children are labeled as a problem, which results in negative self-images that are reinforced by the adults and peers around them. These youth are then more likely to be truant, drop out of school, and thereby increase their interaction with other dropouts and delinquent peers and involvement in delinquency.

A third explanation is the *differential treatment* hypothesis. Studies show that a higher proportion of LD children are arrested and incarcerated. It is estimated that about 10% of children in the general population have learning disorders; and estimates of LD among adjudicated delinquents range from 26% to 73% (Zimmerman, Rich, Keilitz, & Broder, 1981). Some have suggested that such disproportionate representation is additional support for the relationship between learning disabilities and delinquency. Others suggest, however, that youth with LD engage in no more serious or frequent delinquency than other youth, but are more likely to be arrested and adjudicated than other youth (Malmgren et al., 1999).

John Podboy and William Mallory (1978) analyzed intelligence test and aptitude test scores of 250 juveniles in a detention facility in California and found that 12.9% were developmentally disabled and 48.9% were learning disabled (p. 31). The juveniles with learning disabilities tended to come from larger families; they had poorer school performance, poorer English grades, and were likely to have been in a remedial reading class. Podboy and Mallory's findings led them to conclude that approximately 13% of those who enter the juvenile justice system may be below average in IQ, and close to 50% of the juvenile delinquent population may be learning disabled (1978, p. 33). One type of learning disability is attention deficit and hyperactivity (referred to as "ADD" or "ADHD"). David Offord and his associates (Offord, Sullivan, Allen, & Abrams, 1979) compared 31 delinquent children who were also hyperactive with 35 delinquents who were not hyperactive. The hyperactive delinquents had more antisocial symptoms, and an earlier onset of them; and they were characterized as being more reckless and irresponsible, and more involved in fighting and drug abuse than the nonhyperactive delinquents. The two groups did not differ in socioeconomic status, IQ, or in school performance prior to the onset of antisocial behavior.

Terrie Moffitt (1990) analyzed longitudinal data of a birth cohort of 435 boys, comparing self-reported delinquency scores and assessments for attention deficit disorder (ADD). She found that delinquents with ADD began life with significant motor skills deficits and more family adversity; they had difficulty meeting the demands of school; experienced reading failure soon after entering school and fell further behind their peers in reading as they approached high school. The antisocial behavior of the ADD boys was more persistent than that of non-ADD boys and became significantly worse over the years. The link between attention deficit disorder and delinquency appears to be highlighted by her finding that the greatest increase in antisocial behavior of the ADD boys coincided with their entry into school and identified reading failure (Moffitt, 1990). Britt Klinteberg, David Magnusson, and Daisy Schalling (1989) analyzed longitudinal data including scores on personality and impulsiveness scales for subjects in their teens and again at age 26–27 years, and found that early indications of hyperactive behavior was an important predictor of adult impulsivity. They suggested that boys who were hyperactive at an early age are a high risk for delinquency at a young adult age.

Studies that show a link between delinquency and learning disabilities have also been criticized for methodological weaknesses, however. Robert Pasternack and Reid Lyon (1982) found no support for the contention that the majority of juvenile delinquents exhibit learning disabilities. They found no significant difference between prevalence of learning disabled youth from a juvenile delinquent sample and the public school population, when age was held constant. They suggested that the contradiction between their results and those of previous studies supporting a JD–LD link stems from differences in definitions of learning disabilities and in the diagnostic procedures used to identify them (p. 11). Malmgren et al. (1999) conducted a 7-year longitudinal study to examine whether the presence of learning disabilities increases a youth's risk of becoming a juvenile delinquent. They studied self-report data and official court records for 515 students, 51 (10%) of whom were youth with LD. When controlling for demographic variables, their findings did not support any direct relationship between LD and delinquency. Malmgren and her associates suggest that findings of an LD–delinquency relationship by other researchers may actually be explained by confounding effects of age, ethnicity, or socioeconomic status. It may be that LD youths are not involved in more delinquent behavior than non-LD youths, but they may be more likely to be arrested, adjudicated, and incarcerated than other youth.

In summary, while there are some questions about the exact association between juvenile delinquency and learning disabilities, it is clear that many children with learning disabilities do fail in school; many of them do act out in response to their experience of failure and frustration; and many of them do find their way into the justice system. The delinquent behavior of many of these youth justifiably brings them to the attention of juvenile authorities; but it is also apparent that decisions of juvenile justice officials to process them through the system may be influenced by the learning problems and school failure as well as by the antisocial behavior of these youth.

POLICY AND PRACTICE 3.1   EDUCATION, DISABILITY, AND JUVENILE JUSTICE

There appears to be an association between learning disabilities, educational failure, and delinquency. A disproportionate number of youth with educational disabilities are involved in juvenile court cases, and many are committed to juvenile correctional facilities. The National Center on Education, Disability and Juvenile Justice (EDJJ) has examined this national problem with funding assistance from the U.S. Department of Education and the U.S. Department of Justice. Researchers in this national center have found that at least three to five times as many youth with educational disabilities are involved with the courts and corrections compared with other students in the general public school population. The overrepresentation of these youth with disabilities in the juvenile justice system is associated with school failure, dropout, poorly developed social skills, and inadequate school and community services. A number of theories (some noted in this chapter) have been developed to explain the relationship between learning disabilities and delinquency; but the profession still lacks sufficient knowledge and research findings to enable professionals, parents, and policymakers to respond most effectively to this problem. The National Center for EDJJ continues to develop, analyze, and disseminate data to inform policy and practices regarding youth with educational disabilities who may be at risk for involvement in the juvenile justice system. The Center focuses on assisting practitioners, policymakers, researchers, and juvenile advocates to identify and implement effective school-based delinquency prevention programs, special education services in juvenile corrections facilities, and to assist in the transition of youth re-entering schools from secure correctional settings.

SOURCE: National Center on Education, Disability and Juvenile Justice. (2008). *What we do*. College Park, MD: National Center on Education, Disability and Juvenile Justice. Retrieved March 5, 2009, from http://www.edjj.org/aboutedjj/about.html.

Discussion Questions

1. Based on what you have read, personally noticed or experienced, or can imagine: How might educational and learning disabilities lead to school failure, dropout, behavior problems in school, disciplinary actions, and possibly delinquency?

2. Suggest some ways for teachers and principals to identify youth who may be educationally disabled.

3. Suggest some alternatives and strategies for teachers and principals to intervene in school problems such as poor performance, frustration, and discipline with students who are educationally disabled.

4. Suggest some alternatives and strategies for juvenile probation officers to assist and advocate for educationally disabled juveniles who come to their attention.

Psychological Explanations of Delinquency

Personality characteristics and individual differences in learning are the major emphases of psychological explanations of delinquency. August Aichhorn (1936) drew upon the psychoanalytic theories of Sigmund Freud and suggested that juvenile delinquents had difficulty conforming to parental and societal expectations because they had not developed a healthy superego. Fritz Redl and David Wineman (1951) also argued that juvenile delinquents had an inadequate superego so that they tended to follow the impulses and drives of the id. Psychoanalytic theories have been criticized because it is impossible to establish a causal relationship between a person's mental state and delinquent behavior. Sheldon and Eleanor Glueck (1950) compared 500 juvenile offenders and 500 non-offenders and found that the delinquents were more defiant toward authority, extroverted, resentful, hostile, suspicious, and defensive than the nondelinquents. Conger and Miller (1966) found that delinquents were more emotionally unstable, impulsive, suspicious, hostile, irritable, and egocentric than nondelinquents.

Psychological learning theories include behaviorism, social learning, and moral development. According to B. F. Skinner (1953), behavior is conditioned by the reinforcements and punishments that it produces. Reinforcements increase the likelihood that the behavior will be repeated, and punishments decrease the probability of the behavior being repeated. Skinner, who introduced the concept of behaviorism, is regarded as the most influential psychologist of the 20th century. *Behaviorism* has contributed a great deal to understanding human behavior, but critics contend that it falls short of explaining the role of cognitive mental processes involved in behavior. *Social learning theory* attempts to explain why some adolescents engage in delinquent behavior while others, in similar environments, do not. According to this theory, behavior is a reflection of people observing and imitating other persons (see Bandura, 1977). Research evidence suggests that some delinquent behavior is a result of observing the actions of others; and many believe that television and movie viewing may affect aggressive and violent behavior (Josephson, 1987). Child psychiatrists have evidence to indicate that children who view a lot of television violence are more likely to behave more aggressively (American Academy of Child & Adolescent Psychiatry, 2002). Children who view shows in which violence is more realistic, is frequently repeated, and goes unpunished are more likely to imitate what they see. Children with emotional, behavioral, learning, or impulse control problems may be more easily influenced by television violence. The impact of frequently viewing violence may be immediately evident in the child's behavior or may surface years later. Viewing violence can affect young people even when the family atmosphere shows no tendency toward violence.

POLICY AND PRACTICE 3.2   CHILDREN AND TV VIOLENCE

Experts in child development and psychology have recognized an association between viewing violence and the probability of acting out with violence. This problem has become more acute as an increasing number of television shows have portrayed violence, and as more children are viewing television for a greater number of hours each week. The American Academy of Child and Adolescent Psychiatry has expressed concern about the problem of children and television violence. American children on average watch from three to four hours of television daily. Experts tell us that television may be a powerful, influential factor in developing persons' value systems and in shaping behavior. Television therefore may have a positive influence when the programs are educational and present appropriate ethical and pro-social values. The opposite is true, however, when television shows do not present positive values and behavior; and unfortunately much of television programming today is violent. Many studies have been conducted on the effects of television violence. Researchers have found that children and youth who watch many hours of television violence may:

- Be desensitized or become "numb" to the horrors and effects of violence.
- Gradually begin to accept violence as a way to solve problems.
- Begin to imitate and act out the violence that they observe on television.
- Begin to identify with certain violent characters or victims of violence.

According to social learning theory, viewing many hours of television violence may cause children to become more aggressive. The types of television shows viewed make a difference. Cartoons portray a lot of violence, but they are not as realistic and may not be copied by children. On the other hand, children who view shows in which violence is more realistic, repeated often, and goes unpunished, are more likely to imitate what they see. Some children are more vulnerable to the effects of watching television violence. Children with emotional, behavioral, learning, or impulse control problems may be more influenced by violence than other children. Finally, the effects of viewing television violence may be either more immediate or more long-term. Some children may exhibit violent behavior shortly after watching violence, while for others the violent behavior may not surface until years later.

SOURCE: American Academy of Child & Adolescent Psychiatry. (2002). *Facts for Families: Children and TV Violence.* Washington, DC: The American Academy of Child & Adolescent Psychiatry. Retrieved March 5, 2009 from http://www .aacap.org/cs/root/facts_for_families/children_and_tv_violence.

Discussion Questions

1. Given that almost all human behavior (learning to walk, talk, ride a bike, etc.) is learned, is it so surprising that violence may also be "learned behavior"? Give examples from your own experience (observed, or practiced; perpetrated, or victimized) to support this.

2. Contrary to many other social science research findings, this is one on which many citizens, policymakers, and industry leaders agree. Cite examples of how the television and movie entertainment industry have acted on this (television and movie ratings).

3. Television and movie ratings (for sex, violence, "tough" language) work only if parents do their part in monitoring and supervising their children's viewing. Suggest additional ways that the entertainment industry and technology have already acted to assist parents.

4. What other technological, educational, or policy changes would you recommend to reduce the amount of violence on television, the movies, and video games?

Entertainment industry executives argue that overregulation of their industry amounts to unfair censorship and a violation of their First Amendment right ("freedom of speech and expression"). Offer arguments to balance or counter this argument, in the interest of reducing violence, serious injury, death, and enormous costs in dollars and human lives.

Moral development theories (see Piaget, 1932; Kohlberg, 1964) focus on how children learn social rules and make judgments on the basis of those rules. In terms of Kohlberg's theory, delinquents are at a lower level of moral development than nondelinquents. They are more likely to define right and wrong in absolute terms, they focus more on external consequences, act to avoid punishment, and show little concern for the feelings of others. Nondelinquents, in contrast, have internalized societal rules and expectations. Research comparing the moral judgments of delinquents and nondelinquents shows mixed results. Critics note that Kohlberg's work focused on reasoning, not behavior; and moral and immoral behavior is inconsistent and situation specific. Psychologists discovered that children at different stages of moral development behave similarly and children at the same stages of moral development behave differently. In summary, psychological theories of delinquency are difficult to test and verify; and the relationship between personality factors and delinquent behavior has not been well supported by research.

Table 3.2 Psychological Explanations of Delinquency

	Major Premise	Strengths
Psychodynamic	Development of unconscious personality, early childhood influences; weak egos, damaged early childhood personality cause delinquency.	Explains onset of deviance and delinquency, across and regardless of social class lines problems or peer influence problems
Behaviorism	Stimulus-response, conditioning; behavior is modeled after others, is reinforced by rewards, and is extinguished by punishment.	Explains the role of parents and peers; the role of family; media and popular culture influence delinquency.
Cognitive	Intelligence (IQ); reasoning processes, perception of environment influences behavior and moral development.	Shows how delinquent behavior patterns change over time; persons mature and develop moral reasoning.

CASE IN POINT 3.3

The Case of Vinnie

Vinnie was the second of four children. His mother was a quiet, hardworking woman; his father, regularly unemployed and seldom at home, drank alcohol nearly every evening. When he drank, Vinnie's father would become physically violent and verbally abusive toward the family. Since birth, and unlike his other siblings, Vinnie was a difficult child. Temper tantrums were frequent for Vinnie until age 2. Vinnie disliked school, his teachers, his counselor, and had few friends. Vinnie repeated the third grade due to numerous truancies and low grades. In addition, Vinnie was expelled from school on two occasions for fighting. Vinnie's mother would regularly attend scheduled school meetings; however, Vinnie's father would not. According to Vinnie's mother, "Vinnie is just an energetic kid; he will eventually grow out of it. Regardless, school doesn't teach kids about the 'real world'; Vinnie's father knows what is best." Vinnie started stealing, first from his parents at the age of 8, and then shoplifting from local stores at age 9. By the age of 12, Vinnie was drinking alcohol; and by age 13, Vinnie was detained in a juvenile center for fighting.

Discussion Questions

1. How does Vinnie's case illustrate one or more of the explanations and theories in this chapter?

2. What contributing factors may have influenced Vinnie's behavior?

3. What interventions may be appropriate for Vinnie and his parents?

Biochemical Explanations of Delinquency

Biochemical factors focus on chemical imbalances in the body that may influence delinquent behavior. Researchers have found evidence that chemical imbalances in the body bring about changes in perception and hyperactivity (Hoffer, 1975). The connection between nutrition and delinquent behavior has received considerable attention in the juvenile justice system (Schauss, 1981). Stephen Schoenthaler and Walter Doraz (1983) observed that a reduction in the sugar diets of institutionalized youths brought about a corresponding reduction in the number of assaults, fights, thefts, and defiant acts. In another study they found that improving the diets of public school students was correlated with improved school performance (Schoenthaler, Doraz, & Wakefield, 1986).

CASE IN POINT 3.4

Crime and a Junk Food Diet

Researchers have observed over the past 30 years that biochemical factors may influence delinquent behavior. We noted in this chapter that chemical imbalances in the body may cause changes in perception and hyperactivity; that reducing sugar in the diets of institutionalized youths has reduced the number of assaults, fights, and thefts; and improving the diets of public school students has been associated with improved school performance. The findings of American studies funded by the National Institutes of Health are being applied by researchers and prison administrators throughout the world, from Great Britain to Australia and The Netherlands. Researchers have found an association between violence and diets that are high in omega-6 fatty acids, which are mainly from cooking oils such as soya, corn, and sunflower. In the past 100 years the use of soya oil in the United States increased from only 0.02% up to 20% of all calories consumed. Omega-6 fatty acids come mainly from deep-fried fast foods, snack foods, chips, ice cream, and margarine. In contrast, researchers have observed that industrial countries such as Japan, which is higher in the consumption of omega-3 fatty acids primarily from eating more fish, have low rates of violence, murder, and depression.

British researchers conducted a study of 231 volunteer prison inmates, half of whom were placed on a diet of more multi-vitamins, minerals, and essential fatty acid supplements; and half of whom received placebos. Results showed that those receiving the extra nutrients committed 37% fewer serious violent offenses and 26% fewer offenses overall; while those receiving placebos showed no change in their behavior. The Dutch and Australian governments are conducting similar studies to determine whether changing the diets of imprisoned offenders has positive effects on improving mood disorders and reducing violent behavior.

SOURCE: Based on "Crime, punishment and a junk food diet." (2006, November 16). *The Sydney Morning Herald*. Retrieved March 5, 2009, from http://www.smh.com.au/news/national/crime-punishment-and-a-junk-food-diet/2006/11/15/1163266639865.html.

Discussion Questions

1. Does it make sense that our diet, mood, and behavior are related? Give examples of foods or beverages that clearly have effects on mood and behavior.

2. Based on the research findings on the association between food, diet, and behavior, would you support policy changes for institutional practices in public schools? . . . juvenile residential and correctional facilities? Give examples of suggested changes.

3. Based on these research findings, would it be feasible and a good idea for judges to order juveniles on probation and their parents to reduce intake of omega-6 fatty acids and increase intake of omega-3 fatty acids? Support your answer with some examples.

4. Science and technology are increasingly improving detection of crimes (using DNA) and correction and supervision of offenders (urinalysis, electronic bracelets, GPS). Is it time to require dietary changes as another crime reduction tool? Would the courts support such a requirement? Offer your arguments to support this.

Researchers have discovered that exposure to toxic substances such as lead interferes with brain functioning and affects behavior. Herbert Needleman and his colleagues (1979) found that children with higher dentine lead levels had lower IQ test scores and exhibited more attention difficulties that resulted in poor classroom performance. Research on the long-term effects on many of the same lead-contaminated children indicated that they were more likely to have a reading disability, lower class standing in high school, increased absenteeism, and more likely to have dropped out of high school (Needleman, Schell, Bellinger, Leviton, & Allred, 1990). In a recent study, Needleman and his associates found a relationship between lead poisoning and delinquency (Needleman, Riess, Tobin, Biesecker, & Greenhouse, 1996). The most common cause of lead poisoning is lead-based paint. Though it is no longer produced, lead-based paint is still on the walls, woodwork, and windows of many older homes and apartment buildings. The children of lower-income families are more vulnerable to the effects of lead toxicity. Fortunately, lead poisoning as a cause of school failure and delinquency is preventable. Knowledge of the dangers of lead poisoning and proper building maintenance can minimize this source of learning and behavior problems among children.

The relationship between drugs and behavior is a third biochemical factor in explaining delinquency. Pharmacology experts know that drugs affect human emotions, but drugs have not been proven to cause aggressive behavior. Persons react differently to the influence of drugs, and certain personality types are affected more by drugs (McCardle & Fishbein, 1989). Whether a person engages in aggressive or antisocial behavior while under the influence of drugs depends on individual and environmental conditions (Fishbein, 1990). Alcohol and drugs are clearly associated with aggressive behavior and violent crimes; but criminologists do not agree on the exact causal relationship. Studies have not clearly demonstrated that alcohol and drug use is a cause of crime and delinquent behavior (Huizinga, Loeber, & Thornberry, 1995). Relatively few juvenile offenders have reported committing a crime while using drugs, and most youths appear to commit crime for reasons other than drug use (Altschuler & Brounstein, 1991). Elliott, Huizinga, and Ageton (1985) concluded that delinquent peer associations increase the likelihood of delinquency and drug use. That is, youths who associate with friends who use drugs and engage in delinquency are more likely themselves to use drugs and commit crime. In summary, psychological and biochemical factors are associated with delinquency, but whether they cause individuals to commit crime depends on environmental circumstances and social influences.

Individual Explanations and Justice Responses

From a juvenile justice perspective, the primary purpose for studying and understanding causes of delinquency is to develop policies and programs for preventing juvenile crime and correcting delinquents. In an ideal world, if we could eliminate the causes we could eliminate the problem. Every theory of crime has a proposed solution or strategy for reducing criminal behavior. Classical theorists who believe that crime is a free will, voluntary, and rational choice hold that the best response to crime is punishment, as we discussed above. Laws and sanctions that are designed to deter individuals from engaging in crime are the most logical response based on a rational choice explanation of crime.

Positivists hold that behavior is determined or influenced by factors that are beyond the control of the individual. The recommended responses to crime based on positivist theories therefore differ from those based on classical or choice theories. Positivists question the assumption that crime is a rational choice and that legal sanctions and harsher punishment alone are the best responses to crime. They believe that individual and social factors that cause crime must also be addressed.

Reducing crime and preventing delinquent behavior must include individual treatment programs and social change strategies that are directed at the causes and sources of criminal behavior. It is important to recognize that both theoretical perspectives, the classical and the positivist, contribute to understanding and explaining delinquent behavior. Throughout the history of juvenile justice, responses to crime and delinquency that are based on both theoretical explanations have shaped the juvenile justice system. Over the past century the juvenile justice system has implemented punitive responses as well as individual and social change strategies in attempting to reduce and prevent delinquency.

In summary, we recognize that the study of crime theories is not simply an academic or intellectual exercise. Understanding the causes of crime is essential in order to make rational, informed responses to the problem of crime. All policies, laws, and crime prevention programs are based on some beliefs about what causes the problem. Those who argue in favor of passing tougher laws to combat crime assume that offenders are acting rationally, and may be deterred by tougher laws and harsh punishment. Those, on the other hand, who argue for more rehabilitation and treatment programs assume that some underlying psychological problems, or alcohol or other drug abuse, have impaired offenders' judgment and influenced their delinquent involvement. Both of these explanations and responses are correct and appropriate for given offenders under certain circumstances. No single theory can explain all offenders, and no single crime prevention strategy can work effectively for all offenders under all circumstances. As with any problem facing society, it is important to understand the origins and causes of crime in order to make policy decisions that are more realistically in line with the true nature of the problem. Most of the major explanations of delinquency do offer accurate descriptions for why youth engage in delinquent behavior. Just as there are a variety of causes, policymakers must also take a variety of approaches to deal with the problem.

SUMMARY

- A good theory is one that explains the causes of delinquency for most youth under a variety of circumstances.
- We study theories of crime and delinquency in order to better understand why youth engage in criminal and delinquent behavior; but also to develop policies and strategies for preventing delinquency and correcting delinquents.
- Explanations of delinquency fall into one of two broad categories: classical or rational theories and positivist theories.

- Individual explanations focus on the biological, genetic, and psychological causes of delinquency.
- All of the major theoretical explanations make some contribution to our understanding of delinquent behavior, but some theories have received more extensive research support and offer more viable answers for how to prevent delinquency.
- Classical and positivist theories offer different policies and solutions for responding to crime.
- Punishment and individual change strategies are both appropriate as justice responses to delinquent behavior.

KEY TERMS

Criminological theories

Classical theory

Rational or choice theory

Routine activity theory

Positivist theory

Determinism

Individual explanations

Specific deterrence

General deterrence

DISCUSSION QUESTIONS

1. Most persons have some opinion or "theory" of what causes delinquency. Before reading this chapter, what have you believed are the five most important causes of delinquency?

2. Based on what you have read in this chapter about the individual explanations of delinquency and the research studies supporting them, what explanations would you add to your list?

3. Most of us have done some delinquent acts and have known persons who have frequently committed crimes and delinquent acts. What explanations or theories best describe some delinquent youth you have known?

4. Which of the individual explanations do you believe offer the best solutions for preventing crime and delinquency today?

WEB RESOURCES

American Academy of Child & Adolescent Psychiatry (Children and TV Violence): http://www.aacap.org/cs/root/facts_for_families/children_and_tv_violence

OJJDP Bulletin on Juveniles with Disabilities:http://www.ncjrs.gov/pdffiles1/ojjdp/179359.pdf

The National Center on Education, Disability, and Juvenile Justice: http://www.edjj.org/

Sociological Explanations of Delinquency

The academic discipline of sociology is a study of group behavior, descriptions of social groups, social problems, and how society and social factors influence individual behavior. The field of criminology was originally developed by sociologists and is a specialized area of study within the discipline of sociology. Criminologists have traditionally viewed the causes of delinquency and criminal behavior *not* as biogenetic or psychological in nature, but as a social problem. Sociological explanations of delinquency emphasize social influences on individuals caused by the structure of society, societal change, social disorganization, subcultural differences, and social processes that influence behavior. In this chapter we discuss and summarize the predominant criminological theories that have been developed by sociologists. Sociological explanations of delinquency fall into three main categories: social structure, social process, and social reaction theories. More recent criminological explanations include developmental and life-course theories. No single theory can explain all of the causes of criminal behavior. A number of criminologists have therefore developed general and integrated theories to explain crime and delinquency. Most criminological theories have been based on studies of male delinquents and focus primarily on explaining delinquent involvement of boys. With the increase in female crime and delinquency, criminologists have developed theories to explain the different reasons that girls and young women engage in criminal behavior. We conclude the chapter with a discussion of the applications of sociological theories for developing and implementing delinquency prevention programs and juvenile justice responses to delinquency.

Social Structure Theories

Social structure theorists claim that forces such as social disorganization, status frustration, and cultural deviance lead lower-class youths to become involved in delinquent behavior. Social structure explanations of delinquency focus on the social and cultural environment in which adolescents grow up and on the subcultural groups with which they become involved. Social structure theorists, relying on official statistics as the primary measure of crime, claim that such forces as cultural deviance, social disorganization, and status frustration lead lower-class youths to become involved in delinquent behavior. Three categories of social structure explanations are social disorganization theory, strain theory, and cultural deviance theory.

Social disorganization theory was developed by Clifford Shaw and Henry McKay (1942) who were in the School of Urban Criminology at the University of Chicago. They were joined by Walter Miller (1958), a social anthropologist at the university. They studied Chicago's urban development and noted changes in the quality of life as industrialization changed the city. They noted that urban growth produced a condition of social disorganization characterized by urban density, overcrowding, substandard housing, low income, unemployment, poor schools, and family problems. Large numbers of European immigrants were moving to the city and taking advantage of jobs available in the factories, businesses, and stockyards. Juvenile delinquency was commonly believed to be a problem of "morally inferior" ethnic groups, and many upper-class citizens believed in the stereotype that foreign immigrants had low moral values and were responsible for the increase of crime. The Chicago School sociologists challenged this prejudiced view with a scientific approach to the study of delinquency. Based on their research, they held that urban growth produced a condition of social disorganization, characterized by urban density, overcrowding, substandard housing, low income, unemployment, poor schools, and family problems. The increase in crime that occurred with urban growth was due not so much to immoral, crime-prone immigrants but to social disorganization and the conditions over which individuals had little control. Social disorganization theory has made a significant impact on the study and understanding of crime and delinquency since its development by Shaw and McKay a century ago. This theory directs attention *not* to individual responsibility for crime, but rather to the need for adequate housing, quality public schools, equal employment opportunities, and other social institutions as metropolitan areas experience unbridled growth.

SOURCE: © Lambert/Getty Images.

Photo 4.1 Juveniles vandalizing an abandoned
inner-city building illustrates the social
disorganization explanation of delinquency.

Strain theory is the second type of social structure theory. This theory explains delinquency as being caused by the "strain" or frustration of not having an equal opportunity or means to achieve commonly shared goals such as economic or social success. Robert Merton (1957) was an eminent criminologist who formulated strain theory around the concept of "anomie" or "normlessness." Merton applied the concept of anomie to rapidly changing conditions in society where competition for success, wealth, and material goods is highly valued. Persons with little formal education and few economic resources are denied the ability to acquire the goals of American society, thus producing a sense of alienation, hopelessness, and frustration. Merton claimed that this sense of anomie often leads to attaining socially desired goals through criminal or delinquent means. Social disorganization leads to uncertainty, confusion, and shifting moral values, referred to as anomie or normlessness. Conditions of anomie exist when the rule of law is weakened and becomes powerless to maintain social control. Under conditions of anomie, crime may be considered a "normal" response to existing social conditions.

The emphasis is that most people share similar values, goals, and aspirations; but many people do not have an equal ability or the means to achieve those goals, such as economic or social success. The discrepancy between what persons want and their limited opportunities to achieve them produces frustration, or "strain." Because opportunities for success are more open for the middle- and upper classes, strain is experienced most by those in the lower socioeconomic class, where quality education and employment opportunities are more limited. The strain and frustration resulting from blocked opportunities increases the likelihood that some individuals will use deviant and illegitimate means to achieve their goals. Strain theory explains why many lower-class youth resort to theft, drug dealing, and other delinquent behavior when they perceive fewer legitimate means and opportunities to achieve their goals. Strain and social disorganization are similar because they emphasize the relationship between social variables such as poverty, economic opportunity, and available goods and services to crime and delinquency. Strain is more common among lower-class persons, who live in inner-city urban areas that are characterized more by social problems and crime. Strain theory has been expanded and further developed by other criminologists. The opportunity–structure theories (Cloward & Ohlin, 1960) prompted government-funded policies such as "Head Start" and jobs programs for lower-class youths as a way to enhance educational and employment opportunities and reduce delinquency.

Robert Agnew (1992) extended Merton's theory of strain and anomie to better explain varieties of delinquent behavior through the general strain theory. Agnew identified three sources of strain:

1. Strain caused by the *failure to achieve positively valued goals,* basically the same as Merton's theory of anomie.

2. Strain caused by the *removal of positively valued stimuli* from the individual. Examples include the loss of a girl- or boyfriend, death of a loved one, divorce or separation of parents, or leaving friends and moving to a new neighborhood or school.

3. Strain as the *presentation of negative stimuli,* such as child abuse and neglect, physical punishment, family and peer conflict, stressful life conditions, school failure, and criminal victimization (see Agnew, 1992, p. 57).

Agnew's general strain theory has made an important contribution to explaining delinquency. The theory helps to explain how stressful incidents and sources of strain in the life course influence patterns of offending. There is ample research support for the general strain theory. Youth who report being "hassled" by peers, have bad peer relationships, or experience victimization or similar "negative life events" are also the persons most likely to engage in delinquency (Agnew & White, 1992). Research shows that indicators of strain such as family breakup, unemployment, moving, feelings of dissatisfaction with friends and school are positively related to delinquency (Paternoster & Mazerolle, 1994).

Cultural deviance theory, also referred to as subcultural theory, is the third type of social structure theory. Subcultural theorists point to observations that values and attitudes of lower-class youth differ from mainstream middle-class values. Youth from socially disorganized neighborhoods marked by unemployment, poverty, and social problems develop values and attitudes of that subculture. Cultural deviance theory suggests that youth violate the law because they follow the values of their lower-class community. Honesty and hard work make little sense to youth growing up in a neighborhood where poverty, unemployment, and crime are part of life. Drug dealing and prostitution are viewed by many lower-class youth as a way to overcome unemployment and poverty. Youth learn to value being tough and "street smart." Threats and physical attacks are preferred over verbal negotiation for resolving conflicts in some subcultures.

Walter Miller (1958) described a number of "focal concerns" that dominate lower-class cultures and often run counter to lawful, middle-class behavior:

1. *Trouble:* Getting into trouble and being able to handle trouble are valued, so trouble-making behavior such as fighting, drinking, and sexual misconduct are quite accepted.

2. *Toughness:* Surviving in lower-class subcultures requires toughness, so physical strength, fighting ability, and mental toughness are valued over being soft and sentimental.

3. *Smartness:* Formal education is not valued as much as being "street smart" and able to outsmart or "out-con" one's opponent.

4. *Excitement:* Similar to "trouble"; members of the lower class seek to enliven their tough life through excitement such as gambling, fighting, getting drunk, and sexual activity.

5. *Fate:* Members of the lower class believe there is little they can do to change their course in life, and that any good that may come their way is simply through luck and good fortune.

6. *Autonomy:* Lower-class youth learn to value being independent, and not depend on anyone else, particularly authority figures such as police, parents, and teachers (see Miller, 1958).

Miller's "focal concerns" accurately describe the attitudes and behaviors of many lower-class and even middle-class youth today. Getting in trouble is common among many youth, and a reason given for much delinquent activity is excitement ("because we were bored"). Poor school performance among lower-class students may be explained by the value placed on "street smarts" over being smart in the classroom; and one's life success being ruled by fate more than personal goals and achievements. Many youth carry guns in order to protect themselves, thus displaying their toughness and autonomy. The primary reason for weapons in schools is because youth who feel threatened and fearful believe they cannot depend on school officials for protection and must take matters into their own hands. Street-smart youth take care of themselves and do not depend on police for protection.

In summary, social structure, strain, and cultural deviance explanations claim that delinquent acts are often an expression of frustration because of limited educational and employment opportunities, particularly of lower-income and disadvantaged youth. Delinquent acts are viewed as reactions to the frustration caused by blocked opportunity. Social structure and strain theories are supported by considerable research evidence in explaining a great deal of delinquent behavior.

Social Process Theories

Social process explanations of delinquency focus not on societal structures but on social interactions between individuals and environmental influences that may lead to delinquent behavior. Differential association theory holds that delinquency is a learned behavior as youth interact closely with other deviant youth. Control theory is a social process explanation that focuses on social bonds that reduce the risk of delinquent involvement. According to control theory, delinquency is more likely among youth who lack social bonds and positive social interactions among parents and peers.

Differential association theory was developed by Edwin Sutherland, who believed that delinquency is learned behavior as youths interact with each other. The theory is founded on a number of propositions (Sutherland & Cressey, 1970, pp. 75–77):

1. Criminal behavior is learned.

2. Criminal behavior is learned in interaction with other persons in a process of communication.

3. The principal part of the learning of criminal behavior occurs within intimate personal groups.

4. When criminal behavior is learned, the learning includes (a) techniques of committing the crime; and (b) the specific direction of motives, drives, rationalizations, and attitudes.

5. The specific direction of the motives and drives is learned from definitions of the legal codes as favorable or unfavorable.

6. A person becomes delinquent because of an excess of definitions favorable to violation of law over definitions unfavorable to violation of law. This is the principle of differential association.

7. Differential association may vary in frequency, duration, priority, and intensity.

8. The process of learning criminal behavior by association with criminal and anticriminal patterns involves all of the mechanisms that are involved in any other learning.

9. While criminal behavior is an expression of general needs and values, it is not explained by those general needs and values since noncriminal behavior is an expression of the same needs and values.

Sutherland's *differential association theory* remains an important explanation for juvenile delinquency. It is difficult to argue against a theory that maintains crime is learned like other behaviors. This explanation also has a positive appeal as it holds that youth are changeable and can be taught prosocial behavior. Delinquency prevention efforts may be effective when they are directed at reducing the criminal influence among groups of antisocial youths. Sutherland's differential association theory has stimulated considerable research on explaining delinquent behavior. Burgess and Akers (1966) reformulated the differential association theory according to operant conditioning principles, and Akers (1985) further developed an explanation of deviant behavior according to a social learning approach.

CASE IN POINT 4.1

West Side Story and Delinquency Theories

West Side Story is the award-winning adaptation of the classic romantic tragedy, *Romeo and Juliet,* by William Shakespeare. The 1957 Broadway play was based on a book by Arthur Laments, with music by Leonard Bernstein and lyrics by Stephen Sondheim. The 1961 musical film was directed by Jerome Robbins and Robert Wise. The story revolves around two warring New York City gangs: the "Jets," a white gang led by Riff; and the Puerto Rican "Sharks," led by Bernardo. Tony, a former leader of the Jets and Riff's best friend, sees Maria, Bernardo's little sister, at a dance. Their eyes meet across the room, and it is love at first sight. Despite opposition from both sides, they meet secretly and their love grows deeper. The Jets and the Sharks plan one last rumble, and whoever wins gains control of the streets. Maria sends Tony to stop the fight in hopes that he can end the violence. His attempts fail, however, and tragedy strikes as the story comes to a climactic and heartbreaking ending.

SOURCE: Internet Movie Data Base. (2009). *West Side Story*. Retrieved February 7, 2009, from http://www.imdb.com/title/tt0055614/.

Some excerpts from the lyrics of one of the songs in the Broadway musical illustrate the points made in this and the previous chapter. Delinquency has multiple causes, and youth act out according to the roles they have learned from their environment and those around them.

"Gee, Officer Krupke"

Dear kindly sergeant Krupke, You gotta understand

It's just our bringin' up-ke, that gets us out of hand.

Our mothers all are junkies, our fathers are all drunks.

Golly Moses, natcherly we're punks. . . . .

We never had the love that ev'ry child oughta get.

We ain't no delinquents, we're misunderstood. . . .

Dear kindly judge, your Honor, my parents treat me rough. . . .

They didn't wanna have me, but somehow I was had.

Leapin' lizards! That's why I'm so bad!. . . .

This boy don't need a judge, he needs an analyst's care!

It's just his neurosis that oughta be curbed.

He's psychologic'ly disturbed!. . . .

This boy don't need a doctor, just a good honest job.

Society's played him a terrible trick, and sociologic'ly he's sick!. . . .

Juvenile delinquency is purely a social disease!. . . .

SOURCE: Adapted with permission. "Gee, Officer Krupke," *West Side Story.* © Copyright 1956, 1957, 1958, 1959 by Amberson Holdings LLC and Stephen Sondheim. Copyright renewed. Leonard Bernstein Music Publishing Company LLC, publisher. Boosey & Hawkes, Inc., sole agent. International copyright secured.

Discussion Questions

1. Suggest how the characters and actions in *West Side Story* illustrate social structure theory.

2. How do members of the Sharks and the Jets illustrate cultural deviance theory (such as that of Walter Miller's "focal concerns")?

3. Identify some psychological and sociological theories of delinquency that are illustrated by the song "Gee, Officer Krupke."

Control theories begin with the premise that the way to understand delinquency is to know the characteristics of persons who conform, and do *not* engage in delinquency. The focal question therefore is *not* "Why do youth become delinquent?" but rather "Why do most youth *not* engage in repetitive, serious delinquency?" The research supporting control theory was based on self-report measures of delinquency, and not just official police measures of juveniles who were apprehended and arrested. Control theory therefore begins with the assumption that most youth engage in some deviance and delinquency during adolescence. The basic idea of control theory is that human behavior is guided by various controls, some within the person, and some outside the person. An internal source of control, for example, is one's self-concept; and external sources are the family, school, and other social institutions.

Walter Reckless (1961) held that internal factors such as self-control and external factors such as parental supervision, discipline, and social institutions help to "insulate" or "contain" persons from crime. Reckless and his associates emphasized that inner containment, or self-concept, was a major variable in steering youth away from delinquency (Reckless, Dinitz, & Kay, 1956, pp. 744–746). There are problems in developing operational definitions for a valid and reliable measure of self-concept, but studies have confirmed that the greater the self-esteem, the less likely a youth is to become involved in delinquent behavior (Jensen, 1973).

Travis Hirschi (1969) developed the most prominent **social control theory,** based on self-report results of a large sample of youth. Hirschi explained the presence or absence of delinquent involvement based on four elements of the social bond: attachment, commitment, involvement, and belief. *Attachment* refers to the ties of affection and respect that youth have to parents, teachers, and friends; it helps youth avoid the temptation to commit delinquent acts. *Commitment* to socially acceptable activities and values, such as educational and employment goals, helps youth avoid delinquency by increasing the cost and risks involved. *Involvement* in conventional activities keeps youth occupied and reduces their opportunities to commit deviant acts. *Belief* refers to respect for the law and societal norms, and derives from close relations with other positive role models, especially parents. Hirschi tested and supported his control theory by giving a self-report survey to more than 4,000 junior and senior high school youth in California. The theory has generated a considerable amount of research.

Control theory has several strengths. It has clear concepts that lend themselves to empirical research and testing. Others have used the social control model to develop integrated theories patterned on the social bond (Elliott, Ageton, & Canter, 1979). Hirschi's control theory has made valuable contributions to understanding the relationship between delinquency and the major social institutions of family and the school. He examined the role of attachment to parents, and the relative importance of peer relationships as youth mature. The theory addresses educational aspirations and goals, student–teacher relationships, and the role of school performance and behavior in delinquency.

A major emphasis of control theory is the role of parents, peers, and school experiences in explaining delinquency. Hirschi (1969) found that students who perform poorly in school reduce their interest in school and related activities, and increase the likelihood of committing delinquent acts. Students' perceived academic ability and actual performance affect their bond to school, and his data show that these are associated with delinquent involvement (p. 120). Those with weak attachments to parents tend to show less respect for teachers and to dislike school (Hirschi, 1969, pp. 131–132).

The nature of peer relationships has an intervening effect on parental attachment, school experiences, and delinquency. Attachment to peers does not necessarily mean less attachment to parents. It appears to depend on *to whom* one is attached, and the nature of one's peer attachments. Linden and Hackler (1973) found that self-reported delinquency was inversely related to ties to parents and conventional peers, but positively related to ties to deviant peers. Others suggest that parental attachment affects delinquency, which affects school performance, which in turn affects parental attachment (Liska & Reed, 1985, pp. 556–557). Parents, not school, are the major institutional sources of delinquency control, for lower-class more than middle-class youth (pp. 557–558). According to Hirschi's control theory, delinquents are less dependent on peers than are nondelinquents, a finding that has been supported by other research. In a study comparing nondelinquent high school students with a group of court-adjudicated students on supervision and also attending school, the delinquents scored higher on the "self-sufficient" scale while nondelinquents scored higher on "group dependence" (Lawrence, 1985). The role of parents, peers, and school as factors in promoting or preventing delinquent behavior deserves careful examination, particularly for practical and policy implications. A study of school performance, peers, and delinquency using self-report data from the National Youth Survey compared youths' school attachment and how many of their friends had committed delinquent acts (Lawrence, 1991b). Results indicated that peer relationships have a greater influence on delinquent behavior than attachment to school. Youth who had fewer friends who had committed delinquent acts reported less delinquent involvement themselves, regardless of high or low school attachment. Youth with more friends who admitted to some delinquency reported a higher number of delinquent acts themselves, and this held true even for students with higher school attachment. Those with more delinquent friends and lower school attachment reported the highest self-reported delinquency rate. The findings indicate that peer relationships are more important than school attachment in explaining delinquent behavior (Lawrence, 1991b).

School involvement tends to reduce involvement in delinquency. Boys in Hirschi's sample who felt they had nothing to do were more likely to become involved in delinquent acts. He theorized that lack of involvement and commitment to school releases youth from a major source of time-structuring (1969, pp. 187–196). Hirschi's claim for the positive benefit of involvement has been supported by other studies. Sampson and Laub (1997) found that weak school attachment and poor school performance have the strongest effects on delinquency. Gottfredson and Hirschi (1990) explained that the relationship stems from the school system's rewards and discipline, which also increase young peoples' level of self-control. Schools require students to be in a certain place on time, to be orderly and attentive; and schools reward good behavior and performance. The authors also note the important role of parents in support of education. The discipline, structure, rewards, and greater self-control provided by schools can happen only when students have parental support and regularly attend school. Parents and schools share an interdependent relationship as the two most important factors that enable most youth to avoid serious involvement in delinquency.

CASE IN POINT 4.2

Stories, Movies, and Delinquency Theories

Americans fear crime and despise criminals, and yet we have a profound fascination with crime stories. Books, movies, theatrical plays, and television shows illustrate our interest in reading about and viewing stories about crime and criminals. Case in Point 4.1 on *West Side Story* in the previous pages is an example. Writers and Hollywood producers have focused on crime stories for years. These are primarily for entertainment purposes, but we can learn from these stories and examine them for how the writers have captured a piece of life in American cities. Some of the outstanding movies (many based on books) on juvenile delinquency are briefly summarized below. We encourage you to view these films and consider how the characters in each story illustrate one or more of the theories of delinquency causation.

The Outsiders. Director: Francis Ford Coppola; Writers: S. E. Hinton (book), Kathleen Rowell (screenplay). Release date: March 25, 1983. This is a story about two rival gangs, the Greasers—an urban gang of lower-class youth; and the Socies (or "socials")—a group of popular, snobbish, rich kids.

(Continued)

(Continued)

The story involves boy–girl jealousy, "turf battles," threats, weapons, and fights. The story takes a turn when members of the Greasers help rescue children from a burning building. Risk of injury and death are ever-present realities for them. Despite rays of hope, getting tired of the fighting, and wanting to get out of the urban gang life, the youth seem trapped by their environment and lifestyle. *The Outsiders* is a very good film (with well-known actors), based on an excellent book that has been used as a learning tool in junior high and high school English classes. See this film and answer the discussion questions below in relation to the plot, story lines, and dilemmas faced by the youth who are considered "outsiders."

Boyz 'n' the Hood. Director: John Singleton. Release date: July 12, 1999. This is a story of a group of childhood friends growing up in an urban ghetto in South Central Los Angeles. John Singleton portrays three friends growing up together in "the hood," taking different approaches to the tough lives they face. "Ricky" is the All-American athlete, seeking a way out through sports and looking to win a football scholarship to USC. "Doughboy," in contrast, succumbs to the violence, alcohol, and crime that surround him in the neighborhood. Their friend "Tre" is lucky to have a father, "Furious Styles," who tries to teach him to have the strength of character to do what is right and always to take responsibility for his actions. The struggles of adolescence are illustrated through a boy–girl relationship, sexual tension, and questions of right and wrong. The violence common in urban neighborhoods is played out with the death of Ricky by members of a local gang. Tre, Ricky's best friend, has to decide whether he will seek revenge for the murder or whether to stop the cycle of violence.

SOURCE: The Internet Movie Data Base. Retrieved February 9, 2009, from http://www.imdb.com/.

Discussion Questions

1. Suggest how the characters and actions in *The Outsiders* and *Boyz 'n' the Hood* illustrate the social structure or social disorganization theories.

2. How do the characters in the films illustrate strain theory or opportunity–structure theory? Do you believe that if they had equal opportunities to achieve goals through education or employment that they might choose to get out of the gang, or out of the 'hood?

3. How does cultural deviance theory (such as that of Walter Miller's focal concerns) explain the struggles in *The Outsiders* and *Boyz 'n' the Hood*?

4. What characters in either of these movies illustrate Hirschi's social control theory and the social bonds that help youth avoid delinquent behavior? What positive social bonds might have helped the Greasers or boys in the 'hood to escape the violence and crime in their lives?

Social Reaction Theories: Labeling and Conflict

Social reaction theories focus more on how society, social institutions, and government officials react to crime and delinquency than on why offenders commit crime. The theories we have discussed so far explain juvenile delinquency as a function of individual choices or characteristics, social structure, or social processes that influence delinquent involvement. Social reaction theories are different in that they explain crime as being caused by how laws are written and enforced, and how social institutions and justice agencies react to crime and criminals.

Unlike the biological, psychological, and sociological explanations that have been developed and tested for many years, social reaction theories developed in the 1960s and 1970s. Agencies of government and justice were being scrutinized and criticized in the years following the Vietnam War and the Nixon administration. Critical scholars noted that criminal laws and their enforcement tended to focus more on crimes committed by the lower class, while many white-collar crimes were ignored or punished lightly. They contended that laws written by those in power were created to serve the interests of those in power, and to keep the lower class in its place. Theorists also point to the stigmatizing effect of the judicial and correctional processes, in which offenders tend to be labeled and restricted from reintegration back into society even after serving their sentence. Despite not being as popular or having as much research support as many other theories, labeling and conflict theories do offer interesting insights on societal reactions to crime, and how changes in laws and policies will help in crime reduction.

Labeling Theory

Labeling theory begins with the understanding that most youth engage in some deviant acts, and labeling theorists use findings from self-report studies to support that contention. The initial involvement of youth in deviant and delinquent activities can be explained by many factors. Labeling theory focuses more on why some youth continue to repeat delinquent acts and often escalate to more serious delinquency. The primary assumption of the labeling perspective is that repeated delinquent behavior is caused by society's reaction to minor deviant behavior. Frank Tannenbaum (1938) first suggested that the very process of identifying and segregating deviant persons as criminals increased the likelihood that the behavior would continue. Lemert (1951) and Becker (1963) are the other major proponents of labeling theory. Lemert differentiated between "primary deviance," referring to behavior of the individual, and "secondary deviance" resulting from society's response to that behavior and that resulted in a status, role, or individual identity. Becker proposed that those in society who make and enforce the rules "create" deviants by labeling persons, who in turn tend to act out the deviant behaviors consistent with their new identity.

There has not been a great deal of research support for labeling theory. Jensen (1973) found that having a delinquent record was related to having a delinquent self-concept for young white males (but not for black youth). Jensen concluded that an official label of delinquency may not affect black youth because such labels are more common, and because the label is given by outsiders. Ageton and Elliott (1974) studied youths over a 6-year period, and concluded that police contact was followed by a greater delinquency orientation, among both lower- and upper-class boys. Other studies show mixed or negative support for labeling theory. Foster, Dinitz, and Reckless (1972) found no changes in personal relationships or parental attitudes toward boys following a juvenile court appearance. Most (90%) of the boys showed no evidence of being negatively labeled, and they believed that their official delinquency record would not pose difficulties with their finishing school. Hepburn (1977) compared the self-concepts and attitudes of nondelinquent and delinquent males. He found that the delinquents did have greater definitions of themselves as delinquents, more commitment to future delinquency and to other delinquents, lower self-concepts, and less respect for the police. However, when other variables such as socioeconomic status and self-reported delinquency were considered, he found that an arrest record had no direct effect on self-concept or delinquency identification.

Labeling theory does have a number of strengths. It provides an explanation for why many youths who become involved in minor deviant acts often continue offending and may escalate to more serious delinquent acts following initial contact with police and juvenile authorities. The theory emphasizes the important role of rule-making, power, and reactions of society and justice system authorities. As part of the symbolic interactionist perspective, labeling theory points out that some persons *do* tend to take on the roles and self-concepts expected of them. Labeling theory has many weaknesses. It lacks clear-cut definitions and testable hypotheses (Gibbs, 1966). It does not explain why youth initially commit deviant or delinquent acts, and tends to minimize the importance of delinquency. The theory appears to excuse the behavior of the delinquent and make society the culprit. The reasons or motives for why youth engage in delinquency are not explained. Overall, labeling theory has been widely criticized by criminologists and has little empirical support.

Conflict Theory

Conflict or "critical" theory shares a similarity with labeling theory in its focus on social and political institutions as causes of crime, rather than individual characteristics and criminal tendencies of offenders. Conflict theorists or critical criminologists point to the presence of conflict and competition among social classes and groups in society (Quinney, 1974). Examples that come to mind are the differences in values and beliefs between gender, race, ethnicity, political parties, and religious groups. Conflict results when competing groups vie for power, and attempt to implement laws and policies that support their views. Nowhere is this conflict more evident than in the criminal justice system, where law enforcement practices, judicial sentencing policies, and correctional trends have changed dramatically over the years. Competing groups try to convince others that their beliefs and policies offer the best answer to solve what they believe to be the most urgent types of crime problems in the nation. Conflict theory offers an explanation for why certain deviant and illegal behaviors are enforced and punished more severely. The theory explains why the number of persons arrested, convicted, and sentenced to prison has increased with criminal law and sentencing changes, despite the fact that criminal and deviant behavior has remained fairly stable over the years. That is, certain laws "criminalize" behavior that is not a crime in other countries; that was not a serious crime in this country in the past; and that is considered by some persons more of a medical or social deviance problem than a crime. A clear example is the emphasis placed on drug enforcement in America. Certain drugs have been identified as dangerous and addicting drugs and the use, possession, and sale of those drugs results in severe sentences, including jail and prison time. Other drugs, such as tobacco and alcohol, despite causing serious medical, behavioral, and social problems, do not receive the same severe criminal sanctions as marijuana and other drugs. Conflict theorists claim that economic forces, business interests (such as the alcohol and tobacco lobbies), and public sentiment of those in power are responsible for the differential enforcement of drug use. Criminal laws and their enforcement tend to focus more on crimes committed by the lower class, while many white-collar crimes are ignored or punished lightly. Critical or conflict theorists contend that laws written by those in power are done so in order to serve their own interest, and to keep the lower class in its place. An examination of the crimes committed by the thousands of persons in our growing prison population is evidence that conflict theorists have raised a critical issue in the administration of justice in America (Reiman, 1990). Most prisons and jails in America today house more persons convicted of drug offenses than property or violent offenses.

Race, Social Class, and Delinquency. Critical theorists view juvenile delinquency and juvenile justice in terms of a capitalist, class-structured society. They point to economic and social inequities that increase the probability of lower-class youth turning to crime because so few opportunities are open to them. Critical criminologists contend that the origin of the concept of "delinquency" and juvenile justice in America is based on economic and class differences. Anthony Platt (1974) argued that the role of the "child savers" in creating a separate system of juvenile justice was not so much to save wayward children, but an effort by wealthy upper-class persons to maintain the existing class structure and to control the behavior of lower-class youth. Conflict theorists view schools as social control institutions whose primary purpose is to prepare young people for entry into the work world, and to ensure that they conform to the existing capitalist structure. Lower-class and minority youth do not enjoy the same social, economic, and educational opportunities as middle- and upper-class white youths in America (Ferguson, 2000). Most youth and families look to education as the primary means by which they can compete for good jobs and improve their social standing. Equal quality education is not available to all youth, however, as differences in school funding have resulted in what one critic described as "savage inequalities" in schools throughout the United States (Kozol, 1991). Conflict theorists argue that competition among social classes restricts equal quality education and employment opportunities for some youth.

Race. Race is a significant factor in any study of juvenile delinquency and juvenile justice. African Americans and other racial and ethnic minorities are disproportionately lower class with fewer social and economic opportunities. There is evidence that black Americans suffer disproportionately both as victims and as offenders. A higher proportion of blacks live in high-crime areas, where they face a higher probability of being victims and of witnessing crime as an everyday fact of life. Young black males growing up in high-crime neighborhoods are more likely to join a gang and to engage in antisocial and delinquent behavior. Ferguson (2000) noted that school disciplinary practices such as after-school detention, suspension, and expulsion are disproportionately enforced against black males. Teachers tend to view the attitudes and behaviors of African American males as threatening and intimidating, and their behavior is monitored more closely so that minor infractions may result in sanctions while similar misbehavior by white youths is overlooked or treated more leniently. Ferguson notes that black males are not totally innocent and play an active role in this labeling process, for they view challenging teachers or school rules as a way to enhance their own "bad boy" image. Ferguson's observations offer at least a partial explanation for the disproportionate alienation, academic failure, and dropout rates of racial minorities.

News media depictions of crime and criminals tend to focus more on blacks as offenders (Lawrence & Mueller, 2003). Newspapers are more likely to identify race in a crime story when an African American is the suspect (Dorfman & Schiraldi, 2001); and minorities are overrepresented as perpetrators of crime (Romer, Jamieson, & deCoteau, 1998; Weiss & Chermak, 1998). Despite higher rates of black victimization, white victims are shown at a much higher rate on television news and in newspaper coverage (Romer et al., 1998; Sorenson, Manz, and Berk, 1998; Weiss & Chermak, 1998). Persons of color are shown primarily for their role as perpetrators of crime, whereas whites are shown primarily for their role as victims of crime (Romer et al., 1998). School violence and shooting incidents are more prominently covered by the media when they involve white victims than when minorities are victims (Males, 2000). News media researchers explain this phenomenon as a focus on those events that are most "newsworthy," meaning those that are most shocking, surprising, or unexpected.

The implication is that crime and violence involving blacks and other minorities are considered normal, everyday events in lower-class communities. This supports what critical criminologists claim is a differential response by law enforcement and the judicial system to blacks and other racial and ethnic minorities. Race has played a prominent role in recent legislative changes in juvenile laws, and in juvenile court practices (Feld, 1999a, 2003). In an analysis of historical events, political developments, and media studies, Feld (2003) argued that recent "get-tough" crime policies have unfairly targeted blacks so that they are overrepresented at every stage of the justice process, despite federal mandates to examine and reduce the disproportionate confinement of minorities in detention and correctional facilities.

Feminism and Delinquency. The feminist perspective on delinquency is a form of conflict theory that focuses on victimization of women, gender differences in crime, and differences in judicial and correctional policies for women offenders. Research and theory in criminology and criminal justice have traditionally focused on male offenders and ignored women. Feminist theory is critical of traditional criminological theories that focus almost exclusively on male crime and delinquency, and fail to account adequately for gender differences. Feminist theory claims that the patriarchal structure of society and the justice system results in laws and policies that are unfair to women. They claim that the male-oriented system creates gender bias, fails to protect women victims, and oppresses women offenders through unfair sentencing policies and unequal correctional resources and services (Chesney-Lind, 1989; Chesney-Lind & Shelden, 1998). Chesney-Lind (1989) claimed that juvenile laws and their enforcement by police, the courts, and prisons reinforce women's place in male society. Female delinquency frequently begins with victimization experiences in the home. Girls are victims of sexual abuse to a greater extent than boys. Leaving home to avoid victimization increases the likelihood of being arrested as runaways, and places them at risk of other crimes perceived as necessary for street survival, such as theft, dealing drugs, and prostitution. A double standard is still applied to young women in the belief that they need protection more than boys. As a result, a major reason for girls' referral to juvenile court was that their parents insisted on their arrest (Chesney-Lind, 1989). Feminist theory points to the differences in male and female delinquency, emphasizing that the discrepancies are due primarily to paternalistic responses by parents and the justice system.

In summary, conflict or critical theory is focused on social and political institutions as causes of crime, rather than individual characteristics and criminal tendencies of offenders. Conflict theorists and critical criminologists point to the presence of conflict and competition among social classes and groups in society. The critical perspective contributes to our understanding of the causes and solutions of juvenile delinquency by challenging our current thinking on social, political, and justice system responses to delinquency and crime. Critical criminologists remind us that changes in laws and policies are an essential step toward effective delinquency prevention and crime reduction.

Life-Course Development and General Integrated Theories

Research on delinquency causation and theory testing is a recurring process in the field of criminology. Recent work by criminologists raises questions about many of the traditional sociological theories for explaining crime and delinquency (Sampson & Laub, 1997; Thornberry, 1997). Criminologists have argued that theories explaining delinquency as a function of social structure, cultural deviance, or learning and social process fail to recognize that delinquent involvement is not constant throughout childhood, adolescence, and adulthood. Delinquent involvement varies with age, and youthful offenders vary as to the onset of delinquency and whether their offending persists into adulthood. Sampson and Laub (1997) point to research evidence that delinquency varies by age. Although delinquency tends to peak in the teenage years, there is an early onset of delinquency, as well as continuity of criminal behavior over the life course. Sociological criminology has failed to recognize age variations in delinquency, so recent theorists have turned to developmental psychology to better understand delinquency over the life course. Moffitt (1993) studied the psychological development of children and youth and found that most adolescents who engage in delinquency do not persist into adult crime. Social factors may diminish their tendency to continue delinquent careers, in contrast to "life-course persistent" delinquents who are likely to continue deviant, antisocial, and criminal conduct as adults.

Developmental or Life-Course Explanations. These attempt to account for differences among offenders who begin offending at an early age and continue offending, and those who begin in adolescence and seem to grow out of it. There is a distinction, for

example, between "adolescent-limited" antisocial behavior, that is, temporary normative behavior among teens; and "life-course persistent" delinquent behavior, typified
by a smaller group whose antisocial behavior begins early in life and develops into an
adult career in crime (Moffitt, 1993, p. 696). Others have noted the differences between
early and late starters in delinquency, and the different effects of parenting and deviant
peers on these two types of delinquents (Simons, Wu, Conger, & Lorenz, 1994). The
developmental, life-course perspective points to the importance of longitudinal studies of antisocial behavior beginning in infancy and childhood. While most adolescents
do not persist in delinquent careers, most adults who engage in antisocial and criminal behavior are the same persons who began antisocial behavior in early childhood.

General and Integrated Theory

Most criminological research has proceeded with the assumption that delinquency is
the result of a social environment or social processes that are common to all delinquents. Criminologists now acknowledge that no single theoretical orientation can
adequately explain the multiple variables and factors that cause delinquent behavior.
Some have examined whether there are multiple paths to the same types of delinquency. For example, some youth may run away from home because of a poor family
environment, some because they are pushed out, and others may run away for fun and
excitement (Huizinga, Esbensen, & Weiher, 1991). A number of criminologists have
taken the best parts of different theories and combined them in a single general or
integrated theory. Strain, social control, and social learning theories have been combined into an integrated theoretical explanation of delinquency and drug use (Elliott
Ageton, & Canter, 1979; Elliott, Huizinga, & Ageton, 1985).

Gottfredson and Hirschi (1990) combined the strong points of the traditional
classical theory (also referred to as the rational choice model) and positivist theories
that crime is caused by biological, psychological, or socioeconomic factors. In the *general theory of crime* they begin with the question, "What is crime?" rather than "What
causes crime?" They claim that crime in fact bears little resemblance to criminological
theories or to explanations offered by law enforcement or the media. Crimes are illegal acts that are for the most part simple, trivial, and mundane. Gottfredson and
Hirschi even explain homicides as "mundane" and easily explainable, because most
involve acquaintances, alcohol, or drugs, and are often impulsive crimes of passion
with little rational gain (p. 32). In an extension of Hirschi's (1969) control theory, they
describe the offender as an individual who lacks self-control and tends to be impulsive, insensitive, physical (more than mental), a risk-taker, short-sighted, and nonver-
bal. These traits predispose the individual to pursue immediate pleasure, including
criminal acts and noncriminal behavior such as smoking, drinking, drug use, gambling, and illicit sex (Gottfredson & Hirschi, 1990, p. 90). The general theory of crime
aptly describes juvenile delinquents whose lack of self-control draws them to criminal
acts that offer excitement, risk, deception, and power; and criminal or antisocial adults
whose lack of self-control results in unstable marriages, friendships, and jobs (p. 89).

Table 4.1 Sociological Explanations of Delinquency

	Major Premise	Strengths
Social disorganization	Social changes cause a breakdown of formal and informal controls, an increase in crime.	Explains urban crime rates, increase in crime with change and growth in cities.
Strain	Persons who lack the means to attain goals legitimately do so illegally; lower-class persons feel strain or frustration trying to meet middle-class goals.	Explains crime among lower class, and among those who lack equal education and employment opportunities.
Cultural deviance	Persons from groups having different life patterns or "focal concerns" are judged by the dominant culture.	Explains why lower-class and minority groups are overrepresented in the justice system.
Social process	Persons learn delinquent behavior from others; the presence of social bonds helps reduce the probability of delinquent involvement.	Explains why delinquency occurs among middle- and lower-class youth; shows the importance of parents, positive peers, and school.
Social reaction	Deviance and initial delinquent behavior are perpetuated and made worse by reactions of society and juvenile justice officials' reactions to crime and delinquency.	Explains why minor offenders often get worse after arrest and referral to juvenile detention and probation intake.
Critical theory	Points to the presence of conflict and competition among social classes and groups; focuses on social and political institutions as causes of crime.	Directs attention to laws and justice policies focused unfairly on lower class, racial and ethnic minorities, and women.
Developmental life-course theories	Study differences among youth who begin offending at an early age and continue offending, compared with others who begin in adolescence and grow out of it.	Accounts for age variations in onset of delinquency; and the majority of delinquents who "age-out" versus some who persist on to adult crime.
General, integrated theories	Combine the strengths of rational choice, strain, social control, and social learning theories to explain delinquency and drug use.	No single theory can explain the varied, complex causes of delinquency.

Explanations of Female Delinquency

Most juvenile crimes are committed by boys. Crimes committed by girls are less frequent and less serious than those by boys, but the rate of increase of female juvenile arrests has been greater than for boys. A total of 621,670 girls under age 18 were arrested in the United States in 2005, and girls accounted for 29% of the 2.1 million total juvenile arrests (Snyder, 2007, p. 3). The same report shows that girls accounted for 24% of juvenile arrests for aggravated assault, 33% of other assaults, and 42% of larceny–theft (see Table 1.2 in Chapter 1). The Office of Juvenile Justice and Delinquency Prevention (OJJDP) convened the Girls Study Group to examine reported increases in violence by teenage girls. The group of criminologists is focusing attention on the latest statistics showing that girls accounted for one third (33%) of simple assaults and one quarter (24%) of all juvenile arrests for aggravated assaults (Zahn et al., 2008). These are the largest proportions of female arrests for any type of violent crimes.

The increase in female delinquency has been apparent the past several years. Between 1993 and 2002, the rate of increase in arrests of girls under age 18 was greatest for drug abuse violations (120%), liquor law violations (37%), DUI (94%), and curfew and loitering (50%) (Snyder, 2004, p. 8). This is a marked increase over past years. From 1965 to 1977, arrest statistics from the Uniform Crime Reports indicated that females were *not* catching up with males in the commission of violent, masculine, or serious crimes; but there were rising levels of female delinquency in the categories of larceny, runaway, and liquor law violations (Steffensmeier & Steffensmeier, 1980, p. 80). Girls' share of all juvenile arrests remained fairly steady over that time period, ranging from about 15% to 29% (p. 66). Official measures of juvenile crime underestimate their actual involvement, and this is even more so for females. The ratio of male to female arrests is 3.4:1, but self-report studies report a male to female ratio of only 2:1 (Cernkovich & Giordano, 1979; Canter, 1982). Cernkovich and Giordano found that while males report more delinquent acts than females, the differences in self-reported delinquency are considerably smaller than those for arrest rates. They found no significant gender differences for school problems, suspension, and expulsion; status offenses such as truancy, defying parents' authority, and running away; and drug-related offenses such as smoking marijuana, using and selling hard drugs, and driving under the influence of hard drugs.

The types of offenses for which most youth are arrested are for less serious crimes. The crime for which most girls are arrested is larceny/theft (usually shoplifting). Arrests of boys is generally three to four times greater than that for girls, but larceny/theft is an exception, where nearly half (about 40%) of the arrests were girls; and more than half (62%) of the arrests for runaway involved juvenile females (Snyder, 2004). This is not to suggest that more girls than boys were runaways, but that law enforcement officers arrested more girls than boys. Minor offenses are most characteristic of juveniles, and this is especially true for girls. In fact, status offenses play a major role in girls' official delinquency. Status offenses accounted for 24.1% of all girls' arrests in 1990 but only about 8% of boys' arrests (Chesney-Lind, 1995, p. 74). Arrests of juveniles for status offenses declined during the 1970s with the passage of the Juvenile Justice and Delinquency Prevention Act (JJDPA) in 1974, which called for diversion and deinstitutionalization of youth arrested for noncriminal offenses. Arrests of juveniles, and especially girls, for status offenses began increasing again in the 1980s, however. Meda Chesney-Lind (1995) suggests that girls are arrested disproportionately more than boys for such status offenses as running away and curfew violations because of a tendency to sexualize their offenses and to control their behavior under the patriarchal authority of the juvenile justice system. There is evidence that many young women run away to escape sexual victimization at home; and once on the streets they are vulnerable to further sexual victimization (Chesney-Lind, 1995, p. 83).

Little attention has been paid to female delinquency, primarily because delinquency is generally associated with boys. Most research and explanations of the juvenile crime problem in fact focus on boys. Except for some early work (Lombroso, 1920; W. I. Thomas, 1923), research and writing on delinquency involving girls was virtually nonexistent until the past 50 years (Pollak, 1950; Konopka, 1966). Much more attention has been given to female delinquency since a dramatic increase in arrests of girls beginning in the 1970s. Freda Adler (1975) believed the increase in female crime could be explained by a "liberation hypothesis," that as women have become more active and taken advantage of opportunities outside the home and in the workplace, so also have they begun to engage in more crimes originally committed almost entirely by men. Rita Simon (1975) believed that as women have become more liberated and more are working outside the home, they have had more opportunities and incentives to commit property crimes.

Other researchers have found only partial support for the liberation hypothesis to explain the increase in female delinquency. Cernkovich and Giordano (1979) surveyed girls in three high schools and two state institutions to examine their attitudes on traditional versus liberated feminist views, and found that the more delinquent girls were less liberated and held more traditional views of marriage and children. Rankin (1980) interviewed 385 students in several Wayne County (Detroit), Michigan, high schools to examine their attitudes toward education and involvement in delinquency. He found that negative attitudes toward school and school performance were associated with more delinquency involvement for both boys and girls; but surprisingly, the relationship was stronger for girls than for boys (p. 431). The findings seem to indicate that with more women in the workforce today, the perceived occupational consequences of negative attitudes toward education or poor grades seem to be just as serious for girls as for boys. Rankin suggested that school factors thus may inhibit female delinquency as much as male delinquency (p. 432).

John Hagan and his associates (Hagan, Gillis, & Simpson, 1985) developed their power–control theory to explain variations of delinquency among males and females. The theory examines social class, whether husbands and wives work outside the home, and the degree of power and control they have in the workplace. According to the theory, in the "patriarchal" family with traditional gender role definitions, mothers have the primary socializing role and a daughter is more controlled than a son. Gender differences result because girls, more than boys, are taught to avoid risks in general, and particularly illegal behavior. Thus girls appear to be more easily deterred by the threat of legal sanctions, an effect that Hagan et al. believe is produced more through maternal than through paternal controls (p. 1156). In an "egalitarian" family, control over daughters and sons is more equal, and both are encouraged to be more open to risk taking. That is, daughters are encouraged to be more decisive and willing to take control and assume responsibility, though risk taking may have unintended consequences, such as involvement in delinquency (Hagan, Simpson, & Gillis,1987, p. 793). Thus in egalitarian families daughters are more like sons in their involvement in risk taking, including some delinquency.

Jill Rosenbaum and James Lasley (1990) found support for the power–control theory to explain male–female differences in delinquency. Findings from the Seattle Youth Study of 1,508 adolescents indicated that positive attitudes toward school and achievement produced stronger reductions in delinquency for boys than girls; while involvement in school activities and positive attitudes toward teachers led to more delinquency reduction for girls than for boys (p. 510). They also found social class differences, and suggested that school conformity is instilled socially in females and in middle-/upper-class youths more strongly than in males and lower-class youths. Meda Chesney-Lind (1995) is critical of power–control theory as an explanation of variations in female delinquency. The argument that mothers' employment leads to daughters' delinquency in more egalitarian families is little more than a variation on the earlier liberation hypothesis; but "now, mother's liberation causes daughter's crime!" (pp. 81–82). She also notes methodological problems with the theory, and a lack of evidence to suggest that girls' delinquency has increased along with women's employment. A reanalysis of the 1981 National Survey of Children indicated that gender differences in delinquency were present regardless of patriarchal or egalitarian family structures (Morash & Chesney-Lind, 1991, p. 347); and female delinquency has declined or remained stable in the last decade, as women's employment in the labor force has increased (Chesney-Lind, 1995, p. 82). Merry Morash and Meda Chesney-Lind (1991) argue for a feminist theory of female delinquency, noting that both boys and girls who identify with a nurturing parent who cares for them are likely to be more caring and have concern for others, rather than harm others. They believe that nurturing roles are not gender specific. Sons can identify with a nurturing parent as readily as daughters, and can learn prosocial behaviors (p. 351). A significant amount of female delinquency can also be accounted for by patriarchal tendencies of the juvenile justice system. Girls' delinquent involvement is often a result of physical and sexual abuse, since running away from victimization experiences leads to more serious criminal involvement. They are referred to juvenile court for behaviors that parents and authorities generally ignore or overlook when committed by boys, because of a perceived need to protect girls from engaging in more serious delinquency (see Chesney-Lind, 1995, pp. 82–85).

Further research is needed to explain more clearly the causes of female delinquency and the extent to which girls' involvement in crime is different from boys'. Boys still commit more serious and violent offenses, but girls' involvement in property and drug-related offenses is a matter of concern. More research is needed on how differences in family, peer relationships, and school factors contribute to female delinquency. Further research is also needed to examine how the juvenile justice system responds to female delinquency, from police referral to juvenile court decisions. The Office of Juvenile Justice and Delinquency Prevention (OJJDP) convened the Girls Study Group to examine the increase in violence by teenage girls and to establish a theoretical and empirical basis for developing strategies to reduce girls' involvement in delinquency and violence (Zahn et al., 2008). Relying on official arrest data, self-report data, and victimization data, the analysts have suggested a number of factors that may explain the apparent increase in violence among teenage girls:

- Changes in law enforcement policies such as responses to domestic violence, may explain the increased arrests, rather than actual increases in assaults by girls.
- Family dynamics may contribute to gender differences in juvenile arrests for assault.
- Research indicates that girls fight with family members or siblings more frequently than boys.
- Policies of mandatory arrest for domestic violence provide parents with a method for controlling their "unruly" daughters.
- School officials' zero-tolerance policies toward youth violence may increase the number of girls referred to police for fights at school that previously were handled internally (Zahn et al., 2008, p. 7).

Application of Sociological Explanations of Delinquency

The best criminological theories of delinquency have been tested repeatedly to determine how well they explain delinquency causation among the greatest number of youth and in a variety of social settings. The theories that are cited the most and tested most frequently using different samples of youth in different geographical regions and social settings are those that are considered the best theories to explain delinquency. Perhaps the most important criterion of a good theory, according to juvenile justice researchers, practitioners, and policymakers, is whether the theory recommends policies, programs, and strategies for crime reduction and delinquency prevention. Explanations of delinquency may be fairly judged by seasoned criminologists as well as by students of juvenile justice as to whether they make sense, are observable and testable, and whether they answer the "so what" question: "so what does the theory recommend to prevent delinquency?" The most effective delinquency prevention policies are those that have a firm theoretical and empirical basis. The OJJDP initiative discussed above (see Zahn et al., 2008) is an example of current efforts to find better explanations for causes and correlates of girls' delinquency, risk, and the protective factors associated with delinquency, toward the goal of implementing effective strategies to reduce juvenile crime and violence.

SUMMARY

- Sociological explanations of delinquency emphasize social influences on individuals caused by the structure of society, societal change, social disorganization, subcultural differences, and social processes that influence behavior.
- Social structure theories claim that forces such as social disorganization, status frustration, and cultural deviance lead lower-class youths to become involved in delinquent behavior.
- Social process explanations of delinquency focus not on societal structures but on social interactions between individuals and social group influences that lead to delinquency.
- Social reaction theories focus more on how society, social institutions, and government officials react to crime and delinquency than on why offenders commit crime.
- Developmental or life-course explanations attempt to account for differences between offenders who begin offending at an early age and continue offending, and those who begin in adolescence and grow out of it.

- No single theoretical orientation can adequately explain the multiple variables and factors that cause delinquent behavior, so a number of criminologists have taken the best parts of different theories and combined them in a single general or integrated theory.
- Most criminological research and theories to explain delinquency are based on boys, so criminologists have developed theories to explain gender differences in delinquency.
- For juvenile justice researchers and practitioners, the best theory is one that recommends policies, programs, and strategies for effective crime reduction and delinquency prevention.

KEY TERMS

Social disorganization theory	Subcultural theories
Strain theory	Differential association theory
Opportunity–structure theories	Social control theory
General strain theory	Race, social class, and delinquency
Cultural deviance theory	Feminism and delinquency

DISCUSSION QUESTIONS

1. Think of your personal observations of small towns, suburbs, and large cities or metro areas and describe the reasons for different levels of crime and delinquency according to the social structure theories.

2. Give an example of delinquent behavior that can be explained by "differential association" or social learning.

3. Think of two examples of young people: some who are characterized by at least two or three elements of the "social bonds" and others for whom the social bonds are weak or absent. Explain how the absence of social bonds place those youth at risk of delinquent behavior.

4. Think of an example of how a rule, law, or policy (in school, at work, or in government) favors some individuals or groups and seems unfairly targeted against other individuals or groups.

5. Pick one of the theories discussed in this chapter that makes most sense to you. Next, suggest a legislative change, policy, or program that may be an effective delinquency prevention strategy based on your favorite theory.

WEB RESOURCES

Girls Study Group: Understanding and Responding to Girls' Delinquency: http://www.ncjrs.gov/pdffiles1/ojjdp/218905.pdf

Juvenile Offenders and Victims: 2006 National Report: http://ojjdp.ncjrs.gov/ojstatbb/nr2006/downloads/NR2006.pdf

The Office of Juvenile Justice and Delinquency Prevention (OJJDP): http://www.ojjdp.ncjrs.org/

Correlates and Causes of Delinquency

Many factors are associated with delinquency. In this chapter we examine more closely some of the *correlates* of delinquency. Factors such as the parent–child relationship, family experiences, peer relations, school experiences, gang involvement, and drug use are important in determining whether or not youth engage in delinquent behavior. These factors are called correlates rather than causes because every young person experiences them in varying degrees in the normal process of growing up. Despite being exposed to some family problems, negative peer influence, and drug use, most youth do not become serious delinquents. The difference is in the nature and extent of their exposure to these problems, and how youth cope with or respond to these factors throughout childhood and adolescence. The Office of Juvenile Justice and

Delinquency Prevention (OJJDP) has funded a program of Research on the Causes and Correlates of Delinquency, and includes the Denver Youth Survey, the Pittsburgh Youth Study, and the Rochester Youth Development Study in New York. The program was begun in 1986 to improve the understanding of serious delinquency, violence, and drug use by examining how youth develop in the context of family, school, peers, and community. The research program involves analyses of longitudinal data collected over several years from samples of youth. Researchers conducted personal interviews with inner-city youths who were considered at high risk for delinquency and drug abuse. They also collected information from parents and legal guardians, teachers, police, courts, schools, and social service agencies. Samples from each of the three cities involved in the research program include 1,000 to 1,500 males and females who were in the eighth grade in the spring of 1988 (Browning, Huizinga, Loeber, & Thornberry, 1999). The causes and correlates research program is the largest shared measurement approach ever done on juvenile delinquency research.

In this chapter we introduce the primary correlates, discuss their relationship with delinquency, and examine whether there is evidence to show they are causes of juvenile offending. We include a discussion of the programs that have been developed to address these problems and to prevent juvenile delinquency.

The Family and Delinquency

The family is the most important source of socialization in a child's life. Parents are role models for children, providing examples for interacting with others, for ethical and legal behavior, for instilling work habits and being responsible. Nurturing parents who are positive role models and who maintain a positive home environment provide support to help children resist negative peer influence in schools and on the streets. Good parents provide the kind of home environment that helps youth succeed in school and resist antisocial behaviors even when growing up in high-crime neighborhoods. In contrast, children who grow up in families marked by parental conflict and tension, with parents who are absent, neglectful, and/or verbally or physically abusive, have a greater risk of engaging in delinquency. Family problems are related to negative peer relations, alcohol and drug use, school problems, absenteeism, and failure; and to deviant and delinquent behavior. There is little question whether family problems, negative peer pressure, school problems, and alcohol and drugs are major contributing factors to juvenile delinquency. Exactly how and under what conditions the process occurs are issues on which not all social scientists are in agreement.

The Broken Home. **Broken home** refers to a family structure that has been disrupted (or "broken") by separation, divorce, or death of a parent. Research by Sheldon and Eleanor Glueck (1950) showed that 60% of delinquents, but only 34% of nondelinquent youth, came from broken homes. In a longitudinal study of men who had been involved in a delinquency prevention program, McCord (1982) found that over half of the fathers of boys reared in broken homes were known to be alcoholics or criminals; and close to half of the sons of alcoholic or criminal men had been convicted of serious crimes (p. 123). McCord found that the quality of home life rather than the number of parents was most important in explaining youths' criminal behavior; and concluded that the lack of supervision in these broken homes accounted for much of the criminal behavior of these children raised by only one parent. Gove and Crutchfield (1982) noted gender differences in the family–delinquency connection, finding that boys in single-parent homes are more likely to be delinquent but there was little impact on girls' delinquency. Researchers caution that the broken home may only be associated with a greater risk of running away and truancy (Rankin, 1980), and that there is a weaker relationship for serious delinquent behavior (Wells & Rankin, 1991). Other researchers have concluded that there is a relationship between official measures (those who get caught by police), but not self-report measures of delinquency, and the broken home (Laub & Sampson, 1988). The Glueck study noted above was based on official delinquency measures, not on self-report data. Laub and Sampson (1988) concluded that self-report measures of delinquency show few if any differences between youth from intact homes and those from broken homes. Decisions by school and juvenile justice officials are often influenced by family status. Youth from single-parent homes are believed to be in greater need of intervention and supervision than youth with two parents, so officials often process cases that might be dropped for youth with two parents, who are perceived less in need of court intervention. Thus, youth from broken homes are disproportionately represented in referrals to the justice system (Laub & Sampson, 1988). Most research on single-parent homes has focused on the absence of fathers. Single fathers, however, are becoming the fastest growing family form and account for about 15% of all single-parent families. Demuth and Brown (2004) analyzed data from the 1995 National Longitudinal Survey of Adolescent Health and found that levels of delinquency were greatest among adolescents living in single-father families and lowest among adolescents living with two biological parents. They concluded that parental absence weakens direct and indirect controls, which in turn leads to higher levels of delinquency. To reduce delinquency among adolescents, parents and communities should strengthen the balance between nurture and control (Demuth & Brown, 2004).

The effects of the single-parent family appear to be experienced more negatively in disadvantaged neighborhoods. Lauritsen (2003) analyzed data from the National Crime Victimization Survey (NCVS) and found that children in single-parent families were at higher risk for violent victimization regardless of the quality of the neighborhood in which they lived; but this risk was magnified in disadvantaged neighborhoods. Using two data sources from Denver, Huizinga (2005) failed to replicate the Lauritsen study. Living in single-parent families in disadvantaged neighborhoods was a significant risk factor for violent victimization among youth, but the highest rates of violent victimization and offending were *not* in the most disorganized neighborhoods but rather in the moderately disorganized neighborhoods with moderate to high arrest rates. Thus, living in a single-parent family had a greater negative effect in "good neighborhoods" than it did in disadvantaged neighborhoods. Thornberry and Hall (2005) also attempted to replicate the Lauritsen (2003) findings, using data from the Rochester (New York) Youth Development Study. They found that youth in families with frequent changes in structure were more likely to engage in violent offending; and youth living in disadvantaged neighborhoods were more likely to be involved in violent offending. There was no interaction between the two variables, however. That is, the neighborhood impact on violent offending was the same regardless of the number of family structure changes.

There is a relationship between family problems and delinquency, but we cannot conclude that broken homes are a cause of delinquency. Most youth from broken homes, after all, are *not* delinquent; and having two parents in the home is not a guarantee that youth will not engage in delinquency. Rather it is the quality of the parent–child relationship, regardless of whether there are one or two parents, that is more important in explaining youth involvement in delinquent behavior. Single-parent families *do* face more difficulties in discipline, supervision, and economic pressures. The single parent (usually a woman) faces more challenges to maintain employment, a household, and to devote time to numerous childrearing tasks, often without the psychological, social, and financial support of the noncustodial parent. Given the high rate of divorce in this country, it is appropriate that family courts have placed a high priority on the well-being of the child in custody and support decisions. Increasing attention has been given to enforcing child-support responsibilities of the noncustodial parent. This is an important step in minimizing the difficulties faced by children of broken homes.

Family Size. The number of children in a family is also related to delinquency. A sizeable number of youth who come in contact with police are from larger families. Loeber and Stouthamer-Loeber (1986) suggest three reasons for this apparent relationship: (1) it is harder for a parent to discipline and supervise a larger number of children; (2) parents often delegate the authority to supervise younger children to the older siblings; and (3) larger families are often associated with other social problems, such as illegitimacy, poverty, and crowding in the home (pp. 100–101). Families of any size with adequate financial means, quality parent–child relations, and good discipline and supervision are less likely to have children who are involved in delinquent behavior. Studies indicate that a broken home is less important than the quality of the parent–child relationship in explaining delinquency (Matsueda & Heimer, 1987; Laub & Sampson, 1988).

Family Relationships. The quality of the parent–child relationship is more important than whether there are one or two parents present in the home. Research has established a relationship between delinquency and parental rejection, a term for parent–child relationships that are lacking in warmth, love, affection, and appreciation of parents for their children. Loeber and Stouthamer-Loeber (1986) found that 12 of 15 studies measuring parent–child relations reported a significant relation between rejection, delinquency, and aggression (p. 55). Rosen (1985) found lower delinquency rates among African American youths who had more father–son interaction. Hirschi (1969) found that delinquency is less likely among youth who have a positive "attachment" with their parents. Other research supports Hirschi, that the quality of family life and degree of parental attachment are more important predictors of delinquency than family structure (Laub & Sampson, 1988; Rankin & Kern, 1994). Parents influence their children's behavior through positive interaction, emotional closeness, and through gaining respect. Parents are positive role models. Children who feel loved, respect their parents, and identify with them are less likely to get into trouble.

Discipline and Supervision. Parents differ greatly in parenting skills. Some parents are inconsistent in their discipline, and when they do correct their child they are nagging or too harsh. Parents who are preoccupied with their own concerns often neglect their children, fail to monitor their whereabouts, do not know their children's friends, or are simply too lenient or inconsistent in their discipline. Parents in broken homes and in large families face more difficulties administering consistent discipline and supervision. Inconsistent parental discipline and limited supervision are strong predictors of delinquent behavior (Patterson & Stouthamer-Loeber, 1984; Cernkovich & Giordano, 1987). There is a stronger relationship between lack of supervision and official delinquency than between lack of supervision and self-reported delinquency (Loeber & Stouthamer-Loeber, 1986, p. 61). Wells and Rankin (1988) concluded that direct parental controls such as close supervision and monitoring of youngsters' behavior have as great an impact on delinquency as that of "indirect controls" such as "attachments" or positive parent–child relations.

Child Abuse and Neglect

Child abuse is a serious problem with a long history in America. It has endured because harsh discipline, corporal punishment, and cruelty to children have not always been recognized as serious problems. Dr. C. Henry Kempe first brought attention to child abuse when he reported survey results of medical and law enforcement agencies that showed high rates of child abuse. He originated the term battered child syndrome to describe the numerous incidents of non-accidental physical injuries of children by their parents or guardians (Kempe et al., 1962). Kempe and his associates have since recommended the terms *child abuse and neglect* as more inclusive terms that refer to physical abuse and failure to care properly for children's development and emotional well-being (Helfer & Kempe, 1976). Research on the problem of child abuse increased in the 1960s and 1970s, and several states passed laws requiring mandatory reporting of child abuse and neglect cases. The U.S. Congress passed the Child Abuse Prevention Act and established the National Center on Child Abuse in 1974.

CASE IN POINT 5.1

Child Abuse Facts and Findings

- The American family and home are among the most violent places in the nation.
- Three of every 100 parents admitted they had kicked, punched, bitten, beat, or threatened their children with a weapon.
- 1–2 million children are seriously injured each year by child abuse.
- 3–4 million children have been kicked, bitten, or punched by a parent at some time in their lives.

(Continued)

(Continued)

- More than 5 of every 1,000 children are victims of some type of emotional, physical, or sexual abuse in this country every year.
- Reports of child abuse and neglect have nearly doubled in the past couple of decades.
- Neglected and abused children act out through truancy and disruptive behavior in school, run away from home, and use alcohol and other drugs.
- Abuse causes self-rejection and low self-esteem that youths attempt to deal with through substance abuse, attention-getting behavior, and association with deviant peers or gangs.
- Children who are victims of physical aggression often act out later with aggressive violent behavior.
- Children of abusive parents are more likely to become abusive parents themselves.
- Family violence is associated with youth accepting attitudes that violence is a part of life and committing violent crime as adults.
- As many as two thirds of female juvenile offenders have been victims of physical or sexual abuse.
- Many offenders convicted of first degree murder had been severely abused by their parents.
- An estimated 899,000 children in the United States and Puerto Rico were determined by child protective services (CPS) agencies to be victims of abuse or neglect in 2005.
- An estimated 1,460 children died of abuse and neglect nationwide in 2005.

SOURCE: Straus, Gelles, & Steinmetz, 1980; Zingraff & Belyea, 1986; Gelles & Straus, 1988; Gray, 1988; Lawrence, 2007; U.S. Department of Health & Human Services, 2007.

Discussion Questions

1. Which of the above research facts and findings are most surprising to you? Is it possible or likely that violence and physical aggression is a learned behavior? If so, how and why?

2. Most parents have learned and believe that strict discipline that may include spanking is necessary to raise children. What is your experience and belief?

3. Many private or church-related schools have supported some forms of physical punishment to maintain order and discipline. Do you support the use of spanking, slapping, or a "heavy hand" to control unruly or disruptive students? Argue for or against your belief.

NOTE: The U.S. Supreme Court has ruled that corporal punishment in schools is *not* a constitutional violation of the Eighth Amendment right against "cruel and unusual punishment."

Definitions of Child Abuse and Neglect. Child abuse includes neglect and physical beating. The terms describe physical or emotional trauma to a child where no reasonable explanation, such as an accident or acceptable disciplinary practices, can be detected. Child abuse is usually a pattern of behavior rather than a single beating or act of neglect. Its effects are cumulative, and the longer it persists, the more severe are the physical and emotional effects on the child. *Neglect* refers to parental deprivation of children, such as lack of food, shelter, clothing, care, and nurturance. Neglect is more passive in nature, yet over time results in emotional or physical problems. Children who are identified as "dependent and neglected" ("D & N") are differentiated from delinquent children. *Abuse* is a more overt, physical mistreatment of a child, often resulting in injuries requiring medical care. The two terms are often used interchangeably, and do often occur together in the same family (see Helfer & Kempe, 1976; Kempe & Kempe, 1978).

The Extent of Child Abuse. The American family and the home setting have been called one of the most violent institutions in the nation (Straus, Gelles, & Steinmetz, 1980). The risk of assault, physical injury, and even murder is greater in the home, by a family member, than on the street by a stranger. Straus and his associates (1980) conducted a nationwide survey of families and found that an astounding number of the parents who were interviewed in 1975 reported that they kicked, punched, bit, beat, or threatened their children with a gun or a knife. About 3 parents in 100 kicked, bit, or punched their child; 1% had beaten their child up in the past year, and 4% had done that at some point in the child's life. Three of 100 children have had a parent threaten to use a gun or knife on them at some time in their lives; 1 in 1,000 children faced a gun or knife threat from parents during 1975; and an estimated 3.1 to 4 million children have been kicked, bitten, or punched by a parent at some time in their lives; while between 1 and 1.9 million were kicked, bitten, or punched in 1975 (Straus et al., 1980, p. 62). The national survey showed that family violence was not limited to children, but includes spousal assaults and intra-family violence. The National Center on Child Abuse and Neglect in 1982 estimated that each year 3.4 children per 1,000 were victims of some physical abuse in this country; 5.7 children per 1,000 were victims of some type of emotional, physical, or sexual abuse; and 5.3 per 1,000 have experienced educational, emotional, or physical neglect (Gray, 1988). The 1985 National Family Violence Survey found that each year about 1.5 million children were kicked, bitten, punched, beaten up, burned or scalded, or threatened or attacked with a knife or gun (Gelles & Straus, 1988). In 1996, the U.S. Department of Health and Human Services estimated that the number of child abuse and neglect reports nearly doubled between 1986 and 1993, rising 98% from 1.42 million to 2.81 million; and the number of seriously injured children nearly quadrupled, increasing from 141,700 in 1986 to 565,000 in 1993 (Bavolek, 2000, p. 2). On average, three children die of child abuse and neglect each day in the United States (National Clearinghouse on Child Abuse and Neglect Information, 1998). During 2005, an estimated 899,000 children in the United States were determined by child protective services (CPS) agencies to be victims of abuse or neglect. The rate of abused children in 2005 was 48.3 per 1,000 children, a significant increase from the 43.2 per 1,000 in 2001. Rates of victimization by maltreatment type have varied only slightly in recent years. The majority of the reported abuse and neglect cases in the United States involved neglect (62.8%); 16.6% were physically abused; 9.3% were sexually abused; and 7.1% were emotionally or psychologically maltreated. An estimated 1,460 children died of abuse or neglect nationwide in 2005 (U.S. Department of Health and Human Services, 2007).

Victims of child abuse and neglect suffer the worst forms of family conflict and parental rejection. Neglect and abuse have serious effects on a child's emotional development. Abused children often act out through truancy and disruptive behavior in school; run away from home; and use alcohol and other drugs. Abuse causes self-rejection and low self-esteem that youth may attempt to deal with through substance abuse, attention-getting behavior in school, or association with other deviant peers. The parent–child relationship is so damaged that parents do not have the respect of their children, so are not accepted as role models or positive authority figures. Children who have been victims of physical aggression often act out later with aggressive violent behavior against them (see Zingraff & Belyea, 1986).

The relationship between child abuse and delinquency has been widely accepted. Curtis (1963) suggested that "violence breeds violence." Abused and neglected children often act out as juveniles and young adults with acts of violence. The process by which child abuse often leads to delinquency has been described as a "cycle of violence" (Widom 1989b, p. 3). Studies show a relationship between child abuse and aggressive, delinquent, and violent behavior (Zingraff & Belyea, 1986; Gray, 1988). Family violence including physical fighting between parents and among siblings is associated with youth accepting violence as a part of life, and with committing a violent crime in adult life (Fagan, Hansen, & Jang, 1983). A large proportion of juvenile female offenders have been victims of physical or sexual abuse or exploitation. An American Correctional Association study reported that 62% of female juvenile offenders said they were physically abused, usually by a parent (Bergsmann, 1989, p. 73). Other researchers have argued that there is a relationship between child abuse and later adult criminal behavior. Persons who have been victims of abuse or have witnessed abusive family environments purportedly view violence and aggression as an appropriate way to deal with problems. Zingraff and Belyea (1986) reviewed a number of studies documenting cases in which offenders convicted of murder reported having been physically or emotionally abused by their parents. Many offenders convicted of first degree murder had been severely abused by their parents; 85% of a group of 53 murderers reported that they had experienced severe corporal punishment during their early childhood; and a group of 112 felons reported significantly more abusive treatment than a comparison group of 376 noninstitutionalized male adults (Zingraff & Belyea, 1986, p. 52). There is some evidence that abuse breeds abuse. Widom (1989b) reviewed studies that showed there appears to be a higher likelihood of abuse among parents who were abused themselves, although the majority of abusive parents were not themselves abused as children. She estimated that about a third of the persons who were abused as children will abuse their own children (Widom 1989b, p. 8). A connection has also been made between abuse, neglect, and delinquency. One study found that, for both men and women, a history of abuse or neglect significantly increased one's chances of having a criminal record as an adult (Widom, 1989a, p. 260). In summary, we know there is a connection between child abuse and neglect and later criminal behavior as juveniles or adults. We know that many abused children become abusive parents. Most abused children, however, do *not* become abusive parents, juvenile delinquents, or violent adult criminals (Widom, 1989a; Wright & Wright, 1994). The Office of Juvenile Justice and Delinquency Prevention (OJJDP) has addressed prevention of child abuse as an important delinquency prevention strategy. The Nurturing Parenting Program is part of the OJJDP's Family Strengthening Series and is directed at helping to stop the generational cycle of abuse and neglect by building nurturing parenting skills (Bavolek, 2000).

POLICY AND PRACTICE 5.1	REPORTING CHILD ABUSE TO POLICE

When a child is assaulted or molested, it is not only a child welfare problem, but also a crime. Until recently, no law enforcement data were available on child abuse; and cases reported to law enforcement were not included in the National Child Abuse and Neglect Data System (NCANDS). The National Incident-Based Reporting System (NIBRS) is being implemented to include more information on crime and its victims, including child abuse.

Child abuse is reported to police in a variety of ways:

- The victims and other family members
- Concerned neighbors and community members
- Professionals such as teachers, nurses, and doctors
- Other authorities such as child welfare agencies
- Professionals in all states, and even citizens in some states, are required by law to report child abuse to responsible authorities
- Laws in many states now require child welfare authorities to share all child maltreatment reports with law enforcement

Reports of child abuse or maltreatment are investigated by authorities to confirm the accuracy of the report. The investigation process and results include the following:

- Child welfare investigations confirm about one third of all child maltreatment reports.
- In some states, child welfare workers and police conduct these investigations jointly.
- In a few jurisdictions, responsibility for investigation lies with law enforcement only.
- Police have become increasingly involved in child abuse cases, but their role in the reporting and investigation of child abuse varies from jurisdiction to jurisdiction.
- The National Incident-Based Reporting System (NIBRS) data confirm that large numbers of offenses against children by caretakers are reported to the police.
- These incidents are largely physical assaults, involve older youth more than younger children, and involve more male than female caretakers.

SOURCE: Finkelhor, D., & Ormrod, R. (2001). Child abuse reported to the police. *OJJDP Juvenile Justice Bulletin.* Washington, DC: Office of Juvenile Justice and Delinquency Prevention. Retrieved April 24, 2009, from http://www .unh.edu/ccrc/pdf/jvq/CV32.pdf.

Discussion Questions

1. Why do you believe lawmakers felt it was necessary to pass a law requiring persons to report suspected cases of child abuse? Is it possible that the requirement to report suspected cases to law enforcement may explain the increase in reported child abuse cases? Explain.

(Continued)

(Continued)

2. Do you believe that many neighbors, child-care providers, teachers, doctors, and nurses may be hesitant to comply with the law requiring the reporting of suspected child abuse? Suggest reasons for their reluctance to report suspected cases.

3. Suggest reasons why reports of child abuse are investigated by police and child welfare officials to confirm and substantiate the reports. Would this investigation process alleviate any concerns raised in No. 2 (above) about being accused of making a false report or of being wrongly accused of child abuse? Explain your answer.

Parents and Delinquency Prevention

Research shows that parents play a vital role in helping their children grow and mature through a healthy and normal child development. Parents cannot shield their children from all antisocial behavior and deviant influences from peers, popular culture, and the media. Parents can, however, reduce the risk that their child will be victimized or engage in deviant and delinquent behavior by following at least three effective parenting practices:

- *Awareness:* Be aware of popular culture and peer influences on youth.
- *Communication:* Maintain communication, encourage sharing, listen as much as or even more than talking.
- *Engagement with youth:* A combination of the above, remaining in touch with youth, their issues and concerns, school progress and problems, and decisions they are expected to make.

Awareness and Communication. The level of communication and quality of parent–child relations is important in youths' prosocial development, and avoidance of drugs and delinquency. Parents' awareness of youth problems and behavior is essential in order for meaningful communication, monitoring, and parental supervision to take place. A statewide survey of parents and their adolescent children examined associations between parenting strategies and self-reported teen drinking (Haynie, Simons-Morton, Beck, Shattuck, & Crump, 1999). Less teen drinking was associated with parents' reports of checking to see if other parents would be present at teen parties, particularly among white parents. Parents who reported more awareness and monitoring of their teens' involvement with alcohol expressed more competence in taking a proactive approach. Research has also established a relationship between parental influences on students' aggressive behaviors and weapon carrying. Orpinas, Murray, and Kelder (1999) examined the association between parenting and fighting and weapon-carrying among junior high school students. Parental monitoring, positive parent–teen relations, and lack of parental support for fighting had an inverse relationship with aggression, fighting, and weapon-carrying. Students who lived with both parents were less likely to report aggression. Youths' perception of parents' attitudes toward fighting was the strongest predictor of aggression (Orpinas et al., 1999).

Parental Engagement. The quality of the parent–child relationship is important in helping children form positive peer relationships; make a commitment to education; and avoid use of tobacco, alcohol, and other drugs and involvement in delinquent behavior. In a study of more than 20,000 American teenagers from nine high schools, researchers found that adolescents who had the most problems came from families in which parents were hostile, aloof, or uninvolved (Steinberg, Brown, & Dornbusch, 1996; Steinberg, 2000). Steinberg and his associates found that children from homes characterized by negative parenting were at risk for problems regardless of their ethnicity or income and regardless of whether their parents were married, divorced, single, or remarried. The quality of the parent–child relationship therefore matters much more than the social demographics of the household (Steinberg, 2000, p. 35). The most worrisome finding of their research was what they described as the high level of **parental disengagement** they saw in their sample (p. 35). Examples of "parental disengagement" cited by Steinberg were:

- One fourth of students were allowed to decide what classes to take in school without discussing the decision with their parents.
- Thirty percent of parents did not know how their child was doing in school.
- One third of parents did not know how their child spends his or her spare time.
- One fourth of the students said their family "never" did anything together for fun.
- Only 30% of the students said their parents spend some time talking with them each day.

Based on their study of 20,000 youth, Steinberg estimated that 25% to 30% of families with teenagers nationally may be characterized by some degree of parental disengagement (Steinberg, 2000, p. 35). Adolescents from disengaged homes were more likely to show psychological immaturity and adjustment difficulties, were less interested and less successful in school, and were more likely to become involved in misconduct, drug use, and delinquency (Steinberg, 2000, p. 36). Parental involvement in their children's lives is perhaps the most important factor in their healthy psychological development. Steinberg asserts that we need a public health campaign in America to inform parents how to raise psychologically healthy children, and to remind parents of their responsibility for active and involved parenting (p. 37).

The role of parents in delinquency prevention has been recognized at the highest levels of government, to the U.S. Department of Justice. The Office of Juvenile

Justice and Delinquency Prevention (OJJDP) has funded several research and program development initiatives with the goal of providing information, resources, and technical assistance to juvenile justice agencies to help strengthen families (Kumpfer & Alvarado, 1998; Thornberry, Smith, Rivera, Huizinga, & Stouthamer-Loeber, 1999). We have noted that delinquency is often a result of child abuse, and the "nurturing parenting program" is one of the efforts to reduce child abuse and train parents in proper child nurturing (Bavolek, 2000). Family-based approaches to delinquency prevention also emphasize the need to develop prosocial conflict resolution skills, and to recognize gender differences in addressing family problems. Hinton and associates (Hinton, Sheperis, & Sims, 2003) noted that gender plays a role in development of delinquent behaviors due to differing social expectations for girls and boys. Our culture often gives females negative messages about their bodies, minds, and worth; and sexual abuse is a common experience of female delinquents. Other family problems related to delinquency include weak parental decision making and guidance, lack of positive parent–child bonds, and aggressive communication. Effective delinquency prevention approaches include multisystemic therapy, functional family therapy, behavioral parent training, and family skills training (Hinton et al., 2003).

Research results indicate that early family/parent training programs reduce child behavioral problems, including antisocial behavior and delinquency (Piquero, Farrington, Welsh, Tremblay, & Jennings, 2008). The effective programs involved either individual or group-based parent training sessions that were conducted in a clinic, school, or other type of community-based site. The programs included parenting intervention training and parent–child interaction therapy. Piquero and his associates recommended that family and parent training should be used for the first 5 years of a child's life in order to prevent child behavioral problems.

POLICY AND PRACTICE 5.2 FEDERAL INITIATIVES TO STRENGTHEN FAMILIES

The Office of Juvenile Justice and Delinquency Prevention (OJJDP) and Center for Substance Abuse Prevention (CSAP) jointly conducted a search for best practices and found a number of effective family-focused prevention strategies that target a variety of family needs and help numerous family types.

- The 35 programs identified as best practices range from structured programs with standardized written curriculums to open-ended support groups.
- Some programs work exclusively with parents, while others work with the entire family and encourage extended family participation.

- Programs use strategies designed for biological families, foster families, single-parent families, teen parents, and ethnic families, as well as with families with an incarcerated parent, families in which both parents work outside the home, and rural and inner-city families.
- The programs work with families of children of varied ages, from the prenatal stage through high school.

The following are examples that illustrate the broad spectrum of programs that were selected as best practices:

- *The Incredible Years: Parents, Teachers, and Children Training Series* is a parent training curriculum designed for parents of children ages 3 to 12; focuses on strengthening parents' monitoring and disciplinary skills and building their confidence.
- *Strengthening Families Program* is a 14-week family skills training program designed to reduce risk factors for substance abuse and other problem behaviors.
- *Prenatal and Early Childhood Nurse Home Visitation Program* is designed to improve the health and social functioning of low-income first-time mothers and their babies.
- *Multisystemic Therapy (MST)* is an intensive home-based family treatment program to reduce rates of antisocial behavior in youth ages 10 to 18, reduce out-of-home placements, and empower families to resolve difficulties.
- *Project SEEK (Services to Enable and Empower Kids)* is a program that focuses on families with children from birth through age 11 in which a parent is in prison.

SOURCE: Alvarado, R., & Kumpfer, K. (2000). Strengthening America's families. *OJJDP Juvenile Justice Bulletin.* Washington, DC: Office of Juvenile Justice and Delinquency Prevention. Retrieved April 24, 2009, from http://www.ncjrs.gov/pdffiles1/ojjdp/184746.pdf.

Discussion Questions

1. Family problems are local problems that occur in private homes in cities and towns. Can you suggest reasons why the federal government, under the U.S. Department of Justice, would spend time, money, and resources on ways to reduce this local problem?

2. Based on what you have read in previous chapters about the causes of delinquency and in this chapter about the "correlates" of delinquency, suggest how the above programs may reduce delinquency and youth crime.

3. Imagine you are the Administrator or Research and Training Director of a local county juvenile court services or juvenile probation agency. How might you incorporate one or more of these federal government initiatives into your local county program?

Peers and Delinquency

Youths' relationships with peers and close friends are very important factors in whether they become involved in delinquent behavior. As youth reach the teenage years, peer group influence often interferes with parental and family ties, encouraging alienation between youth and their parents. The role of parents and peers are thus closely related in the emergence of delinquent behavior. Youth are more vulnerable to the temptations and pressures of peers, and are more likely to violate laws when they are with their friends, especially if ties with their parents are weaker. The nature and extent of peer influence on young people varies according to a number of factors. First, the influence of peers varies depending on the behavior or attitude in question. Peers play an important role in young peoples' alcohol and substance use, but Ronald Akers (1985) emphasized that the process is not one of peer "pressure" but of peer *influence* (p. 115). Akers found that for the majority of teenagers, peers are more likely to reinforce conforming behavior than deviant behavior; most of them reported feeling no pressure from peers to use any substances; and they said parents were more important than peers as sources of influence and knowledge in their decisions whether or not to use tobacco, alcohol, and other drugs (p. 117). Second, peer influence tends to vary by gender, race, and social class. Peer group influence has a greater impact on delinquency among males than among females (Johnson, 1979). Girls are more likely to commit a delinquent act when they are in a group of other girls and boys than when alone, and white females seem to be influenced by peers more than African American females (Giordano, Cernkovich, & Pugh, 1986, p. 1195). Merry Morash (1986) found that adolescent females belong to fewer delinquent groups than males, and this helps explain their lower levels of delinquent involvement. Female characteristics of being less aggressive and having more empathy also helps restrain them from engaging in delinquent and violent behavior with peers (Morash, 1986). Mark Colvin and John Pauly (1983) claimed that the difference in peer relationships between working-class and middle- or upper-class youth was explained by their parents' workplace experiences. Lower-class workers tend to experience a coercive working environment, which reduces their capacity as parents to deal with their children in any other way than a repressive manner, using harsh verbal or physical punishment. The coercive family environment places a strain on parent–child relations, and the negative peer group associations increase the likelihood of these youth engaging in delinquency and violent behavior (Colvin & Pauly, 1983, pp. 542–543).

Travis Hirschi maintained that youth who have a closer bond to parents and prosocial peers are less likely to commit delinquent acts (1969). Attachment to others refers to the affection and respect that children have for parents and friends; and these are important considerations when youth are tempted to engage in delinquent behavior. He found that youth with a greater attachment to parents reported less delinquent involvement. Youth with weak ties to parents reported little concern for the opinions of teachers and disliked school, and were more likely to become involved in delinquent behavior (Hirschi, 1969). The peer attachment–delinquency relationship as explained by social control theory has received a great deal of support among criminologists. Hindelang (1973) found a direct relationship between peer attachment and self-reported delinquency among rural males and females; and concluded that it appears to depend on the kinds of friends youth have and the characteristics of their peer associations. Linden and Hackler (1973) studied youths' relationships with parents, conventional peers, and deviant peers; they found that youth who had closer relationships with deviant peers than with their parents and conventional peers had the highest rates of self-reported delinquency. Johnson, Marcos, and Bahr (1987) found that peer associations influence adolescent drug use. Thornberry (1987) concluded that associating with delinquent peers, not being committed to school, and engaging in delinquent behavior are contradictory to parents' expectations and therefore diminish the attachment between parent and child. Agnew (1991) analyzed data from the National Youth Survey and concluded that peer attachment strongly affects delinquency when an adolescent spends much time with serious delinquents, feels they approve delinquency, and feels pressure to engage in delinquency (p. 64). Youth whose friends are positive and law-abiding are at less risk of delinquent involvement than those who associate with peers having a higher level of self-reported delinquency. Close relations with parents and the family reduce delinquent influences, but alone they are not enough. Lawrence (1991b) analyzed data from the National Youth Survey to determine the relative effects of parental attachment, commitment to school, and delinquent peer relations on delinquency; he found that the influence of delinquent friends is more important than school attachment in explaining delinquent behavior (Lawrence, 1991b).

The effects of peer associations on delinquent involvement have important implications for juvenile justice and correctional programs. Elliott, Huizinga, and Ageton (1985) suggested that treatment approaches that use adolescent peer group processes may actually have the unintended effect of contributing to closer delinquent friendships. They believe that incarceration of juvenile offenders together in institutional settings inevitably results in closer ties among serious young offenders; they recommended efforts to integrate high-risk youth into conventional peer groups (p. 149). Gary Gottfredson (1987) reviewed studies of the effects of peer group interventions conducted in schools (e.g., Guided Group Interaction, Positive Peer Culture, peer group counseling) and arrived at a similar conclusion. Gottfredson suggested that it may be better to seek ways to avoid delinquent peer interaction entirely rather than to try to change its nature (p. 710).

In summary, parents should be concerned about their children's friends; closely monitor what their children do, where they go, and with whom. Parents, schools, and correctional programs cannot entirely control or eliminate associations with delinquent peers. The evidence is clear, however, that failure to minimize such associations promotes delinquency. The more effective delinquency prevention strategies are those that encourage stronger attachments to family, school, and nondelinquent friends. Supporting the efforts of parents, schools, and juvenile justice programs in collaborative efforts is a worthwhile goal for effective delinquency prevention.

Schools and Delinquency

Public schools have been cited as a source of delinquency. A Presidential Crime Commission report some 40 years ago cited several school practices and deficiencies that were causes of academic failure and could lead to delinquency. Irrelevant instruction, inappropriate teaching methods, "tracking" students, inadequate remedial education, inferior teachers and facilities in low-income schools, and economic and racial segregation all contribute to school failure and delinquency (Schafer & Polk, 1972, pp. 185–208). Other education critics and criminologists have cited evidence suggesting that delinquency results in part from youths' negative school experiences.

Experiences in a young person's life course influence the likelihood of engaging in delinquent behavior, and the institution that has the greatest impact next to the family is the school (Sampson & Laub, 1997). School experiences are critical as adolescents are developing morally, socially, and psychologically and are most at risk of delinquent involvement. Schools can be a turning point in a young person's life, and education can reduce the potential for criminal behavior and risk of imprisonment (Arum & Beattie, 1999). Schools play an important role in society and face a number of challenges in meeting societal expectations. Three factors summarize the important role of schools in society and in the lives of children and youth.

1. A Social Institution. Because they are important social institutions, high expectations are placed on schools to provide students with critical skills and personal values, and to prepare young people to be productive and responsible citizens in a democratic society. Education has played an important role in developing America. The framers of the U.S. Constitution understood that democratic government would not succeed without an informed, educated citizenry. Thomas Jefferson and Benjamin Franklin, among others, advocated strongly for the development of schools that were publicly supported. America's leaders have placed high expectations on education for its role as an important social institution in forming a democratic society.

2. Demands on Education for Social Change. Schools have been expected to serve as the primary institution for social change. Thousands of immigrants came to America in the early decades of the 20th century, and schools were charged with the responsibility of ensuring that the children of these new citizens were given American values and to socialize them. The school teacher became a parent-substitute for many immigrant children. School leaders responded to demands to assist needy children by developing special schools and educational programs in cities across the country where immigrants were working and struggling to make it. For more than a century, schools have attempted to meet the demands of business and industry, immigration, and the social effects of urbanism. The idea that schools should be instruments of social change and take on responsibilities beyond basic education has been promoted through regular legislative initiatives by the U.S. Congress.

3. Expectations and Demands on Schools. In addition to meeting educational demands, schools have assumed responsibility for youths' personal and social development, tasks traditionally belonging to the family and the church. At the same time, the demands of an increasingly technological society have brought criticism that American schools are weak on academic standards. Presidential administrations and Congress regularly propose new legislation and policies to improve the state of education in America.

Politicians and the public regularly call for school reform to "get back to basics." Educators are criticized for students' school failure, and the political response has been to raise educational standards and require competency tests. In the face of higher expectations and demands, public funding of education to help meet those demands has been diminishing throughout the United States (Lawrence, 1995).

Truancy, Dropout, and Delinquency

School problems and low academic achievement have been linked to deviant and delinquent behavior. Students who are not committed to school and not positively involved in school activities are at risk of school failure and antisocial behavior. The academic demands and discipline of school are frustrating for many students. Those who do not receive support and encouragement from parents, siblings, and peers are at risk of absenteeism and truancy. School truancy is considered to be the first step to a lifetime of problems (Garry, 1996), and is associated with substance abuse, gang involvement, and delinquency (Dryfoos, 1990; Bell, Rosen, & Dynlacht, 1994; Huizinga, Loeber, & Thornberry, 1995). Truancy has been linked to higher rates of crime that increase the cost of law enforcement. Additional costs attributed to truancy are for lost revenues to school districts from federal and state funds that are based on attendance figures; higher welfare costs to taxpayers; and costs to businesses that must pay to train uneducated workers (Garry, 1996). There is evidence that truancy may have long-term effects. Adults who were frequently truant as teenagers are more likely to have poorer physical and mental health, lower paying jobs, likely to live in poverty, likely to depend on welfare support, have children with problem behaviors, and have an increased risk of incarceration (Dryfoos, 1990; Bell et al., 1994).

Ten percent to 30% of students are absent from school on any given school day in the United States. In the New York City public school system, about 150,000 (15%) of the 1 million public school students are absent on a typical day; the Los Angeles school district reports an average of 62,000 (10%) of students are out of school each day (Garry, 1996). The school dropout rate has gradually declined over the years but it is still a serious problem. The problem is particularly acute in inner-city urban schools. School principals have rated absenteeism and tardiness among the worst discipline problems they face (Heaviside et al., 1998).

Factors Associated With Dropping Out. Research studies have identified several factors associated with dropping out of school. The most prominent factors noted by the majority of studies include race, ethnicity, and gender; family, parents, and peers; school-related factors; economic factors; and individual factors (Rumberger, 1983, 1987; Ekstrom, Goertz, Pollack, & Rock, 1986; Dunham & Alpert, 1987; Drennon-Gala, 1995).

Dropout–Delinquency Relationship. There is clearly a relationship between dropout and delinquency, but there is disagreement as to the exact causal order of the association. The question is whether dropout causes delinquency, whether delinquency causes dropout, or whether other social factors may be responsible for truancy, dropout, and delinquency.

According to *strain theory,* delinquency is a response to the frustrations or "strains" of school experiences. Elliott and Voss (1974) hypothesized that dropping out occurred after school failure led to frustration. Feeling alienated from successful achievers and students who are positively involved in school activities, the failing students associate with peers who are also failing, dislike school, and are skipping classes. Based on their observations of a sample of youth, Elliott and Voss concluded that delinquent behavior occurs more frequently while youth are in school, and declines after they drop out. According to strain theory, school failure and delinquency cause dropout. An alternative explanation is offered by *social control theory* with an emphasis on social bonds that help youth avoid delinquent involvement. Delinquency is more likely when young peoples' bonds to conventional society are weak (Hirschi, 1969). Youth who see the positive benefits of school, who have educational goals, and are involved in school are less likely to be involved in delinquency. According to Hirschi, dropping out of school causes delinquency; and other studies have supported the causal relationship of dropout leading to delinquent behavior (Thornberry, Moore, & Christenson, 1985; Farrington et al., 1986). A *third explanation* of the dropout–delinquency relationship is offered by Jarjoura (1993), who analyzed data from the National Longitudinal Survey of Youth and found that delinquency does not always cause dropout nor does dropout necessarily cause delinquency. Rather, it depends on the reasons youth drop out of school. Jarjoura found that those who dropped out because they disliked school and those who were expelled for school misconduct were more likely to engage in delinquency; but dropping out for personal reasons such as marriage or pregnancy had no effect on later involvement in drugs or theft. In subsequent analyses, Jarjoura (1996) noted that dropouts are not a homogeneous group; they differ by social class, the reasons for dropping out, and the level of criminal involvement after dropping out. In summary, research shows that multiple factors are associated with dropout and delinquency. Strain and control theories offer the best explanation, but no single criminological theory provides an adequate explanation for dropout and delinquency. It is clear that preventing truancy and dropout is an important step in delinquency prevention.

Truancy and Dropout Prevention Programs. The Office of Juvenile Justice and Delinquency Prevention has developed and funded a number of truancy and dropout prevention programs, including Communities in Schools (CIS), a network of local, state, and national partnerships working together to help prevent youth from dropping out of school (Cantelon & LeBoeuf (1997). Families and Schools Together (FAST) is a program that provides support to parents to help their children avoid school failure, prevent alcohol and other drug abuse in the family, and reduce the stress that parents and children often experience in daily family life (Cantelon & LeBoeuf, 1997). Truancy reduction programs have been implemented by county attorneys' offices, law enforcement agencies, as juvenile court diversion programs, and with probation officers working in schools. Concentrated efforts by the Dallas Police Department to enforce truancy and curfew laws had a positive impact on reducing gang violence (Fritsch, Caeti, & Taylor, 1999). Results of a combined school–law enforcement Truant Recovery Program in California showed slight improvements in attendance, behavior, and grades a year after the program began (White, Fyfe, Campbell, & Goldkamp, 2001). A Truancy Reduction Demonstration Program (TRDP) was initiated in 1998 through the combined resources of the OJJDP, the Justice Department's Weed and Seed program, and the Safe and Drug-Free Schools Program of the Education Department (Baker, Sigmon, & Nugent, 2001). Effective truancy reduction programs have been reported throughout the United States that have made some positive initial steps in better school attendance and delinquency prevention (Mueller & Giacomazzi, 2003; McCluskey, Bynum, & Patchin, 2004).

Crime in Schools

School crime reports based on the National Crime Victimization Survey (NCVS) show that students ages 12–18 were victims of about 2 million nonfatal crimes (theft plus violent crime) while they were at school and about 1.7 million crimes while they were away from school in 2001. These figures represent victimization rates of 73 crimes per 1,000 students at school, and 61 crimes per 1,000 students away from school (DeVoe et al., 2003, p. 6). Thefts are the most frequently occurring crimes at school. In 2001, about 1.2 million thefts occurred at school, and about 913,000 occurred away from school. Students were victims of about 603,000 simple assaults (fighting, hitting, kicking, and punching that do not result in serious injury). Students were victims of about 161,000 serious violent crimes (rape, sexual assault, robbery, and aggravated assault) at school, and 290,000 serious violent crimes away from school. Younger students (ages 12–14) were more likely than older students (15–18) to be victims of crime at school, while older students were more likely than younger students to be victimized away from school (DeVoe et al., 2003, p. 6).

School crime and victimization have remained fairly stable over the years, but schools continue to have higher rates of crime than many other places in the community. The most recent available data on school crime is from *Indicators of School Crime and Safety: 2007.* Key findings from this most recent report indicate that during the 2005–2006 school year

- There were 17 school-associated violent deaths
- There were about 1.5 million victims of nonfatal crimes at school
- The victimization rate of students ages 12–13 at school declined between 1992 and 2005
- Eighty-six percent of public schools reported one or more violent crimes, theft, or other crime
- Eight percent of students in Grades 9–12 reported being threatened or injured with a weapon
- Twenty-five percent of students reported that drugs were made available to them on school property
- Twenty-eight percent of students ages 12–18 reported having been bullied at school (see Dinkes, Cataldi, Lin-Kelly, & Snyder, 2007)

Bullying at School. Teasing, verbal harassment, shoving, kicking, and other physical assaults have been a part of the school experience for most persons. According to the School Crime Supplement to the National Crime Victimization Survey, 8% of students ages 12–18 reported that they had been bullied at school in the last 6 months

(DeVoe et al., 2003, p. 16). Males were more likely than females to report being bullied (9% vs. 7%). Bullying varied by race and ethnicity of students. White students were more likely than black students to report being bullied (9% vs. 6%); and 8% of Hispanic students reported being bullied. Bullying was reported more frequently among lower- than upper-grade students. In 2001, 14% of 6th graders, 9% of 9th graders, and 2% percent of 12th graders reported that they had been bullied at school (DeVoe et al., 2003, p. 16). The problem of bullying is one of the most serious victimization problems in school for a number of reasons. Research shows that bullying not only affects students' attendance and school performance, but also has long-lasting consequences that affect victims for months and years after the bullying incidents (Olweus, 1980, 1991; Farrington, 1993; Juvonen & Graham, 2001). There is evidence that bullying is one of the factors in fatal school shooting incidents (Lawrence, 2007, pp. 153–159), and anti-bullying programs are a part of most school safety and violence prevention initiatives. Bullying has taken a new angle as modern technology has enabled bullies to harass their peers through what Patchin and Hinduja (2006) refer to as "cyberbullying." Results of a pilot study revealed that 74% of youth reported that bullying occurs online and nearly 30% of them reported being victimized by others while online (Patchin & Hinduja, 2006).

CASE IN POINT 5.2

School Shootings Involving Multiple Fatalities in the United States, 1974–2008*

Date	Location	Alleged Perpetrator (Age)	Victims
December 1974	Olean, NY	Anthony Barbaro (18)	3
May 1992	Olivehurst, CA	Eric Houston (20)	3
January 1993	Grayson, KY	Scott Pennington (17)	2
October 1995	Blackville, SC	Toby Sincino (16)	3
February 1996	Moses Lake, WA	Barry Loukaitis (14)	3
February 1997	Bethel, AK	Evan Ramsey (16)	2
October 1997	Pearl, MS	Luke Woodham	3
December 1997	W. Paducah, KY	Michael Carneal (14)	3
March 1998	Jonesboro, AR	Andrew Golden (11) Mitchell Johnson (13)	5
April 1998	Pomona, CA	Unknown gang member(s)	2
May 1998	Springfield, OR	Kip Kinkel (15)	4
April 1999	Littleton, CO	Eric Harris (18) Dylan Klebold (17)	15
March 2001	Santee, CA	Charles Andrew Williams (15)	2
April 2002	Red Lion, PA	James Sheets (14)	2

September 2003	San Diego, CA	William Hoffine (58) (killed son, Evan Nash, 14)	2
September 2003	Cold Spring, MN	Jason McLaughlin (15)	2
March 2005	Red Lake, MN	Jeff Weiss (17)	8
September 2006	Bailey, CO	Duane Morrison (53)	2
October 2006	Nickel Mines, PA	Charles Roberts (32)	6

*The listed cases are those involving multiple fatalities in "school-associated violent deaths," including suicides, that occurred in or around K–12 schools, on the way to or from school, or at school events (not including colleges and universities).

SOURCE: Lawrence, 2007; National School Safety Center, 2008.

Discussion Questions

1. Based on reports in the news media, including television and the Internet, do most people believe that violent school deaths are a recent occurrence (especially since Columbine in Littleton, Colorado, in 1999)? Do the reported fatalities in the above table surprise you?

2. This table includes only the "multiple fatality" school shooting incidents. Note the Web site sources at the end of this chapter, go to the National School Safety Center (NSSC) Web site, and the "school-associated violent deaths." How many school shooting deaths occurred in your state over the years? Do more states or regions of the country seem to have more school shootings?

3. After the Columbine High School tragedy in 1999, school safety and violence prevention became a high priority among schools throughout the country. Reviewing the table above and the NSSC Web site, does it appear that school shootings have decreased somewhat since 1999?

School Safety and Violence Prevention

Shooting incidents at schools involving multiple fatalities have drawn extensive media coverage and public attention. School shootings are newsworthy events because they are so shocking. We expect schools to be safe havens, free of the dangers of street crime. School shootings are actually rare, infrequent events in comparison with most juvenile violence; and therefore receive extensive media coverage. School shootings are tragic events, but the number of youth killed in schools each year averages only about 1% (20–25) of the approximate 2,000 youth who are victims of homicide each year (Lawrence & Mueller, 2003). School shootings, nonfatal assaults, and the presence of guns and other weapons in schools nevertheless creates a climate of fear, making impossible the safe and orderly environment necessary for learning. State and federal education and justice agencies have made school safety a top priority and have provided funding and program support for school violence prevention (see Lawrence, 2007, pp. 161–163).

Gangs and Delinquency

We discussed above how peer associations take on great importance for adolescents and that for most youth these friendships are positive and supportive, indeed a normal part of adolescent development. Youth who have poor relations with their parents, on the other hand, are likely to experience school problems and to associate with delinquent friends. The resulting negative peer influence leads to involvement with delinquency and drugs, even to serious criminal and violent behavior. The formation of juvenile gangs is an extension of adolescent peer groups, and youth join gangs for a variety of reasons: a need for peer acceptance, belonging, and recognition; for status, safety or security, power, and excitement (Spergel, Curry et al., 1994, p. 3). Youths who are especially drawn to gangs include those raised under socially deprived conditions; those who are failing in school and not involved in school activities; and those who are unemployed with few if any perceived job goals or opportunities.

Gangs and crime committed by gang members are evident in many American cities. A National Institute of Justice (NIJ)–sponsored survey of metropolitan police departments in the 79 largest U.S. cities showed that in 1992 all but 7 were troubled by gangs, as were all but 5 departments in 43 smaller cities (Curry, Ball, & Fox, 1994). In 110 jurisdictions reporting gangs, the survey found that during the previous 12-month period there were

- 249,324 gang members
- 4,881 gangs
- 46,359 gang-related crimes
- 1,072 gang-related homicides (see Curry et al., 1994, p. 1)

A gang problem of this magnitude clearly presents a challenge for law enforcement, and calls for a concerted community-wide effort to respond to the problem.

Definitions and Characteristics of Gangs. Despite the existence of youth gangs since the early part of the 20th century, delinquency experts have not been able to agree on a precise definition of a "gang." The term is sometimes used (even by some youth themselves) to describe any group of teenagers who participate together in deviant and delinquent activities. Police departments and researchers generally prefer a narrower definition of *gang* to include violent behavior, group organization, leadership, and territory (see Horowitz, 1990; and Curry et al., 1994). Jeffrey Fagan (1989) defined gangs according to their primary purpose and activities. Some are basically social groups, involved in few delinquent activities and little drug use; some gangs are involved in drug use and sales, and in vandalism; other gangs have members who are serious delinquents, and are extensively involved in property and violent offenses (pp. 649–651). In a study of gangs in Cleveland and Columbus, C. Ronald Huff (1989) identified three types of gangs: (1) informal hedonistic gangs whose primary interest was in "getting high" and "having a good time"; (2) instrumental gangs that commit property crimes for economic reasons; and (3) predatory gangs that commit robberies, street muggings, and are actively involved in drug use and sales (pp. 528–529).

Gangs appear to be more structured than delinquent groups, but some loosely organized groups may still be regarded as gangs. Most gangs tend to be organized on a geographical basis, such as neighborhoods; and many are focused around racial or ethnic origin, age, or gender. Males make up the vast majority of gang membership, but female participation in gangs is increasing (Campbell, 1990). Gangs tend to be concentrated in communities that are in low-income, public-housing project, and poor black and low-income Hispanic sections of the city (Curry & Spergel, 1988, p. 399).

Gangs and Delinquency. Most delinquency is committed by youth who are not gang members; and gang membership is not necessarily synonymous with delinquent behavior. Huff (1989) observed that gang members spend more time in deviant adolescent behavior (skipping school, disobeying parents), and only the more delinquent gangs and gang members engage in serious criminal behavior. Jeffrey Fagan (1990) surveyed samples of students and dropouts in Chicago, Los Angeles, and San Diego and observed that the involvement of both gang and non-gang youths in delinquency and drug use suggests that gangs are only one of several deviant peer groups in inner cities; but gang members in his sample were more heavily involved in both delinquency and substance use than non-gang members. City police departments in the NIJ survey reported far more gang members than gang-related incidents. The Los Angeles Police Department reported 503 gangs and 55,258 gang members but only 8,528 gang-related crimes in 1991; and the Chicago Police Department reported that 29,000 gang members in 41 gangs accounted for only 4,765 gang incidents in 1991 (Curry et al., 1994, p. 7). Thornberry and his associates (Thornberry, Krohn, Lizotte, & Chard-Wierschem, 1993) conducted a longitudinal study to compare youths' crime patterns prior to, during, and after gang involvement. They found that gang members did not have higher rates of delinquency or drug use before entering the gang, but once they became members their rates increased substantially; and the rates of delinquency decreased when gang members left the gang. Esbensen and his associates had similar conclusions from their studies of youths in high-risk urban neighborhoods. Gang members are already delinquent before joining the gang, but gang membership does slightly increase their delinquent activity (Esbensen & Huizinga, 1993). Gang members were found to be similar to youths who were self-reported serious offenders but were not members of a gang (Esbensen, Huizinga, & Weiher, 1995).

Why Youth Join Gangs. Gangs are more widespread and diverse than the stereotypical group of lower-class minority youth from inner-city urban areas. Gangs are now found in smaller cities, suburban areas, and even youth in small town and rural communities are emulating gang behavior. It is still true, however, that the majority of gangs are located in larger cities, primarily in the lower socioeconomic urban areas. However, because most youth from those areas do *not* join gangs, additional factors are required to explain why youth join gangs. Researchers have identified a number of *characteristics or risk factors* that are associated with *gang membership* (Esbensen, 2000):

> *Individual and Family Demographics.* Gang members are primarily male, though females may account for up to one third of youth gang members (Esbensen & Winfree, 1998), and join gangs and participate for reasons that differ from male members (Campbell, 1990). Gangs in urban areas are believed to be primarily African American or Hispanic, but whites accounted for 30% of gang members in small cities and rural counties (Esbensen, 2000). Some gang youth do come from two-parent families, but gangs are made up primarily of minority youth residing in single-parent households.

> *Personal Attributes.* Gang members have more antisocial beliefs (Hill, Howell, Hawkins, & Battin-Pearson, 1999), and more delinquent self-concepts (Maxson, Whitlock & Klein, 1998). Gang members tend to be more impulsive, engage in more risk-seeking behavior, are less committed to school, and have less communication and attachment with their parents (Esbensen, 2000).

> *Peer Group, School, and Community Factors.* The strongest predictor of gang membership is a high level of interaction with and influence from antisocial peers (Battin, Hill, Abbott, Catalano, & Hawkins, 1998). Gang youth are less committed to school than non-gang youth (Maxson et al., 1998; Hill et al., 1999). Community factors predominate in gang research, and studies indicate that poverty, unemployment, the absence of meaningful jobs, and social disorganization contribute to the presence of gangs (Fagan, 1990; Huff, 1990). Gangs are clearly more prevalent in urban areas and are more likely to emerge in neighborhoods characterized by economic distress and social disorganization (Esbensen, 2000).

Responding to Gang Problems. Five strategies have been variously used in dealing with youth gangs: (1) neighborhood mobilization; (2) social intervention; (3) provision of social and economic opportunities like special school and job programs; (4) gang suppression and incarceration; and (5) special police gang units and specialized probation units (Spergel et al., 1994b). There are limits to what schools can do about family and community factors that contribute to youth gang problems, but there is much they can do in cooperation with community agencies. Public schools, especially middle schools, are among the best resources for preventing and intervening early in youth gang problems. The peak period for recruitment of new gang members occurs between the fifth and eighth grades, among youth who are doing poorly in class and are at risk of dropping out (Spergel, Curry et al., 1994). One suggested approach is the delivery of a flexible curriculum targeted to youth gang members who are not doing well in their classes. The goal is to enhance the students' basic academic and work-related problem-solving skills (Spergel, Chance et al., 1994). Experts have made several recommendations for an effective gang control and suppression strategy by schools:

- Create training programs to inform and prepare teachers and administrators to recognize and respond to gang problems in schools.
- Ensure programs make a clear distinction between gang- and non–gang-related activity so as not to exaggerate the scope of the problem.
- Develop clear guidelines and policies for responding to gang behavior; controlling intimidation, threats, and assaults among students; and strictly forbidding any weapons.

- Enforce rules and regulations through open communication and positive relationships between school personnel, students, and parents.
- Work closely with police and probation agencies, communicating regularly and sharing information for monitoring gang activity (see Huff, 1989, pp. 53–55; Spergel, Chance et al., 1994, pp. 18–19).

The most recent comprehensive effort to respond to the youth gang problem is the Gang Resistance and Education Training (G.R.E.A.T.) Program funded by the National Institute of Justice, developed by the Bureau of Alcohol, Tobacco and Firearms and the Phoenix, Arizona, Police Department. Objectives of the program are to reduce gang activity, and to teach youths to set goals for themselves, how to resist peer pressure, how to resolve conflicts, and the consequences of gang involvement (Esbensen & Osgood, 1999). The program is offered to middle school students (primarily seventh graders) and taught by law enforcement officers. A national evaluation involving more than 5,000 eighth-grade students reported small but positive effects on students' attitudes and their ability to resist peer pressure. The G.R.E.A.T. students reported less delinquency and had lower levels of gang affiliation, higher levels of school commitment, and greater commitment to prosocial peers (Esbensen & Osgood, 1999; Esbensen, 2000).

Many other gang intervention and prevention programs are conducted in schools throughout the United States. A survey of school-based gang prevention and intervention programs conducted on a national sample of schools estimated that there were 781,800 gang prevention activities and 159,700 gang intervention activities under way in the nation's schools (Gottfredson, 2001). Most of the programs were not limited to a gang prevention focus but also covered other forms of problem behavior. The quality and effectiveness of the programs varied greatly, but research findings show that school-based gang prevention programs can have a positive impact on the gang problem.

POLICY AND PRACTICE 5.3   A MODEL FOR GANG INTERVENTION AND DELINQUENCY PREVENTION

Racine, Wisconsin, developed the community–university model for gang intervention and delinquency prevention in small cities. This team model consists of six major steps that communities experiencing an emerging gang problem can take:

- *A genuine commitment to youth.* This can be demonstrated by working directly with youth, developing an understanding of their problems and concerns, building trust, and empowering them to solve problems.
- *Gang problem assessment.* The team will need to investigate, observe, and document the developing gang problem while learning from neighboring jurisdictions through the exchange of information. . . . Meetings with community leaders and individuals must be organized.

(Continued)

(Continued)

- *Initial networking.* A task force should be formed to collaborate on possible solutions. Its work includes organizing community meetings and neighborhood hearings to identify solutions and develop a collaborative response to gangs.
- *Local study of the gang situation.* The task force should identify a local college, university, or other community resource that can study the local gang problem.
- *Timeout.* In this stage, the task force should publish and disseminate research findings, expand its network via conferences and other communication outlets, identify funding sources, establish political foundations for funding, and prepare grant/contract applications for the second set of awards.
- *Development of new programs.* The final stage is program development and implementation. The overall plan should include long-term goals and a master plan. New programs should be implemented through continued collaborative efforts. Research and program development would continue during the implementation of the program.

SOURCE: Office of Juvenile Justice and Delinquency Prevention. (2000). Youth gang programs and strategies: Strategies using multiple techniques. *OJJDP Juvenile Justice Bulletin.* Washington, DC: Office of Juvenile Justice and Delinquency Prevention. Retrieved September 30, 2008, from http://www.ncjrs.gov/html/ojjdp/summary_2000_8/strategies.html.

Discussion Questions

1. Note the Web site sources at the end of this chapter (NCJRS, and the National Gang Crime Research Center). How do some other programs compare with the Racine, Wisconsin, program above?

2. Do an Internet search for any gang prevention programs in your state, region, or city. How do they propose to reduce gang involvement and juvenile crime?

3. The Racine program above works with local colleges and universities to help study the local gang problem. Suggest how your class or student organization might propose a similar project, working with your local police department. What might be some challenges or difficulties with such a project?

Alcohol, Drugs, and Delinquency

Drug use among youth continues to be a serious problem despite some downturns in use levels. Youth alcohol and drug abuse may lead to other problems, including antisocial behavior, school problems, delinquency, and health-related issues; and those who begin drug use at a younger age are more likely to develop drug problems later in life. The causes of drug abuse and addiction vary among users according to biological and environmental factors, but abuse of alcohol and other drugs has significant and long-lasting effects on individual development of children and youth.

Extent of Drug Use. According to the 2008 Monitoring the Future Survey, 16% of 10th graders and 22% of 12th graders reported using illegal drugs in the past month; and 27% of 10th graders and 37% of 12th graders reported some illegal drug use in the past year (Johnston, O'Malley, Bachman, & Schulenberg, 2008). Results of the 2007 Youth Risk Behavior Surveillance System indicated that 38% of high school students had used marijuana during their lifetime and 20% reported current use (Centers for Disease Control, 2008). In 2007, state and local law enforcement agencies reported 109,444 drug abuse arrests of juveniles under 18, representing about 11% of drug arrests among all age groups (Federal Bureau of Investigation, 2008). According to data from the Arrestee Drug Abuse Monitoring (ADAM) Program, an average of 60% of male detainees and 46% of female juvenile detainees tested positive for drug use in 2000 (National Institute of Justice, 2003). In 2004, juvenile courts in the United States handled an estimated 193,700 delinquency cases in which a drug offense was the most serious charge. Between 1991 and 2004 the number of juvenile court cases involving drug offenses more than doubled. Drug offense cases accounted for 12% of all delinquency cases during the year of 2004 compared with 7% in 1985 (Stahl, 2008). According to a census of juvenile offenders in residential placement in October, 1999, there were 9,882 juvenile offenders in custody for drug offenses, about one third of them for drug trafficking (Sickmund, 2004).

Research reports indicate a problem of alcohol and drugs in schools. Twenty percent of students ages 12 through 18 reported that alcohol was available at school, and 37% reported that drugs were available (Addington, Ruddy, Miller, DeVoe, & Chandler, 2002, p. 18). The presence of alcohol and drugs in schools is associated with other problems, such as the presence of gangs, victimization, and student reports of knowing about a student who brought a gun to school. According to the 2000 School Survey on Crime and Safety (SSOCS), 12% of public school principals (K–12) reported some distribution of illegal drugs at their school, and 27% reported possession or use of illegal drugs by students at school (Miller & Chandler, 2003). No significant differences were reported in drug possession based on city size, crime level where students lived, or percentage of minority enrollment at the schools. Drug possession was reported by principals in urban, suburban, and rural schools; schools in both high and low crime areas; and where minority enrollments ranged from less than 20% to than 50% (p. 67). Alcohol and illegal drug possession or use was associated with discipline problems, disruptions, and percentage of students absent without excuses. Twice as many principals who reported some alcohol or drug possession also reported problems with discipline, disruption, or absenteeism (p. 69).

Effects of Drug Abuse. Persistent substance abuse by young people often leads to academic difficulties and health-related problems including mental health, family conflicts, poor peer relationships, and involvement with the juvenile justice system. Results from the 2001 National Household Survey on Drug Abuse show that the earlier in life people begin drug use, the more likely they are to develop a drug problem. Greater use of cigarettes, alcohol, or any illegal drug had a negative effect on students' grades (Substance Abuse and Mental Health Services Administration, 2002). Findings from the National

Longitudinal Survey of Youth indicate that youth who reported use of alcohol and drugs also engaged in selling drugs and other delinquent behaviors (McCurley & Snyder, 2008). Estimates indicate that substance abuse and addiction will have added at least $41 billion to the costs of elementary and secondary education for the 2000–2001 school year. The costs include truancy (and resulting reduction of per pupil funding of education), drug testing, employee training to increase alcohol and drug awareness, and special education programs for students with substance abuse problems.

CASE IN POINT 5.3

Correlates and Causes of Delinquency in the Movies

We noted in the previous chapter that crime is a popular form of entertainment in America, and many Hollywood movies focus on crime and criminals. Many of the movies (some based on true stories) illustrate some of the **causes and correlates of delinquency.** The book and screenplay writers also force the viewer to critically examine the background, sources, and broader implications of such delinquency correlates as family and school problems, peer pressure, and drugs and alcohol. We encourage you to view these films and consider how the characters in each story illustrate some of the correlates and causes of delinquency.

The Breakfast Club. Director and Writer: John Hughes. Release date: Feb. 15, 1985. Five teenagers, students at a suburban high school, come together for an all-day Saturday Detention Hall. They were all strangers with little or nothing in common, but that day changed their lives forever. The five students represent a brain, a beauty, a jock, a rebel, and a loner. What they did have in common was that they had broken a school rule. Before the day was over, they broke more rules, bared their souls, and touched each other in a way they never dreamed possible.

Dangerous Minds. Director: John Smith. Written by LouAnn Johnson (book) and Ronald Bass (screenplay). Release date: August 11, 1995. LouAnn Johnson is an ex-Marine who is hired as a teacher in a high school in a poor area of the city. Her friend, who is also a teacher in the school, got her the temporary job. After a rocky reception from the students she tries unconventional methods of teaching to gain the trust of the students and to get them interested in learning, such as using Bob Dylan lyrics to develop an appreciation for poetry. She makes such an impact on their education and personal lives that they plead with her to not leave what she had intended to be a temporary, one-year teaching position.

Lean on Me. Director: John Avildsen; written by Michael Schiffer. Released March 3, 1989. Eastside High School in Patterson, New Jersey, faced the threat of being taken over by the state because of poor academic performance, discipline problems, and crime. In desperation, the superintendent turns to the controversial Joe Clark to become the principal and turn the school around. With a bullhorn in one hand, a baseball bat in the other, Clark took a tough approach to take control of the school. Parents fought him, teachers resented him, even his own boss doubted him; but many students loved him. Clark did turn the school around and got national attention for his achievement. He told the students, "If you don't succeed in life, don't blame your backgrounds. Don't blame the Establishment. Blame yourselves." His message was simple and direct: "Don't lean on excuses, drugs, crime, or anger. Lean on me . . . and learn."

Traffic. Director: Steven Soderbergh; Writer: Stephen Gaghan. Release date: January 5, 2001. This movie is a contemporary look at America's war on drugs told through four separate stories that are connected in one way or another. A conservative politician just appointed as the U.S. drug czar learns that his daughter is a drug addict. A trophy wife struggles to save her husband's drug business, while two DEA agents protect a witness with inside knowledge of the spouse's business. In Mexico, a corrupt yet dedicated cop struggles with his conscience when he learns that his new boss may not be the antidrug official he made himself out to be. The intertwining stories in this film challenge our thinking and the policies of America's escalating War on Drugs.

SOURCE: The Internet Movie Data Base. Retrieved February 9, 2009, from http://www.imdb.com/.

Discussion Questions

1. How do the stories depicted by these films illustrate one or more of the correlates or causes of juvenile delinquency? Comment on one or more of the following factors: family relationships; peer relationships and influence; school problems; alcohol and drug use.

2. As Hollywood films and sources of entertainment, are the stories exaggerated? Or, do they depict real-life situations and experiences of youth? Support examples in the films, or statements of characters in the films, with research findings in this chapter.

Alcohol, Drugs, and Delinquency. Alcohol and substance use are forms of deviant behavior to which most young people are exposed from late childhood through adolescence. Possession and use of alcohol and illegal drugs are of course delinquent acts in themselves that may result in arrest and referral to Juvenile Court. Even if youth avoid police arrest and judicial sanctions, drug use will have adverse effects on their lives. Youths who take drugs do poorly in school, have high dropout rates, and continue to use drugs after they leave school (Krohn, Thornberry, Collins-Hall, & Lizotte, 1995). Based on the research evidence and findings of numerous studies, it is clear that drug use is associated with delinquency along with the other risk factors discussed in this chapter, including family problems, peer influence, school problems, and gang involvement. It less clear, however, whether drug use is a *cause* of delinquency. Elliott and his associates (1985) have reported on delinquency and drug use based on findings of the National Youth Survey. In longitudinal studies of self-reported delinquency and drug use, they found a strong association between the two, but believe that drug abuse is a type of delinquent behavior and not necessarily a cause of it (Elliott et al., 1985; Huizinga, Menard, & Elliott, 1989). They found that most youths engage in delinquent acts before they begin using drugs, and they conclude that both delinquency and drug use appear to reflect a developmental problem that is part of a disturbed socialization process and lifestyle. Researcher directors of the Program of Research on the Causes and Correlates of Delinquency have analyzed data from their study sites in Denver, Pittsburgh, and Rochester to examine the co-occurrence or over-lap of serious delinquency with drug use, problems in school, and mental health prob-lems. Preliminary findings indicate that a large proportion of serious delinquents are *not* involved in persistent drug use, and they do *not* have persistent school or mental health problems (Huizinga, Loeber, Thornberry, & Cothern, 2000). The problem that does co-occur most frequently with serious delinquency, however, is drug use; and for males, as the number of problem behaviors other than delinquency increases, the like-lihood that an individual will be a serious delinquent also increases. Analyses of data from the National Survey on Drug Use and Health found that illegal drug use was sig-nificantly associated with self-reported delinquency as well as self-reported arrest (Ford, 2008). Results of a survey administered to a large sample of 7th- to 12th-grade students in New York state indicated that early initiation into alcohol use is likely to increase the risk of further alcohol abuse, other substance use, and delinquency (Barnes, Welte, & Hoffman, 2002).

These research findings have important implications for drug abuse and delin-quency prevention. Programs targeted solely at substance abuse prevention may have little effect on delinquency rates because drug use is a symptom and not a cause of delinquent behavior. The Drug Education for Youth (DEFY) is a multiphased drug edu-cation prevention program for youth ages 9 to 12 (Executive Office for Weed and Seed, 2004). The program is designed to deter at-risk behavior by giving youth the tools to resist drugs, gangs, and alcohol by developing relationships between youth and positive adult role models and providing life-skills training. Researchers and juvenile justice program administrators have known for years of the link between alcohol, drug use, and juvenile crime. Several promising strategies have now emerged for intervening in the juvenile drug–crime cycle. The balanced and restorative justice (BARJ) approach (discussed in Chapter 13 of this volume) combines the traditional rehabilitative philos-ophy with juvenile accountability and shows promise for confronting the problem of drugs and delinquency. Other promising strategies involve integrated case management and collaboration among social service agencies and the traditional juvenile justice sys-tem (VanderWaal, McBride, Terry-McElrath, & VanBuren, 2001). The most effective delinquency prevention and intervention programs are those that take a comprehensive and multidimensional approach. In later chapters of this text we will highlight research on delinquency prevention, juvenile corrections, and the balanced and restorative approach that addresses these multiple correlates and causes of delinquency.

SUMMARY

- Parents and families play a major role in the development of youth.
- Research evidence shows that the chances of youth becoming involved in delinquent behavior are greater when they have experienced problems in parent–child relations, inconsistent supervision and discipline, and/or parental rejection and abuse.
- Child neglect and abuse are serious problems that affect thousands of children and youth and have serious consequences, including involvement in juvenile crime and violence.

- Peers have a significant influence on a youth's behavior, and association with negative peers is more likely when there are problematic relations with parents.
- School problems including academic failure, truancy, and dropout are associated with delinquency, both as causes and as consequences.
- Bullying, assaults, verbal harassment, and threats create a fearful environment in schools that affect learning and lead to more serious violent and delinquent behavior.
- Youth gangs often provide a feeling of acceptance and belonging for youth lacking a positive family relationship, and who are experiencing problems in school.
- Alcohol and substance abuse adversely affect young peoples' family and peer relationships and school performance, and are associated with delinquent involvement.
- Correlates of delinquency are factors that may or may not cause delinquency, but place young people at greater risk of delinquent involvement.

KEY TERMS

Broken homes

Parental rejection

Parental attachment

Parental disengagement

"Battered child syndrome"

"Cycle of violence"

Teenage gang

Gangs and delinquency

DISCUSSION QUESTIONS

1. What are some causes and "correlates" of juvenile delinquency? Explain why some are "correlates" but not necessarily causes, and what research findings must establish before they could be considered "causes."

2. Based on the research findings you have read, do you believe that it is more important that a young person has two parents in the home; or that the quality of the family relationships is good, whether one or two parents? Explain your answer.

3. Child abuse is a problem in which a young person is a victim, not a delinquent. Explain how and why the problem may lead to delinquency.

4. Does dropout cause delinquency, or delinquency cause dropout? Based on research studies, is it possible that both, or neither, may be true for some students? Explain.

5. If a juvenile gang problem was evident in your city, what recommendations would you offer to the police department, human services, schools, and other community agencies to reduce the problem?

6. Based on research findings and any of your experiences and observations, what three main recommended strategies would you offer to reduce young peoples' abuse of alcohol and other drugs?

WEB RESOURCES

Causes and Correlates of Delinquency Program: http://www.ncjrs.gov/pdffiles1/fs99100.pdf

Problem behaviors and delinquency: http://www.ncjrs.gov/pdffiles1/ojjdp/182211.pdf

Child Abuse and Neglect: http://www.ncjrs.gov/app/Search/Abstracts.aspx?id=240753

OJJDP Parent Training Programs Example: http://www.ncjrs.gov/pdffiles1/ojjdp/172848.pdf

National Gang Crime Research Center: http://ngcrc.com/

Highlights of the National Youth Gang Survey: http://ojjdp.ncjrs.gov/publications/PubAbstract.asp?pubi=245263

Indicators of School Crime and Safety: 2007: http://www.ojp.usdoj.gov/bjs/pub/pdf/iscs07.pdf

National Center for Education Statistics; resources on school crime and safety: http://nces.ed.gov/programs/crime/surveys.asp

School Survey on Crime and Safety (SSOCS): http://nces.ed.gov/surveys/ssocs/index.asp

National School Safety Center ("school-associated violent deaths"): http://www.schoolsafety.us/School-Associated-Violent-Deaths-p-6.html

Office of National Drug Control Policy, Juveniles and Drugs: http://www.whitehousedrugpolicy.gov/drugfact/juveniles/index.html

Police and Juveniles

CHAPTER HIGHLIGHTS

- ❖ The Police and Juvenile Crime
- ❖ Police Roles and Responsibilities
- ❖ Police–Juvenile Relations
- ❖ Police Discretion
- ❖ Race as a Factor in Juvenile Arrests
- ❖ Alternatives to Police Arrest and Custody

The first contact that a young juvenile offender has with the juvenile justice system is with a police officer. The nature and circumstances of this police contact are likely to be significant and have a lasting impression on a young person. In this chapter we examine police roles and responsibilities in general, and the unique roles that police have when dealing with juvenile offenders. Children and juveniles are involved in a variety of law violations ranging from status offenses to more serious offending, and present special challenges for the policing function. We discuss alternatives to traditional law enforcement strategies, such as community- or problem-oriented policing; curfew enforcement; preventive efforts such as D.A.R.E. and School Resource Officers; police procedures for taking juvenile offenders into custody; legal guidelines for interrogation and gathering evidence; and police officers' discretion in deciding whether to refer a case to juvenile court or to use other alternatives.

The Police and Juvenile Crime

For juveniles, the police role is considered especially important, because young persons' views and attitudes toward law enforcement are shaped by their first encounter with a police officer. Juvenile offenders are involved in a disproportionately large number of crimes relative to their percentage of the population, so they present a special challenge for law enforcement. In 2005, law enforcement agencies in the United States made an estimated 2.1 million arrests of persons under age 18. Juveniles accounted for about 16% of all violent crime arrests and 26% of all property crime arrests in 2005 (Snyder, 2007, p. 1).

The police role with juveniles is expanded because they handle many noncriminal matters referred to as *status offenses,* including running away, curfew violations, and truancy as well as nondelinquent juvenile matters such as neglect, abuse, and missing persons reports. Most urban police departments have special police units or juvenile bureaus for handling the increasing number of juvenile cases. Duties of special juvenile officers include taking missing children reports; examining runaway cases; investigating juvenile crimes; contacting and interviewing juveniles, their parents, school officials, and complainants regarding the circumstances of an offense; maintaining juvenile records; and appearing in juvenile court.

Juveniles are less predictable than adults, and often exhibit less respect for the authority of officers. The immaturity of many children and youth means that they are more susceptible to the dares of other youth, and they often engage in deviant behavior when in the company of their peers. Many youth view the police officer on patrol not as a deterrent to delinquent behavior, but as a challenge to avoiding detection and confrontation while loitering at night or engaging in behaviors ranging from petty mischief, to property damage and vandalism, to more serious crimes of theft and assaults. The immaturity of youth coupled with limited parental supervision and negative peer influence presents special problems for police, who frequently encounter juveniles with little respect for law and authority. Juveniles also present a special problem for police because they are less cognizant of the consequences of their actions and of the effects of their delinquent behavior on their victims, their parents and families, their peers, and themselves. Before discussing police roles with juvenile offenders, we provide an overview of police roles in general.

Police Roles and Responsibilities

Police officers are the most visible officials in the criminal justice system. They introduce citizens to the justice process. That introduction ranges from taking a report from a victim or witness to a crime, issuing a traffic citation, to questioning or taking into custody a suspect in a misdemeanor or felony offense. Police are charged with preventing crime and enforcing the law. They are given the authority to make arrests, to use reasonable physical force when necessary, and to take persons charged with crimes into custody. Society entrusts a great deal of authority to police, but also expects a lot from them. Police are expected to provide public order and safety; to prevent crimes from occurring, and find and apprehend offenders when crimes occur; and to perform a variety of law enforcement functions without violating constitutional rights. In reality, traditional police patrol does little to prevent crime. Police in most cases react to crime after it has already happened, responding to citizen calls, reporting to crime scenes, conducting investigations, and tracking and apprehending offenders. The fact that police are called upon for many services besides law enforcement makes their job even more difficult.

Police officers actually perform three roles in fulfilling their law enforcement responsibilities: law enforcement, order maintenance, and service (Wilson, 1968). The public and the police themselves have viewed the law enforcement function as the primary and most important task, and little attention was given to the others, which were considered less important, and not "real law enforcement."

Law Enforcement

The traditional law enforcement role of police is to detect and investigate crimes, and to apprehend those responsible for committing crimes. Police attempt to detect crimes through regular police patrols and by responding to complaints of victims and statements of witnesses. The traditional law enforcement role gives police visibility to the public as they "protect and serve." There are some additional challenges in policing crimes such as drug dealing, gambling, and prostitution, where there are no witnesses or clearly identified victims. To enforce laws against the so-called victimless crimes (or more appropriately termed *consensual* crimes, because persons involved are willing participants), police work as undercover officers to detect the crimes and make arrests. The law enforcement role includes enforcement of traffic laws and parking violations, and it is here that officers have the most interaction with the general public as law enforcers. To finalize their law enforcement role and ensure that suspects are brought to trial, police engage in interrogation of suspects, collection of physical evidence at a crime scene, and presentation of the evidence in court.

SOURCE: © Ruaridh Stewart/ZUMA/Corbis.

Photo 6.1 A juvenile offender suspect awaits verification of juvenile status and questioning by police.

Order Maintenance

The order maintenance function of the police involves crowd control during events such as parades, large public gatherings, music concerts, sports competitions in indoor and outdoor stadiums; patrolling on foot, bicycle, horseback, or in vehicles; and patrolling on streets, sidewalks, and in public parks. The order maintenance function parallels the law enforcement role when officers intervene to control disorderly behavior. The order maintenance role is less clear (both to the public and to many police) than the law enforcement role, mainly because the behaviors being controlled are less clearly defined. "Disorderly behavior," for example, generally refers to behavior that disturbs the public peace, but the exact definition and an officer's determination whether the behavior warrants official intervention depends on the neighborhood location and the time during which the disturbance occurs. The officer's role may be that of telling participants of a loud party to quiet down, or dispersing a group of juveniles who are loitering on a street corner or in front of a business establishment.

Service Function

The third role of police is that of providing services to the public. This may include providing aid or assistance to persons in need, such as calling a tow truck for a stranded motorist; transporting abandoned or neglected children to a hospital or shelter facility; delivering a baby whose mother did not make it to the hospital on time. The service function often results in a combination of functions, such as when one officer transports abandoned children to a shelter, and another officer locates the parent(s) and initiates a child abuse investigation (a law enforcement function). The service function more recently has come to include an educational component, such as when police are assigned to schools to assist in the education of children and youth on the dangers of drugs and how to avoid drug abuse.

The three primary roles of police are very different on a number of dimensions: criminal versus noncriminal, urgent versus routine, and dangerous versus relatively safe (Dorne & Gewerth, 1995). Police officers generally view the law enforcement function as the primary role, while order maintenance and service tasks have been typically regarded with mixed feelings, ranging from ambivalence to disdain (Moore, 1992). Police officers hold varying opinions of the importance of each of the roles, and they do not undertake these three functions with equal degrees of enthusiasm. They are given considerable autonomy and independence in carrying out their law enforcement roles, and are allowed to place greater or lesser importance on a given role depending on their assigned patrol area and individual circumstances.

The service functions of policing take on a special emphasis in relation to juveniles. Police are expected to *protect children* and to *prevent delinquency* (Sanborn & Salerno, 2005). Child protection may involve intervening in suspected cases of child neglect (being left at home alone, or left inside a vehicle in cold or hot weather conditions); endangering a child's safety (failure to use a car seat or seat belts); or child abuse such as physical punishment that may involve serious injury or even death. Child neglect and abuse have been shown to have a relationship with status offenses such as running away, which in turn often lead to more serious delinquency. The primary reason for the inclusion of status offenses in all juvenile statutes, in fact, is for child protection and delinquency prevention. Laws giving police the authority to intervene in noncriminal behaviors such as running away, truancy, and curfew violations are intended to protect them and to prevent worse delinquent behavior.

POLICY AND PRACTICE 6.1	CONSIDERATIONS FOR CHILD ABUSE INVESTIGATIONS

Police officers have a number of alternatives available for handling situations that involve child abuse. Officers must be objective and proactive in their investigations of abuse. Questions concerning who, what, where, when, how, and why must be answered. It is important to remember that child abuse is a crime, and law enforcement has a legal duty and responsibility to respond accordingly. Police departments must establish policies and procedures to investigate child abuse cases, and they need to consider many important factors:

When You Receive the Referral

- Know department guidelines and State statutes.
- Know what resources are available in the community . . . and provide this information to the child's family.
- Introduce yourself, your role, and the focus and objective of the investigation.
- Assure that the best treatment will be provided for the protection of the child.
- Interview the child alone, focusing on corroborative evidence.
- Don't rule out the possibility of child abuse with a domestic dispute complaint; talk with the children at the scene.

Getting Information for the Preliminary Report

- Inquire about the history of the abusive situation. Dates are important to set the timeline.
- Cover the elements of crime necessary for the report. Inquire about the instrument of abuse or other items on the scene.
- Don't discount children's statements about who is abusing them, where, how, or what types of acts occurred.
- Save opinions for the end of the report, and provide supportive facts.

Preserving the Crime Scene

- Treat the scene as a crime scene . . . and not as the site of a social problem.
- Secure the instrument of abuse or other corroborative evidence.
- Photograph the scene and, when appropriate, include any injuries to the child.

(Continued)

(Continued)

Follow-up Investigation

- Be supportive . . . to the child and the family.
- Arrange for a medical examination and transportation to the hospital.
- Be sure the child and family have been linked to support services or therapy.
- Be sure the family know how to reach a detective to disclose further information.

During the Court Phase

- Visit the court with the child; familiarize her or him with the courtroom setting.
- Prepare courtroom exhibits to . . . support the child's testimony.
- File all evidence in accordance with state and court policy.
- Unless they are suspects, update the family about the status and progress of the investigation and stay in touch with them throughout the court process.
- Provide court results and case closure information to the child and the family.
- Follow up with the probation department for preparation of the presentence report and victim impact statement(s).

SOURCE: Hammond, B., Lanning, K., Promisel, W., Shepherd, J. R., & Walsh, B. (2001). *Law enforcement responses to child abuse: Portable guides to investigating child abuse.* Washington, DC: U.S. Department of Justice. Retrieved September 3, 2008, from http://www.ncjrs.gov/pdffiles/162425.pdf.

Discussion Questions

1. Compare the guidelines above with the police roles in this chapter, and indicate whether child abuse reports involve the police role of law enforcement, order maintenance, or service (or a combination of them).

2. Give an example of how police involvement in a child neglect or abuse case could involve both the law enforcement and service functions.

3. Explain why many police officers believe that investigating a child abuse case is more difficult than investigating assaults involving teenagers or young adults.

Police–Juvenile Relations

Police officers encounter a wide variety of deviant and delinquent behavior among children and youth, ranging from minor status offenses to serious crimes. The majority of police encounters with juveniles are in response to minor offenses that involve an order maintenance function of law enforcement (Friedman, Lurigio, Greenleaf, & Albertson, 2004). Regardless of the seriousness of the behavior, however, the nature of the police–juvenile encounter can make a significant difference on police–juvenile relations. Sherman (1997) noted that police themselves often create a risk factor for crime by using "bad manners." Research evidence indicates that when police are less respectful toward suspects and citizens in general, then citizens also tend to have less respect for police officers and for the law (Sherman, 1997, p. 8–1). Juveniles are critical of police practices such as stopping to question them, asking them to "move on" and not loiter on street corners, parking lots, or in front of stores. African American and Hispanic youth, and those living in urban areas, are more critical of police than white students or those living in suburban or rural areas (Taylor, Turner, Esbensen, & Winfree, 2001). Students often have ambivalent or mixed feelings about police. Taylor et al. (2001) found that a majority of students in their study believed that police are friendly and hard working, but they also believed that officers are racially prejudiced and dishonest. They did *not* believe that police officers contribute directly to the negative feelings, however. The reasons for juveniles' negative attitudes toward police are likely the inevitable result of police officers' fair but unpopular restrictions on young peoples' behaviors (Taylor et al., 2001). Lieber, Nalla, and Farnsworth (1998) suggested that community policing practices and problem-oriented policing can positively influence youths' perceptions of police, but Hurst and Frank (2000) have noted that attempting to involve youths in community-oriented policing is a challenge because of their negative views and disapproval of many police functions. Friedman and his associates (2004) have noted that both police and youth's demeanors affect the perceived nature and outcomes of their encounters, so there is reason to believe that juveniles' negativity toward the police might have triggered officer disrespect, which in turn feeds juveniles' negative attitudes. In short, they believe that police–juvenile interactions are a two-way street. Young people react to how police officers treat them, and officers often respond in kind to juveniles' disrespectful behavior. Working with juveniles is a challenge, and police departments do well to provide officers with cultural awareness training to enhance their skills in working and interacting with juveniles (Friedman et al., 2004).

Community Policing. A new approach and philosophy of policing was developed in the 1990s based on the concept that police officers and citizens working together can help solve community problems related to crime, neighborhood decay and disorder, and fear of crime. Community policing is based on the belief that crime reduction requires police departments to develop a new relationship with the law-abiding citizens in the community, seeking their input and involvement to improve the quality of life in their neighborhoods (Trojanowicz & Bucqueroux, 1990). Community policing is a significant change in the philosophy and structure of law enforcement in the United States, and is defined by some new and innovative organizational strategies, including:

- *Community Partnerships:* Collaboration between law enforcement agencies and the individuals and organizations they serve to develop solutions to community problems and to increase trust in the police.
- *Organizational Transformation:* Realigning organizational management, structure, personnel, and information systems to support community partnerships and perform problem-solving tasks.

- *Problem Solving:* The process of engaging in proactive and systematic examination of identified problems in order to develop effective responses (Office of Community Oriented Policing Services, 2008).

The value of community policing and its potential for making a greater impact on community crime than the traditional reactive style of responding only to dispatchers' calls for service has been recognized by local police administrators and officers, and by the U.S. Department of Justice. The Advancing Community Policing (ACP) Grant Program was established by the Office of Community Oriented Policing Services (COPS Office) in 1997 to help law enforcement agencies develop community policing strategies in communities and cities throughout the nation (Schneider, 2003).

Two law enforcement initiatives that are applications of the community policing approach and that have helped to improve relations between police and juveniles include D.A.R.E. (Drug Awareness Resistance Education) programs and the emergence of School Resource Officers (SROs) working in an increasing number of schools throughout the United States.

D.A.R.E. Officers. The most prominent program involving police with children and youth is the Drug Awareness Resistance Education (D.A.R.E.) program that has been implemented in schools throughout the United States. Originally begun by the Los Angeles Police Department, D.A.R.E. programs have been established in large and smaller cities throughout the country. Special juvenile officers undergo several weeks of training in order to be a D.A.R.E. officer and present the structured curriculum of educational materials primarily to fifth and sixth graders. D.A.R.E. programs have operated in all 50 states and in six foreign countries (Rosenbaum, Flewelling, Bailey, Ringwalt, & Wilkinson, 1994). D.A.R.E. is unique with its collaborative effort between education and law enforcement, and for the use of trained, uniformed police officers in the classroom to teach a highly structured drug prevention curriculum. The program targets students in their last years of elementary school. The D.A.R.E. program is focused on this age group because it is assumed that these students are most receptive to antidrug messages and are entering the drug experimentation phase where intervention may be most beneficial. Officers teach the D.A.R.E. curriculum in one-hour sessions for 17 weeks. Teaching strategies include lectures, workbook exercises, question and answer sessions, audiovisual materials, and role-playing sessions. The strategies support the objective of D.A.R.E., to teach peer resistance skills by offering students several ways to say "no" to drugs. D.A.R.E. is a comprehensive program that includes a variety of teaching objectives including the effects and consequences of using alcohol, marijuana, and other drugs; media influences and advertising techniques for tobacco and alcohol; and developing assertiveness skills and strategies for resisting peer pressure to use drugs.

The results of studies evaluating the effects of D.A.R.E. programs do not show them to have a consistent or significant impact on students' drug use, however. Michele Harmon (1993) examined the effectiveness of a D.A.R.E. program in South Carolina and found that students in the D.A.R.E. group used alcohol less, had higher levels of belief in prosocial norms, reported less association with drug-using peers, showed an increase in attitudes against substance use, and were more assertive. However, no significant effects were found for self-reported cigarette, tobacco, or marijuana use in the past year; frequency of any drug use in the past month; coping strategies, attitudes about police, school attachment and commitment, and rebellious behavior. Susan Ennett and her associates (Ennett, Tobler, Ringwalt, & Flewelling, 1994) conducted a meta-analysis of several D.A.R.E. program outcome evaluations representing six states and a Canadian province and found that the D.A.R.E. programs had very little effect. Except for reduced tobacco use, the effects of the D.A.R.E. programs were slight and not statistically significant. They noted that some features of D.A.R.E. may be more effective in school districts where the D.A.R.E. curricula for younger and older students are in place; and its impact on improved relations with the community, schools, and students may have important benefits. The results showing D.A.R.E.'s limited influence on adolescent drug use behavior contrasts with the popularity and prevalence of the program. Ennett et al. (1994) cautioned that proponents of the D.A.R.E. program may be overstating expectations that it will change adolescent drug use.

Dennis Rosenbaum and his associates (1994) evaluated the D.A.R.E. program in 12 urban and suburban schools in Illinois, involving 1,584 students. A matched group of 24 schools were selected for the study, 12 of which were randomly assigned to receive D.A.R.E., and 12 that served as controls for comparison. The D.A.R.E. program had no significant overall impact on students' use of alcohol or cigarettes about one year after completion of the program. The only significant effect of D.A.R.E. was on perceived media influences regarding the portrayal of beer drinking: more of the D.A.R.E. students' recognized the media's portrayal of beer drinking as desirable. The program had some effect on encouraging females to quit using alcohol but seemed to have the opposite effect for males. The failure of D.A.R.E. to produce any measurable differences in students' attitudes and use of drugs raises questions about the commitment of time and funds to D.A.R.E. programs. Rosenbaum et al. suggested that more attention should be given in drug prevention programs to changing students' inaccurate perceptions about their peers' supposed approval and use of drugs. There *has* been an overall decline in the prevalence of drug use among U.S. students; and this raises the question of whether factors other than school-based drug prevention programs are responsible for the decline, or whether the evaluation measures are not precise enough to detect the effectiveness of the programs (Rosenbaum et al., 1994). It is possible that the decline in drug use may be due to the current emphases on the health risks of drug use, declining social acceptance, and the fact that youth are getting these messages from multiple sources, including the media, parents, family members, and their peers. A review of D.A.R.E. programs also led Denise Gottfredson (2001) to conclude that they do not work to reduce substance use. She suggested that the program's content, teaching methods, and use of uniformed police officers rather than teachers might explain the weak evaluations; and added that the D.A.R.E. curriculum is unlikely to reduce substance use without instruction that is more focused on social competency development.

D.A.R.E. officers and schools have made well-intentioned efforts to prevent drug abuse among youth, but research does not clearly show long-term positive results for the programs. D.A.R.E. programs nevertheless are widely supported by educators, by parents, and by police departments that sponsor the officers who conduct the courses. The programs do have the potential for providing early drug education and awareness for young people; they also serve the function of improving relations with children and youth and are regarded as an important community policing component of law enforcement agencies. For these reasons, there has been considerable incentive for developing a new program. The new D.A.R.E. program is designed to keep students away from high risk behaviors, and it focuses on teaching life skills and resistance to drug use. New components of the revised program include new leadership, increased research activities to maintain program effectiveness, and science-based curricular components (Perin, 2008). The new program has a revised training model and instructional methodology, and 10 lessons with a selection of enhancement lessons. The lessons are now interactive versus a lecture format, and the focus is on applying the D.A.R.E. decision-making model to real-life situations. The new D.A.R.E. has also revised the original program to place more emphasis on the high-risk group of seventh and ninth graders. Initial reports on the new D.A.R.E. program indicate that the new curriculum is having a positive effect on participants' normative beliefs and refusal skills regarding drug use and on students' awareness of the consequences related to substance use (Carnevale Associates, 2005). Carter (1995) has noted that integrating community policing with D.A.R.E. programs can better serve all citizens because both initiatives are intended to establish effective communication links with the community. D.A.R.E. supports the philosophy of community policing as a law enforcement initiative that is designed to respond to changing social problems and community demands.

School Resource Officers. Many school administrators have employed police officers full-time or part-time during school hours. The practice is more common in inner-city urban schools or in schools that have experienced an increase in juvenile crime activity. The origin of police–school liaison officers has been traced to Liverpool, England, in 1951. The concept was soon introduced to the United States as the Flint, Michigan, school district hired police officers in 1958; schools in British Columbia, Canada, began placing police–school liaison officers in many schools in 1972 (LaLonde, 1995). School liaison officers in Canada are not armed, and place more emphasis on the crime prevention and educational role than on law enforcement and patrol functions. School liaison officers may:

- Counsel, advise, and talk informally with students
- Teach classes on alcohol and drug use prevention
- Advise school personnel and students on security precautions
- Offer safety and crime prevention education to students, staff, and parents
- Work to improve the safety and security of the school
- Gain students' trust and be aware of bullying behavior, harassment, alcohol and drug use, and gang activities
- Investigate, document, and record critical incidents
- Serve as a liaison between the school and the criminal justice system (see LaLonde, 1995).

School police officers in the United States fulfill all of the above roles, but they are now usually called School Resource Officers (SROs). The Omnibus Crime Control and Safe Streets Act of 1968 (Part Q, Title I) defines the SRO as "a career law enforcement officer, with sworn authority, deployed in community-oriented policing, and assigned by the employing police department or agency to work in collaboration with school and community-based organizations." In contrast with officers in Canada, SROs in the United States generally focus on traditional police functions and are usually armed, although not all officers may be in uniform. They patrol school grounds, parking lots, hallways, stairways, and bathrooms; check student identification; handle trespassers, class cutters, and truants; investigate criminal complaints; handle disruptive students; and prevent disturbances at after-school activities (Blauvelt, 1990). Police assigned to schools also provide services beyond traditional law enforcement functions. They are available to counsel students and faculty on crime and security issues; they also improve school safety and prevent crime through educational programs. Experts have recommended that school administrators should carefully assess the frequency and seriousness of crime and disruption in their schools before determining whether to hire police or security professionals (Blauvelt, 1990). School administrators and police officials generally develop mutually agreeable policies for the specific duties and responsibilities of the officers. Larger metropolitan schools districts have developed an independent school district police force (Dorn, 2004). Regardless of the exact structure of the SRO program, the important factor is the selection of highly qualified officers and proper training for working in schools. The U.S. Department of Justice funded $68 million that would be awarded through the Office of Community Oriented Policing Services (COPS) to hire and train 599 SROs in 289 communities throughout the nation (Girouard, 2001). The special funding is in recognition that the SRO's multifaceted role as law enforcement officer, counselor, teachers, and liaison between law enforcement, schools, families, and the community requires training beyond that traditionally offered in police academies (Girouard, 2001).

School resource officers have been effective in helping to control disciplinary problems and school crime. A study comparing incidents before and after the placement of officers in schools showed a significant reduction in the number of crimes and disciplinary infractions and in suspensions related to such incidents (Johnson, 1999). Studies have found that SROs reduce the time and effort that school administrators and teachers spend addressing illegal and disruptive behavior; they support educational objectives through classroom presentations (Atkinson, 2001); they counsel students on behavioral and attitudinal issues relating to school security and delinquency prevention (Benigni, 2004); and they help provide a safe environment in public schools (May, Fessel, & Means, 2004). SROs are instrumental in helping to reduce the number of crime incidents in the neighborhood around schools, and during nonschool hours. They have been able to obtain valuable information through their communication with students that has helped in the investigation of crimes in the community. The most effective programs emphasize close working relationships between police, school staff, and students; and clear communication regarding the police role, policies, and actions to be taken in crime incidents. SRO programs are another law enforcement strategy for improving juvenile and police relations through better understanding of police roles and functions. Funding provided by the Community Oriented Policing Services (COPS) Office has supported the development of several School Resource Officer (SRO) programs throughout the United States (Office of Community Oriented Policing Services, 2003).

POLICY AND PRACTICE 6.2 | **FACTORS THAT INFLUENCE PUBLIC OPINION OF THE POLICE**

The National Institute of Justice (NIJ) conducted a study in an attempt to answer what contributing factors influence public opinion on police. The survey, administered to Los Angeles residents in 2003, revealed a number of important factors. The study reported that police can improve public opinion and increase residents' approval of their job performance by

- Increasing their informal contacts with citizens
- Participating in community meetings
- Increasing officers' visibility in neighborhoods
- Talking with citizens

The survey also revealed that

- Residents' perception of the level of crime and disorder in their neighborhood was a significant factor shaping their opinion of the police.
- Residents with informal police contacts had more positive perceptions than residents with formal contacts.
- Residents' opinion of police performance did not vary by race or ethnicity in disorderly neighborhoods.
- Media [television and print news] did not affect residents' approval of police job performance or their perception of officers' demeanor.

SOURCE: Maxson, C., Hennigan, K., & Sloane, D. C. (2003). *Factors that influence public opinion of the police.* Washington, DC: U.S. Department of Justice. Retrieved September 4, 2008, from http://www.ncjrs.gov/pdffiles1/nij/197925.pdf.

Discussion Questions

1. How do the residents of your city view their police department? How do the young people in your city schools view the police department?

2. What have the police in your city done to improve the local opinion of police?

3. What have the police in your city done in local schools that might influence students' opinion of police?

Curfew Laws. In contrast to D.A.R.E. and School Resource Officer programs that generally help to enhance police officers' relations with juveniles, the enforcement of curfew violations tends to aggravate the relationship. Curfew laws have been challenged on constitutional grounds, but the courts have generally upheld them as a tool in supporting parental monitoring of children and of delinquency prevention (Hemmens & Bennett, 1999). Many cities have implemented curfew laws in an effort to get children and youth off the streets at night, reduce their opportunities to get into trouble, and therefore prevent delinquency. Curfew laws generally apply only to youth under the age of 16, and the hours during which youth are required to be off the streets may vary according to the age of the youth (the limit may be 10:00 p.m. for those under 14, and 11:00 or midnight for youth aged 15 or 16, for example). Violation of curfew laws is a status offense, illegal only for those of juvenile age, and not punishable by referral to juvenile court. Police responses to curfew violations vary, but may include a warning to get home, telephoning the parents, delivering the youth to their home in a patrol car, or bringing the youth to a shelter, where parents are asked to come to pick them up. Evidence of the effectiveness of curfew laws varies, with some researchers claiming that juvenile crime is reduced (McDowall, Loftin, & Wiersema, 2000); while others found no evidence of crime reduction that could be explained by the curfew (Reynolds, Seydlitz, & Jenkins, 2000). Curfew laws may have little effect on juvenile crime because there is evidence that a significant proportion of juvenile crimes occur immediately after school hours between 3:00 and 6:00 p.m. (Sickmund, Snyder, & Poe-Yamagata, 1997). Some cities have therefore attempted to enforce day-time, after-school curfews, but these present countless problems in intervening with youth who are not or would not engage in criminal activity (Bannister, Carter, & Schafer, 2001).

Police officer responsibilities under D.A.R.E., as School Resource Officers, and enforcing curfew violations fall under a service and order maintenance role more than law enforcement. Under a community policing philosophy, however, these roles are equal to that of the law enforcement role in terms of their potential for problem solving and improving police–community relations. Other juvenile problems that require the special roles of police include truancy, gang activity, and firearm possession and violations. These problems involve police officers in challenging demands for combining their order maintenance and law enforcement roles on a regular basis in cities throughout the country.

POLICY AND PRACTICE 6.3   OPERATION LINEBACKER

Juvenile offenses and status offenses remain a problem in many major cities throughout the nation. To combat such problems in Fort Wayne, Indiana, the Fort Wayne Police Department (FWPD) developed a juvenile interdiction sweeps program, nicknamed Operation Linebacker. Coinciding with a 1998 spring break, Fort Wayne community schools and the FWPD initiated this program with four goals in mind: (1) to reduce

(Continued)

(Continued)

gang violence, (2) to curb vandalism, (3) to decrease juvenile criminal activity, and (4) to act as an ongoing deterrent during the spring and summer months. To accomplish these goals, the FWPD targeted status crimes such as alcohol-related offenses committed by individuals under the age of 21, underage possession of tobacco products, and curfew violations.

Prior to the first Operation Linebacker sweep, the FWPD held a public meeting to explain the concepts of the program. Concerned citizens, parents, and other interested parties attended the meeting and obtained general information about the operation. Specific dates or times of the sweeps were kept confidential, so as to not let juvenile offenders know the dates or times of sweeps. For two consecutive weekends teams patrolled for juvenile crime. The patrols conducted the first weekend sweeps from 7 p.m. to 3 a.m. and the following weekend from 9 p.m. to 5 a.m. During these first two sweeps, the teams arrested roughly 200 juveniles for various offenses.

The FWPD indicated that during and immediately following the sweeps, the calls for police service and the number of criminal incidents declined noticeably. Vandalism, gang crimes, and juvenile violence were reduced. Reports indicated that Operation Linebacker resulted in a dramatic and successful decrease in crime and an increase in neighborhood safety. The police department indicated that the program was implemented at little or no cost to the agencies and helped to combat crime and violence in Fort Wayne.

SOURCE: Girod, R. J. (1999). Operation linebacker: Using status offenses to reduce crimes in communities. *FBI law enforcement bulletin 68*(7), pp. 7–9. Retrieved April 25, 2009, from http://www.fbi.gov/publications/leb/1999/jul99leb.pdf.

Discussion Questions

1. Are there juvenile problems similar to those in Fort Wayne, Indiana in your city, or a city near you?

2. Are there any programs similar to Operation Linebacker within your city, county, or region?

3. Imagine a program of similar law enforcement sweeps in your city during the late night hours. What kinds of juvenile behaviors and activities might they detect and reduce with sweeps like Operation Linebacker?

Police Discretion

Police are permitted to exercise a great deal of discretion in their duties. That is, they have the ability to choose between different courses of action, depending on their particular assignment. Individual autonomy and discretion is not unique to the police role, but tends to get more attention than in other professions. Employees in many organizations are given some discretionary authority and flexibility in carrying out job functions. In most organizations, however, discretion among personnel at the lower levels is very limited; and flexibility in decision making expands as one moves farther up organization levels. In police organizations the opposite is true. Discretionary authority among police is greater at the lowest levels of the organization, giving the line-level officer on patrol a considerable amount of discretion in carrying out and discharging his or her duties (Goldstein, 1977). In other organizations, the actions of line-level personnel are under close scrutiny. In police organizations, officers on patrol are out of sight of their superiors, and the low visibility means they are frequently beyond the commanding officers' control. Because of the considerable amount of discretion, much research and writing has been devoted to studying and understanding police discretion.

The nature of police discretion varies with the different police roles. In law enforcement situations, police must resolve whether a crime occurred and whether there is sufficient evidence to justify stopping a suspect for questioning, taking the suspect into custody, or making an arrest. Officers receive extensive training in the *law enforcement* function, including thorough education on the legal statutes and the appropriate legal interventions they are authorized to make for law violations. *Order maintenance* situations leave more room for police discretion, as "public order" and "disorderly conduct" are not so clearly defined. It is difficult or even impossible to determine, for example, whether a loud exchange of words on the street, in a public gathering, or in a home amounts to a violation of the "public order." It may depend on the context and circumstances of the verbal exchange. Police decisions and discretion in the *service function* are equally difficult. The police role in service situations has generally not been discussed in police training manuals, or in books and research articles on policing (Moore, 1992). Many police regard calls for service, such as rendering first aid or helping a stranded motorist, as a waste of time and interference with the real job of policing. Some police would maintain that calls for service can be better handled by other agencies and individuals.

A number of arguments have been made for reevaluating the negative attitude toward the service function of police: (a) police response to requests for service might result in more effective law enforcement; (b) response to such calls may prevent a crime later; (c) response to service calls helps establish a positive community presence; and (d) response to service calls helps enhance the flow of information from community sources and aids in crime detection and prevention (Moore, 1992). The emergence of community policing has diminished to a great extent some of the earlier sense of frustration and resistance of police officers in fulfilling service functions. Community policing includes emphases on police–community relations, citizen input, team policing, crime problem solving, and crime prevention (Cordner, 2005). With the emergence of community policing, officers have come to accept more readily that order maintenance and service functions are important functions of law enforcement. Police agencies that have adopted a community policing perspective accept and recognize that all three functions are equally important in carrying out effective police operations.

Police Discretion and Juvenile Offenders. Police can stop, question, and arrest juveniles in every situation that applies to adults. Juveniles can be arrested for committing a crime (misdemeanor or felony); for escaping and running away from a correctional facility; or for violating a court order, probation, or parole. Unlike adults, juveniles can also be taken into custody by police for status offenses such as truancy, incorrigibility, and running away from home. "Status offenses" are not crimes as such, but are considered violations of the law based on the "status" of the juvenile's age as defined by the particular juvenile code of each state (generally under the age of 18, but in some states it is age 17 or 16). The inclusion of status offenses in juvenile codes is to protect juveniles from their bad judgment; to reinforce the authority of parents and legal guardians; and because it is believed (and there is evidence to show) that status offenders often become involved in delinquent behavior. Enforcement of status offenses is therefore a delinquency prevention tool of police.

The question of how much evidence a police officer needs before arresting a juvenile is not always clear. For crimes or delinquent acts, the standard used by most jurisdictions since the *Gault* decision (discussed in Chapter 7) is the same as for adults, which is *probable cause*. Some states, however, use a lesser standard of evidence for juvenile arrest, using terms such as "reasonable suspicion," "reasonable grounds," or "reasonable cause" (Sanborn & Salerno, 2005, p. 132). The lesser standards of evidence generally apply to status offenses or where the physical protection and "best interests" of the juvenile are being considered by the police officer. Based on the *Gault* decision, the higher standard of *probable cause* is necessary when the arrest is for a crime (or delinquent act) that is likely to result in court referral that may lead to institutional placement. The important point is that juveniles are subject to police intervention for a broader array of behaviors than are adults. This is often a point of contention for many juveniles and some parents, who may not be aware of or may disagree with the intent of laws pertaining to status offenses including curfew violations.

Police have considerable discretionary power in handling juvenile matters, ranging from reprimand and release, to transporting a juvenile to detention and referral to juvenile court. Discretion is important in police work, for the officer's decision to intervene in any suspected law violation is the first stage in the juvenile justice process. Officers use their discretion in deciding whether or not to take official actions with offending juveniles or simply order them to "move on," "break it up," or "get on home." Most police contact with juveniles is nonofficial; police make an arrest and take juveniles into custody in only a small percentage of cases. In a study of police responses with juveniles in two cities, Myers (2002) found that police took juveniles into custody in only 13% of their encounters with juveniles. Most of the police–juvenile encounters involved noncriminal matters, such as public disorder (22%), traffic offense (14%), nonviolent conflicts (9%), and suspicious situations (7%); and about one fourth (27%) involved violent or nonviolent crimes (Myers, 2002, p. 123). In 2003, 20% of juvenile arrests were handled within law enforcement agencies, 71% were referred to juvenile court, and 7% were referred directly to criminal court. The remaining 2% were referred to a welfare agency or to another police agency. The proportion of arrests referred to juvenile court increased from 1980 to 2003, from 58% to 71% (Snyder & Sickmund, 2006, p. 152).

Factors That Affect the Decision to Arrest. We noted above that "probable cause" is generally required by police to meet legal grounds for stopping a person for questioning, taking into custody, or making an arrest when there is clear evidence that the person is a suspect in a crime. Examples of *legal factors* that may affect the arrest decision include the following:

- *Factors related to the offense:* type of offense, seriousness, whether gang related, use of weapon, amount of evidence to prove guilt in court.
- *Factors related to the juvenile's record:* previous police contact(s), status offense(s), delinquent acts, whether on probation or parole, or escaped from placement.

Police discretion has been criticized because some believe that police abuse their broad discretionary powers, and that they base their decisions on *extralegal factors* other than the offense. Extralegal factors are those that have nothing directly to do with the offense for which the juvenile suspect is being questioned, taken into custody, or arrested. Several kinds of extralegal factors have been known to influence police officers' decision to make an arrest and referral to juvenile court (see Sanborn & Salerno, 2005, pp. 134–139). Examples of extralegal factors that may affect the arrest decision include the following:

- *Factors related to the offender:* age, gender, race, social class, attitude, demeanor, condition (drunk or high on drugs), belligerence, refusal to answer questions, or resisting arrest.
- *Factors related to complainant or victim:* able to identify the perpetrator, desire to prosecute, prominence in the community, social class, age, gender, or race.
- *Factors related to the neighborhood or location of crime:* crime level, police patrol level, socioeconomic level, disorganized or well-structured, offender is a community member, bystanders present (especially if hostile).
- *Factors related to parent(s) or home:* belligerent parental attitude, parent not home or not located, parents or home present a problem, parent fails or refuses to appear at police station.
- *Factors related to the officer:* age, gender, race, class status, training and experience, view of juvenile system and diversion, previous contact with the accused, and officer's workload (Sanborn & Salerno, 2005, pp. 135–139).

In summary, police decisions to arrest must be based on legal factors. Police discretion, however, does allow them *not* to make an arrest even when there are legal grounds to do so. They may exercise their option to use a lesser alternative (discussed below). Police are working in a "real-world" setting and their decisions are affected by their judgment and perceptions of the degree of risk and threat to public safety—and often by their personal judgments of the circumstances of the alleged crime. Police arrest decisions based on "legal" and "extralegal" factors often have differential effects, depending on the gender or the racial or ethnic group of the juvenile offender. Girls are less likely than boys to be arrested and referred to juvenile court, but they are often referred more than boys for status offenses such as running away or disobeying parents (Armstrong, 1977; Chesney-Lind, 1977). Researchers have reported differing results on the importance of race in police discretion. Some studies report few differences when controlling for offense seriousness and prior record. African Americans and other minority youths seem to be involved in more frequent and serious offenses than whites, so it is difficult to determine whether they are singled out more by police for official action. There is some evidence of racial bias, however, as minority youths have often been targeted more by police for official intervention (Wolfgang, Figlio, & Sellin, 1972, p. 252). Some critics of police discretion also contend that lower-class youths are processed into the justice system for the same offenses for which middle- or upper-class juveniles are simply reprimanded and released to their parents. Police and juvenile officers justify this use of discretion on the basis that middle- and upper-class youth are more likely to be corrected without referral to the justice system because their parents have the resources to provide their children with the necessary supervision and corrective services. Merry Morash (1984) found that an older juvenile with a prior record who fits the image of a serious delinquent is more likely to be referred by police to the juvenile court. A juvenile's demeanor and attitude make a difference in a police officer's use of discretion. A youth who is polite and respectful is more likely to get off with a reprimand, while a negative and hostile attitude is likely to result in a court referral (Piliavin & Briar, 1964; Lundman, Sykes, & Clark, 1990).

CASE IN POINT 6.1

Yarborough v. Alvarado (2004)

This case raises several questions. Should police treat juvenile suspects different from or the same as adult suspects when interrogating them about a crime? Are juveniles entitled to the Miranda warning? If so, under what circumstances and at what point does that warning apply to police interrogations of suspects? When deciding whether a suspect is "in custody" and therefore entitled to his Miranda warnings, must an officer consider the suspect's age and previous history with law enforcement?

Police interviewed Michael Alvarado, age 17, without his parents present at a police station about his involvement in a crime. Police had not arrested Alvarado, and did not give him a Miranda warning. During the interview, Alvarado confessed involvement in the crime. Based in part on these statements, Alvarado was convicted of second degree murder and attempted robbery. His appeals in the California courts and request for a writ of habeas corpus in federal district court in California were unsuccessful. The Ninth Circuit Court of Appeals reversed the criminal court decision. The Appellate Court recognized the "in custody" standard to be whether a reasonable person would feel free to end interrogation, and held that a juvenile is more likely to feel that he is in custody. Because Alvarado was "in custody," the Fifth Amendment required that his rights under *Miranda v. Arizona* (1966) be read to him.

In a 5-to-4 decision written by Justice Anthony Kennedy, the U.S. Supreme Court ruled that the purpose of the Court's *Miranda* decision was to provide an objective rule readily understandable by police officers. When interrogating a suspect who is "in custody," an officer must first read the suspect his Miranda rights. Determining whether a suspect is actually in custody has always been based on objective criteria like whether he had been brought to the police station by police or had come of his own accord. Requiring officers to consider individual characteristics of a suspect when determining whether he is "in custody," such as the suspect's age or previous history with law enforcement, would make the test a subjective one that would be more difficult for officers to understand and abide by. Justice Kennedy wrote that the *Miranda* decision "states an objective rule designed to give clear guidance to the police, while consideration of a suspect's individual characteristics—including his age—could be viewed as creating subjective inquiry."

SOURCE: *Yarborough v. Alvarado* 541 U.S. 652 (2004).

Discussion Questions

1. What is your understanding of the "Miranda warning"? What does it state?

2. Michael Alvarado was being questioned by police at a police station but was not "Mirandized" because police had not arrested him. Did the police have him in custody? What did the Court say about his being "in custody"?

3. Do you believe police should question a juvenile without his or her parent(s) and or legal guardian or an attorney being present? Is there a difference in police questioning a juvenile or an adult suspect? Explain your answer.

4. What is the majority opinion of the Court regarding whether police should treat juveniles any different from adults regarding the "Miranda warning" and interrogations?

Race as a Factor in Juvenile Arrests

The issue of race is a concern in the criminal and juvenile justice systems. It is an undisputed fact that racial and ethnic minorities (especially African Americans) are disproportionately represented at each stage of the system: in police arrests, in jails and detention centers, in courts, and in correctional facilities. Research studies are mixed, however, as to whether that disproportionate representation is a result of racial bias in police arrest, prosecutors' decisions, and judicial sentencing (Conley, 1994; Wordes, Bynum, & Corley, 1994). African American youth are overrepresented in juvenile arrests when compared to their proportion of the population (i.e., racial disparity). Black youth, who accounted for 17% of the juvenile population in 2005, were involved in a disproportionate number of juvenile arrests for robbery (68%), murder (54%), motor vehicle theft (43%), and aggravated assault (42%) (Snyder, 2007, p. 9).

The question is whether the overrepresentation of black juveniles in police arrest rates is due to racial bias or to the greater involvement of black youth in violent crimes. Violent crimes are more likely to be reported, detected, and result in a police arrest. To answer this question, Pope and Snyder (2003) analyzed National Incident-Based Reporting System (NIBRS) data from law enforcement agencies in 17 states, with a large sample of 102,905 juvenile offenders. They found no significant effects of race in police arrest decisions, and they were able to identify some characteristics that

SOURCE: © Barry Lewis/Corbis.

Photo 6.2   Police arrest a suspected juvenile offender for drug dealing.

differentiated the crimes of white and nonwhite juvenile offenders. Compared to non-whites, white juvenile offenders were:

- Less likely to have multiple victims
- More likely to act alone
- More likely to commit crimes indoors
- Less likely to possess a nonpersonal weapon (firearm, knife, or club)
- Less likely to offend against adults
- Less likely to offend against members of another race
- More likely to commit crimes against family members; equally likely to commit crimes against acquaintances; but less likely to commit crimes against strangers (Pope & Snyder, 2003, p. 4)

The findings revealed that the crime incident characteristics that increased the odds of arrest for violent crimes were largely the same for white and nonwhite offenders, with one important exception: victim's race was correlated with arrest probability for nonwhite juvenile offenders, but *not* for white offenders. A nonwhite juvenile offender therefore was more likely to be arrested if the victim was white than if the victim was nonwhite. More research must be conducted on police arrest patterns, using larger samples that are more representative of the nation. Arrest patterns may differ among states, and within regions of states and the nation.

Race and ethnic background may be a factor in police decisions to arrest juvenile offenders, but based on research evidence it is clear that several other factors also influence officers' decisions. In summary, the factors noted above that may affect police officers' decisions to arrest a juvenile or to take less formal actions without court referral include factors relating to the following:

- Offense (seriousness, type, time of day, gang related, use of weapon)
- Youth's record or status (prior police contact or arrest, school record, probation status)
- Offender (age, gender, race, social class, demeanor)
- Complainant (present at the scene, desire to prosecute, age, gender, and race)
- Location of the offense (type of neighborhood, low- or high-crime area)
- Parents (attitude, present at the scene or at home, concern and ability to supervise)
- Officer (training and experience, view of justice system and diversion, workload)
- Police department (enforcement policies, community policing, or problem-solving emphasis) (Sanborn & Salerno, 2005, pp. 137–139)

Police discretion is necessary, and the juvenile justice system could not function without some use of discretion. Juvenile courts in urban areas have a backlog of cases, probation officers' caseloads are too high for them to provide adequate supervision, and correctional facilities are becoming overcrowded. The system must concentrate on those juvenile offenders who pose the greatest risk and need official intervention to prevent further offending.

POLICY AND PRACTICE 6.4   CRIME ALERT BULLETINS

The Minneapolis Police Department (MPD) issues Crime Alerts via the Web when MPD notices a crime pattern. MPD notes that the crime pattern may be specific to geographic area, a time-period, or specific method of crime. At times, MPD issues Attention Residents Flyers to the public for less serious, yet important crime prevention information. Crime Alerts and Attention Residents Flyers aim to provide accurate information, increase the chance for arrests, prevent future crimes, and reduce fear. In addition, MPD conducts free Personal Safety Workshops. The key part of the notices and workshops is crime prevention information, and providing simple steps that persons can take to reduce victimization. The following is an abbreviated posting of a Crime Alert issued by the MPD.

Minneapolis Police are investigating nine robberies of persons that have occurred since September 4 in the area between East 42nd Street and East 56th Street, from Portland Avenue to Elliot Avenue. The neighborhoods within the geographical area are Field, Regina, Northrop, Hale, and Diamond Lake. The two most recent robberies occurred about 2 hours apart on Tuesday, September 23. About 6:00 p.m., as a resident approached his home on the 4900 block of Park Ave., a young male confronted him with a handgun. The robber took his briefcase, demanded his wallet, and then fled on foot. The victim described him as a thin black male, 5'8" to 5'10," dark complexion, and a narrow face with some chin whiskers. He wore a black, lightweight winter "hoodie" jacket with the hood up. At 7:45 p.m., a resident was walking on the south bike path by Minnehaha Creek east of 51st Street and Chicago Avenue. A male with a handgun approached him from behind and demanded his wallet. The resident's description of the robber was close to that in the earlier robbery except he wore a gray hoodie and dark pants. Most of the other robberies

(Continued)

(Continued)

occurred between 4:45 p.m. and 11:30 p.m. Suspects threatened victims with handguns in several of the robberies, but no one was injured. Suspect information was varied. Third Precinct officers, investigators from MPD's citywide Robbery and Juvenile units, and the Park Police are conducting intense investigations.

SOURCE: Minneapolis Police Department. (2008, September 26). Robbers strike in Field, Regina, Northrop, Hale & Diamond Lake. *Crime Alert Bulletin.* City of Minneapolis, Minnesota. Retrieved October 17, 2008, from http://www.ci.minneapolis.mn.us/police/crimealert/C1-2434167.pdf.

Discussion Questions

1. Access other recent crime alerts at www.ci.minneapolis.mn.us/police/crimealert/. Note the race, gender, and age of the alleged offenders. Do you see any patterns in suspected perpetrators, or in the reported offenses?

2. Do an Internet search for similar "police alerts" in other cities. How are they similar to, or different from, those of the Minneapolis police?

3. In addition to alerting the public to potential crimes, is it possible that police departments may get assistance from the community in helping to detect and reduce crimes in this way? Explain.

4. Do "crime alerts" increase public fear? Or, might crime alerts increase public support and police satisfaction? Explain your response.

Alternatives to Police Arrest and Custody

A police officer may refer a minor offender to a youth services bureau, a community agency such as a Big Brother or Big Sister program, or a similar delinquency prevention program. In the majority of cases where police have reason to believe that a juvenile has committed an offense, the youth will be taken to the police department juvenile bureau for questioning, may be fingerprinted and photographed, and then taken to the intake unit of the juvenile probation department where a decision will be made to detain the youth or release to the parents.

- *Questioning, Warning, and Release in the Community.* The least severe sanction is when an officer questions a youth for a possible minor offense, and gives a warning and reprimand on the street without taking formal actions.

- *Station Adjustment.* Police may take a youth into custody and to the station, record the alleged minor offense and actions taken, give the youth an official reprimand, and release the youth to the parents. The parents are generally contacted first and may be present when the youth is reprimanded. In smaller cities the youth may be placed under police supervision for a short period of time.

- *Referral to a Diversion Agency.* Police may release and refer a juvenile to a youth service bureau (YSB), Big Brother/Big Sister program, runaway center, or a mental health agency. Diverting minor offenders from the juvenile justice system to a YSB that provides counseling and social services is considered preferable for many first-time offenders and troubled youth.

- *Issuing a Citation and Referring to Juvenile Court.* The police officer can issue a citation and refer the youth to juvenile court. The intake probation officer accepts the referral, contacts the parents if the police have not already done so, and releases the youth to the parents on the condition that they will report to the court when ordered to do so. The intake officer then determines whether a formal delinquency petition should be filed. In some states the decision is made by the prosecuting attorney assigned to the juvenile court.

- *Taking to a Detention Center or Shelter Home.* The police officer can issue a citation, refer the youth to the juvenile court, and take him or her to a detention center. The intake officer at the detention center then decides whether to hold the juvenile or release him or her to the parents. Juveniles are detained when they are considered dangerous, when there is a lack of parental supervision, or when there is a high probability that they will not report to the court when ordered to do so. If a detention center is felt to be too restrictive, and an appropriate parent or foster home is not available, the youth may be placed in a shelter care facility, which might be either a private home or a group home. Most states now provide for a detention hearing within a day after the youth's referral in which a judge or referee must determine whether there is sufficient reason to continue to detain the juvenile. In cities without a separate juvenile detention center, juveniles who cannot be released to their parents are confined in a separate section of the county jail, or may be transported to a juvenile facility in another county. There has been a national effort to remove juveniles from adult jails. Removing juveniles from their homes and detaining them in juvenile centers is considered a last resort.

In Chapter 8, we discuss the topics of Juvenile Court Intake, assessment, and the temporary detention of juvenile arrestees (after a discussion of Due Process and Juveniles' Rights next, in Chapter 7).

SUMMARY

- The police role with juvenile offenders is especially important because young persons' views and attitudes toward law enforcement are shaped by their first encounter with a police officer.
- Police face special challenges when dealing with juvenile offenders, because they must enforce noncriminal (status) offenses in addition to criminal violations; because of youths' immaturity; and because of their susceptibility to group influence.
- Police officers actually perform three roles in fulfilling their law enforcement responsibilities: law enforcement, order maintenance, and service functions.
- Community policing is a recent development in law enforcement that aims to involve the citizens and community in crime prevention; police work together with the community in problem solving to reduce crime.
- Community policing initiatives focused on children and youth include programs such as D.A.R.E. and School Resource Officers.
- Police discretion is a normal and necessary part of the law enforcement decision-making process that is often influenced by extralegal factors; it may result in disproportionate processing of racial and ethnic minorities.

- Research findings on police discretion show mixed results as to whether disproportionate representation of minorities is due to racial discrimination in decision making, or to the greater involvement of minorities in offenses that are more likely to result in court processing and sentencing.
- Police officers have a number of alternatives to arrest and custody of offenders, and using these alternatives appropriately benefits the offender, the community, and the justice system.

KEY TERMS

Status offenses

Law enforcement role

Order maintenance

Service function

Racial disparity

DISCUSSION QUESTIONS

1. Can you think of any experiences as a teenager when you or any of your friends had any encounters with a police officer that were negative and/or created poor relations with the police? Give an example.

2. Do you think police should spend much of their time responding to status offenses of juveniles? Explain why, or why not. Do you think there is any relationship between status offenses and more serious juvenile crime?

3. Can you think of any examples when you, your friends or family, or any neighbors were affected or benefited by the police roles of order maintenance and service functions? Give an example.

4. Have you had a personal experience with a D.A.R.E. program, or with a School Resource Officer? Explain the effects of that program, from your perspective.

5. Have you or an acquaintance ever experienced police discretion, such as getting a warning rather than a citation or arrest; or getting a citation or arrest when you believe a warning was more appropriate?

WEB RESOURCES

The following Web sites provide information and discussion on the role of police in the juvenile justice system:

Juvenile offenders and victims: 2006 national report: http://ojjdp.ncjrs.gov/ojstatbb/nr2006/downloads/NR2006.pdf

Community-oriented policing: http://www.cops.usdoj.gov/

D.A.R.E. Web site: http://www.dare.com/home/default.asp

National Association of School Resource Officers: http://www.nasro.org/home.asp

Crime Alert Bulletins (City of Minneapolis, Minnesota: http://www.ci.minneapolis.mn.us/police/crimealert/

7

Due Process and Juveniles' Rights

❖

CHAPTER HIGHLIGHTS

❖ The U.S. Supreme Court on Juvenile Justice
❖ Due Process Rights of Juveniles
❖ Juvenile Versus Criminal Court: Legal and Procedural Distinctions
❖ Purpose Clauses of Juvenile Courts

The U.S. Supreme Court on Juvenile Justice

The policies and practices of the juvenile court went unchallenged for the first 60 years following its origin and development. The stated purpose of the juvenile court was for treatment rather than punishment, so the most severe sanctions for adjudicated delinquents were generally less than one year in a residential facility. The juvenile court process resembled an informal civil proceeding more than a criminal trial. Despite the fact that juveniles did not receive the same due process protections in court as those accorded adult offenders in criminal court, the attorneys who provided legal counsel for juveniles saw little reason to question the juvenile court process or dispositions. This began to change in the 1960s, however, as it became apparent in a number of court cases that juveniles were being sentenced to institutions resembling adult prisons or transferred to criminal court, but without the due process protections common to criminal court. Criticisms of some of the longstanding practices of the juvenile court were highlighted in a number of U.S. Supreme Court cases beginning in the 1960s.

Kent v. United States (1966)

Morris Kent, age 16, was on probation when in 1961 he was charged with rape and robbery. He confessed to the offense, and his attorney filed a motion requesting a hearing on the issue of jurisdiction, because he assumed that the District of Columbia juvenile court would consider waiving jurisdiction to criminal court. The judge did not rule on the motion for a hearing, but waived jurisdiction after making a "full investigation," without describing the investigation or the grounds for the waiver. Kent was found guilty in criminal court and sentenced to 30 to 90 years in prison. Appeals by Kent's attorney were rejected by the appellate courts. The U.S. Supreme Court ruled that the waiver without a hearing was invalid, and that Kent's attorney should have had access to all records involved in the waiver, along with a written statement of the reasons for the waiver. *Kent* is significant because it was the first Supreme Court case to modify the longstanding belief that juveniles did not require the same due process protections as adults, because treatment and not punishment was the intent of the juvenile court. The majority statement of the justices noted that juveniles may receive the "worst of both worlds"—"neither the protection accorded to adults nor the solicitous care and regenerative treatment postulated for children" [383 U.S. 541, 86 S.Ct. 1045 (1966)].

In re Gault (1967)

Gerald Gault, age 15, was on probation for a minor property offense when he and a friend made what was described as obscene comments in a telephone call to a neighbor woman. Gerald was picked up by police and held in a detention facility until his parents were notified the next day. Gerald was not represented by counsel at his court hearing. The victim was not present, and no evidence was presented regarding the charge; but Gerald was adjudicated delinquent and committed to a training school. (The maximum sentence for an adult making an obscene phone call would have been a $50 fine or 2 months in jail.) An attorney obtained later by the Gaults filed a writ of habeas corpus that was rejected by the Arizona Supreme Court and the appellate court, but was eventually heard by the U.S. Supreme Court. The Court found that Gerald's constitutional due process rights had been violated; and it ruled that in hearings that could result in commitment to an institution, juveniles have the right to notice and counsel, to question witnesses, and to protection against self-incrimination [387 U.S. 1, S.Ct. 1428(1967)].

In re Winship (1970)

Samuel Winship, age 12, was accused of stealing money from a woman's purse in a store. A store employee stated that Samuel was seen running from the store just before the money was reported missing, but others in the store disputed that account, noting that the employee was not in a position to see the money actually being taken. At the juvenile court hearing, the judge agreed with Winship's attorney that there was some "reasonable doubt" of Samuel's guilt, but New York juvenile courts (like those in most states) operated under the civil law standard of "preponderance of evidence." Winship was adjudicated delinquent and committed to a New York training school. Winship's attorney appealed the case on the issue of the standard of evidence required in juvenile court. The Supreme Court ruled that the standard of evidence for adjudication of delinquency should be "proof beyond reasonable doubt" ([387 U.S. 358, 90 S.Ct. 1068 (1970)].

McKiever v. Pennsylvania (1971)

Joseph McKiever, age 16, was charged with robbery and larceny when he and a large group of other juveniles took 25 cents from three youths. At the hearing, the judge denied his attorney's request for a jury trial, and McKiever was adjudicated and placed on probation. McKiever's attorney appealed the case to the state supreme court, which affirmed the lower court. The case was then appealed to the U.S. Supreme Court, which upheld the lower court rulings. The Court argued that juries would not enhance the accuracy of the adjudication process, and could adversely affect the informal atmosphere of the non-adversarial juvenile court hearing process [403 U.S. 528, 91 S.Ct. 1976 (1971)]. The significance of *McKiever* is that it is the only one of these first five cases in which the U.S. Supreme Court did *not* rule that juveniles must receive all the same due process rights as adults in criminal court.

Breed v. Jones (1975)

Gary Jones, age 17, was charged with armed robbery and appeared in Los Angeles juvenile court, where he was adjudicated delinquent. At the disposition hearing, the judge waived jurisdiction and transferred the case to criminal court. Jones's attorney then filed a writ of habeas corpus, arguing that the waiver to criminal court after adjudication in juvenile court violated the double jeopardy clause of the Fifth Amendment. The court denied the petition on the basis that juvenile adjudication is not a "trial." The case was appealed to the U.S. Supreme Court, where the Justices ruled that adjudication is equivalent to a trial, because a juvenile is found to have violated a criminal statute. Jones's double jeopardy rights had therefore been violated, and the Court ruled that double jeopardy applies at the adjudication hearing as soon as any evidence is presented. A juvenile court waiver hearing must therefore take place before or in place of an adjudication hearing [421 U.S. 519, 95 S.Ct. 1779 (1975)].

Effects of the Cases on Juvenile Courts. These U.S. Supreme Court cases profoundly affected the legal process and procedures in juvenile courts throughout the United States. Additional procedures and legal forms were instituted, from the county or state's attorney prosecuting the cases down to the intake probation officer working with juveniles referred from police departments for delinquent behavior. The overall purposes of the juvenile court remained the same, but court personnel were now required to inform the youth and their parents of due process rights. State legislation quickly followed to amend juvenile court procedures in accordance with the Supreme Court rulings. Juvenile court procedures did not change overnight in jurisdictions throughout the nation, but it was clear to juvenile court authorities that many of the informal processes had to be changed. Changes were apparent within months after the Supreme Court decisions (especially the *Gault* case) in most if not all metropolitan juvenile courts where the majority of cases are heard. Juvenile court experts have noted, however, that some changes were slow in coming in many courts throughout the country. The effects of *Kent* and *Breed v. Jones* on juvenile court cases involving waiver and transfer to criminal court were more immediate than the overall due process procedures mandated by *Gault*. The courts have been more attentive to procedural justice where the consequences involve the criminal court and more serious sanctions.

Due Process Rights of Juveniles

Arrest, Interrogation, and Counsel (*Fare v. Michael C.*)

When police arrest an adult suspect they are required under the Miranda warning to inform the person in custody of the right to silence and to legal counsel. The Miranda "warning" applied to persons who might be tried in criminal court, and the courts had not established the same rights for juvenile offenders (1966). The U.S. Supreme Court clarified the application of the Miranda warning to juvenile offenders in the case of *Fare v. Michael C.* [442 U.S. 707(1979)]. Michael C. was stopped by police and before being questioned was Mirandized, but did not trust the police when they offered him the assistance of a lawyer. He instead asked to see his probation officer, who was the one person he trusted and who had told Michael to contact him if he got into trouble. Police declined his request to see the probation officer, as *Miranda* specifically provides only for assistance of legal counsel. Without consulting legal counsel, Michael then eventually confessed to the homicide with which he had been charged. The juvenile court accepted the confession as admissible and adjudicated Michael C. delinquent. He then appealed to the California Supreme Court and won a reversal of his adjudication. The California court examined the way in which the confession was obtained and determined there was a violation of *Miranda,* based on Fifth Amendment grounds of a right to silence. The court reasoned that asking for a probation officer was equivalent to asking for silence, for help, or advice. The police denial of that request therefore amounted to a constitutional violation, according to the California Supreme Court. The same court had ruled similarly in a previous case years earlier when a juvenile asked to see his parents. The California court reasoned that youths in custody are more likely to call for help from the persons with whom they are closest and trust, their parents or guardian, than from an attorney.

The state of California appealed the state supreme court ruling to the U.S. Supreme Court, which reversed the state court's decision. The Court acknowledged the right to remain silent, but emphasized that asking for a probation officer is *not* the same as asking for a lawyer. The police had not committed a violation of *Miranda* because Michael had asked for the wrong person. The decision was a very narrow 5–4 majority opinion that took a strict and technical reading of *Miranda* that allows suspects to ask for silence and for only the presence and advice of one person, a lawyer. The implications of the U.S. Supreme Court decision in *Fare v. Michael C.* is that when juveniles are given the Miranda warning, it applies the same way as it does to adults. Most jurisdictions do require police to give juveniles Miranda warnings before any interrogation while they are in custody. It is important to note, however, that the Miranda warning applies only in situations when juveniles (or adults) are in police custody.

CASE IN POINT 7.1

Police Interrogation

Woods v. Clusen established the right of juveniles against aggressive police interrogation tactics by failing to observe juveniles' constitutional rights and provide for fundamental fairness. On September 10, 1979, Henry and Beryl Schwab were beaten to death in their Shawano County, Wisconsin, home. While local police were investigating the murder scene, Burdette Woods was observed watching the events unfold from a distance. His presence and interest caused him to become a prime suspect. However, several days into the investigation police had no probable cause to arrest him. Later, the police received information that Woods had attempted to sell a stolen chain saw to a local resident approximately 17 months earlier. Although the police lacked any probable cause to arrest Woods for the Schwab murders, the police decided to arrest Woods on the stolen chain saw charge in order to bring him into custody to question him about the Schwab incident.

On September 23, 1979, two Shawano police officers drove to the trailer where the 16-year-old Woods was residing with his grandparents. After gaining entrance with the consent of a family member, the police walked into Woods's bedroom, woke him up, and arrested him. Woods was then handcuffed and placed in a police car. During transit to the police station, Woods was read his Miranda rights and asked if he understood them. Woods responded that he did. He was also asked if he wished to consult an attorney, to which he answered "no." When asked if he would like to answer any questions or make a statement, Woods did not respond. Woods arrived at police headquarters, and a juvenile intake worker asked Woods many of the same questions concerning his understanding of his Miranda rights and his opportunity to consult an attorney. Woods continued to state that he understood his rights and did not wish the presence of counsel. At this point Woods was fingerprinted, photographed, and asked to remove his clothes and don jail overalls. He was not issued shoes or socks and was left barefoot.

After approximately 45 minutes the booking process was completed and Woods was taken to a room to be interrogated. Approximately one to two feet away from Woods were pictures of the Schwab murder scene. The officers did not repeat the Miranda warning to Woods. They did ask several times if Woods was willing to talk to them, but he never responded. Without Woods's explicit consent, the officers proceeded to interrogate Woods about the Schwab case for approximately 15 to 20 minutes. Several intimidating and deceptive tactics were employed by the officers to get Woods to talk. First, there were the disturbing pictures of the murder scene. In addition, one officer misrepresented that police officials had enough evidence to convict Woods regardless of whether he talked. The other officer suggested things would "be better" or "go easier" if Woods talked, in view of the fact he knew Woods committed the murders. The officers reported that Woods became visibly emotional during the interrogation. At one point Woods was asked why he was in the woods the day after the murders and Woods responded, "I never went in the woods the next day." Nonetheless, except for this statement and despite the police tactics mentioned above, Woods—although clearly emotionally involved—remained unresponsive.

Having reached an apparent impasse, the two officers left and were replaced by two investigators. One asked Woods if he had been advised of his rights and Woods replied affirmatively, at which time the two new officers began their own questioning. More deceptive tactics were employed to elicit an

(Continued)

(Continued)

incriminating response from Woods during this second interrogation. After 20 to 30 minutes of continuous interrogation, Woods began to cry. One of the officers then put his hand on Woods's shoulder in a paternal manner. It was at this point Woods orally confessed to the Schwab murders. Burdette Woods pled guilty and was subsequently adjudged guilty of second degree murder and manslaughter in the Circuit Court for Shawano County, Wisconsin, for the beating death of Henry and Beryl Schwab. An oral confession obtained from Woods while in police custody played a pivotal role in his pleading guilty.

The 7th Circuit Court of Appeals ruled that Woods's confession was inadmissible because the juvenile had been taken from his home at 7:30 a.m., handcuffed, stripped, forced to wear institutional clothing, but no shoes or socks, showed pictures of the crime scene, and intimidated and interrogated for many hours. The court criticized the tactics used by the police, and the investigators were reprimanded for their failure to uphold and respect the offender's constitutional rights and provide fundamental fairness.

SOURCE: *Woods v. Clusen,* 794 F.2d 293 (7th Cir. 1986).

Discussion Questions

1. Compare this case with that of *Fare v. Michael C.* How is it similar? How is it different?

2. Since *Fare v. Michael C.* was a U.S. Supreme Court case in 1979, suggest whether and how the appellate court justices may have relied upon the precedent case in this 1986 ruling.

3. Imagine you are a police officer interrogating a juvenile suspect in this or similar cases. How might you proceed with your interrogation? What questions or statements in this *Woods* case would you *not* make?

Students' Rights in School

Very few young people ever experience arrest, custody, and interrogation by police officers, so due process rights relating to the justice process affect only a relatively few youth. On the other hand, most youth are affected by a number of court decisions that defined students' rights relating to school rules and policies. About the same time that the U.S. Supreme Court was examining and redefining juvenile court procedures, a number of cases scrutinized and redefined school officials' discipline policies and students' rights. Many school officials were convinced that the growing problems of student disruption and general lack of respect for authorities were attributable directly to an overemphasis on students' rights. Many believed that the balance had shifted from teachers' authority to students' rights. The fact is that students *do* have rights. They do *not* (in the words of Justice Abe Fortas) "shed their rights at the schoolhouse gate." The U.S. Supreme Court in *Tinker v. Des Moines* reminded educators and school boards that schools may not be operated in a totalitarian manner, with absolute authority over students.

It can hardly be argued that either students or teachers shed their constitutional rights . . . at the schoolhouse gate. . . . In our system, state-operated schools may not be enclaves of totalitarianism. School officials do not possess absolute authority over their students. Students in school as well as out of school are "persons" under our Constitutions. They are possessed of fundamental rights which the State must respect. . . . [Justice Abe Fortas, *Tinker v. Des Moines Independent Community School District*, 309 U.S. at 506, 511, (1969)]

The authority of school principals and school boards in developing and enforcing school rules must be balanced with consideration for students' rights and responsibilities relating to school rules. State and federal courts have determined what is considered to be reasonable and fair enforcement of rules, and a number of decisions by the courts have extended legal protection to students against school sanctions that have been deemed unreasonable and unconstitutional. We can see a direct analogy and comparison here to the responsibilities of police officers and juvenile court officials when dealing with juvenile offenders. Treating students as young citizens of the community, with rights and responsibilities, is a valuable lesson in their preparation for life in a democratic society. Many young people and their parents are quick to demand their rights. Responsibilities go hand in hand with rights, however, and schools have an opportunity to teach students that the former must be learned before the latter may be enjoyed (Wilkinson, 1996, p. 313).

CASE IN POINT 7.2

Zero Tolerance

Crime and violence in schools have presented challenges for administrators and juvenile justice officials. In Chapter 5, we discussed the problems of school failure, truancy, dropout, and delinquency. School administrators and lawmakers have responded to public demands to reduce violence and ensure that schools are safe places for students and teachers. A focal part of the response has been the emergence of "zero tolerance" policies for any students bringing weapons to school or making threats of violence. Violation of such policies brings automatic suspension or expulsion from the school. The enforcement of such policies, however, must consider students' constitutional rights. A report issued by the Justice Policy Institute and the Children's Law Center cites several questionable examples of school administrators implementing zero tolerance policies that arguably may go beyond what would be considered a fair and balanced approach.

- A student was expelled from school after he shot a paper clip with a rubber band at a classmate, missed, and broke the skin of a cafeteria worker.
- A 9-year-old was suspended for a day after he found a manicure kit with a 1-inch knife on the way to school.
- A 12-year-old who had been diagnosed with a hyperactive disorder warned the kids in the lunch line not to eat all the potatoes, or "I'm going to get you." The student was suspended for 2 days, referred to police, and charged with making "terroristic threats." He was incarcerated for 2 weeks while awaiting trial.

(Continued)

(Continued)

- Two 10-year-old boys were suspended for 3 days for putting soapy water in a teacher's drink. At the teacher's urging, police charged the boys with a felony that carried a maximum sentence of 20 years. They were formally processed through the juvenile justice system before the case was dismissed months later.

- A 13-year-old was asked to write a "scary" Halloween story for a class assignment. He wrote a story that referred to shooting up a school and received a passing grade by his teacher, but was then referred to the principal's office. The police were called and the child spent 6 days in jail before the courts confirmed that no crime had been committed.

- A 14-year-old disabled student was referred to the principal's office for allegedly stealing $2 from another student. The principal referred the child to the police, where he was charged with strong-armed robbery, and held for 6 weeks in an adult jail for this, his first arrest. The local media criticized the prosecutor's decision to file adult felony charges, but he stood behind his decision. The prosecution dropped charges when a *60 Minutes* crew showed up at the boy's hearing.

SOURCE: Brooks, K., Schiraldi, V., & Zeidenberg, J. (2000). *School house hype: Two years later.* Justice policy institute/Children's law center. Retrieved April 27, 2009, from http://www.justicepolicy.org/images/upload/00-04_REP _SchoolHouseHype2_JJ.pdf.

Discussion Questions

1. Which of the above cases, if any, do you agree should be handled with zero tolerance, resulting in suspension or expulsion from school? Give reasons for your response.

2. Can you think of any similar incidents by students in your school experience? How were those handled by the teacher and principal?

3. For what types of school rule violations or offenses do you feel that zero tolerance and suspension/ expulsion are appropriate?

4. Do you believe that some exceptions should be made in zero tolerance policies for students who misbehave as a result of emotional problems, or other disabilities, or who merely forget what is in their pocket after legitimate nonschool activities?

School suspension or expulsion is like a juvenile court "sentence" that relates to students' legal rights to an education and affects their life. What due process rights should students have before being expelled from school?

Freedom of Speech and Expression

School officials are charged with the responsibility to provide a quality education for students, in a safe environment that is conducive to learning. What students say and express in written communication and how they dress sometimes interfere with educational objectives. The First Amendment rights relating to freedom of speech and expression are more misunderstood and less clear than, for example, the Fourth

Amendment relating to unreasonable search and seizure. The U.S. Supreme Court has used the test of "material and substantial disruption" to determine whether a school can deny a student the right of freedom of expression. In the case of *Tinker v. Des Moines Independent Community School District* [393 U.S. 503, 89 S. Ct. 733 (1969)] the U.S. Supreme Court ruled that students wearing black armbands to protest the Vietnam War did *not* pose a substantial disruption to the educational process, and that the school officials violated the students' right to freedom of expression. In the more recent case of *Bethel School District No. 403 v. Fraser* [478 U.S. 675, 106 S. Ct. 3159 (1986)], the Supreme Court supported school officials' suspension of a student who made a lewd speech full of sexual innuendos that offended the teachers and other students of the school. The Court thus made a distinction between the "political message" in the *Tinker* case and expression that includes vulgar and offensive terms. The two cases also serve as contrasting examples of how the First Amendment right to freedom of expression may have positive educational value. In the *Tinker* case, the silent protest of the Vietnam War (through wearing black armbands) presented an opportunity for organized class discussions that might have positive educational value. School officials, teachers, and students could also choose not to recognize the students making the silent protest, whose actions did not interfere with the educational process or the rights of other students. In contrast, the delivery of an indecent speech containing vulgar and offensive terms can hardly be said to have any positive educational value, so the Bethel School District was justified in curtailing the student's right to freedom of expression.

Student Appearance. Personal appearance as freedom of expression pertains to the issue of whether school officials may regulate students' dress and personal appearance, including haircuts. Students and parents have relied on the First Amendment and the equal protection clause of the Fourteenth Amendment to contest school regulations regarding student attire, and available court cases reveal a lack of consensus as to whether various dress styles pose a "material and substantial disruption" of the educational process. Students wearing gang colors and paraphernalia in some schools pose a potential risk and disruption, and some schools have considered policies that ban the wearing of gang-related clothing. No court cases to date have tested the legality of any bans, however.

School regulations banning unkempt or long hair have been challenged in some court cases, but school officials are hard-pressed to prove that the length or style of students' hair would significantly disrupt the school educational process. A federal appellate court refused to become involved in haircut disputes, writing that "we refuse to take our judicial clippers to this hairy issue" (Alexander & Alexander, 2005, p. 318). Federal Circuit Courts of Appeals have been involved in considerable litigation regarding school regulations on student hairstyles, but the rulings are not consistent. Some courts have determined that hairstyles may be a distraction in schools and could be regulated; other courts have ruled that hairstyles are constitutionally protected. Some federal judges have expressed indignation at having to rule on matters relating to hairstyles, in light of court calendars filled with weightier criminal and civil matters. Despite ruling in favor of one school district's good grooming rule, the federal court nevertheless noted that the entire problem seemed minuscule in light of other matters involving the school system (Alexander & Alexander, 2005, p. 318).

Constitutional Due Process

The Fourteenth Amendment to the United States Constitution provides that no state shall deprive a person of life, liberty, or property without due process of law. This post–Civil War amendment has come to be of special importance because it applies the rights guaranteed to citizens under the federal constitution to actions of state and local agencies of government. Thus, for example, the right against unreasonable search and seizure (Fourth Amendment), against self-incrimination (Fifth Amendment), and the right to legal counsel and to a fair and impartial hearing (Sixth Amendment) are all applied to the state government agencies through the Fourteenth Amendment. A state *may* therefore deprive a person of life, liberty, or property as long as the individual is given due process.

There are two kinds of due process: *procedural* and *substantive due process.*

Procedural Due Process. This means that a constitutionally prescribed procedure must be followed before a person may be deprived of life, liberty, or property. The U.S. Supreme Court has identified three components that make up procedural due process. First, the person must be given proper notice that he or she is about to be deprived of life, liberty, or property; second, the person must be given an opportunity to be heard and to present his or her side of the issue or case; and third, the person is entitled to a fair hearing. The procedures prescribed for and expected to be followed by all police and court officials, including probation officers, all routinely include careful measures to ensure that no persons are stopped, questioned, temporarily detained, or taken into custody for law violations unless these three procedures are provided for in the process. It is now (or should be) common practice for school officials to include these three procedures when any student is deprived of the liberty to attend school or deprived of property such as illegal substances or weapons.

Substantive Due Process. This refers to the objectives and appropriateness of legal interventions. To satisfy this constitutional requirement, before a state may deprive someone of liberty or property, it must show that the objective and methods used are reasonable and appropriate for accomplishing the objective. An Arizona court defined substantive due process:

> The phrase "due process of law," when applied to substantive rights . . . means that the state is without power to deprive a person of life, liberty or property by an act having no reasonable relation to any proper governmental purpose, or which is so far beyond the necessity of the case as to be an arbitrary exercise of governmental power. [*Valley National Bank of Phoenix v. Glover,* 62 Ariz. 538, 159 P.2d 292, (1945)]

Substantive due process is a major factor in court decisions relating to corporal punishment in schools. Courts have upheld the right of school authorities to use physical punishment as a means of discipline. Corporal punishment in schools has *not* been found to violate the Eighth Amendment against cruel and unusual punishment as long as school officials can show that the punishment is not excessive and reasonably relates to educational objectives.

Search and Seizure

The Fourth Amendment to the United States Constitution provides for "the right of people to be secure in their persons, houses, papers, and effects"; and for the right "against unreasonable searches and seizures." School officials are frequently confronted with the question of whether to search a student's pockets, book bag, purse, locker, or automobile. Educators often must make an instantaneous decision whether to initiate a search, particularly in cases of bomb threats and dangerous weapons, in order to protect the safety of students and teachers. The Fourth Amendment as applied to persons conducting searches generally pertains to law enforcement, court, and security officers. The right of school officials to search students depends upon whether any illegal evidence seized may be turned over to law enforcement officers and be used as evidence in juvenile or criminal prosecution. In that case, a search warrant would be required.

The Fourth Amendment in Schools. There are three parts to the Fourth Amendment as applied to students' rights in school. First, students have a right to privacy ("to be secure in their persons, papers and effects"); second, they have a right against unreasonable searches and seizures; and third, any search must be specific as to the location of the search and what is being sought. The courts have not required school officials to show probable cause for a search or to obtain a search warrant from a judge before initiating a search. School officials must have "reasonable suspicion" before conducting a search, but this requirement is less rigorous than the requirement of "probable cause," which is required for police to obtain a search warrant (see Alexander & Alexander, 2005). "Reasonable suspicion" means that school officials must have some facts or knowledge that provide reasonable grounds to search, and a school search may be conducted only if it is necessary to fulfill educational objectives. Thus, a student's freedom from unreasonable search and seizure must be weighed against the need for school officials to maintain order, discipline, and a safe learning environment.

New Jersey v. T.L.O. The U.S. Supreme Court in the case of *New Jersey v. T.L.O.* [105 S.Ct. 733 (1985)] defined students' Fourth Amendment rights and provided guidelines for officials in conducting school searches. The case originated when a teacher at a New Jersey high school found two girls smoking in the restroom. The teacher took them to the principal's office because smoking in restrooms was in violation of a school rule. When questioned by the Assistant Vice Principal, T.L.O., a 14-year-old freshman, denied that she had been smoking and claimed that she did not smoke at all. The vice principal demanded to see her purse, and upon opening it he found a pack of cigarettes and also noticed a package of cigarette rolling papers, which are commonly associated with the use of marijuana. A further search of the purse produced some marijuana, a pipe, plastic bags, a substantial amount of money, an index card containing a list of students who apparently owed her money, and two letters that implicated her in marijuana dealing. The evidence was turned over to the police and she was charged with delinquent conduct. The juvenile court denied her motion to suppress the evidence found in her purse, held that the search was reasonable, and adjudged her delinquent. The state appellate court affirmed the juvenile court's finding, but the New Jersey Supreme Court reversed, ordered that the evidence found in her purse be suppressed, and held that the search was unreasonable.

On appeal, the U.S. Supreme Court ruled that the Fourth Amendment prohibition against unreasonable searches and seizures does apply to school officials, who are acting as representatives of the State. Students do have expectations of privacy when they bring to school a variety of legitimate, noncontraband items; but the Court noted that school officials have an equally important need to maintain a safe and orderly learning environment. In balancing students' Fourth Amendment rights and school officials' responsibilities, the Court ruled that school officials do not need to obtain a warrant before searching a student as long as the search was reasonable in light of educational objectives, and not excessively intrusive in light of the student's age and sex and the nature of the violation (p. 736).

A "Reasonable" Search. The Court cited two considerations in determining whether a warrantless search was "reasonable" or not. First, "one must consider whether the . . . action was justified as its inception"; and second, "one must determine whether the search . . . was reasonably related in scope to the circumstances which justified the interference in the first place" (p. 744). The first involves justification or grounds for initiating the search, while the second relates to the intrusiveness of the search (see Alexander & Alexander, 2005, pp. 339–340). In one case, a school administrator had heard reports that a student was involved in drugs. A search of the student's locker and car revealed drugs and was found reasonable and constitutional [*State v. Slattery,* 56 Wn.App. 820, 787 P.2d 932 (1990)]. In another case, a student's car was searched and cocaine was found, after the assistant principal noticed that the student smelled of alcohol, walked unsteadily, had slurred speech, glassy eyes, and a flushed face. The court found that the observations were sufficient to support reasonable suspicion [*Shamberg v. State,* 762 P.2d 488, Alaska App. (1988)]. School officials must also be able to justify the extensiveness and intrusiveness of searches, and show that there was reasonable suspicion. In one case in which money was missing from a schoolroom, a teacher searched the books of two students and then required them to remove their shoes. The court found the search to be reasonable and not excessively intrusive, because the two students had been alone in the room where the stolen money disappeared [*Wynn v. Board of Education of Vestabia Hills,* 508 So. 2d 1170, Ala. (1987)].

Beyond T.L.O.: Expanded Search Powers. The Court in *T.L.O.* held that when the purpose of a search was to maintain a safe environment conducive to learning, it falls within the category of the "special needs" exception to the warrant and probable cause requirements. Since *T.L.O.,* courts have expanded the special needs doctrine to areas beyond those considered in the original case, including searches conducted by law enforcement officials (Vaughn & del Carmen, 1997). The U.S. Supreme Court expanded school search powers 10 years after *T.L.O.* in *Vernonia School District 47J v.*

Acton [515 U.S. 646 (1995)]. The Court allowed the consideration of special circumstances to give school officials the right to conduct random searches without reasonable individual suspicion. After experiencing several instances of drug possession and use at school, the Vernonia School District had instituted a policy that required students who wanted to participate in extracurricular sports to sign a form consenting to random urinalyses to search for drug use among student athletes. The Court upheld the policy, resting the decision on three factors: (1) School officials may determine that "special needs" exist to conduct random searches for the use of drugs that place students at risk. (2) Students in sports programs have a lower expectation of privacy than students who do not participate. The Court noted in *Acton* that student athletes undress and dress in uniforms, and shower together. (3) The Court ruled that the method of the search, conducting urinalyses, was not overly intrusive, since the samples were collected by the students themselves in the privacy of enclosed stalls.

The Court used reasoning similar to *Acton* in a 2002 case, once again upholding random, suspicionless drug testing of students. The School District of Tecumseh, Oklahoma, adopted a drug testing policy that required all students who wanted to participate in any extracurricular activities to consent to random urinalyses. The student plaintiffs in this case were not student athletes, but members of the choir, marching band, and academic team. Writing for the Court majority opinion in *Board of Education of Independent School District No. 92 of Pottawatomie County v. Earls* [536 U.S. 822 (2002)], Justice Thomas argued that "special needs" may justify the searches among students in activities beyond those required of all students; second, students in extracurricular activities have a lower expectation of privacy; third, the method of the search was minimally intrusive on students' privacy; and fourth, the designation of "special needs" does not require the school district to show a pervasive drug problem to justify random suspicionless drug testing. Evidence collected in the search was kept private, and not turned over to any agencies of the justice system. Critics of the Court's decision in *Earls* have expressed concern about the reduced privacy of students involved in extracurricular activities; and that information obtained from the searches might not be kept private. Evidence in the case indicated that test information was not handled carefully; school file cabinets containing test data were left open; and test results were made available to all school activity sponsors, regardless of whether they had a need to know about each case (see Beger, 2003).

Juvenile Versus Criminal Court: Legal and Procedural Distinctions

Distinctions between juvenile and adult offenders are based on English common law, which formed the basis for a separate juvenile justice system. At the core of this distinction is the question of what age and under what circumstances children are capable of forming criminal intent. More than 1,000 murders are committed by juveniles every year. Many citizens and policymakers react to what is perceived as a growing trend toward more juvenile violence with demands to punish violent juvenile offenders like adult criminals. Under law, however, two elements are necessary in order to find a person guilty of a crime. Most attention is focused on the first element, the criminal act itself. The second element, criminal intent, is equally important, though often overlooked. In weighing evidence against a suspect, a court must determine that there is sufficient evidence for both a criminal act and criminal intent, known as **mens rea** or "guilty mind." The critical question is at what age is a child capable of understanding the differences between right and wrong and of comprehending the consequences of a criminal act before it occurs. The answer to the first question appears clear to most persons, who would argue that even very young children know that killing a person is wrong. It is less clear whether children charged with violent crimes have carefully weighed the consequences of their actions, however, or whether they have formed criminal intent comparable to that of an adult. Laws and policies that place limitations on youths' drinking, driving, marrying, and entering into other contracts illustrate our belief that they are not as equally prepared as adults to engage responsibly in these activities. Based on the belief that youth do not have equal capacity for careful thinking and awareness of the consequences of their behavior, young people are treated differently and allowed limited responsibility under the law for most other critical decisions while they are minors. Judicial experts generally agree that legal sanctions for criminal behavior should be consistent with laws limiting juveniles' legal rights in other areas. Distinctions between legal procedures for juveniles and adults therefore stem from the differences in juveniles' maturity, limited knowledge of the law and its consequences, limited legal responsibility, and the belief that youth should be processed separately from adults throughout the judicial system.

Juvenile justice grew out of the criminal justice system, so there is common ground between the two. The *main features that distinguished juvenile court proceedings* from criminal court proceedings may be summarized as follows:

- *Absence of legal guilt.* Because juveniles are generally less mature and often unaware of the consequences of their actions, they are not held legally responsible for their actions to the same extent as adults. Legally, juveniles are not found guilty of crimes, but are "found to be delinquent." Juvenile status, generally being under 18 years of age, is a defense against criminal responsibility, much like the insanity defense. Exceptions are made in cases of more mature juveniles who have committed serious offenses. The juvenile court may waive jurisdiction and transfer the case to criminal court.

- *Treatment rather than punishment.* The stated purpose of the juvenile court is treatment of the child and community protection, not punishment as for adult felony offenders in criminal court.

- *Informal, private court proceedings.* Juvenile court hearings are more informal and in many states they are not open to the public, with usually only the child, parents, attorneys, and probation officer present. Hearings were often held in the judge's chamber. The majority of hearings are informal, noncontested, nonadversarial proceedings that take less than 10 minutes. This practice is rooted in the original child-saving philosophy that the purpose of the court was for treatment, not punishment. Proceedings for more serious juvenile offenders are now often open to the public.

- *Separation from adult offenders.* Juvenile offenders are kept separate from adult offenders at every stage of the juvenile process, from arrest (or "taking into custody") to detention, pretrial, and court proceedings, to probation supervision and institutional corrections. All juvenile records are also maintained separately from adult criminal records, including in computerized information systems.

- *Focus on a juvenile's background and social history.* A juvenile's background and the need for and amenability to treatment are considered of equal importance with the offense committed when making decisions on handling each case. This is consistent with the stated purpose of treatment rather than punishment. The assumption that court officers can assess and treat juveniles' needs is open to question. Basing the length of "treatment" on the child's needs as well as the offense has come under criticism. Children committing relatively minor crimes but with "greater needs for treatment" are often supervised for longer periods of time than more serious offenders who have been determined to be less "in need of treatment."

- *Shorter terms of supervision and incarceration.* The terms of probation supervision, confinement in a detention center, or commitment to a correctional facility are usually shorter in duration than for adult offenders—generally not much longer than 1 to 2 years, on average. In recent years many states have revised their juvenile statutes, extending jurisdiction over and length of incarceration for violent juvenile offenders.

- *Distinctive terminology.* Consistent with the need to treat juveniles differently from adults because of their immaturity and limited legal accountability, different terms are used when handling juveniles at each stage of the process. Juveniles are taken into custody, not arrested; transported to a detention center, not booked into jail; a petition for delinquency is filed with the court, not a criminal indictment; the result is an adjudication of delinquency rather than conviction of a felony or misdemeanor crime; juvenile court cases result in a disposition, not a sentence.

Purpose Clauses of Juvenile Courts

The distinctions noted above indicate that the primary purpose of the original juvenile courts was prevention and treatment more than punishment. There is variation among states in how they describe the purposes of the juvenile court, and many states' juvenile codes have been amended in recent years. The purpose clause of several states is based on the Standard Juvenile Court Act that was originally issued in 1925. The 1959 revision used by some states declares that a child who comes within the jurisdiction of the juvenile court shall receive care, guidance, and control appropriate for the child's welfare; and when removed from parental custody the court shall provide care equivalent to what the parents should have provided (Snyder & Sickmund, 2006, p. 98). Other states have drawn from the *Legislative Guide for Drafting Family and Juvenile Court Acts* (Sheridan, 1969). This publication from the late 1960s lists four purposes for the juvenile court: (1) to provide for the care, protection, and wholesome mental and physical development of children involved with the juvenile court; (2) to remove from children committing delinquent acts the consequences of criminal behavior and offer a program of supervision, care, and rehabilitation; (3) to remove a child from the home only when necessary for his or her welfare or in the interests of public safety; and (4) to ensure their constitutional and other legal rights (Sheridan, 1969; Snyder & Sickmund, 2006, p. 99). The most common purpose clauses among states today have components of *balanced and restorative justice* that give equal attention to three concerns: (1) public safety, (2) individual accountability to victims and the community, and (3) the development of skills to help offenders live law-abiding and productive lives (Snyder & Sickmund, 2006, p. 98; discussed in Chapter 13 of this volume).

In summary, jurisdictions vary in the extent of their distinctions between juvenile and criminal justice. Some of the distinctions are less visible today as states modify the purpose clauses of their juvenile laws and place more emphasis on public safety and individual accountability, which are common in criminal codes applicable to adult offenders. As many of the traditional distinctions between juvenile and adult laws have begun to fade, there has been considerable discussion recently about the possibility of merging the juvenile and criminal justice systems. These changes are based upon beliefs and assumptions about juvenile crime, its causes, and whether juvenile offenders are amenable to treatment or should be held accountable and punished similar to adult offenders. Laws and policy decisions should ideally be based upon an understanding of delinquency, and what research findings have indicated as the most effective sanctions and responses for preventing juvenile crime and changing young offenders.

SUMMARY

- Juvenile court procedures went unchallenged for 60 years, until some of the longstanding practices of the juvenile court were overturned in a number of U.S. Supreme Court cases beginning in the 1960s.
- Five U.S. Supreme Court cases that marked a change toward more constitutional rights for juveniles include *Kent, Gault, Winship, McKiever,* and *Breed v. Jones.*
- The case of *Fare v. Michael C.* clarified juveniles' right to counsel following arrest and during interrogation.
- School rules and disciplinary practices provide good examples of young peoples' constitutional rights and responsibilities under the law.
- Juveniles and students are protected by the Fourth Amendment right against unreasonable search and seizure, but the courts have applied slightly different restrictions for school personnel than for police officers.
- Juvenile justice procedures have traditionally been distinguished from criminal justice procedures for adults by different terms, practices, and emphases.
- Purpose clauses of state juvenile codes and statutes provide an example of the differences between juvenile justice and criminal justice procedures.

KEY TERMS

Fourth Amendment rights

Criminal intent/*mens rea*

Purpose clauses

DISCUSSION QUESTIONS

1. Summarize the changes that the U.S. Supreme Court ordered for the juvenile court in the 1960s and 1970s.

2. Can you think of any rules and disciplinary procedures in your junior or senior high school that could have been legally challenged by a court today? Discuss and explain.

3. What procedures taken by teachers, principals, or school police officers in your school were clearly within current constitutional guidelines as defined by recent appellate court decisions?

4. Students are expected to give up certain rights to privacy in order to maintain safe schools that are free of drugs and weapons. Offer arguments *for* and *against* the following court-supported procedures in schools: (a) no privacy in school lockers, which are subject to random searches; (b) the presence of surveillance cameras in schools; (c) the presence of metal detectors at the entrance of some schools; and (d) the right to drug testing of any students who want to participate in any extracurricular activities.

5. Summarize the distinctions between juvenile and criminal justice procedures. Do you believe the distinctions are appropriate when considering the age, maturity level, understanding, and types of delinquent behavior of most juvenile offenders? Explain your answer.

WEB RESOURCES

Information on due process and juveniles' rights (Juvenile Confessions/Right Against Self-Incrimination): http://www.familyrightsassociation.com/info/law/all_about_miranda/juvenile_confessions.htm

School safety: http://www.ncjrs.gov/spotlight/school_safety/Summary.html

Access to juvenile courts: http://www.rcfp.org/juvcts/index.html

Juvenile Detention and Court Intake

In this chapter we provide an introduction to the post-arrest process for juvenile offenders, the detention decision for youth who pose a risk to the community, assessment of youth risks and needs, and the prosecutor's role in the intake decision that may result in diversion, informal adjustment, or a petition for adjudication in juvenile court. In 2005 slightly more than half (56%) of the 1.7 million delinquency cases referred by police to the juvenile court were formally processed with a petition for delinquency; and nearly half (44%) of the cases were processed informally (Puzzanchera & Sickmund, 2008, p. 36). The decision process for formal or informal processing is the responsibility of juvenile court intake.

Juvenile Court Intake

Intake is the next major step in juvenile justice processing for youth who are taken into custody by police and referred to juvenile court. The role of probation intake is a unique feature of the family and juvenile court that distinguishes it from adult criminal court (Lindner, 2008). The intake probation officer accepts referrals from police and is charged with the decision-making authority involving screening cases, detention, diversion, or referral for court processing. The intake officer must verify that the court has jurisdiction in each case. This involves determining from the police report that the youth is allegedly in violation of a provision in the state juvenile code. The range of forbidden juvenile behavior is quite broad, ranging from status offenses to felony offenses. The intake officer must also verify the juvenile's date of birth to ascertain that the department has jurisdiction. State juvenile codes vary, but most legal definitions of *juvenile* are youth between the ages of 10 and 17. The intake officer must immediately inform the parents of the referral, and decide whether to turn the youth over to the parents pending further action, or to detain the child temporarily. A considerable amount of information may be gathered and reviewed in the intake process, including a police officer's report of the arrest and charge, offense history and record, past indications of violent or aggressive behavior, mental health and medical needs, substance abuse, family problems, peer relationships, gang membership, school attendance and progress, and amenability to diversion or treatment programs (Mears & Kelly, 1999). This information is generally gathered during an *intake conference* with the juvenile and parent(s) that may take up to an hour.

Intake alternatives that an officer can make after gathering information on each case include:

1. Take *no action* other than to advise and counsel the juvenile and parents, and perhaps refer them to social services outside the justice system on a *voluntary* basis (sometimes called "reprimand and release").
2. *Divert* the case to a social service agency outside the court system, on *conditions* that they will agree to a diversion agreement and follow up on recommendations and services provided.
3. *Informal adjustment* or informal supervision of the intake division, usually with *conditions* of paying restitution or doing community service; and short-term supervision and counseling by the intake officer or a community agency.
4. *Referral* of the case to the prosecutor's office for filing *formal charges* or a delinquency petition in juvenile court.

Diversion programs include a variety of services operated by community organizations, churches, or schools such as teen court, drug court, Big Brothers Big Sisters, mentoring programs, and victim–offender mediation programs (discussed in more detail in Chapter 13). Diversion and informal adjustment are intake alternatives that must be agreed upon by the juvenile and his or her parent(s). The case usually remains on file as "active" or "pending" for a short period of 3 to 6 months, during which the intake officer monitors the juvenile's progress.

Various terms are used to describe youth recommended for informal supervision, such as a "child in need of supervision" (CINS) or "child in need of protective services" (CHIPS). These referrals are informal and voluntary, but they require admission of delinquent involvement and may be accompanied by the threat of more formal action if the youth does not comply. Failure to comply with the agreements and conditions specified could result in the intake officer referring the case to the prosecutor for processing in court. Under the "least restrictive" philosophy of the juvenile justice system, the goal of probation agencies is to divert minor juvenile offenders from processing through the juvenile court, and refer them to other agencies for short-term intervention and guidance. Diversion is considered most appropriate for status offenders and youth who have allegedly committed minor property crimes.

The intake officer serves a screening function, separating those cases that seem appropriate for diversion from cases that should be petitioned to juvenile court. The officer has considerable discretionary authority in this decision-making process. The decision of whether to file a petition for adjudication is made in consultation with the prosecuting attorney. Juvenile justice reforms in many states are placing the legal decisions solely in the office of the prosecuting attorney (discussed in more detail later in this chapter). Legal factors (current charge and previous record) are foremost in the decision of whether to release the youth to parents rather than detain, and whether to divert the youth to informal supervision or refer for juvenile court adjudication. Extralegal factors also play an important role in this decision-making process, however, and extensive research has been done on the effect that variables such as race, ethnicity, gender, socioeconomic level, and family history have on intake and detention decisions.

Diversion and Alternatives to Juvenile Court Referral

Diversion programs have been promoted as a way to reduce the number of minor offenders processed through the juvenile justice system, while still providing supervision or services on an informal basis. Criminologists argued that processing minor offenders through the justice system had a stigmatizing effect that was likely to perpetuate rather than reduce the chance of further delinquent behavior. Proponents of diversion argued that court referrals should be restricted to juvenile offenses that would be crimes if committed by adults. Status offenders should be diverted to agencies outside the formal justice process, which would provide needed supervision and services but would not be adjudicated delinquent and placed on official probation. Diversion was a recommendation of the 1967 President's Commission on Law Enforcement and Administration of Justice, and the Juvenile Justice and Delinquency Prevention (JJDP) Act of 1974 promoted diversion of minor juvenile offenders to community treatment programs in lieu of formal juvenile justice processing. Youth service bureaus (YSBs) were among the diversion agencies that were developed through federal funding to provide an alternative source of referrals by police and probation intake officers. The YSBs and similar diversion agencies provide services such as counseling, educational assistance, job training, and recreational opportunities as a means of preventing further delinquent involvement among minor and first-time young offenders. Diversion programs provide more flexible and efficient services than formal juvenile court processing, and offer an alternative for youth in need of some supervision.

Deinstitutionalization *of status offenders* (DSO) was a major provision of the JJDP Act. The Act required states to provide that juveniles who were charged with offenses that would not be criminal if committed by an adult not be placed in juvenile detention or correctional facilities, but rather in shelter facilities Amendments to the original act (in 1977, 1980, and 1992) required that states receiving JJDP Act grant funds provide assurance that they were taking action to remove status offenders and non-offenders from detention and correctional facilities and not detaining juveniles in adult jails (Holden & Kapler, 1995). A comprehensive national evaluation of DSO programs found that they were successful in significantly reducing the number of status offenders in detention and institutions (Schneider, 1985b). Other studies have found mixed results, however. Kobrin and Klein (1982) conducted a national evaluation of DSO programs and found problems in the definition of status offenders. They found that "pure" status offenders were relatively rare; most status offenders had prior delinquent experiences. Some jurisdictions limited their programs to pure status offenders; many otherwise eligible youth were therefore not served by the programs. In other areas the number of juveniles referred to court intake actually increased, and many youngsters whose behavior did not justify police intervention were referred to diversion programs. This tendency led to a problem referred to as "net widening." Many status offenders who previously would have been handled by police or intake probation officers through a "reprimand and release" were drawn into diversion or DSO programs. Diversion programs have therefore been criticized because they have received referrals of youth who otherwise would not have been referred to probation intake or court (Decker, 1985). Recent juvenile justice reforms in many states have limited the discretionary decisions of intake probation officers and shifted most of those decisions to the responsibility of the prosecutor.

Prosecutor Role in Intake and Court Referral

The prosecutor is primarily responsible for the decision whether to file a petition for adjudication in most jurisdictions today. Under the traditional rehabilitative or "medical model" of juvenile justice, the intake probation officer had a considerable amount of discretion in deciding whether to handle the case informally or refer the case to juvenile court. Police referred a juvenile to the intake officer, who reviewed the charges, checked for previous arrest records, and interviewed the juvenile and the parents. Based on the information, the intake officer then made the decision either to divert the case, handle it on informal adjustment, or refer the case to the prosecutor with a recommendation to file a petition for court adjudication. The traditional intake model has given way to a more formal process with the prosecutor as the central figure responsible for the decision whether to file a petition. A prosecuting attorney is the more appropriate court official to make a determination whether to petition a case based on the evidence and the factors necessary for court jurisdiction (Whitehead & Lab, 2006). An example of the current trend is the state of Washington, which now gives sole responsibility of the intake decisions to the prosecutor. Juvenile justice reform legislation in that state includes intake and sentencing guidelines based on seriousness of the offense, prior offenses, and age of the youth. The practice of informally adjusting cases at intake was completely eliminated (Schneider & Schram, 1986). The intent of the legislative reform was to hold juveniles accountable for their crimes and to hold the system accountable for what it did to juveniles. The traditional rehabilitation philosophy was replaced by a "justice" or "just deserts" model that emphasized fairness, uniformity, and proportionality in the court's response to juvenile offenses. In support of this emphasis, status offenses were removed entirely from court jurisdiction (Schneider & Schram, 1986, p. 211). The current trend is for more states to move toward this more formal, legal approach in the intake process. The intake decision now is based not on the "need for treatment" but on legal criteria and on holding juveniles accountable for their crimes.

Juvenile Detention

Juvenile detention centers were established to serve as an alternative to placing juveniles in adult jails. The federal Juvenile Justice and Delinquency Prevention Act of 1974 (see Table 2.1 in Chapter 2) requires that detained juveniles be separated by "sight and sound" from adults (Snyder & Sickmund, 2006, p. 97). This requirement specifies that juveniles may not be detained or confined in any institution in which they have contact with adult offenders who have been convicted of a crime or are awaiting trial on criminal charges. This means that juvenile and adult inmates cannot be held in the same detention facility where they could see each other or where conversation between them might be possible. Any states in violation of this requirement may lose federal funding.

City, county, or state governments administer detention centers, though most are run by the county in conjunction with the juvenile court and the probation department. Detention centers serve as temporary holding facilities for juveniles who need to be held for their own safety or that of the community. They may be held temporarily after arrest and referral to the probation intake unit pending release to their parents. Juveniles are usually detained for a week or less, with exceptional cases being held up to 3 to 4 weeks or longer while awaiting their court hearing. The National Juvenile Detention Association (NJDA) adopted this definition:

> Juvenile detention is the temporary and safe custody of juveniles who are accused of conduct subject to the jurisdiction of the court who require a restricted environment for their own or the community's protection while pending legal action. . . . [J]uvenile detention provides a wide range of helpful services that support the juvenile's physical, emotional, and social development. Helpful services . . . include education, visitation, communication, counseling, continuous supervision, medical and health care services, nutrition, recreation, and reading. Juvenile detention includes or provides for a system of clinical observation and assessment that complements the helpful services and reports findings. (Roush, 2004, p. 219)

POLICY AND PRACTICE 8.1   ADMISSION TO JUVENILE DETENTION

Admission to detention is the act of taking custody of a juvenile on the basis of the statutory authority specified in each state's juvenile code. Admission is a legal act involving the physical transfer of the juvenile into a detention facility. Until admission, the juvenile is usually in the custody of law enforcement. Each detention facility should provide policies and procedures for the admission process, as outlined in the "Desktop Guide to Good Juvenile Detention Practice" (Roush, 1996, p. 89). These policies and procedures should include the following:

- Determination that the juvenile is legally committed to the facility.
- Complete search of the juvenile and possessions.
- Disposition of personal property.
- Shower and hair care.
- Issue of clean and laundered clothing.
- Issue of personal hygiene articles.
- Medical, dental, and mental health screening.
- Assignment to a housing unit.
- Recording of basic personal data information to be used for mail and visiting list.
- Assistance to juveniles in notifying their families of admission and procedures for mail and visiting.
- Assignment of a registered number to the juvenile.
- Provision of written orientation materials to the juvenile. (Roush, 1996, p. 89)

Unlike state correctional facilities for juveniles, most county juvenile detention facilities do not use a complete and well-developed classification system for detained youth at admission. Juvenile detention facilities have a constitutional requirement to protect the safety of youth in their care, however, so it is essential that they use some method to identify and separate violate offenders from nonviolent offenders. The separation is intended primarily for housing assignment and sleeping arrangements, and not necessarily during waking hours when there are more staff to supervise the activities. The minimal classification of juvenile detainees involves three basic factors: "(1) separation of violent and nonviolent detainees, (2) separation of male and female detainees, and (3) separation of detainees based on level of sophistication or on some arbitrary assessment of age, size, and mental maturity" (Roush, 1996, p. 90). Information used in a detention classification system should include:

- Sex and age.
- Physical characteristics.
- Nature of offense.
- Prior offense history.
- Behavioral reports and summaries from prior detentions.
- Social history.
- Psychological assessment.
- Conversations with admitting police officers.
- Information from probation officer or case workers.

(Continued)

(Continued)

- Status of gang membership.
- Physical indicators of violence (e.g., scars from fights or gunshots).
- Reports from other agencies.
- Self-reported data. (Roush, 1996, p. 90)

SOURCE: Roush, D. W. (1996). *Desktop guide to good juvenile detention practice.* Washington, DC: Office of Juvenile Justice and Delinquency Prevention. Retrieved November 5, 2008, from http://www.ncjrs.gov/pdffiles/desktop.pdf.

Discussion Questions

1. Review the steps in the detention admission process (search, inventory personal property, shower and hair care, etc.). Suggest reasons why these are considered important for every detention admission. Are there any procedures that do not seem as important for all new admissions? Why? Or, are all admission procedures equally important?

2. Review the list of information recommended for a detention classification system (sex, age, physical characteristics, etc.). Which of those pieces of information do you believe might be most difficult to obtain? Suggest ways in which a detention intake officer might get that information.

Which items of detention admission information may be most interesting or helpful in explaining why the juvenile was arrested and detained? Can you think of some personal characteristics or personal problems that may justify having detention staff members treat a detainee with special care or considerations?

All states have a provision in their juvenile statutes requiring that a detention hearing be held within a day or two to determine whether a juvenile may be held longer or must be released. In the detention hearing a judge reviews the decision to detain a youth, the reasons for detention, and either orders the youth released or continues the detention. Detention may be used either pre-adjudication or post-adjudication; as a case is processed through the justice system, a juvenile may be detained and released more than once between referral and disposition. Juveniles who are on probation supervision and who commit another crime or violate probation conditions may be detained pending further court actions. Juveniles who have been committed to a correctional facility will also be detained while they are awaiting transportation.

Trends and Variations in Detention

The number of delinquency cases involving detention was 341,300 in 2004, an increase of 42% since 1985 when 232,400 cases were detained (Stahl et al., 2007, p. 30). Person offenses comprised 29%; property offense cases made up 29%; public order cases were 32%; and drug offense cases made up the smallest proportion of detained

SOURCE: © Robert Essel/NYC/Corbis.

Photo 8.1 A juvenile in custody awaiting further processing by an intake officer.

cases at 10% (Stahl et al., 2007, p. 30). The use of detention varies not only by offense type, but also by gender, race, and age. Twenty-two percent of males who were charged with delinquency were detained, compared to 17% of females. Delinquency cases involving youth age 16 or older were more likely to be detained than were youth age 15 or younger. The greatest variation among cases detained was for race. In 2004, the black proportion of detained delinquency cases (37%) was much greater than the black proportion of the juvenile population (16%); and greater than the black proportion of delinquency cases handled during the year (29%). The overrepresentation of black juveniles in detention was even greater (42%) for person offenses, although black youth accounted for 39% of the person offense processed in 2004 (Stahl et al., 2007, p. 31). Black juveniles were detained at a disproportionately higher rate for property offenses (28% of cases, 35% detained); drug offenses (22% of cases, 34% detained); and public order offenses (32% of cases, 35% detained). Black youth were about twice as likely as white youth to be detained for drug offense cases (28% vs. 15%). In summary, cases involving black youth were more likely to be detained than cases involving white youth in each year between 1985 and 2004, across all offense categories (Stahl et al., 2007, p. 33). Detention decisions are generally based on a judge's determination of whether a youth presents a risk of committing another offense, of not appearing for the court hearing, or presents a risk to self or others if not detained. Previous arrests would therefore be a logical factor in detention decisions. Studies have found, however, that after controlling for present offense and prior arrests, a juvenile's race is a significant factor in detention decisions (Feld, 1999a, p. 148). In fact, a youth's race affects both police referral and detention, even after controlling for weapons use, victim injury, and socioeconomic and family structure (Wordes, Bynum, & Corley, 1994).

CASE IN POINT 8.1

A Juvenile Is Arrested and Detained

Frank was arrested for bringing a gun to school. He is 15 years old, the oldest of three children living with his mother, a single parent. After the arrest by a Minneapolis police officer, Frank was transported to the Hennepin County Juvenile Detention Center (JDC). The police officer drove the squad car into the vehicle sally port, opened the door for Frank (who was in handcuffs) and escorted him inside the JDC. Frank was pat searched by one Juvenile Correctional Officer (JCO) while another took the required paperwork from the police officer and began to document his personal effects on a property inventory form. The intake officer looked over the paperwork to ensure that the charges were appropriate for detention. Frank was then led through a metal detector and taken to the intake office to be interviewed.

The intake officer used a Risk Assessment Instrument (RAI) to assess Frank's risk level and whether he needed to be detained. The RAI helps officers differentiate between youth who need to be detained and those who can be released to parents or referred to one of the many detention alternatives developing in Hennepin County. The Juvenile Detention Alternatives Initiative (JDAI), funded by the Annie E. Casey Foundation, selected Hennepin County as a site needing reduction in its juvenile detention population. The JDAI has helped reduce overcrowding at juvenile detention centers in the United States in the past decade. Youth who do not pose a risk to public safety and do not need secure detention can be transported to one of the alternative agencies, thereby preventing exposure of the youth to the detention environment and reducing cost to the county.

Based on the police officer's charge and the risk assessment process, Frank was admitted to the JDC. The assessment screening also helps place each detained juvenile in a module according to age, physical size, and suicide risk. The entire intake process—from the exchange of custody from the police officer, pat search and weapons screening, intake interview, fingerprinting, photograph, and unclothed search and shower—took about 30 minutes. Frank was then led to his module to begin the resident orientation process.

Frank's concrete cell measures 6 feet by 9 feet, and is designed for only one person. Being confined to such a small space and isolated from other juveniles can be a traumatic experience for most detained youth. Each resident is closely observed on a regular basis, for signs of emotional trauma or suicide tendencies. Detained juveniles who become physically assaultive are physically and mechanically restrained. JDC staff members are trained in behavior management and physical restraint. The JDC is licensed by the Minnesota Department of Corrections, which provides staff training on the emotional and psychological effects of being locked up. Staff members are trained to use verbal skills rather than physical restraint whenever possible to deescalate residents who are assaultive and out of control. Major rule violations such as fighting receive additional consequences such as "disciplinary room time."

Frank, along with all detention residents, is expected to participate in daily educational programming provided by Minneapolis public school teachers in the detention center classroom. He can earn points toward incentives for positive behavior and is sanctioned for negative behavior by losing incentive points. Treatment and correctional change are not an emphasis or focus of detention centers, as they are temporary holding facilities for juveniles awaiting trial or transportation to a residential facility following court disposition. The JDC does, however, have programs that teach basic living skills as well as a type of cognitive behavioral therapy to teach youth to practice thinking through problems before taking actions. Frank's temporary incarceration in JDC will have an impact on him, and the close association with other delinquent peers may have negative consequences. The programs provided during his temporary stay are intended to reduce the adverse influences of other delinquents, and to offer Frank and other detention residents some basic life decision making skills.

SOURCE: Adapted from a juvenile detention case in Hennepin County, Minneapolis, Minnesota.

Discussion Questions

1. Consider the detention intake process of Frank and the hundreds of other juveniles who are placed in detention in cities throughout the nation every week. What are some of the skills and qualifications of JDC staff members who must respond to youth who may be verbally or physically assaultive, traumatized and possibly suicidal, or who exhibit similar reactions?

2. Based on your understanding of some psychological and sociological causes of delinquency (Chapters 3 & 4) suggest how the detention experience of Frank and other juveniles may (a) encourage further delinquency; or (b) deter him from delinquency.

3. Access one or more of the Web sources related to juvenile detention practices, and suggest three important practices to follow in working with juveniles in detention.

Conditions of Confinement in Detention

More juveniles were confined in correctional facilities in 2003 (65,636) than in detention centers (25,019), but between 1991 and 2003 the detained population increased more (38%) than the 28% increase in correctional facilities (Snyder & Sickmund, 2006, p. 200). Nearly half (48%) of detained juveniles were in large urban detention facilities that held more than 200 residents. The number of delinquency cases involving detention increased 42% between 1985 and 2002, although the proportion of cases (20%) detained was the same in 2002 as in 1985 (Snyder & Sickmund, 2006, p. 168). Cities and counties in the United States have been struggling to keep up with the growth of detention cases. Overcrowding affects a substantial proportion of juveniles in detention centers. According to the Juvenile Residential Facility Census in 2002, 34% of juveniles were held in facilities operating at or above their standard bed

capacity; and detention centers were more likely than other types of juvenile corrections facilities to be at or above their rated capacity (Snyder & Sickmund, 2006, p. 223).

The physical structure of most metropolitan juvenile detention centers resembles
adult jails. They are generally built of concrete and steel construction with small individual cells or rooms containing a bed, toilet, and sink. If the cell has a window, it is
only a small opening that allows some natural light into the tiny room. Detention centers are built and programmed almost entirely around custody and security concerns.
Educational, recreational, and treatment programs are secondary. The emphasis on
security over correctional programming is justified by the short-term nature of detention; preventing additional crimes or harm to the individual juvenile and others before
the court appearance; and to ensure presence in juvenile court on the assigned date.

Modern detention facilities are now built in a modular or "podular" architectural
design that features a more open environment, with small rooms surrounding a day
room. Residents are generally segregated by age and physical size, with just 10 to 15
rooms in each "pod." This design enables better supervision and control in a more
relaxed setting that is less institutional in appearance, with space designed for educational, recreational, and treatment programs. Most new detention centers being
constructed throughout the United States now incorporate this new design.
Unfortunately, allocation of funds for building new juvenile detention centers is not a
top priority among cities and counties. They are very expensive to build and operate,
and county government officials are unable to allocate funds for better detention facilities in the face of competing budgetary demands. Many cities are therefore detaining
children in facilities that are overcrowded and in worse condition than many adult
jails. Juvenile courts in many nonurban settings often lack detention facilities and
therefore must detain juveniles in a section of the adult jail, or transport youth more
than an hour's drive away to the nearest available county detention center or regional
facility. In addition to the travel costs, this practice presents clear disadvantages for visits by family members; and probation officers are unable to make regular visits for
gathering information relating to intake decisions and preparing predisposition
reports. It is ironic that less attention is given to the conditions of confinement in
detention than to training schools and juvenile correctional facilities, especially considering that detention centers house children as young as 10 or 12 years of age, those
who have been arrested and incarcerated for the first time, and youth who have not yet
been adjudicated delinquent.

Consequences of Being Detained

The detention experience has lasting effects on children and youth, and may have
a number of negative consequences. Despite the intended purpose of detention—for
the protection of the charged youth and the community, to prevent additional crimes,
and to ensure the youth's appearance in court—detention itself may have a number of
unintended consequences. Detention centers, much like juvenile correctional facilities,
may promote rather than prevent delinquency by bringing offenders together and
isolating them from the community (Elliott, Huizinga, & Ageton, 1985). Detention
adversely affects juveniles' school attendance and educational progress, current

employment and future job prospects, and separates youths from their families (Fagan & Guggenheim, 1996). There is research evidence that detention increases the likelihood of a juvenile being adjudicated and committed to a training school. McCarthy (1987) found that even after controlling for crime severity and prior records, juvenile courts processed more detained youth further into the justice system, adjudicated them delinquent more frequently, and sentenced them more severely than youths who were not detained prior to the court hearing. Being detained appears to exert a greater influence on court decisions than other legal or social factors, acting in a manner that McCarthy (1987) referred to as a self-fulfilling prophecy. Once a juvenile is identified in a detention hearing as one who is predicted to pose a greater risk of danger and future delinquent involvement, that preliminary decision appears to have an influence on the adjudication and disposition decisions, which in turn have greater and long-lasting consequences for the youth. The fact that judges disproportionately detain more minority youths means that the consequences of detention affect them even more. The negative effects of detention and the influence of detention on judges' court decisions are matters of concern for juvenile justice experts and child advocates. The practice of **preventive detention** also involves a prediction that a juvenile poses a risk and danger if not detained while awaiting court action.

CASE IN POINT 8.2

The Effects of Detention on a Juvenile

The experience of being incarcerated in detention can have a significant impact on juveniles. This is true whether it is just overnight or for several days or weeks. Detained juveniles are temporarily separated from their parents and siblings, in an institutional setting. Their forced absence from school may have serious consequences for their educational status; and research has shown that being detained often has negative consequences for their court adjudication and disposition. They are exposed to many serious and chronic juvenile offenders, and are at risk of taking on the attitudes, behavior, and demeanor of other delinquents. Detained juveniles are at the mercy of juvenile corrections staff, who often respond to the conditions of their work with hopelessness and resentment. The callous and negative attitudes of some detention workers are often expressed through inhumane and inconsistent treatment of the youth under their care.

Carl Taylor (1996) explored the impact of detention on juveniles under age 16 and presented his findings to highlight the unintended consequences of incarceration. The shock of being detained is vividly illustrated by the words of a young woman (now age 21) who recalled her stay in a detention center when she was 14, after getting caught selling drugs in Detroit, Michigan. Her rough street language is offensive, but is the kind of talk regularly heard by police and juvenile detention officers. The following narrative illustrates how detention reminds juveniles of the consequences of doing crime; but the detention experience also brings unintended consequences. Her case depicts the horrors that many youngsters experience daily in American prisons and detention centers (Taylor, 1996, pp. 41–42):

(Continued)

(Continued)

It was hard. . . . I hated being in there 'cause I wanted my freedom. I figure, hey, I can do it. It ain't s—. But when dem m— f— doors closed, oh, it wasn't all dat 'cause I cried like a m— f—. I was real hurt. I wanted to be out there in the world. . . . I was like, d—, I can't believe this s—. . . .

And all the time I was there, I kept on saying, Oh, God, please help me, God. Please give me one more chance, God. I swear I ain't gonna do it no more. I ain't gonna try to sell drugs. I know it's wrong. Please, God, please, God. Dat's all I was saying. Cause dat's the first person anybody holler for, when dey get in trouble, is God.

The staff, dey was f— up. Dey ain't give a f—. Only thing dey do was sit there and watch us. You ask them a question, dey look at you like dey crazy or like dey don't know s—. The teachers was f— up, too, Dey didn't give a f—, anyway. Dey figure like, ya'll m— f— criminals. I don't give a f—, you know, if you learn or not. I'm just here to get paid. And dat was real sad. You know, we know we was in there for wrong things. I was in there for drugs; people was in there for killing people, people was in there for running away, people was in there for all type of little dumb s—. But no matter what we was in there for, we was human beings, and we deserved to be treated like it. . . . And . . . at night . . . when you go all in your room, dey lock the doors and s—. So, I used to be knockin' on the door at night, 'cause I used to have to use the bathroom 'cause I had a bad bladder infection. And I used to be bam, bam, bam, Ms. Doe, Ms. Doe. Bam, bam, bam. The b— ain't never answered the door. And so I was like, f— it. She didn't give a f—, so I didn't give a f—. So I pulled my m— f— shorts down and I p— on the m— f— floor. And I know I was a criminal, and I know what I had done was wrong by sellin' drugs, but I do got my m— f— rights, and I know dat b— is supposed to open the door and let me p—. I know dat m— f— much.

SOURCE: Adapted from Taylor, C. S. (1996). Growing up behind bars: Confinement, youth development, and crime. In Vera Institute of Justice (Ed.), *The unintended consequences of incarceration* (pp. 41–65). New York: Vera Institute of Justice. Retrieved November 7, 2008, from http://www.vera.org/publication_pdf/uci.pdf.

Discussion Questions

1. We do not know the prior record or risk level of the young woman in this case, but can you suggest some goals of detention and incarceration that were supported in this case?

2. Some *intended consequences* of detention and incarceration may be for deterrence, and to remind young offenders of the consequences of crime. Explain whether this case may illustrate any of those purposes.

3. The original purpose of the author presenting this case was to illustrate the *unintended consequences of detention*. What are the unintended consequences in this case?

4. Compare this case with the admission procedures presented in this chapter, and suggest any apparent deviations from acceptable policies and practices.

Under the Eighth Amendment protection against "cruel and unusual punishment," what do you believe are some rights of juvenile detainees and responsibilities of detention workers?

Preventive Detention and Predicting Dangerousness

The pretrial detention of youths who have been arrested and charged with a crime but not yet found guilty and adjudicated has met with legal challenges. In *Schall v. Martin* (467 U.S. 283[1984]) the U.S. Supreme Court upheld the constitutionality of the preventive detention of juveniles. The Court ruled that a juvenile may be held in preventive detention if there is sufficient reason to believe the juvenile may commit additional crimes while the case is pending court action. The Court also ruled that the juvenile has the right to a hearing on the detention decision and a statement of the reasons on which the detention decision is based. The dissenting opinion of Justices Marshall, Brennan, and Stevens is especially noteworthy in this case, as they questioned the ability to predict dangerousness or to identify which juveniles will engage in serious violent crime while awaiting court action. The dissenting justices argued that because preventive detention infringed youths' "fundamental" liberty interests, the state must demonstrate a "compelling" interest to justify restrictions and provide more adequate procedural safeguards. They argued that judges could not accurately predict dangerousness and therefore the use of preventive detention could not significantly reduce crime. The majority ruling in *Schall* had rejected the lower courts' findings that judges lacked the ability to accurately predict future criminal conduct, asserting that juvenile and criminal court judges could and did predict "dangerousness" regularly. The majority opinion relied on past and current judicial practices to uphold the argument. The dissenting opinion, on the other hand, relied on criminological, clinical, and legal studies that have concluded that there are no risk assessment instruments currently available that enable even the best experts to reliably predict which juveniles will engage in violent crime. Dissenting justices noted that the decision to detain is made by a Family Court judge in a brief hearing lasting between 5 and 15 minutes, with very limited information on which to base the detention decision. Feld (1999a) has noted that in most cases the statutes relating to preventive detention lack objective standards and clear criteria and allow judges broad discretion in detention hearings. The result is the detention of many juveniles who pose no threat to themselves or to others.

In contrast to the broad and nonspecific statutory limits on juvenile detention, the statutory criteria and limits on adult preventive detention are very clear and specific. Federal statute 18 U.S.C. § 3142(f) [1984], for example, authorized courts to detain only those defendants charged with crimes of violence, crimes punishable by death or life imprisonment, major drug offenses, or a felony committed by a defendant with two prior convictions of certain listed offenses. The prosecutor is expected to support the need for preventive detention "by clear and convincing evidence" that the defendant will flee and present a "demonstrable danger to the community" (see Feld, 1999a, p. 138). The Court in *Schall v. Martin* (467 U.S. 255), in contrast, authorized a juvenile court judge to preventively detain a juvenile if it found a "serious risk" that the child "may . . . commit an act which if committed by an adult would constitute a crime." The Court did not specify the nature of the alleged offense, burden of proof, specific criteria, the probability of occurrence of future crime, or the type of evidence that the judge should consider when predicting that a youth posed a "serious risk" of committing a new crime.

Judicial and corrections officials regularly make predictions of dangerousness every day, so researchers in criminal justice and criminology have conducted extensive research in an attempt to identify characteristics that may differentiate dangerous offenders from those who pose no serious risk of violent crime. Research findings do not support the view that judges can predict dangerousness from a legal point of view with an acceptable level of accuracy and reliability. Psychologists, psychiatrists, criminologists, and lawyers criticize the assumption that judges or mental health professionals can make valid and accurate predictions about future dangerousness (Monahan, 1981). Auerhahn (2006) asserts that our ability to predict violent behavior is severely limited. In contrast to "true positives" (accurately predicting who will commit another serious crime), "false positives" (wrongly predicting as dangerous offenders those who if released actually would not commit another dangerous crime) occur at an unacceptably high level. Research shows that when judges attempt to predict dangerousness they will make mistakes. False positive errors of 50% or more of offenders are common in prediction decisions (Auerhahn, 2006), resulting in the preventive detention and incarceration of numerous offenders who pose no risk to society and a significant impact in cost and allocation of resources on the justice process. When wrongly identified in need of preventive detention, judges

> deprive these youths of liberty because they share the characteristics of a . . . group of "potentially dangerous" youths. . . . If a judge erroneously predicts and detains a "false positive," the court imposes unwarranted incarceration on an innocent individual and obtains no incapacitative or crime prevention benefit because that person would *not* have offended if left at liberty. (Feld, 1999a, p. 142)

In addition to the inherent inaccuracy of predictions, judges tend to overpredict offenders believed to pose a risk to public safety. Errors will inevitably be made when predicting dangerousness, and the justice process prefers to err on the side of caution and in favor of the community over the loss of individual liberty. The judicial tendency to overpredict dangerousness nevertheless raises legal, moral, and policy questions. Feld poses an important question:

> How many false positives . . . can a morally defensible legal system incarcerate for no benefit in order to confine those fewer but unidentifiable individuals who actually will reoffend? Should judges speculate about a "serious risk" of future crime . . . if doing so means that they erroneously will preventively detain larger numbers of presumptively innocent false positives? How can a society balance predictive marginal crime reduction versus actual loss of individual liberty? (Feld, 1999a, p. 142)

CASE IN POINT 8.3

Schall v. Martin (1984)

Between December of 1977 and March of 1978, police arrested three 14-year-old juveniles, Gregory Martin, Luis Rosario, and Kenneth Morgan, in three separate incidents on a variety of charges including robbery, assault, and possession of a loaded gun. The New York Family Court Act allowed short-term detention of accused juveniles prior to having their cases resolved. A probation officer would determine if the case should go to juvenile court based on an interview with the juvenile and the arresting officer. If so, an "initial appearance" hearing was held and a judge determined if preventive detention was justified based on whether the juvenile was at "serious risk" to commit more offenses prior to a final hearing. Juveniles could be detained for up to 17 days, and were kept separate from adult criminals. The detention facilities included educational and recreational programs and counseling by social workers.

Martin was detained for 15 days until his court hearing, where he was found guilty and placed on 2 years' probation. Rosario, who had other assault charges pending, was detained for 6 days. His case was later dropped. Morgan, who also had charges pending from another incident, was detained for 8 days, found guilty, and placed in custody for 18 months. While in detention, Martin filed a suit on behalf of all detained juveniles challenging the legality of preventive detention. He claimed pretrial detention violated the Due Process and Equal Protection Clauses of the Fourteenth Amendment.

The U.S. District Court ruled the Family Court Act did violate due process and ordered the release of the three detained juveniles. The state appealed to the U.S. Court of Appeals, which affirmed the district court decision. In 1984 the Supreme Court granted *certiorari* to the *Schall* case to determine the constitutionality of juvenile preventive detention. The Court split the question concerning detention into two parts. First, does preventive detention serve a legitimate state interest, such as protection of property or citizens' safety? Second, are procedural safeguards adequate to ensure fairness? Justice Rehnquist, writing for the majority in a 6–3 vote, found that preventive detention of juveniles does serve a legitimate state objective of protecting both the juvenile and society from pretrial crime. Regarding the second question, he argued that the detention hearings to review each case satisfied "fundamental fairness" required by due process. Regarding prediction of future criminal conduct, the Court held that such predictions could be made through experienced assessments by the Family Court judge based on a variety of factors.

Justice Marshall, joined in dissent by Justices Brennan and Stevens, wrote that neither the argument of state interest nor the existence of procedural safeguards justified preventive detention of juveniles. Marshall noted that contrary to protecting juveniles from wrongdoing, preventive detention may instead unintentionally promote further crime. Detained juveniles were often given institutional clothing and mixed with juveniles already convicted of serious crimes. Given the impressionability of juveniles, pretrial detention is likely to have effects equivalent to adult imprisonment. Secondly, in regard to procedural safeguards, Marshall highlighted that "initial appearance" hearings to determine if detention is justified usually lasted less than 15 minutes. He noted that juvenile court-assigned lawyers usually knew little of the juvenile's background and character and had very little knowledge of the incident in question, so the limited information available at the detention hearing made the process arbitrary and did not measure up to the fairness standard of due process.

The significance of the *Schall* case is the Court's finding that pretrial detention does *not* violate juveniles' constitutional rights. The decision has nevertheless been criticized on the basis that future criminal behavior by individuals cannot be reliably predicted. Many individuals can be and often are wrongly detained. Some judicial experts have recommended that the likelihood of guilt should be a major factor to be considered in addition to a history of violent behavior.

SOURCE: *Schall v. Martin*, 467 U.S. 283 (1984).

(Continued)

(Continued)

Discussion Questions

1. Detaining a juvenile following arrest but before a court hearing amounts to incarcerating the youth (temporarily) before finding the youth guilty of a crime. Offer arguments for and against the practice of detaining a youth who is presumed innocent until the youth's appearance at the court hearing.

2. This case is another step toward treating juvenile offenders more like adult criminal offenders. Based on what you have read in this and previous chapters, in what ways are juvenile offenders different from adult offenders that may make it harder to make a fair decision whether or not detention is needed?

3. Offer arguments that support (a) the majority opinion that judges can accurately predict after a brief hearing which juveniles need to be detained; and (b) the dissenting opinion that accurate predictions of "dangerousness" or likelihood of committing further crimes cannot be accurately predicted by judges after a brief detention hearing.

The available research on predicting dangerousness through clinical methods and using assessment tools does not show a high degree of accuracy and reliability. Auerhahn (2006) adds a cautionary note in support of Monahan (1981), Feld (1999a), and others, concluding that the practice of depriving offenders of liberty based on questionable predictions is, at the least, ethically questionable and is potentially detrimental to the administration of justice. Ongoing research on violence risk screening (e.g., Davies & Dedel, 2006) shows promise of improving on the reliability of predicting dangerousness, and more court services and community corrections agencies are utilizing instruments for risk assessment. Critics remain concerned, however, about the unacceptably high rate of false positives that result in the unnecessary incarceration of hundreds of individuals. We turn next to a discussion of risk assessment instruments.

Assessment of Juvenile Risks and Needs

Assessment is a term that has appeared in juvenile justice literature only in the past couple of decades, but it is actually based on one of the original concepts of probation. In order for probation to be a viable alternative to incarceration, probation officers have always had to identify those offenders who posed a lower risk of reoffending, could be safely supervised in the community, and who were considered amenable to treatment. A fundamental concept of juvenile justice has always been an emphasis on individualized treatment as opposed to court sanctions and punishment. The emphasis on individual offender treatment requires identification of the specific treatment needs of each juvenile. Gathering information for and writing a predisposition report has been a central responsibility of juvenile probation officers. The reports have traditionally been very comprehensive, including information on the juvenile's childhood and family background, educational progress, and prior arrest and court records. A psychological evaluation to assess intelligence and personality factors might be requested (depending on available resources) in serious cases involving violence, when the case may be waived and transferred to adult court. Predisposition reports nevertheless involve subjective judgments of probation officers. Individual officer judgments vary considerably, so that similar cases by different officers are likely to receive different recommendations. It has been readily apparent for some time that there was a need for more objective assessment instruments that would provide more accurate, consistent, and standardized results on offenders' risk levels and treatment needs. It is generally accepted that when offender needs are clearly identified, the probation client can be provided with or referred to the appropriate rehabilitation programs, resulting in more efficient and effective probation outcomes.

A variety of assessment and classification systems have been developed and tested with juvenile and adult offenders. A nationwide survey found that corrections agencies in most states have some form of juvenile needs assessment (Towberman, 1992). The most common juvenile needs and risks that were assessed included substance abuse by juveniles or family members; mental and emotional health of the juvenile or family members; sexual or physical abuse in the family; education achievement and intellectual ability of the youth; vocational training needs of the youth; peer relationships; family dysfunction; medical or physical problems; and self-reported delinquency, including violent behavior (Towberman, 1992, p. 232). In a study of juvenile justice practitioners in Texas, Mears and Kelly (1999) found that there is considerable variation among probation officers as to the need for and the goals of assessment in the intake process. They recommended that greater attention should be given to clarifying the purposes and goals of assessment. Young, Moline, Farrell, and Bierie (2006) reported on the lessons learned from developing and implementing assessment tools in the Maryland juvenile justice system. They noted the importance of involving staff, supervisors, and judicial personnel in the process of developing and implementing assessment tools.

SUMMARY

- The intake probation officer accepts referrals from police and with the prosecutor decides whether to divert youth for informal adjustment or refer to court for adjudication.
- Detention centers serve as temporary holding facilities for juveniles who need to be held for their own safety or that of the community.
- A juvenile's race is a significant factor in detention decisions, and African American juveniles are detained at disproportionately higher rates.
- The number of delinquency cases involving detention increased dramatically in the past 20 years, and overcrowding affects a significant number of juveniles in detention centers.
- Being detained has a number of adverse consequences on juveniles, including the increased likelihood of being adjudicated and committed to a training school.
- Despite research evidence that questions the ability of a judge to predict dangerousness with certainty, the U.S. Supreme Court has upheld the constitutionality of preventive detention for juveniles.
- Assessment tools have been developed to assist in juvenile court decision making, including intake, detention, and disposition alternatives.
- Diversion programs were developed to reduce the number of minor first-time offenders referred to juvenile court, while still providing supervision and services on an informal basis.
- Juvenile justice reforms in many states have reduced the discretionary authority of the intake probation officer, giving the prosecutor primary responsibility for case processing.

KEY TERMS

Intake

Diversion

Detention

Deinstitutionalization

Preventive detention

Dangerousness

Assessment

DISCUSSION QUESTIONS

1. If intake and detention decisions are to be fair and just, is it appropriate that detention involves a disproportionate number of racial and ethnic minorities? What changes or reforms would you suggest?

2. Explain the difference between "false positives" and "false negatives" in predicting dangerousness and identifying offenders likely to pose a risk to public safety. Is it acceptable to have a false positive error rate of up to 50% if that means reducing the false negative rate to less than 5%? Explain and justify your response.

3. Based on the available research evidence, does it seem likely that risk and needs assessment instruments may reduce disparities due to extralegal factors used in juvenile court decision making? Explain.

4. Is there research support for the practice of giving intake officers some discretionary authority to divert or refer minor first-time offenders charged with a minor offense for informal adjustment? Explain and cite the research evidence.

5. The current trend is to move away from the rehabilitative "medical model" and toward the "justice model," giving the prosecutor primary authority for decisions at the intake stage. What are some arguments for each model and which seems to be the most convincing argument, based on the research evidence?

WEB RESOURCES

The following Web sites provide information and discussion on the detention and intake procedures of the juvenile justice system:

National Juvenile Detention Association: http://www.njda.com/

Annie E. Casey Foundation, on detention reform: www.aecf.org

Juvenile offenders and victims, 2006 national report: http://ojjdp.ncjrs.gov/ojstatbb/nr2006/downloads/NR2006.pdf

Youth Law Center, on juvenile confinement: http://www.buildingblocksforyouth.org/issues/

Roush, D. (1996). *Desktop Guide to Good Juvenile Detention Practice*: http://www.ncjrs.gov/pdffiles/desktop.pdf

Transfer to Criminal Court

Overview of Waiver and Transfer

Throughout the history of the juvenile court, all crimes involving juvenile-age offenders have first been filed in the juvenile court, regardless of the seriousness of the charge. All states and the District of Columbia, however, have laws that provide for criminal court prosecution of juveniles under certain circumstances. Transferring juveniles to criminal court is not a new practice. Juvenile courts have always had the authority to waive jurisdiction and transfer the case to criminal court. The statutes and the terms describing the process for waiver of juvenile court jurisdiction and transfer to criminal court differ somewhat from state to state. Traditionally the decision has been left to the discretion of the judge, who could waive juvenile court jurisdiction, certify the juvenile as an adult, and transfer the case to criminal court. The waiver decision essentially is a choice between either punishment in adult criminal court or rehabilitation in juvenile court (Podkopacz & Feld, 1996). The juvenile court must determine whether the seriousness of the present offense and the juvenile's prior record justify transferring the case to criminal court. This is still the case in most jurisdictions, but recent "get-tough" legislation has led to statutory or automatic transfer of chronic or violent juvenile offenders (Torbet et al., 1996).

Judicial waivers were exceptionally rare in juvenile court through the 1970s when the focus of the court was on the needs and "best interests" of the child. The traditional juvenile justice philosophy began to change in the 1980s and 1990s, to more of a focus on the criminal acts of juvenile offenders and a presumed need for more coercive intervention. The change in philosophy brought changes in waiver policies. The number of juvenile cases waived to criminal court had never been more than between 1% and 2% of the total number of juvenile court cases, but the rate of increase in the 1990s was dramatic. Person offenses are the types of cases most likely to be waived to criminal court, with a smaller percentage being waived for property, drug, and public order offenses. The early 1990s witnessed a dramatic increase in waived cases, and particularly for drug offenses, part of the result of the federal government initiative of the "war on drugs." This increase of waivers for drug offenses in comparison to person, property, and public order offenses is depicted in Figure 9.1. The overall trend in juvenile court waivers has been primarily for person offenses.

The number of delinquency cases waived to criminal court from 1985 to 1994 increased from about 7,200 to 13,000, an 83% rate of increase. The number then began a steady decline, dropping to 6,300 in 2001, which was 1% below the number in 1985 and less than 1% (0.8%) of all petitioned delinquency cases (Snyder & Sickmund, 2006, p. 186). The most recent available figures indicate a total of 6,900 juvenile cases waived in 2005 (Sickmund, Sladky, & Kang, 2008). The number of delinquency cases and the demographic percentages of juveniles waived to criminal court in 1985, 1994, 1999, 2004, and 2005 are presented in Table 9.1. The majority of juveniles waived to

| Figure 9.1 | Juvenile Court Cases Waived to Criminal Court, 1985–2005 |

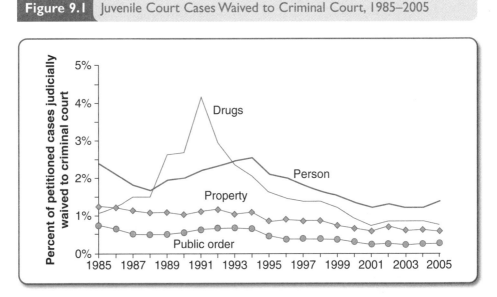

SOURCE: Puzzanchera & Sickmund, 2008, p. 41.

criminal court are males and juveniles aged 16 and over. A slightly higher percentage of white juveniles are waived than are blacks and other races; but a disproportionate percentage of black youth are waived to criminal court in comparison to their proportion of the juvenile population (see Table 9.1).

The number of juvenile cases waived by judges to the criminal court has decreased since the 1990s. This decrease in court waivers is because of legislative changes in many states that provide for *prosecutorial discretion* and *legislative exclusion* as additional mechanisms to try juveniles as adults (Griffin et al., 1998). Therefore, many more juveniles have been tried in criminal court following prosecutorial discretion or legislative exclusion than the 6,600 recorded cases of juveniles transferred to criminal court following juvenile court waiver in 2004. Howard Snyder of the National Center for Juvenile Justice (NCJJ) has estimated that there are well over 100,000 juveniles tried in criminal court each year, but those numbers are not reported to the NCJJ, the OJJDP, or to the Bureau of Justice Statistics (Snyder, personal communication, July 31, 2007).

Some states have now developed an alternative to juvenile transfer known as "extended juvenile jurisdiction prosecution" (or EJJP), also referred to as "blended

Table 9.1	Delinquency Cases Waived to Criminal Court by Demographic Characteristics, 1985–2005				
Characteristic	**1985**	**1994**	**1999**	**2004**	**2005**
Total Cases*	7,200	13,000	8,800	6,600	6,900
Gender					
Male	95%	95%	93%	91%	91%
Female	5%	5%	7%	9%	9%
Race					
White	59%	54%	60%	60%	58%
Black	40%	43%	36%	36%	39%
Other races*	1%	3%	4%	4%	3%
Age					
15 and under	7%	13%	16%	16%	15%
16 and over	93%	87%	84%	84%	85%

SOURCE: Adapted from Sickmund, Sladky, & Kang (2008). *Easy access to juvenile court statistics: 1985–2005.*

NOTE: *Numbers are rounded, so percentages may not equal 100. Native Americans and Asian Americans are included in "other races."

sentencing" (Snyder, Sickmund, & Poe-Yamagata, 2000; Sanborn & Salerno, 2005) that will be discussed in Chapter 10 ("The Juvenile Court Process"). In this chapter we examine developments in waiver and transfer; legislative changes providing for prosecutorial discretion and statutory exclusion; legal factors and scientific evidence relating to transfer; and research evidence on the effects of transferring juvenile offenders to criminal courts and adult corrections.

Judicial and Legislative Developments in Juvenile Transfer

There are basically three ways in which juveniles can be prosecuted in the adult criminal justice system. They differ according to the terms used to describe them and according to who makes the transfer decision. The three different processes are: judicial waiver, statutory exclusion, and concurrent jurisdiction (Griffin et al., 1998; Snyder et al., 2000).

Judicial Waiver

Under judicial waiver the juvenile court judge has the authority to waive juvenile court jurisdiction and transfer a case to the criminal court. A total of 46 states give juvenile court judges this authority (Griffin et al., 1998). Judicial waiver is usually requested by the prosecuting attorney and is granted by the court after a hearing. States vary in the degree of flexibility they allow the court in decision making, but waiver decisions must comply with guidelines spelled out in the U.S. Supreme Court case of *Kent v. United States* [383 U.S. 541 (1966)]. As we noted in Chapter 7, the U.S. Supreme Court, in *Kent*, reversed the conviction of a 16-year-old youth who had been tried as an adult. The waiver to adult court was ruled invalid because the juvenile was denied a hearing with assistance of legal counsel, and no written statement was made giving reasons for the waiver to criminal court. The waiver hearing is to consider evidence that relates to the criteria for waiver. The evidence presented is *not* to determine guilt on the present charge. The U.S. Supreme Court ruled in the 1975 case of *Breed v. Jones* (421 U.S. 519) that it was in violation of the double jeopardy clause of the Fourteenth Amendment to prosecute a juvenile in criminal court following adjudicatory proceedings in juvenile court. The purpose of the waiver hearing is not to determine guilt or innocence, but to assess the juvenile's threat to public safety and amenability to treatment under the juvenile justice system. Under most waiver statutes, the juvenile court judge considers such factors as the circumstances and seriousness of the alleged offense, prior adjudications, and the age and maturity of the youth. Most states that specify factors to be considered in waiver hearings either list or paraphrase some of the factors in the U.S. Supreme Court decision in *Kent* (Griffin et al., 1998, p. 4). Two variations of judicial waiver that exist in several states are mandatory waiver and presumptive waiver.

Mandatory Waiver

Mandatory waiver (in the statutes of 14 states) makes waiver mandatory in cases that meet certain age, offense, or other criteria (Griffin et al., 1998, p. 4). Proceedings are initiated in the juvenile court, but the court has no role other than to confirm that the statutory requirements for mandatory waiver are met. The juvenile court must then transfer the case to criminal court. Mandatory waiver is different from statutory exclusion because the case originates in the juvenile court. Under statutory exclusion (discussed below), a case that meets statutory criteria originates in criminal court. The juvenile court's involvement under mandatory waiver is minimal, but it does initiate proceedings, conducts a preliminary hearing to confirm that the case meets the criteria for mandatory waiver, and issues a transfer order and other orders that may include appointment of counsel and pretrial detention (Griffin et al., 1998, p. 4).

Presumptive Waiver

Presumptive waiver (in the statutes of 15 states) designates a category of cases for which waiver to criminal court is presumed to be appropriate (Griffin et al., 1998, p. 6). In such cases, the juvenile rather than the State has the burden of proof in the waiver hearing. If a juvenile who meets the age, offense seriousness, prior offense history, or other statutory criteria prompting the presumptive waiver fails to make a convincing argument against transfer, the juvenile court must send the case to criminal court.

Prosecutorial Discretion

The provision for prosecutorial discretion allows prosecutors to file certain juvenile cases in either juvenile or criminal court (Torbet et al., 1996). The statute, also referred to as **direct file** or **concurrent jurisdiction**, has been adopted by 15 states (Griffin et al., 1998, p. 7; Sanborn & Salerno, 2005, p. 279). These direct file provisions give both juvenile and adult criminal courts the power to hear cases that have been specified in the statute according to seriousness of offense and age of offender. Prosecutorial transfer, unlike judicial waiver, is not subject to judicial review and is not required to meet the due process requirements established in *Kent* (Snyder et al., 2000, p. 4). Discretion is left up to the prosecutor whether to file the case in juvenile or criminal court. Prosecutors have broad discretionary authority under this provision, especially given the concurrent jurisdiction of either juvenile or criminal court for the stated offenses and age criteria in the statute. The direct file or concurrent jurisdiction process represents a dramatic departure from the waiver procedures specified in *Kent,* in which juvenile court judges were to determine through a preliminary hearing whether a youth was "amenable to treatment" in the juvenile justice system, or whether a combination of age, maturity, offense, and prior record constituted a risk to public safety. The waiver hearing generally has included social background information compiled by a probation officer, and often a psychological assessment. States also vary widely regarding the applicable offense categories and other criteria. For example, Arkansas authorizes direct file for soliciting a minor to join a street gang; and Florida allows even misdemeanors to be prosecuted in criminal court if the juvenile is 16 and has a prior serious record (Griffin et al., 1998, p. 8). Because prosecutor discretion does not involve a juvenile court hearing and transfer, no national data exist on the number or characteristics of the cases that prosecutors exclude from juvenile court jurisdiction (Snyder et al., 2000).

Critics of prosecutorial waiver have expressed concerns about giving exclusive authority to prosecutors and removing the judge from the transfer decision process. The practice runs contrary to the traditional principles of juvenile justice, whereby judicial decisions were made based on not only the offense but also on the sophistication, culpability, maturity, and amenability to treatment of the offender. Feld (2004) has expressed concern over the practice of allowing elected prosecutors who are subject to political pressure and are not likely to rely on any social background information to make the important decision of jurisdictional waiver: "The shift of sentencing discretion from the judicial branch to the executive branch via 'direct file' legislation raises a host of sentencing policy questions about institutional competencies and justice administration" (Feld, 2004, p. 600). He suggests that prosecutors are not likely to make better informed and appropriate transfer decisions than would judges in an adversarial waiver hearing in which they are assisted in the decision with clinical and social background evidence and guided by specific waiver criteria. A study of prosecutors' direct certification and waiver in Virginia found that only a small percentage of eligible offenders were actually transferred, suggesting that factors other than seriousness of offense may have been considered (Sridharan, Greenfield, & Blakley, 2004). Certifications varied across localities in the state, however; and the authors acknowledged the mixed findings and generally critical assessments of prosecutorial waiver. Critics of direct prosecutorial waiver have vehemently questioned the practice of allowing waiver decisions based on a punitive orientation without the balanced due process safeguards of a judicial hearing to consider relevant evidence and without a requirement to consider specific criteria for waiver, as specified by the U.S. Supreme Court in *Kent* (Feld, 2000; Bishop, 2004; Kupchik, 2004).

Statutory Exclusion

A total of 28 states have statutes that remove certain offenses or age and offense categories from juvenile court jurisdiction (Griffin et al., 1998, pp. 8–9; Sanborn & Salerno, 2005, p. 287). Most of these apply to cases of murder by juveniles 16 or older; but some states include juveniles 14 or older who commit person offenses. In practice, the laws simply exclude anyone fitting the criteria from being defined as a "child" for purposes of juvenile court jurisdiction. A juvenile charged with an excluded offense is therefore treated as an adult from the beginning of the judicial process. The prosecutor does not have discretion regarding the court in which the case is filed. Once the decision is made to charge the juvenile with an excluded offense, the case must be filed in criminal court. Statutory exclusion is part of the same trend toward "get-tough" legislation that has shifted decision-making from judges to legislators and prosecutors (Feld, 2000). As with prosecutorial discretion discussed above, legislators have removed the judge from the decision-making process with statutory exclusion. The evidentiary hearing process mandated by the U.S. Supreme Court in *Kent* is circumvented by statutory exclusion in the same way it is with prosecutorial discretion. Statutory exclusion provisions also circumvent most current state laws for transfer of juveniles to criminal court. Juvenile transfer laws in 46 states today explicitly direct the judge to consider the age, mental maturity, and capacity of the juvenile (Sanborn & Salerno, 2005).

Additional Transfer Laws

Reverse Waiver

Lawmakers in 23 states have added a provision referred to as reverse waiver whereby a juvenile who is being prosecuted as an adult in criminal court may petition to have the case transferred to juvenile court for adjudication or disposition (Griffin et al., 1998, p. 910; Sanborn & Salerno, 2005, p. 294). This statute basically authorizes the adult criminal court to consider the appropriateness of a juvenile case for criminal prosecution, regardless of whether the juvenile case is there due to waiver, transfer, or exclusion. The reverse waiver provision is an attempt to provide some balance to the broad discretion given to prosecutors under "direct file" statutes. In considering a juvenile's petition for juvenile court jurisdiction, the criminal court must consider the same criteria that are used by juvenile courts in transferring juveniles to criminal court (Griffin et al., 1998, 10).

SOURCE: © Reuters/Corbis.

Photo 9.1   Lee Malvo leaves court following his transfer from juvenile court and conviction as an adult for sniper killings in the Washington, D.C., area.

"Once an Adult, Always an Adult"

Laws have been passed in 31 states that apply to juveniles who have been prosecuted and convicted as adults and are subsequently accused of new offenses. Most of the states with "once an adult, always an adult" provisions require criminal prosecution for all subsequent offenses committed by the juvenile (Griffin et al., 1998, p. 10). Others exclude or require waiver of juveniles of a certain age or for sufficiently serious subsequent offenses.

The Law, Science, and Juvenile Transfer

A basic principle underlying the separate system of justice for juveniles is that they are different from adults. This principle is not disputed for most juvenile offenses and offenders. The difference between adult and juvenile offenders becomes blurred in cases of older juveniles who commit serious crimes (Zimring, 1998). Regardless of the age of the offender, however, a fundamental legal premise in the justice system requires that a crime must include both an act and an intent to commit the act (or the *actus reus* and *mens rea*). The offender must be shown to have caused harm and be culpable for the offense. The principle of fundamental fairness was demonstrated in a recent U.S. Supreme Court ruling that banned the execution of mentally retarded persons who had committed murder. In support of the reduced culpability of mental retarded defendants, the Court held that

> [They] frequently know the difference between right and wrong and are competent to stand trial. Because of their impairments, however, by definition they have diminished capacities to understand and process mistakes and learn from experience, to engage in logical reasoning, to control impulses, and to understand the reactions of others. . . . Their deficiencies do not warrant an exemption from criminal sanctions, but they do diminish their personal culpability. *Atkins v. Virginia* [536 U.S. 304, 318(2002)]

The Court's reasoning in relation to the mentally retarded is similar to reasons given for the reduced culpability of young people. All Western nations, including the United States, have separate systems of justice for juveniles based on the understanding that juveniles are less mature than adults, and therefore are less culpable (Zimring, 2000).

Research findings in developmental psychology show that there is ample evidence and support for the reduced culpability of juveniles based on their lower level of maturity. Youth deserve to be treated as less culpable for a number of reasons (see Zimring, 1998, 2000; Feld, 1999a, pp. 306–313; Bishop, 2004, pp. 635–636): (1) the lower cognitive development of youth means they do not process information and consider alternatives as well as adults; (2) adolescent judgment and emotional and social maturity are not as well developed as in adults; (3) youth are less aware of risks, and are more likely to take risks that may harm themselves and others; (4) youth have a different perspective on time than adults, and think more in terms of short-term rather than long-term consequences; (5) juveniles are more vulnerable to peer pressure than adults; (6) youth make poorer judgments because they have less experience in decision making; and (7) recent research in neuroscience indicates that portions of the brain responsible for impulse control and decision making are underdeveloped compared to adults.

The American Bar Association (ABA) (2004) has recognized the reduced culpability of youth based on differences in brain development between adults and juveniles. Based on neuroscientific studies of brain development of adolescents, the ABA supports the assertion that adolescents are less morally culpable for their actions than competent adults, and are more capable of change and rehabilitation. The ideal of not holding violent juveniles accountable and blameworthy the same as adults is difficult for many to accept. This is especially true for juveniles who are physically as big and strong as adults. Appearance and physical size may be deceiving, however. The appearance of physical maturity does not mean an adolescent has the same reasoning capacity as an adult. Research reported by the ABA (2004) indicates that because of slower development of the parts of the brain that support clear reasoning and decision making, youth often rely on emotional parts of the brain. Another misconception is that commission of a serious crime is a sign of maturity. Some children and adolescents do tragically commit serious crimes and cause serious harm. Murder and violent crimes are not strictly "adult" activities, however, and it is illogical to reason that a youth who kills is more mature than a youth who steals (Bishop, 2004). It is understandable that the crime of murder triggers a desire for punishment, retribution, and vengeance. It is no more appropriate to hold an adolescent accountable the same as an adult than it is to hold a mentally retarded offender accountable the same as a person of normal, average intelligence. The fact that adolescents are less mature than adults does not excuse them from punishment for violent crimes. It does, however, reduce their culpability and therefore the level of punishment. For this reason it is important to have a fair and just process of determining through a hearing whether a juvenile offender is "amenable to treatment" in the juvenile system, or may be held accountable for a crime the same as an adult. The American Bar Association (2004) reminds us that the concept of adolescents being less mature and less culpable is not new. We refer to those under 18 as "minors" and "juveniles" for a reason: They are less than adult.

POLICY AND PRACTICE 9.1	RESEARCH ON THE EFFECTS ON TRANSFERRING JUVENILE OFFENDERS TO CRIMINAL COURT

Reasons for Transfer Laws

- Many lawmakers believe that juveniles commit crimes because the juvenile court consequences and punishments are too lenient.
- The increase in transfer laws—for younger juveniles and for a wider range of offenses—is based on the assumption that more punitive adult criminal sanctions will act as a deterrent to juvenile crime.

Increase in Transfer Laws

- In 1979, 14 states had automatic transfer laws to try certain juvenile offenders as adults.
- In 1995, 21 states had automatic transfer laws for juvenile offenders.
- In 2003, 31 states had automatic transfer laws for juvenile offenders.
- The age at which juveniles could be tried as adults has been lowered to 15 or 16 years of age in 13 states.
- The number of delinquency cases waived to criminal court increased from 7,200 in 1985 to 13,000 in 1994, then decreased to 8,800 in 1999 and to 6,900 in 2005.

(Continued)

(Continued)

- Transferred juveniles convicted of violent offenses typically receive longer sentences than those sentenced in the juvenile court for similar crimes.
- On the other hand, many youth incarcerated in adult facilities serve no longer than the maximum time they would have served in a juvenile facility.
- Seventy-eight percent of transferred juveniles were released from prison before age 21; 95% were released before age 25; the average time served on their criminal court sentence was 2 years, 8 months (Redding, 2008; Snyder & Sickmund, 2006).

General Deterrence: Do Transfer Laws Prevent Juvenile Crime?

- A transfer law in Idaho did *not* result in a *decrease,* but had the opposite effect: a 13% increase in arrest rates after the new law; while juvenile arrest rates in Montana and Wyoming (where new transfer laws were not passed) decreased (Jensen & Metsger, 1994).
- An automatic transfer law in New York State had *no effect* on violent juvenile crime (Singer & McDowall, 1988).
- A study of prosecutorial transfer laws in 14 states found that transfer laws had *no general deterrent effect* (Steiner & Wright, 2006).
- In sum, research evidence suggests that transfer laws have little or no general deterrent effect in preventing serious juvenile crime (Redding, 2008).

Specific Deterrence: Do Transferred Juveniles Have Lower Recidivism Rates?

- A study comparing offenders charged in New Jersey juvenile courts with juvenile offenders tried under New York's automatic transfer law found that more youth (91%) tried for robbery in criminal court than those tried for robbery in juvenile court (73%) were rearrested; and they were rearrested sooner and more often (Fagan, 1996), suggesting that criminal court processing alone produces a higher recidivism rate.
- A study comparing juvenile offenders transferred to criminal court in Florida with a matched sample of juvenile offenders retained in juvenile court found that the rearrest rates were higher among the transferred juveniles; and the average time to reoffending was shorter (Bishop, Frazier, Lanza-Kaduce, & Winner, 1996).
- A Pennsylvania study found that youth who were transferred to criminal court were twice as likely to be rearrested and were rearrested more quickly (and often for more serious offenses) than youth who were retained in juvenile court (Myers, 2003b).
- A second Florida study found that transferred juvenile offenders were significantly more likely to reoffend. Overall, 49% of transferred offenders compared with 35% of retained offenders were more likely to reoffend; and results were similar for violent offenders, drug offenders, and property offenders (Lanza-Kaduce, Lane, Bishop, & Frazier, 2005).

- In sum, six large-scale studies (in Florida, New Jersey, New York, Minnesota, and Pennsylvania) on the specific deterrent effects of transfer found higher recidivism rates among juvenile offenders who had been transferred to criminal court compared with those retained in the juvenile system (Redding, 2008).

SOURCE: Singer & McDowall, 1988; Jensen & Metsger, 1994; Bishop et al., 1996; Fagan, 1996; Myers, 2003a; Lanza-Kaduce et al., 2005; Snyder & Sickmund, 2006; Steiner & Wright, 2006; Redding, 2008.

Discussion Questions

1. Are the findings on the lack of deterrent effects of transfer laws surprising to you? What do the results suggest about whether juveniles consider tougher laws, or whether they even believe they may get caught and transferred to criminal court?

2. Do you believe that most state lawmakers are aware of these research findings? Offer ideas of how lawmakers and the public might be informed of these and accept the policy of trying juveniles in juvenile court (without being perceived as "soft" on juvenile crime).

Research on the Effects of Transfer

The laws designed to send more juvenile offenders to criminal court and punish them as adult offenders are based on lawmakers' belief that serious juvenile crime is increasing and the reason for the perceived increase is due to a lenient and ineffective juvenile justice system. Violent juvenile crime has in fact been dropping for years (Snyder & Sickmund, 2006); and the assumption of a lenient, ineffective system is disputed by numerous juvenile justice experts (Bernard, 1992; Zimring, 1998; Feld, 1999a). The stated purposes of most juvenile waiver and transfer laws nevertheless focus on public safety, reduction of serious crimes by juveniles, and punishing young offenders who are believed to be not amenable to treatment in the juvenile justice system. Rising juvenile crime rates in the 1970s led many to assume that the juvenile system had failed, that it was too lenient and was ineffective in deterring juvenile crime. It is generally taken for granted by politicians and the public that getting tougher with harsher punishment is an effective response to crime. Media accounts of violent juvenile offenders tend to portray them as incorrigible young criminals who view juvenile laws, the court, and corrections system as "soft" on crime. Based on limited empirical evidence of what works in juvenile justice, state legislatures have revised juvenile codes with an emphasis on offender accountability, punishment, and public safety. Most of the states have revised their juvenile codes to make it easier to transfer young offenders to the criminal courts (Feld, 1995; Torbet et al., 1996). Does the transfer of juveniles to criminal court make a difference? Several studies have examined the types of cases that have been waived to criminal court, and the question of whether transfers do in fact make a difference. Mears (2003) examined the leading intended and unintended effects of waiver and noted some critical research gaps that must be addressed if we are to develop a balanced and empirically informed assessment of the effectiveness of waiver.

Types of Juvenile Cases Transferred

There is evidence that many juveniles waived to adult court are *not* the most dangerous or serious offenders. Bortner (1986) examined 214 remanded juveniles and found that they were not more dangerous or intractable than nonremanded juveniles. Her analysis suggested that their remand did not enhance public safety, and she concluded that political and organizational factors accounted for the increased number of remands. There is evidence that criminal courts have given less severe sentences to waived juveniles than if those young offenders had been tried in juvenile court. Donna Hamparian and her associates (1982) found that most of the juveniles transferred to adult court in 1978 received sentences of fines, probation, or other alternatives to incarceration; and the small number who were incarcerated received sentences of one year or less. Donna Bishop and her associates (Bishop, Frazier, & Henretta, 1989) examined the practice of prosecutorial waiver in Florida and found that few of the juveniles transferred were dangerous or repeat offenders for whom the waiver would be justified. They found that a lack of statutory guidelines and the ease of prosecutorial waiver without judicial oversight accounted for many inappropriate cases being transferred to criminal court (Bishop et al., 1989, p. 198).

Crime Reduction Through Transfer

Research on the effects of the harsher juvenile code revisions indicates that the effects have not been in the intended direction. Bishop and her associates (1996) compared matched samples of juveniles, some of whom were transferred and others who were not transferred, and found that transfer actually resulted in increased short-term recidivism rates. Despite being incarcerated for longer periods of time, the transferred youths committed more offenses. Even when controlling for time at risk, the rate of reoffending in the transfer group was significantly higher; and they were more likely to commit a subsequent felony offense. More of the matched sample of nontransferred youths improved their behavior over time, leading the authors to suggest that the stigmatizing effect of criminal court conviction and adult sentencing contributes to greater recidivism rather than reducing criminal behavior. The authors concluded that juvenile transfer did not have a deterrent effect, and removal from the streets through incapacitation did not result in improved public safety (Bishop et al., 1996).

Other research has indicated that juveniles waived to criminal court have received more severe sentences than if they had been retained in juvenile court, but there are significant disparities in the sentences for property and personal offenses, and between adult and juvenile courts (Rudman, Hartstone, Fagan, & Moore, 1986; Podkopacz & Feld, 1996). In a study of criminal court data from the Pennsylvania Commission on Sentencing, Kurlychek and Johnson (2004) found that juvenile offenders transferred to adult court were sentenced more severely than their young adult counterparts. Their juvenile status did not act as a mitigating factor, but rather seemed to aggravate the sentence. Because prosecutorial decisions to transfer do not include an assessment of maturity or culpability, one might expect that criminal courts would at least take those factors into account when sentencing young offenders (Bishop, 2004). Contrary to youthfulness being a mitigating factor, the transferred juveniles received what the authors referred to as a "violent juvenile penalty" (p. 506). The findings contrast sharply with those of a 1978 survey of transferred juveniles receiving lighter sentences than adults (Hamparian et al., 1982). The study by Kurlychek and Johnson did not account for different types of transfer (judicial waiver, exclusion, or prosecutor direct file), so further research is needed to examine whether the mode of transfer makes a difference. The finding of transferred juveniles being sentenced more severely in criminal court than similar adult offenders raises serious questions of the effects of transfer policies, especially considering that transferred juveniles often have higher recidivism rates than those retained in the juvenile system (see Bishop et al., 1996).

Racial Disparity in Transfer

Juvenile transfer policies have disproportionately affected black youth. Juvenile arrests disproportionately involve minorities. Black youth accounted for 16% of the juvenile population in 2003, but were involved in a disproportionate number of juvenile arrests for robbery (63%), murder (48%), auto theft (40%), and aggravated assault (38%) in 2003 (Snyder & Sickmund, 2006, p. 125). Black youth are transferred to criminal court more than white youth. From 1985 to 2002, the likelihood of waiver was greater for black youth than for white youth regardless of offense category. Racial differences in case waivers were greatest for person offenses and especially for drug offenses, for which nearly twice as many black youths were waived to criminal court than were white youth (1.2% and 0.7%, respectively; Snyder & Sickmund, 2006, p. 187).

Despite the fact that white youth account for more than half of the violent crime arrests, violent crime has become associated more with black youth. Feld (2003) maintains that media reports and conservative political reactions have resulted in associating crime with racial minorities, specifically young black males. Media reports tend to focus on crimes that are considered more "newsworthy," resulting in disproportionate coverage of urban street crime. The news media exaggerate the true extent of violent crime, present a distorted picture of criminals (Surette, 1998); and news media coverage overreports and overemphasizes the role of minority youth in violent crime (Dorfman & Schiraldi, 2001). Crime policies are a central political agenda, and the public and political perceptions of race and youth crime were inevitably part of the incentive behind the "get-tough" reforms of juvenile statutes (Zimring, 1998). Feld (2003) has argued that media coverage, racial factors, and a conservative political agenda played a major role in punitive changes in juvenile justice laws and practices that have had a disproportionate impact on racial minorities.

Transfer: Solid Policy or Symbolic?

Research evidence suggests that judicial waiver may have little more than symbolic value (Kupchik, 2004), relaying a message to the public that something is being done about violent juvenile crime, and "creating sentencing systems that bark much louder than they bite" (Zimring, 2005, p. 148). Legislative reforms that include "get-tough" provisions for juvenile offenders seem to have been driven more by political rhetoric than sound research. Slogans such as "If you're old enough to do the crime, you're old enough to do the time" resonate strongly with voters. Yet juvenile waiver and transfer may not accomplish much in terms of reducing the growing number of serious and violent juvenile offenders. They do remove more serious offenders from the juvenile system, but there are questions whether the adult system is equipped to handle a growing number of youthful offenders. Rudman and his associates (1986) believe that waiver creates new problems for adult corrections, and it may be counterproductive to send juvenile offenders for several years of punishment with adult offenders rather than a few years of treatment in the juvenile system. According to Rudman et al., the effectiveness of juvenile justice system responses to violent youth will be improved not by removing them but rather by developing appropriate dispositional alternatives for the juvenile court. These might include increasing the age for juvenile corrections jurisdiction and improving the quality of services in secure juvenile corrections institutions. These alternatives would have more immediate impact on violent juvenile crime than simply transferring the problem to already overburdened criminal courts and correctional facilities. Zimring (1998) contends that transfer of juvenile homicide cases to criminal court simply relocates these difficult problems. It does not solve them.

Lessons Learned

Torbet, Griffin, Hurst, and MacKenzie (2000) have summarized a number of lessons learned based on case studies and research on juvenile transfer and waiver practices. Those lessons are highlighted below. Readers are encouraged to review the government document by Torbet et al. (2000), which is available online and listed in the Web Resources at the end of this chapter. More research is needed regarding the effects of juvenile transfer. The research findings currently available are important for lawmakers and justice officials who are considering additional sentencing reforms or applying those currently on the books.

- A disconnect exists between the legislative intent and the actual implementation of new laws
- Blended sentencing laws encourage plea bargaining
- Blended sentencing provisions expand judicial and prosecutorial discretion
- Local application of new sentencing laws varies widely
- New sentencing laws have a disproportionate impact on minorities
- Expanded sentencing laws require new resources and interventions
- More data collection and systematic follow-up are needed to judge the impact of reforms (see Torbet et al., 2000, pp. 43–45)

The experiences, observations, and personal assessments of youths who have been transferred can also reveal much about the consequences and effectiveness of the policy. Jodi Lane and her associates (Lane, Lanza-Kaduce, Frazier, & Bishop, 2002) conducted a study in which they interviewed groups of juvenile offenders, half of whom had been transferred to the adult system and half of whom were retained in the juvenile system. The study focused on the youths' assessments of the impact of their correctional experience in relation to subsequent offending, and whether it had a beneficial or negative impact on them. They found that youths believe they experienced the best attitudinal and behavioral change in intensive treatment programs within the juvenile system. The findings indicate that juvenile treatment programs are better than adult incarceration for changing juvenile offenders, even for serious offenders. Change in attitudes of even serious juvenile offenders is a result of skills gained while in juvenile correctional programs; whereas any changes that occur in adult institutions are a result of something lost, such as safety, self-esteem, and hope. Lane and her associates (2002) hypothesize that juvenile programs reduce recidivism and reduce the likelihood of reentry into the justice system for those who do reoffend.

POLICY AND PRACTICE 9.2 WHY DO TRANSFER LAWS NOT WORK?

Research findings from numerous studies conclude that juvenile transfer laws do not work to deter juveniles from committing crimes, and that juveniles who are transferred to criminal court and committed to adult prisons have higher recidivism rates than juveniles who are tried in juvenile court and committed to juvenile correctional facilities.

Experts have identified several reasons for this negative effect of juvenile transfer policies:

- Many juvenile offenders are not aware that they can be tried as adults.
- Most juvenile offenders do not believe that they will be caught, transferred to criminal court, and face serious punishment.
- Juvenile offenders in general tend to underestimate the risk of arrest.
- Juveniles' immaturity and tendency to focus on the short-term benefits of offending mean that the threat of tougher punishment will have little deterrent effect on them.

Experts have also identified reasons why juveniles tried and punished as adults have higher recidivism rates than juveniles adjudicated in juvenile court:

- Criminal court processing may cause some juveniles to reoffend out of defiance and a sense of injustice.
- Processing juveniles as criminals has a stigmatizing effect, creating a criminal self-concept in some juveniles.
- Adolescents with conduct disorders have a sense of having been dealt with unfairly by authority figures.
- Interviews with transferred juveniles indicate a strong sense of injustice about being tried as adults.
- Youth in juvenile facilities had more treatment, counseling, and correctional services; gained understanding of their problems; learned the consequences of lawbreaking; and were more prepared for release and community reintegration.

(Continued)

(Continued)

- Juveniles in adult prisons learned criminal behavior from the inmates; feared being assaulted and had to prove how tough they were; experienced or witnessed assaults from inmates; and had few if any positive correctional services.
- The brutalizing and criminogenic effects of adult prisons reduced the likelihood that the prison experience would deter juveniles from committing crimes in the future.

SOURCE: Bazemore & Umbreit, 1995; Bishop & Frazier, 2000; Myers, 2003a; Redding & Fuller, 2004; Redding, 2008.

Discussion Questions

1. Laws that are passed are intended to change the behavior of law violators and protect the public. What must occur before laws will have an effect on human behavior?

2. Authority figures often hear young people say, "I know my rights!" Do you believe that most youth *do* know their rights? Do they know their *responsibilities* under the law?

3. Explain some reasons why tougher laws and punishments may not affect the behavior of many juveniles who *do know* about the laws and threats of punishment.

4. Suggest how "teaching by example" may explain why juvenile corrections facilities and programs have a more positive effect on delinquents than adult prisons have.

Future Trends in Juvenile Transfer

There is some evidence that juvenile transfers may be waning in popularity. The number of juvenile transfers in the United States has declined steadily in the past decade, as noted in the introduction to this chapter and in Table 9.1 (Sickmund, Sladky, & Kang, 2008; see also Snyder & Sickmund, 2006). Donna Bishop (2004) cited several reasons for the reduction in juvenile transfers to criminal court: (a) there is less public support for simplistic, punitive responses to youth crime, particularly as we become aware of the monetary costs and ineffectiveness of transfers; (b) some state legislatures have actually reduced the number of crimes that are subject to prosecutorial transfer decisions; and (c) professionals in the juvenile justice system have responded to evaluation research and begun to develop new and more effective juvenile corrections programs and intervention strategies (Bishop, 2004, p. 641). Exclusion of some juvenile offenders from juvenile court will persist in most jurisdictions, however. There are strengths and weaknesses to the arguments for exclusion of juvenile offenders from juvenile court jurisdiction; exclusion policies should be selectively applied in cases of appropriate serious and chronic juvenile offenders (Sanborn, 2003). As with all justice policies and practices, juvenile transfer is an issue that demands further evaluative research to determine its appropriateness for responding to juvenile crime. It is important for legislators to consider policies for responding to juvenile crime that are most effective in producing long-term benefits for the protection of the community and change for juvenile offenders.

SUMMARY

- Transferring juveniles to criminal court is not a new practice. Juvenile courts have always had the authority to waive jurisdiction and transfer cases to criminal court.
- Three different transfer processes include judicial waiver, statutory exclusion, and concurrent jurisdiction (also called direct file or prosecutorial discretion).
- Several states have developed blended sentencing reforms as alternatives to waiver and transfer of juveniles. Extended juvenile jurisdiction (EJJ) is an example of blended sentencing.
- Legal principles and scientific research on mental maturity and culpability of youth raise questions regarding the fundamental fairness of processing juvenile offenders the same as adult offenders, regardless of the offense.
- Research on the effects of juvenile transfer indicate that it may not reduce serious juvenile crime but may in fact have the opposite effect; that its application varies widely across jurisdictions; that it has a disproportionate effect on minorities; and that it places additional demands on the adult corrections system, requiring additional resources and interventions.

KEY TERMS

Waiver	Concurrent jurisdiction
Transfer	Prosecutorial waiver
Certification	Remand
Legislative exclusion	Blended sentencing
Direct file	Extended juvenile jurisdiction

DISCUSSION QUESTIONS

1. Based on the U.S. Supreme Court ruling in *Kent v. United States,* what do you believe is the most appropriate, legally defensible method of transfer of juveniles to criminal court? Explain your reason and legal arguments.

2. Explain how "blended sentencing" is a blend between juvenile and criminal court and what advantages it seems to have over other transfer processes.

3. Based on legal principles and scientific evidence of youths' level of maturity and understanding, do you believe it is legally justifiable to hold juveniles accountable for crimes in the same way as adults? Explain your answer.

4. What research findings on the effects of transfer do you believe offer the strongest support for or against increased use of transfer for juvenile offenders?

WEB RESOURCES

The following Web sites provide information on waiver and transfer of juveniles:

For a listing of state transfer provisions, please see http://www.ncjrs.gov/html/ojjdp/195420/page4.html

National Overview: Trying Juveniles as Adults: http://www.ncjj.org/stateprofiles/overviews/overviewtransfer.asp

For current statistics on waived cases, see *Easy Access to Juvenile Court Statistics: 1985–2005* (National Center for Juvenile Justice): http://ojjdp.ncjrs.gov/ojstatbb/ezajcs/

10

The Juvenile Court Process

The juvenile court process differs from the adult criminal court in several respects. We summarized the distinguishing characteristics of the two court systems in Chapter 7, and we reviewed the history and development of the juvenile court and the juvenile justice system in Chapter 2. You will recall that the juvenile court in America was developed in the 19th century through the efforts of "child savers" and child advocates who recognized that children must be tried in separate courts with a different legal process than that for adult criminal offenders. The juvenile court was based upon the legal doctrines of *parens patriae* ("parent of the country") and *in loco parentis* ("in place of the parent"). The principle of *parens patriae* gives the court the authority over juveniles in need of guidance and protection; the state may then act *in loco parentis* (in place of the parent) to provide guidance and make decisions concerning the best interests of the child and to provide services in assistance to needy and wayward children who were deemed to be in need of care and supervision. It is important to have an understanding of the origins of the court and the foundations upon which it is based as we compare recent developments and trends in the juvenile court process. This chapter examines the changes in the juvenile court process and the developments that have brought juvenile offenders many of the same due process rights as adults in criminal court; the adjudication process; dispositional alternatives available to the juvenile court; and recent changes and trends toward a more punitive approach with juvenile offenders that is similar to policies and punishment in criminal court.

Juvenile Court Cases: Numbers and Trends

In 2005, U.S. juvenile courts processed an estimated 1,697,900 delinquency cases that involved juveniles charged with criminal law violations (Puzzanchera & Sickmund, 2008). The delinquency court cases by offense types in 2005 are summarized in Table 10.1. The number of delinquency cases handled by juvenile courts increased 46% since 1985; but between 1996 and 2005 the nation's juvenile court delinquency caseload decreased 8%, and after that has remained fairly stable with only 1% increases. The number of person offense cases increased dramatically (133%) since 1985, and saw modest increases (8% and 7%) since 1996 and 2001, respectively. Most property offense cases have decreased since 1985; drug law violation cases increased; and public order offense cases increased. The overall increases in delinquency cases have made a significant impact on the juvenile court workload in the past several decades. In 1960, about 1,100 delinquency cases were processed daily in the United States, compared with 4,700 delinquency cases per day in 2005. We have seen an increase of 46% more cases processed by juvenile courts between 1985 and 2005 (Puzzanchera & Sickmund, 2008, pp. 6–7).

Gender

The vast majority of the delinquency cases handled by juvenile courts continued to involve males, but the female proportion of cases increased from 20% in 1985 to 27% in 2005. Females accounted for 30% (128,850) of person offense cases, 27% (161,600) of property offenses cases, 20% (39,100) of drug offense cases, and 28% (132,800) of public order offense cases (Sickmund, Sladky, & Kang, 2008). The rate of growth in female delinquency court cases between 1985 and 2005 was greater than that for males in every offense category, averaging 4% increase each year compared with a 1% rate of growth for males (Puzzanchera and Sickmund, 2008, p. 12).

Age

A total of 54% of the delinquency cases processed in 2005 involved a juvenile younger than 16 at referral. In 2005, juveniles younger than 16 were responsible for 64% (274,900) of person offense cases, 52% (311,300) of property offense cases, 42% (82,000) of drug law violation cases, and 53% (251,400) of public order offense cases (Sickmund et al., 2008).

Race

In 2005, approximately 78% of the juvenile population in the United States was white and 16% was black. (Juveniles of Hispanic ethnicity are usually included in the

| Table 10.1 | Juvenile Court Cases by Offense Type, 2005* |

Most Serious Offense	Number of Cases	Percentage Change			
		20 Year 1985–2005	10 Year 1996–2005	5 year 2001–2005	1 Year 2004–2005
Total delinquency	1,697,900	46	−8	1	1
Total person offenses	429,500	133	8	7	3
Criminal homicide	1,400	11	−45	−10	2
Forcible rape	4,400	22	−15	−7	0
Robbery	26,000	2	−32	19	21
Aggravated assault	49,900	48	−26	3	6
Simple assault	298,600	193	22	6	2
Other violent sex offense	17,700	118	41	24	6
Other person offense	31,600	192	7	6	−2
Total property offenses	598,600	−15	−33	−7	−3
Burglary	97,600	−32	−35	−8	−1
Larceny–theft	265,800	−20	−37	−9	−6
Motor vehicle theft	32,900	−16	−38	−13	−6
Arson	8,500	20	−10	−8	−5
Vandalism	100,900	18	−17	7	4
Trespassing	52,000	−4	−24	0	0
Stolen property offense	19,900	−28	−42	−17	1
Other property offense	20,900	17	−32	−15	2
Drug law violations	195,300	153	8	−4	0
Public order offenses	474,400	146	28	7	3
Obstruction of justice	222,400	238	34	2	3
Disorderly conduct	129,600	191	43	25	4
Weapons offense	43,600	117	−3	19	5
Liquor law violations	24,600	28	59	0	−4
Nonviolent sex offenses	13,700	8	24	−6	−2
Other public order offenses	40,400	31	−5	−11	1

SOURCE: Adapted from Puzzanchera & Sickmund (2008). *Juvenile court statistics 2005*. Pittsburgh, PA: National Center for Juvenile Justice.

*Estimated numbers and percentages. Details may not add to totals because of rounding. Percentage-change calculations are based on unrounded numbers.

white racial category.) White juveniles were involved in 64% of the delinquency cases that juvenile courts processed, compared with 33% of court cases involving black juveniles. White juveniles were involved in 57% (244,800) of person offense cases, 67% (401,100) of property offense cases, 74% (144,500) of drug law violation cases, and 63% (298,900) of public order offense cases. Black juveniles were involved in 41% (176,100) of person offense cases, 29% (173,600) of property offense cases, 24% (46,900) of drug law violation cases, and 34% (161,300) of public order offense cases (Sickmund et al., 2008). The proportion of black youth in the total number of juvenile court cases increased slightly from 25% in 1985 to 33% in 2005. There was no significant change in person offenses, but the increase from 1985 to 2005 for property offense cases was up from 23% to 29%; from 19% to 24% for drug cases; and from 21% to 34% for public order cases (Sickmund et al., 2008). In 2005, property offense case rates were higher for black juveniles than those for youth of all other race categories. Racial disparity in age-specific drug offenses case rates increased after age 13. By age 17, the black drug offense case rate was twice the white rate, more than twice the rate of American Indian youth, and more than eight times the rate of Asian youth. The public order offense case rate for black juveniles was two to three times the rate for white and American Indian youth, in all age groups (Puzzanchera & Sickmund, 2008, p. 21).

Juvenile Court Officials and Their Roles

The Juvenile Court Judge

The juvenile court was originally developed as an informal "quasi-judicial" process that incorporated more civil procedures than criminal court procedures. The judge was viewed as a "father figure" who presumably acted in "the best interests of the child." The first juvenile courts were private hearings not open to the public, informal, and non-adversarial. Juvenile court judges were to be kindly, protective father figures who were concerned with the child's best interests. Julian W. Mack (1909), one of the nation's first juvenile court judges, emphasized the juvenile court judge's significant role in carrying out the court's benevolent, *parens patriae* philosophy. Ted Rubin, a former juvenile court judge, has noted that the ideal juvenile court judge would have

> a special interest in the legal and social problems of children and families, a special sensitivity toward minority groups, an appreciation of different life styles, an absence of rigid moral standards, a basic knowledge of the social sciences and the life experiences that confront court clients in their day to day living, and an ability to listen and to communicate with children and families. (Rubin, 1985, p. 366)

In reality, few juvenile court judges have all these qualities, but there is general agreement that judges should reflect the different purposes of juvenile court and the differences between juvenile and adult offenders.

SOURCE: © Comstock Select/Corbis.

Photo 10.1   Prosecuting and defense attorneys consult with the judge during a hearing in process.

Juvenile court judges were not originally required to have a law degree. After the U.S. Supreme Court required due process procedures during the 1960s and 1970s, the deficiencies of nonlawyer judges became readily apparent. Court rulings following the legal challenges in *Kent* and *Gault* brought an emphasis on legal formality and a more adversarial process. The changes in the adjudication process made it clear that judges must possess some legal training in order to perform their duties adequately. The National Advisory Commission on Criminal Justice Standards and Goals (1976) acknowledged that juvenile courts had relied on quasi-judicial personnel (referred to variably as "referees, commissioners, or masters") to assume much of the workload of juvenile court judges such as detention hearings and hearings resulting in community supervision. The Advisory Commission recommended that all juvenile court proceedings involving detention, shelter care, waiver, arraignment, adjudicatory, and dispositional hearings should be heard only by a judge. The Commission also recommended several qualifications for family court judges, including: have an interest in the problems of children and families; be sensitive to their respective legal rights; awareness of the fields of psychiatry, psychology, and social work; be familiar with local minority groups and the influence of cultural values on family behavior and child rearing; take responsibility for leadership in developing services for children and families (p. 284).

POLICY AND PRACTICE 10.1 **THE JUVENILE COURT JUDGE'S ROLE**

Judge Emanuel Cassimatis of Pennsylvania offers his perspectives on the roles and responsibilities of juvenile court judges. These guidelines illustrate the high expectations and special commitment of judges in the juvenile court. To be most effective in their judicial role, Judge Cassimatis recommends that juvenile court judges:

- Bring the qualities of passion, commitment, and special skills in administering justice for juveniles.
- Serve as presiding judge over a variety of assigned delinquency cases requiring supervision, care, and rehabilitation.
- Oversee operations of the juvenile probation department and use his or her authority to ensure that the probation administrator has resources for hiring and training personnel, and has adequate office space and resources to maintain quality court services.
- Ensure that the prosecutors' and public defenders' offices are staffed with well-trained and prepared attorneys, and encourage a good working relationship with the court.
- Be influential as a community organizer to encourage participation of schools, the business community, churches, and service clubs in delinquency prevention programs.
- Work with the news media, including newspapers, radio, and television, to inform them and the public of the goals and principles of the juvenile justice system.
- Promote respect for and a positive experience of justice among those who appear in the court: the juvenile and family, victim, police, witnesses, probation officers, and attorneys.
- Articulate clearly the court's expectations of all those involved in the court process.
- Hold those involved in the court hearing accountable for accomplishing their specific assignments and responsibilities.
- Treat everyone with respect and courtesy, and insist that all involved do likewise.
- Treat each contact with the juvenile and family as an opportunity to enable the youth to meet the expected program goals of supervision, care, and rehabilitation.
- Promote the principles and practices of balanced and restorative justice, encouraging involvement of the victim and community members in the justice process.
- Strive to improve juvenile justice by participating in meetings and conferences of judges.
- Be informed on all new developments in the law and treatment programs and resources in juvenile justice. Help to create new programs and community resources.
- Create and maintain an aura of the majesty of the law that instills the respect of all those involved in the court process.

SOURCE: Cassimatis, E. (2008). The juvenile court judge. In *Pennsylvania juvenile delinquency benchbook* (pp. 1–7). Harrisburg, PA: Pennsylvania Juvenile Court Judges' Commission. Retrieved November 30, 2008, from http://www.jcjc.state.pa.us/jcjc/cwp/view.asp?a=3&Q=394446&jcjcNav=.

Discussion Questions

1. In what ways does Judge Cassimatis expect a juvenile court judge to be more than just a good "legal expert"?

2. Based on the summary points above, discuss how judges have power and authority to assert their influence in the courtroom to ensure that hearings are punctual and begin on time, with attorneys

prepared with the clients, and with results that are fair and just for the state and the juvenile defendant.

3. Discuss the points above where Judge Cassimatis suggests that judges have power and influence in the community to promote delinquency prevention. Can you suggest ways that an influential juvenile court judge in your county might motivate schools, businesses, and civic and church organizations to work for juvenile justice and delinquency prevention?

Juvenile Court Prosecutors

The original juvenile courts were informal and nonadversarial proceedings and therefore typically did not have prosecuting attorneys to present the evidence against the juvenile offender in court. Intake probation officers generally had the authority to determine whether to file a petition for delinquency. Police officers often performed the role equivalent to a prosecutor, and some police departments had court officers who were assigned the role of presenting the charges and supporting evidence in the informal hearing process. The U.S. Supreme Court cases of *Kent* and *Gault* in the 1960s brought more formality to the juvenile court process, as the Court affirmed that a juvenile has the right to be represented by an attorney. Juvenile courts became more formal and adversarial in most jurisdictions after the demand for more due process rights, so defense counsel became a more common presence in juvenile court hearings. With the presence of defense counsel and a more formal hearing process came the recognition of the need to have prosecuting attorneys to represent the state in presenting evidence to support the petition for delinquency. The National Advisory Commission on Criminal Justice Standards and Goals (1976) recommended that the prosecutor's office should have one or more attorneys devoted to representing the State in family court. Attorneys assigned to juvenile court from the prosecutor's office are generally the youngest attorneys with the least experience. Juvenile court prosecutors may then be reassigned to adult criminal court as they gain more experience. Juvenile court judges in fact tend to constrain overzealous prosecutors and defense attorneys from taking an adversarial approach similar to criminal courts.

Juvenile court prosecutors do have a great deal of discretionary authority in cases referred by the police department. We noted in Chapter 8, on court intake and detention, that the prosecutor has replaced the intake probation officer in deciding whether or not to file a petition for delinquency. The prosecutor, however, will consider the intake officer's recommendation of diversion or unofficial supervision for first-time offenders with no prior referrals who are involved in minor offenses. The decision whether or not to prosecute cases is determined by factors such as probable cause, the quality of evidence in the case, and due process issues. As we noted in the previous chapter on waiver and transfer, lawmakers have limited some prosecutorial discretion through legislative exclusion or mandatory waiver of cases involving serious and violent crimes.

Defense Attorneys

We have noted the relative absence of defense counsel for juveniles until the U.S. Supreme Court cases of *Kent* and *Gault*. Kent (charged with serious offenses of burglary and rape) was interrogated without being warned of his right to counsel and the right to remain silent; and he appeared before a juvenile court judge without legal representation. Justice Abe Fortas, inwriting for the Court majority, emphasized that the status of being a boy did not justify what amounted to a "kangaroo court" (383 U.S. 541, 1966). The Court ordered that juveniles, like adults, had the right to be represented by counsel. In contrast to Morris Kent, Gerald Gault was charged with making an obscene phone call, and following a hearing without an attorney or testimony from the complainant was sent to the Arizona Industrial School. The disposition greatly exceeded the maximum sentence he would have received as an adult: a fine of between $5 and $50, or a maximum of 2 months in jail. The Court majority in *Gault* held that juveniles must receive most of the same due process rights as adults, including notice of charges, right to counsel, and right to confront and cross-examine accusing witnesses (387 U.S. 41, 1967).

Defense counsel may be either private or court-appointed attorneys, or public defenders. Private attorneys may be retained personally by the family, or be court appointed and receive their fees from the county or state government. Public defenders are state employees who specialize in providing legal counsel for lower-income persons who qualify as indigents and are unable to afford a private attorney. Most jurisdictions have either a court-appoint system or public defender office. Because of their experience in representing clients in juvenile and criminal court, public defenders are generally the most qualified to represent juveniles. However, public defenders usually have large caseloads that limit the amount of time for conferring with and advising clients before court hearings. Private attorneys, whether retained or court-appointed, may specialize in areas of law other than criminal or juvenile court matters, and therefore may not provide the most qualified defense counsel.

Research on the right to counsel for juveniles has examined three important questions: first, whether most juveniles actually receive the assistance of legal counsel; second, whether juveniles can make a knowledgeable and informed waiver of their right to counsel; and third, whether representation by a defense attorney makes a difference in juvenile court. First, the *constitutional right to counsel* that the U.S. Supreme Court ordered for juveniles is *not* being applied in practice in many states and jurisdictions throughout the United States. Forty years after the U.S. Supreme Court cases of *Kent* and *Gault,* the presence of defense counsel in juvenile court varies greatly among states and among juvenile courts within the same state. In many states fewer than half of juveniles receive the assistance of legal counsel, and in Minnesota a majority of the juveniles in court appeared without counsel in the 1980s and 1990s (Feld, 1999a, p. 125). The American Bar Association (ABA; 1995) reported that many children throughout the United States go through the juvenile justice system without the benefit of legal counsel.

The second question relates to *waiver of the right to counsel.* A total of 25 jurisdictions require the presence of defense counsel for juveniles in certain circumstances, such as when institutional commitment is a possibility or there is an issue with the parents (Sanborn & Salerno, 2005, p. 319). Parental issues include cases of parental abuse, parents unwilling to retain counsel when they are financially able to do so, or similar adversarial relationships between parent and child. In such cases the judge is likely to appoint a guardian ad litem (an attorney appointed to advocate for and protect the child's best interests). Juveniles in nearly all (43) states are allowed to waive their right to counsel (Sanborn & Salerno, 2005, p. 320). The question is whether juveniles can make a knowledgeable, informed, and voluntary waiver of their right to counsel. Juvenile court procedures in several states work on the presumption that juveniles cannot intelligently waive their right to counsel. Judges are required to find by clear and convincing evidence after questioning the youth that the juvenile understands the right and the implications of waiver; that the waiver is made freely, voluntarily, and intelligently; and that the parent or guardian agrees with the juvenile's waiver (Sanborn & Salerno, 2005, p. 320). Research has documented juveniles' limited understanding of their due process rights (Feld, 1999a, p. 129). Grisso (1981) studied the legal and psychological competence of children and youth, and questioned whether many of them have the maturity, knowledge, and understanding to waive their rights. He found that many juveniles had a poor knowledge and understanding of their legal rights, did not clearly understand the role of an attorney and the meaning of legal counsel and advice, and few understood that they had a right to an attorney before and during interrogation or during court hearings (Grisso, 1981). Lawrence (1983) replicated a part of Grisso's research in a metropolitan juvenile court and found that fewer than 20% of juveniles had a good understanding of their legal rights and the role of an attorney in providing legal counsel. The findings raise serious questions whether juveniles can make an informed and intelligent waiver of their rights to legal counsel. In a study of the right to counsel in juvenile court, Feld (1989) questioned whether the typical advisory and judges' acceptance of juveniles' waiver of rights under the "totality of circumstances" is sufficient to ensure a valid waiver of counsel.

The third question regarding defense attorneys in juvenile court is *whether they make a difference.* We noted above that juveniles may receive legal counsel and representation by either a private attorney, court-appointed attorney, or a public defender. The quality of defense counsel is often compromised by attorneys' lack of training in juvenile law and the court process, by their lack of experience, or by the attorneys' caseload size and time available for each client. The American Bar Association (ABA; 1995) reported that many juveniles who were represented by counsel had attorneys who were untrained in the complexities of juvenile court matters and failed to provide competent legal representation. The ABA surveyed public defender offices, court-appointed attorneys, and children's law centers and found the quality of legal counsel to be low. The caseloads of public defenders and the conditions under which they worked often greatly compromised the quality of legal counsel and representation they could provide their juvenile clients in court (American Bar Association, 1995; see also Feld, 1999a, pp. 131–134). The failure of most jurisdictions to comply with juveniles' constitutional right to counsel has not gone unnoticed. The American Bar Association Center on Children and the Law (2004) reported on developments among states in providing public defenders for juveniles in court. The ABA is particularly concerned that ethnic and racial minorities, who tend to be disproportionately represented in juvenile court, are also the least likely to have defense counsel.

Research on whether defense counsel makes a difference in the court disposition is contrary to expectations. The presence of counsel has been found to be associated with more severe dispositions. In an analysis of court data in six states, Feld (1988) found that juveniles with defense counsel were more likely to receive placement out-side the home or secure confinement than juveniles without attorneys. Recent studies produced similar findings. Guevara, Spohn, and Herz (2004) found that the presence of a defense attorney (especially a private attorney) had a negative impact and resulted in more severe dispositions than for youth without an attorney. Youth with a private attorney were the least likely to have the charges dismissed and the most likely to be committed to a secure facility. Guevara and her associates concluded that the findings of their study "provide evidence that calls into question the basic and fundamental right to counsel in juvenile court" (p. 366).

Juvenile Probation Officer

We have discussed in Chapter 8 ("Juvenile Detention and Court Intake") the role of the intake probation officer in decisions regarding detention and alternatives to court referral, such as diversion or informal adjustment. Probation officers exercise what has been called a "quasi-judicial" role in the juvenile court process, including: (a) at court intake; (b) in recommending and enforcing conditions of probation; and (c) in reporting probation violations and initiating revocation procedures (Czajkoski, 1973). Juvenile probation officers, through their involvement with youth in the pre-judicial process, often supplement the role of attorneys in providing information about legal rights and the court process (Lawrence, 1983). Their role as court officers has not always been well respected by judges and attorneys in some metropolitan juris-dictions, leading to the claim that probation officers were mere "judicial civil servants" who lacked professional status in the court and whose role in the presentence decision was overrated (Blumberg, 1979). A study of probation officers in a southwestern state found that while they were not given equal status by judges and attorneys in the judi-cial process, the majority of probation officers did view themselves as professionals who provide important information in the sentencing process, and who had a positive and respected working relationship with judges and attorneys (Lawrence, 1984). Most research on probation officer roles has been on the supervision, surveillance, and treat-ment functions (Latessa & Allen, 2003); but the officers' role in the juvenile court process is important. Probation officers prepare a predisposition report (PDR, com-parable to a PSI, or presentence investigation) to assist the judge in the predisposition decision following adjudication of a juvenile (discussed below). The juvenile proba-tion officer may play a more critical role in the disposition than a probation officer in adult sentencing in criminal court, because of the treatment orientation of the juve-nile court (Sanborn & Salerno, 2005). Juvenile probation officers routinely spend from 1 to 3 hours or more in meetings with a juvenile and his or her parents prior to the court disposition hearing. They acquire a greater level of knowledge and insight on the juve-nile's background and problems related to the delinquent behavior than either the judge or attorneys involved in the case. Research on the roles of judges, prosecutors, defense attorneys, and probation officers, involving 100 court workers in urban, sub-urban, and rural courts, found that most probation officers conducted thorough investigations and presented comprehensive predisposition reports (Sanborn, 1996). Because the disposition decision relies on a multitude of factors ranging from prior legal history and severity of the crime, to individual and social "extralegal" factors including family background, attitude, school attendance, and behavior, Sanborn (1996) was unable to determine the actual factors that most influenced the disposition decision. It remains clear, however, that the probation officer's role in the courtroom is important; and the judge's disposition is influenced by the probation officer assigned to the case, his or her orientation, experience, and the extent to which the investigation and predisposition report is complete and thorough (Sanborn & Salerno, 2005, p. 358).

The Juvenile Court Process

The juvenile court process consists of two separate parts and therefore is often referred to as a bifurcated hearing. Juvenile court hearings are considered "quasi-civil" and not criminal proceedings. Juveniles found guilty are not convicted of a crime but are adjudicated delinquent. Since the U.S. Supreme Court decisions in *Gault* and *Winship,* juveniles are entitled to most of the same rights as adults in criminal court. Juvenile hearings are nevertheless more informal than criminal court and except for cases involving older, chronic, or serious juvenile offenders are generally closed to the public (see Sanborn & Salerno, 2005, p. 332).

Adjudication Hearing

The *adjudication hearing* is the fact-finding part of the court process, comparable to the conviction phase of a criminal court hearing. Before hearing any evidence the judge will first determine if the juvenile understands his or her rights; and juveniles not represented by an attorney will be questioned as to whether they understand that right and wish to waive the right to counsel. Procedures vary among jurisdictions, but the typical juvenile hearing is brief and quite perfunctory given the lengthy court dockets and limited time available. When the judge is satisfied that the juvenile understands the rights and is willing to waive a full hearing (presentation of evidence, testimony, confrontation and cross-examination of witnesses), the charges and petition for delinquency are generally read by the prosecuting attorney. The judge asks the juvenile if he or she understands the charges and is willing to plead guilty and accept the adjudication of delinquency. Adjudication is based solely on the present charge, *not* on previous arrests, charges, adjudication, or any extralegal information.

Disposition Hearing

Once the juvenile has been adjudicated delinquent, the next stage in the court process is the disposition, comparable to the sentencing phase in adult criminal court. Disposition decisions are based on offense severity, prior offense history, and individual and social factors. The court relies on a juvenile probation officer's *predisposition report* (PDR, comparable to the presentence investigation or PSI in criminal court sentencing hearings). The probation officer's report is based on interviews with the child and the parents; and may include information from school officials, social service agencies, and mental health professionals. The report may include information on the child's family history and quality of parental supervision; peer relationships; attendance, grades, and behavior in school; participation in school and community activities; and previous court or police involvement. In contested hearings or cases that may result in institutional commitment, the disposition hearing may include testimony and cross-examination of the probation officer and any other persons who have provided information in the report. Juveniles may have legal counsel and may challenge the facts and information presented in the predisposition report. The most important factors in the disposition hearing are the seriousness of the offense and the juvenile's prior record. The social background information contained in the probation officer's report and the dispositional options available to the court are also important factors in the court disposition.

Dispositional Alternatives

The *dispositional alternatives* available to juvenile courts vary considerably depending on the correctional services, resources, and residential placements that are available. The primary dispositional alternatives include the following:

1. *Dismissal.* Even though there may have been sufficient evidence to adjudicate a juvenile, a judge can dismiss the case if there is insufficient evidence that the child needs formal supervision by the court.

2. *Court Diversion Alternatives.* Many state juvenile codes include provisions that allow for suspension of the formal adjudication or disposition process, and the juvenile may be supervised under informal adjustment by a community agency (pre-adjudication) or by a probation officer (predispositional). The case may be terminated after 6 months or less of successful adjustment or, otherwise, may be returned to court for adjudication and disposition. Mediation is an alternative for resolving conflicts and disputes outside the courtroom. Mediation can take place as an alternative to trial and adjudication, or after a finding of guilt, to determine the disposition and often to establish restitution conditions. The Victim Offender Reconciliation Program is a form of mediation that operated in a number of courts (Coates, 1990). There is evidence that offenders involved in mediation are more likely to satisfactorily fulfill restitution conditions and are less likely to reoffend. Mediation and conflict resolution are examples of the "restorative justice" emphasis in juvenile justice (Bazemore & Umbreit, 1995).

3. *Probation.* The child may be released to the parents with orders to report to a probation officer and comply with specified conditions and rules of probation supervision. The juvenile may be ordered to pay restitution, complete community service restitution, or participate in counseling or treatment programs for specific identified needs. We will discuss this in more detail in Chapter 12.

4. *Placement in Community Residential Programs.* The court may order placement in a residential facility if there is evidence of inadequate parental supervision or poor parent–child relations. Such placements are short-term and in nonsecure residential programs. The court may also order short-term placement in a mental health facility or a residential drug and alcohol treatment facility.

5. *Institutional Commitment.* Juveniles who are considered a risk to public safety may be committed to more secure facilities, often called training schools or juvenile

correctional facilities. These are generally administered and operated by the state, and range from minimum-security schools with open campuses and cottage-like settings to medium- or maximum-security correctional facilities for juveniles or young adults. We will discuss this dispositional option in more detail in Chapter 11.

"Blended Sentencing"

In Chapter 9 we discussed waiver of juvenile court jurisdiction and transfer of juveniles to criminal court. The process of waiver and transfer is intended primarily for serious or chronic juvenile offenders for whom commitment to a juvenile facility does not provide adequate security or punishment. We noted the problems and consequences of waiver, particularly committing juvenile age offenders to adult correctional institutions. Several states have developed sentencing reforms that are alternatives to waiver and transfer of juvenile offenders to adult criminal court. The most prominent is referred to as "blended sentencing." Under these laws, serious juvenile offenders are sentenced to a juvenile or adult correctional facility after being adjudicated in juvenile court or convicted in criminal court (Torbet et al., 1996). The criteria for selection of cases appropriate for this option are generally the same as for transfer: offense seriousness, age, or a combination of both. Five models of blended sentencing have been developed in various states, and they differ primarily in whether the juvenile court or criminal court retains jurisdiction and responsibility for adjudicating the case (see Torbet et al., 1996, pp. 11–13). The most prominent example of blended sentencing is referred to as "extended juvenile jurisdiction" (EJJ) or "extended juvenile jurisdiction prosecution" (EJJP; Sanborn & Salerno, 2005, p. 295). An EJJ proceeding is generally used for a serious or violent juvenile offender who would meet the criteria for transfer to criminal court. In processing a case as EJJ, a youth is given a hearing before a juvenile court judge to determine the appropriateness of transferring the case to criminal court. The disposition in an EJJ case is a combined or "blended" sentence. The youth is given both a juvenile court disposition and an adult sentence, but the adult sentence is stayed or suspended and the juvenile court disposition is implemented. If the juvenile complies with the requirements of the juvenile court disposition, the adult sentence is dismissed. If the juvenile violates those terms (through a new arrest or violation of probation or institutional rules), the adult sentence may be imposed following a hearing to document the failure (Sanborn & Salerno, 2005).

The state of Minnesota added an extended jurisdiction juvenile (EJJ) option as part of sentencing reforms in 1994. The legislative intent was to give juveniles who have committed serious or repeat offenses one last chance at success in the juvenile system, with the threat of criminal sanctions "hanging over their heads" if they reoffend (Torbet, Griffin, H urst, & MacKenzie, 2000, p. xv). The Minnesota statute (Section 260B.130) provides for the adult criminal sentence to be stayed on the condition that the juvenile not violate the provisions of the disposition order and not commit a new offense. The juvenile disposition in most cases is commitment to a juvenile correctional facility or placement in a private residential treatment center, followed by a period of aftercare supervision until the young offender's 21st birthday.

If the juvenile violates the conditions of the stayed sentence, typically by committing a new offense, the court may revoke the stay and require that the offender be taken into custody. The juvenile is then given written notice of the reasons for the revocation of the stayed sentence, and may have a hearing with representation of legal counsel if the revocation is challenged. If there are sufficient reasons to revoke the stay of the suspended adult sentence, then the court treats the offender as an adult and the adult sentence is implemented, with no credit given for the time served in juvenile facility custody (Minn. Stat. 260B.130, subd. 5). The extended juvenile jurisdiction alternative has a number of advantages over immediate transfer to criminal court. First, the young offender is placed in a juvenile correctional facility rather than the "criminogenic" environment of adult correctional facilities. Second, the juvenile has the opportunity to receive educational and treatment services that are more available in juvenile corrections than in adult corrections. Third, the juvenile is given another chance to prove that he or she may be "amenable to treatment" in the juvenile system and not pose a threat to public safety.

Blended sentencing has been scrutinized by critics of juvenile sentencing reforms. Zimring (2005) has referred to the Minnesota blended sentencing statute as "one of the most dauntingly complicated in the history of criminal sentencing," and added that blended sentences may be "intentional efforts to design systems that sound much tougher just after conviction than they turn out to be in . . . time served in custody" (p. 148). Research on the results of "blended sentencing" or EJJ is limited. Initial results indicate that the policies do provide an alternative to juvenile transfer to criminal court, but may not significantly reduce the number of youthful offenders who are incarcerated. Podkopacz and Feld (2001) found that nearly half (48%) of youth who received an EJJ sentence were revoked, and a majority of the revocations were not the result of new criminal charges. Judges sent nearly as many youths to jail or prison following EJJ revocations as they did directly through certification proceedings. Additional research is needed to evaluate the effects of extended juvenile jurisdiction prosecution and whether the results are significantly different from sentences resulting from juvenile transfer.

Juvenile Court Trends and Reforms

The juvenile court has come under criticism from two sides: (1) those who want more control and punishment to hold juvenile offenders accountable; and (2) those who point to social problems that contribute to delinquency. Those who advocate for more punishment contend that the court is "soft on crime" when it adopts the traditional goal of treating juvenile offenders, rather than holding them accountable for their crimes. Crime control advocates believe that giving repeat offenders too many chances through diversion programs and community treatment alternatives sends a message to them and the community that we do not take juvenile crime seriously. Juvenile training schools, in their opinion, should be more like secure correctional facilities, and more juveniles should be confined for longer sentences in a more punitive setting. Those who argue for harsher punishment generally believe that crime is a function of individual choice and poor moral character, and the answer to crime reduction lies primarily in deterrence through tougher sentences (Garland, 2001).

Criminologists, on the other hand, view juvenile delinquency as a function of individual and social variables that place many juveniles at risk of deviant and delinquent behavior (Hirschi, 1969; Gottfredson & Hirschi, 1990). Crime is a function of social and economic factors and not simply a matter of rational choice. Therefore, hoping to deter delinquency through tougher laws and threats of harsher punishment the same way as criminal justice policy is aimed at adult offenders, is unlikely to be effective. Criminologists and juvenile justice advocates contend that delinquency prevention must address the social problems and lack of equal opportunities and resources for disadvantaged youth that place many children and youth at risk of involvement in gangs, drug use, and delinquency (Howell, 2003). Critics of the "get-tough" approach claim that tougher sentencing and transfers to criminal court often aggravate the problems; and institutional confinement in detention centers and training schools only serves to criminalize juveniles further (Garland, 2001). Judicial critics denounce the lack of procedural safeguards and uniformity in the informal juvenile court process, with many juveniles receiving more punitive sanctions than adults for minor offenses that would result in no more than a fine in adult court.

Practitioners in the juvenile justice system also express dissatisfaction with current juvenile court policies and disagree among themselves. Police and prosecutors want tougher sanctions for juvenile offenders and fewer "second chances" through diversion programs and community alternatives. Probation officers contend that a large group of juvenile offenders have special needs that can be met through treatment and supervision in the community. Given their knowledge of the social and family background of referred juveniles, probation officers are reluctant to take a punitive approach except as a last resort, after treatment alternatives have failed.

The juvenile court has traditionally given secondary importance to due process rights because the primary focus was on "the best interests of the child" and rehabilitation (Feld, 1999a). These concerns are best illustrated by U.S. Supreme Court decisions such as *Gault* and *Kent* in the 1960s (discussed in Chapter 7). Throughout the 1980s and 1990s more criticisms were leveled against the juvenile court. Judicial and legislative changes have transformed the juvenile court from what was originally intended as a social rehabilitation welfare agency into what Feld (1999a) has referred to as a "scaled-down, second-class criminal court for young people" (p. 286). The criticisms also underscore the reality that the juvenile court cannot be both a court of law and an agency for individual and social change. Probation officers, attorneys, and judges who see hundreds of young offenders pass through the courts each week readily acknowledge the numerous social problems that characterize the youth, none of which are their own fault. Most juvenile offenders and their families encounter lack of proper nutrition and healthcare, housing problems, lack of employment opportunities, and unequal access to quality schools. The sole reason juveniles appear before the court, however, is for the commission of a crime, so any compassion or mitigation of a disposition based on a youth's social disadvantages is secondary to his or her legal status as a young law violator (see Feld, 1999a, p. 295). The juvenile court's first responsibility is to impose legal sanctions and attempt to prevent further delinquent behavior; but it cannot fulfill the traditional promise of juvenile rehabilitation (Grubb & Lazerson, 1982, p. 179; Feld, 1999a, p. 296). Changing many of the conditions that lead to juvenile delinquency is not the responsibility of the juvenile court, but lies with society, families, schools, other social institutions, and government social policies.

| POLICY AND PRACTICE 10.2 | TEEN COURT: AN ALTERNATIVE TO JUVENILE COURT |

A teen court (also called a youth court or peer court) is an alternative to juvenile court. In it, youth have an active role in hearing evidence and pronouncing sentence over their teen peers.

Judge James P. Gray described the peer court experience in the Orange County, California, jurisdiction over which he presides.

Purpose. The Orange County, California, Peer Court provides an opportunity for young people to be responsible for getting accurate information, make intelligent decisions, and serve as important role models for their peers and younger siblings.

The Process. The peer court is a diversion program in which real juvenile court cases are screened by the probation department and presented to a group of high school "jurors." Selected cases include shoplifting, petty theft, stolen property, graffiti and vandalism, trespass, alcohol and drug offenses, and driving a vehicle without owner's permission. Violence and weapons offenses are excluded. The juvenile offender must admit to the offense and waive his or her rights to confidentiality. Teen jurors are from schools other than the offender's, so no one knows them personally. A probation officer reads a statement of the facts of the case; the juvenile and his or her parent have an opportunity to make a statement; and the peer jury members then ask further questions about the offense. A county judge presides over each session and may also ask questions. The peer jury then discusses the case under the supervision and guidance of an attorney advisor to reach a recommended sentence to give to the judge. Juveniles or parents who refuse to admit guilt or freely participate in the peer court will have their cases referred to the district attorney for prosecution in juvenile court. Juveniles who refuse to comply with the sentence of the teen jury also have their cases referred to juvenile court.

The Sentence. Peer court sentences can include nearly anything other than incarceration or the payment of a fine. Sentences have included community service such as picking up trash in a park, removing graffiti, and working with the sick or elderly at local hospitals; monetary restitution to victims; writing letters of apology to victims; writing essays on what they have learned from the experience; attending individual and/or family counseling; being ordered to attend school regularly and attend all classes; and participating as a juror in future peer court sessions.

The Results. Of the 207 juveniles who went through the peer court in the 2001–2002 school year, only 12 failed to completed the ordered sentences. Survey results from the 516 students who participated as peer jurors were also positive. A majority of the students and observers said the peer court was an effective way to reduce youth crime, for students to learn about the legal system, a good alternative to the formal juvenile court, and an effective way to keep youth from committing other crimes in the future. Judge Gray also noted that peer involvement in the hearing and sentencing process has been an excellent learning experience that has contributed to an ethical dialogue that has been lacking, and has given the participating youth a sense of individual responsibility and pride.

According to the National Youth Court Center, there were about 900 youth court programs in 46 states and the District of Columbia in 2003. They vary in process and location (some in courtrooms, some in schoolrooms); but most are diversion programs that provide an effective alternative to formal juvenile court hearings and sentences.

SOURCE: Gray, J. P. (2003). The peer court experience. *Perspectives, 27*(4), 31–33. See also www.youthcourt.net.

Discussion Questions

1. Consider the process of asking questions to gather information about each case and offender, and then deciding on an appropriate sentence. What qualifications and skills do youth have to learn to do this seriously while respecting the offender, the victim, and a fair hearing process?

2. In what ways might it be more difficult for a juvenile offender and his or her parents to face a youth peer jury than judges and attorneys in juvenile court?

3. Do you believe that a peer court experience may impress on some juvenile offenders the wrong they committed, and encourage them to take their peer-imposed sentence very seriously?

Juvenile Court Changes

The juvenile court has undergone significant changes and reforms. The reform movement began with U.S. Supreme Court decisions in *Kent, In re Gault,* and *In re Winship* in the 1960s in which the Court required most of the same due process protections provided for adults in criminal courts. Juveniles were provided notice of the charges, right to counsel, and protection against self-incrimination and unlawful searches. Another step in juvenile court reform involved efforts to remove status offenders from formal adjudication and commitment to detention centers and juvenile institutions. Juvenile lockups and training schools housed many youths whose only "crime" was disobeying their parents, running away, or school truancy. Advocates of such practices argued that involvement in status offenses was the first step toward more serious delinquency, and thus early intervention might prevent serious delinquency. Opponents noted the unfairness of punishing youths for minor deviant behavior, and voiced concerns about the adverse effects of status offenders being housed with older, hard-core juvenile offenders. The President's Commission on Law Enforcement and Administration of Justice (1967a) recommended narrowing the range of offenses going before the juvenile court, and groups such as the

American Bar Association–Institute of Judicial Administration (1982) called for an end to adjudicating and incarcerating status offenders in juvenile institutions.

Despite the changes that were implemented following *Gault* and *Kent,* children and youth appearing before juvenile court still do not have the same constitutional safeguards as adults in criminal court (Feld, 1999a, p. 287; Sanborn & Salerno, 2005, p. 503). Juvenile laws still allow officials to intervene in noncriminal behavior, including incorrigibility, runaway, and truancy. Parents may lose custody as their delinquent child is placed in state custody for placement in a juvenile facility. The juvenile justice system may retain control of children beyond their 18th birthday, when they become adults. Juvenile justice advocates would point to the positive side of the system, however. Juvenile justice interventions are justified based on multiple purposes that range from prevention, to treatment, to public safety. Preventing status offenders from becoming more serious delinquents is still considered a viable purpose of the court, since many believe that status offenses such as parental disobedience, leaving home without permission, and school truancy are precursors of delinquent behavior. Juvenile treatment programs that focus on substance abuse prevention, education, and skill development have been effective in reducing delinquency. Finally, the need for crime control and the emphasis on public safety remains true for chronic and violent juvenile offenders.

Abolish or Rehabilitate the Juvenile Court?

The current focus of discussion concerning juvenile court reform revolves around the very purpose of the juvenile court. The question at issue is whether the primary purpose of the juvenile court is for punishment or for treatment. Most of the states have revised their juvenile codes and redefined the purpose of the juvenile court, de-emphasizing rehabilitation and placing more importance on public protection and safety (Feld, 1995; Torbet et al., 1996). Barry Feld (1993) has argued that judicial and legislative changes have "criminalized" the juvenile court. The juvenile court reforms have altered the court's jurisdiction over status offenders, who are diverted from the system, and serious offenders, who are increasingly transferred to adult criminal court. He contends that there are fewer differences between the two courts. Following the tradition of criminal courts, juvenile courts now tend to punish youths for their offenses rather than treat them for their needs (Feld, 1993, p. 197). Beyond being punished for their crimes, however, Feld argues that the procedural safeguards that are standard in criminal courts would be beneficial to juveniles. Juvenile offenders receive an inferior quality of justice in juvenile courts, and this practice has been rationalized and justified because "they are only children" (1993, p. 267). Feld believes that a separate juvenile court must be based on more than simply a treatment-versus-punishment rationale, and he contends that "the current juvenile court provides neither therapy nor justice and cannot be rehabilitated" (Feld 1999a, p. 297).

Feld has therefore argued for abolition of the juvenile court as we know it. A more formal criminal court hearing would ensure that juvenile offenders receive the same due process safeguards and constitutional rights as adults in criminal court. Juveniles would be treated differently only at the sentencing phase, when they would receive a "youth discount" in consideration of their lower level of maturity and culpability (Feld, 1999a, p. 317). The concept of a youth discount is not new or unique. Other juvenile justice policy groups, such as the American Bar Association and Institute of Judicial Administration (ABA–IJA; 1980), have recommended a similar policy. The ABA–IJA noted that age is a relevant factor in determining a youth's level of responsibility for breaking the law, and for establishing an appropriate sentence or disposition in juvenile court (p. 35). In addition to a "youth discount" in sentencing, Feld (1999a) recommended that youths who are sentenced to an institution be placed in separate correctional facilities for youthful offenders (p. 326).

Abolition of the juvenile court is unlikely in the near future, but juvenile justice experts welcome the ongoing reforms and agree that more changes are needed. Supporters of the current juvenile court acknowledge that juveniles receive "unequal" and "dual" processing in court: not the same quality of due process as adults, and for the purpose of both punishment and rehabilitation (Sanborn & Salerno, 2005). They also emphasize that not everything about juvenile justice is negative or unfair, especially when juvenile courts do pursue the "best interests" of the youthful offender and make positive efforts to provide beneficial interventions and programs aimed at offender change. The juvenile court in most cases does take into account the child's needs and risks, and aims to arrive at a disposition that will best facilitate offender change and public safety. Juvenile justice still does focus on both the youthful offender and the offense. "In short, juvenile justice is *still* largely about who the youth is (in addition to what the youth has done)" (Sanborn & Salerno, 2005, p. 503). The concept of individualized justice does risk differential treatment according to gender, race, and social class despite the intention of a court disposition based on perceived risks or needs of youthful offenders. Sanborn and Salerno (2005, p. 504) suggest that maintaining the rehabilitative purpose of juvenile court may require acceptance of some unequal processing in order to assist families who cannot or will not help resolve their child's problems. This is not to say that juvenile court dispositions based on race are acceptable, however, but that racial minorities and lower-class youth who come before the court often have problems for which resources and services available through the court may provide some relief.

The juvenile justice system must be vigilant in preventing the influence of racism in differential sentencing of juvenile offenders. The federal government, through the Office of Juvenile Justice and Delinquency Prevention, has made the elimination of disproportionate minority confinement a high priority. Feld (1999a, 2003) has repeatedly emphasized the tendency of the individualized juvenile justice system to produce racial disparities in sentencing youthful offenders. Those who support the juvenile court believe that it can still provide a fair and just legal process and rehabilitative services better than would be available in the criminal court (Sanborn & Salerno, 2005). The majority of juvenile offenders—those who have not committed serious, violent crimes and who do not have lengthy records—will continue to benefit from the treatment-oriented juvenile court. For violent and chronic juvenile offenders, the options of transfer and blended sentencing are still available. Correctional and treatment services available as juvenile court dispositions are more properly tailored to meet the needs of most juvenile offenders. Professionals in the juvenile justice system have responded to evaluation research and have begun to develop new and more effective juvenile corrections programs and intervention strategies (Bishop, 2004). The National Council of Juvenile and Family Court Judges (2005) has responded to the need to analyze the practices and results of the juvenile process and to identify areas for improvement. With support from the federal Office of Juvenile Justice and Delinquency Prevention (OJJDP), this national organization of juvenile and family court judges has developed resource guidelines that are directed at improving court practices in juvenile delinquency cases. The guidelines will assist juvenile courts in assessing current practices, identify areas in need of improvement, and help in planning and working toward positive change. The guidelines direct courts to a renewed focus on improving court handling of juvenile delinquency cases, innovative community-based collaborative responses to juvenile crime and delinquency, and expanding professional networks for improving government responses to at-risk youth (National Council of Juvenile and Family Court Judges, 2005).

The public looks to the police and the courts to solve the nation's juvenile crime problem. As juvenile crime has become more rampant, and a disproportionate number of young people commit violent crimes, citizens have demanded tougher laws from their legislators. In an effort to show that "something is being done," legislators have enacted more severe punishment for juvenile offenders. It is well to remember, however, that there are "limits to the criminal sanction" (Packer, 1975). Police and the courts cannot prevent crime or the root causes of juvenile delinquency. They can only respond to criminal violations after they occur. Focusing all of our attention on laws and their enforcement is not an adequate approach to reducing the social and family problems that lead to juvenile delinquency (see Feld, 1995, pp. 980–982). As long as society relies solely on tougher laws and their enforcement to respond to juvenile crime, we are unlikely to see any changes in the current trends of increasing numbers of young people who are committing crimes. Juvenile courts and justice officials will continue to respond to the juvenile crime problem; but social institutions such as the family, schools, and community agencies are essential for reducing and preventing juvenile delinquency.

SUMMARY

- The number of delinquency cases in juvenile courts in the United States has increased 46% in the past 20 years, representing a significant workload increase for court officials.
- Juvenile court judges traditionally took a more informal, "parental" role compared with criminal court judges, and in addition to judicial qualifications are now expected to have an understanding of the special needs of juvenile offenders.
- Prosecuting and defense attorneys take a less adversarial role in juvenile court than in criminal court, and are expected to consider the "best interests of the child" in court proceedings.

- Many juveniles appear without a defense attorney despite questions as to their ability to make a valid waiver of the right to counsel; but research indicates that defense attorneys may not be effective or helpful for juvenile clients.
- The juvenile court process consists of adjudication and disposition hearings that are more informal, "quasi-civil" proceedings compared to criminal court.
- "Blended sentencing" laws offer a dispositional alternative for serious or chronic juvenile offenders, providing for commitment to a juvenile facility followed by transfer to an adult facility if necessary.
- The juvenile court changes beginning with U.S. Supreme Court decisions in the 1960s are now accompanied by demands either to abolish the juvenile court or to make further reforms to ensure that the quality of justice and due process rights for juveniles is comparable to that for adults in criminal court.

KEY TERMS

"Best interests of the child"

"Quasi-judicial" personnel

Court-appointed attorney

Public defender

Right to counsel

Institutional commitment

Guardian ad litem

Court diversion

Bifurcated hearing

Dispositional alternatives

Residential placement

Predisposition report

Informal adjustment

Mediation

Probation

DISCUSSION QUESTIONS

1. Based on your reading, what factors do you believe might explain the disproportionate representation of black youth in U.S. juvenile courts? What juvenile justice policy changes or special programs would you recommend to address this issue?

2. What are some arguments for and against all juveniles having defense counsel in court? Should juveniles who are committed to a correctional institution be able to waive their right to counsel? Why, or why not?

3. Is it surprising that juveniles who are represented by a defense attorney often get harsher punishments than juveniles without an attorney? Based on research presented by the authors, what are some possible reasons for that finding?

4. If a lawmaker in your state introduced legislation to abolish the juvenile court and try juveniles in adult court with a "youth discount" during sentencing, how would you argue for or against the proposal?

WEB RESOURCES

The following Web sites provide information and discussion on the juvenile court:

National Center for Juvenile Justice: http://www.ncjj.org/

For current statistics on juvenile court delinquency cases, see *Easy Access to Juvenile Court Statistics: 1985–2005* (National Center for Juvenile Justice): http://ojjdp.ncjrs.gov/ojstatbb/ezajcs/

National Council of Juvenile and Family Court Judges: http://www.ncjfcj.org/

"Best Practices": http://www.ncjfcj.org/content/view/411/411/

11

Juvenile Corrections

Institutional and Residential

The field of corrections is the third major component of the juvenile justice system; it administers the disposition (or sentence) of the juvenile court. The juvenile court disposition options discussed in the previous chapter vary according to the risk level and correctional service needs of the juvenile offender. Corrections programs accordingly range from probation supervision in the community to secure institutional programs. Correctional programs and facilities for juvenile offenders have historically emphasized a treatment objective rather than the goal of punishment that is common in adult corrections. Juvenile institutions often resemble adult prisons, however, marked by abusive and oppressive conditions and with few rehabilitative programs. In this chapter we examine the history and development of institutional and residential corrections for juveniles; the development of intermediate sanctions; disproportionate minority confinement; research on the effectiveness of correctional programs; and future trends in juvenile corrections.

The juvenile justice system recognizes the differences and unique needs of youthful offenders. The guiding principles have been to make judicial decisions that are "in the best interests of the child," and to use the "least restrictive" dispositional alternatives that fulfill the goals of correctional treatment and public safety. Community corrections refers to supervision of adjudicated delinquents in the community on *juvenile probation,* and may be combined with other alternatives to incarceration such as fines, restitution, and community service. The choice of available alternatives and programs varies in different jurisdictions, but the majority of juvenile offenders are placed on juvenile probation. Institutional corrections refers to placement in secure or semisecure institutional and residential facilities, including temporary detention centers or juvenile shelters, state training schools, public or private residential facilities, group homes, and wilderness camps.

History and Development of Juvenile Corrections

Juvenile corrections has a long history in America, beginning with the development of Houses of Refuge and probation in the 19th century (reviewed in Chapter 2). Juveniles are confined in separate correctional facilities from adults, but many state training schools differ very little from prisons for adult criminals. Juvenile training schools came under criticism in the 1960s and 1970s as reformers highlighted the inhumane conditions in them, claiming that housing minor juvenile offenders with more serious and violent offenders made the facilities nothing more than "schools for crime." Jerome Miller received national attention in the early 1970s when, as director of the Massachusetts juvenile corrections agency, he closed all the training schools. Juveniles were placed in alternative public and private residential programs. Research evaluating the effects of closing the state schools indicated that the reform did not result in an increase in delinquency in the state (Coates, Miller, & Ohlin, 1978). Barry Krisberg and James Austin (1993) reported that a cost analysis of the Massachusetts system compared with other state juvenile corrections systems indicated that the Massachusetts system was cost-effective while providing public safety and offender rehabilitation (p. 163). The Massachusetts experience has been closely followed, and many other states have considered reforms similar to those initiated by Jerome Miller.

Incarceration of juvenile offenders is very costly and does little to reduce juvenile crime. The increase in the number of offenders who are being sentenced to correctional institutions has placed enormous demands on state and federal budgets. The cost of building and operating correctional institutions has required states to cut back on other expenditures. From 1960 to 1985, state and local spending per capita increased 218% for corrections, significantly more than the increase for hospitals and healthcare (119%), police (73%), or education (56%) (Bureau of Justice Statistics, 1988, p. 120). The proportion of taxpayer dollars that goes to corrections has increased at a higher rate than the proportion allocated for education. We are in effect taking dollars from school classrooms to pay for more prison cells (Lawrence, 1995). Many correctional experts believe that a better use of taxpayer dollars is to invest in educational programs that have been shown to be effective in reducing delinquency, and to concentrate correctional spending on community-based programs that are more cost-effective than incarceration, while still providing for public safety. Krisberg and Austin (1993) suggested that a better use of tax dollars might be neighborhood-based crime

Photo 11.1 A secure juvenile corrections facility.

prevention efforts that are directed at reducing child abuse, school dropout rates, youth unemployment, and drug dealing. The correctional reform movement of the 1970s was unfortunately replaced by a "get-tough" approach in the 1990s in response to what some believed to be a youth crime plague.

Institutional and Residential Programs

According to the Juvenile Residential Facility Census (JRFC) in 2002, a total of 102,388 juveniles were held in 2,964 facilities (Sickmund, 2006). Listed below are some of the characteristics of the juveniles and the residential facilities in which they were held:

- There were more private facilities (1,773) than public facilities (1,182), but more juveniles (70,243 or 69%) were held in public facilities than in private ones (31,992 or 31%)
- The number of delinquent offenders in residential facilities decreased 7% from 2000 to 2002
- The national U.S. rate of custody for juvenile offenders was 326 per 100,000 juveniles in the population
- The rate of custody among the states varied widely, from 85 to 688 per 100,000 juveniles in the state populations
- Crowding is a problem in many facilities, with a total of 1,069 (36%) of facilities (mostly public) reporting being at or over capacity, affecting 39,200 (34%) of the residents in 2002 (see Sickmund, 2006, pp. 2–9)

A study of trends of children in custody found that the average length of stay for juveniles in a residential facility is about 4 months; the average yearly cost for custody in a public facility was more than $32,000 in 1998; and private facilities had increased in average annual costs to more than $45,000 in 1995 (Smith, 1998, p. 537). Placement in a residential facility is generally used for the most serious or chronic juvenile offenders who require secure confinement and treatment. Yet as many as one fifth (25,000 or 19%) of confined youth in 1999 were not charged or adjudicated for an offense

(Sickmund, 2004). Residential placement is very costly compared with community corrections, and there are questions whether the education, training, and treatment received in juvenile institutions are effective in reducing delinquent behavior.

In 2002, residential placement was ordered in 85% of cases in which youth were adjudicated delinquent. A total of 144,000 (23%) were ordered to placement, and 385,400 (62%) were ordered to probation supervision in the community. From 1985 to 2002, both residential and probation cases had increased proportions of person, drug, and public order offenses. Cases ordered to residential placement in 2002 made up a greater proportion of personal and public order cases and a smaller share of drug cases than cases ordered to formal probation (Snyder & Sickmund, 2006, p. 174). The most recent available data indicate that nearly 92,000 delinquents were held in residential placement facilities in 2003. About two thirds (64,662) were in public facilities and one third (27,059) were in private facilities. In addition to adjudicated delinquents in residential placement, another 4,824 status offenders were in public and private facilities (Snyder & Sickmund, 2006, p. 198). Table 11.1 summarizes the number of juvenile offenders held in public and private residential facilities in 2003, and the percentage change between 1997 and 2003.

Public facilities housed most of the juvenile offenders adjudicated for person offenses such as homicide, robbery, aggravated assault, and weapons. For most offense categories, fewer juveniles were held in 2003 than in 1997. For offenses such as drug offenses other than trafficking, the public facility population decreased but the private facility population increased. More of the public facilities are operated by county or city governments, but they are smaller in size and held fewer than half of all juvenile offenders in public facilities. Most of the local facilities are detention centers that hold a smaller number of youth and for a shorter period of time. State facilities such as training schools hold a larger number of juveniles and for a longer period of time. Private residential facilities such as shelters, group homes, and ranch or wilderness camps serve as alternatives to public state facilities for nonviolent and nonchronic juvenile offenders.

Juvenile Training Schools

The physical structure of juvenile training schools varies from cottage settings to open dormitories, and maximum security facilities may house residents in individual cells. The secure training schools have an institutional appearance inside and out, with high fences surrounding them, locked doors, and screens or bars on windows. Residents' movements throughout the facility are restricted and closely supervised by the staff. The living quarters of the medium security cottage and dormitory-style facilities are more homelike, but they offer little privacy for residents. Medium security training schools often are surrounded by fences, and therefore resemble maximum security juvenile facilities. Few juvenile training schools are minimum security, because most juveniles are sent to a training school because they need restricted confinement.

Juvenile training schools represent the most punitive sanction available in the juvenile justice system. Removing youth from their families, communities, and public school is a significant punishment for many of them. They live under close 24-hour supervision with strict rules and discipline. Serious rule violations such as fighting and

Table 11.1	Juveniles in Residential Placement, 2003

| Most Serious Offense | Juvenile Offenders in Residential Placement, 2003 | | | Percentage Change, 1997–2003 | | |
| | Type of Facility | | | Type of Facility | | |
	All	Public	Private	All (%)	Public (%)	Private (%)
Total offenders	96,655	66,210	30,321	–8	–12	3
Delinquency	91,831	64,662	27,059	–7	–12	11
Person	33,197	23,499	9,671	–6	–13	21
Criminal homicide	878	803	73	–54	–56	–28
Sexual assault	7,452	4,749	2,698	34	20	68
Robbery	6,230	5,157	1,073	–33	–35	–22
Aggravated assault	7,495	5,745	1.741	–21	–24	–7
Simple assault	8,106	4,984	3,113	22	21	25
Other person	3,036	2,061	973	38	22	87
Property	26,843	18,740	8,073	–16	–18	–10
Burglary	10,399	7,481	2,904	–17	–21	–7
Theft	5,650	3,793	1,848	–22	–26	–12
Auto theft	5,572	3,756	1,812	–15	–14	–16
Arson	735	514	220	–19	–25	0
Other property	4,487	3,196	1,289	–4	–4	–6
Drug	8,002	4,851	3,137	–12	–23	15
Drug trafficking	1,810	1,284	522	–37	–41	–24
Other drug	6,192	3,567	2,615	0	–14	28
Public order	9,654	6,782	2,866	0	–5	11
Weapons	3,013	2,346	665	–28	–29	–24
Other public order	6,641	4,436	2,201	20	16	29
Technical violation	14,135	10,790	3,312	14	5	56
Status offense	4,824	1,548	3,262	–29	–11	–36
Ungovernability	1,825	253	1,570	–36	–45	–34
Running away	997	417	577	–33	–14	–43
Truancy	841	207	634	–37	–49	–32
Curfew violation	203	65	138	5	–18	21
Underage drinking	405	210	186	27	86	–10

SOURCE: Adapted from Snyder & Sickmund (2006). *Juvenile offenders and victims: 2006 national report.* Pittsburgh, PA: National Center for Juvenile Justice.

assaults result in short-term commitment to disciplinary segregation, which is a secure detention setting within the training school. Staff members maintain discipline among the residents by withholding privileges or extending the length of stay for those who violate any rules.

Many training schools do have some good programs, including medical and dental care, an accredited school, vocational training, recreation, and treatment programs. Rehabilitation is still the primary purpose of juvenile training schools. The treatment methods that are used most widely are behavior modification, guided group interaction, transactional analysis, reality therapy, and positive peer culture. Efforts are made to prepare the juveniles for return to their families and communities. Juveniles who have made satisfactory adjustment and are within a few weeks of their release may be allowed to make home visits or take part in work-release programs in the community. The goal of rehabilitation has seldom been achieved in most juvenile training schools. Studies indicate that few of the programs being used in training schools are effective in preventing future delinquency, although there is some evidence that institutional treatment may work with some youth. Carol Garrett (1985) reviewed more than 100 studies conducted between 1960 and 1983 on juvenile corrections treatment programs such as counseling, behavior modification, and life-skill improvement. Garrett found no single treatment strategy that was most effective, but she concluded that the majority of interventions did show change in a positive direction. On the other hand, Steven Lab and John Whitehead (1988) analyzed juvenile correctional research done from 1975 to 1984 and concluded that treatment has little impact on recidivism. One problem seems to be that the programs themselves are not being used effectively (Whitehead & Lab, 1989). The youth workers and counselors in juvenile training schools face the dilemma of trying to adapt programs to a diverse and varied juvenile offender population. The institutional setting in which the primary concern is control of some of the most serious delinquents presents a challenge for the correctional staff in fulfilling educational and treatment goals.

Despite the goals of treatment, juvenile training schools remain institutional settings marked by oppressiveness and fear. As states confine dangerous juvenile offenders together with younger, smaller, or less serious offenders in the same institution, even the closest supervision and the best programs have few positive effects. Training school staff members are often powerless to prevent incidents of inmate abuse by other inmates (Feld, 1977). Bartollas, Miller, and Dinitz (1976) examined victimization in a maximum security juvenile institution in Columbus, Ohio, and found that 90% of the residents were either perpetrators or victims of abuse. Juveniles who are confined in training schools find the institutional environment oppressive and stressful. Despite any good intentions of treatment or "training," staff must first be concerned about maintaining security and close supervision among the residents. Wooden (1976) documented multiple examples of abuse of juvenile inmates by oppressive correctional workers in state training schools. Correctional institutions in which employees are responsible for supervising a large number of juvenile residents often become oppressive and abusive settings in which control becomes a higher priority than treatment and rehabilitation for the juvenile residents.

CASE IN POINT 11.1

Do Juveniles Have a Right to Treatment?

Eric Nelson and a group of juvenile residents of the Indiana Boys School filed a class action suit in the federal district court, claiming the policies and practices of the school violated their Eighth and Fourteenth Amendment rights. The court upheld their claims. Robert Heyne, Commissioner of Corrections for the Indiana Department of Corrections, appealed the case. The U.S. Court of Appeals for the Seventh Circuit upheld the district court in this 1974 decision.

Facts of the Case

The Indiana Boys School is a medium security state correctional institution for boys 12–18 years of age. About one third of them were committed for noncriminal (status) offenses. The boys resided in 16 cottages, and the school also has academic and vocational buildings and a gymnasium. The average length of stay at the school was about 6-1/2 months. The school's maximum capacity was less than 300 juveniles, but its population was usually around 400. The counseling staff of 20 persons included three psychologists with undergraduate degrees; a part-time (4 hours per week) psychiatrist; and a medical staff that included one registered nurse, one licensed practical nurse, and one part-time physician.

The plaintiffs alleged that the frequent use of corporal punishment and use of tranquilizing drugs for control violated their Eighth and Fourteenth Amendment rights. Juveniles who were returned from attempted escapes or who were accused of assaults on other students or staff members were beaten routinely by guards, using a "fraternity paddle" up to 2" thick and 12" long. Juveniles were struck five times on their clothed buttocks by a staff member, who was observed by two other staff members. The beatings caused painful injuries, including bleeding and black and blue marks. One juvenile testified the pain was so great that he had to sleep face-down for 3 days; another pleaded not to be beaten again until after the pain and blisters from a previous beating had ceased (he was beaten despite his pleas).

The Court's Decision

In determining whether the beatings constituted cruel and unusual punishment under the Eighth Amendment, the court considered the fact that this was a school, and previous cases had ruled that the use of corporal punishment by school officials did *not* violate the Eighth Amendment when the punishment was reasonable and moderate. Courts have *not* upheld the use of severe corporal punishment in correctional institutions, however; and the court in this case drew upon previous rulings in declaring that the beatings violated the juveniles' Eighth Amendment rights, for a number of reasons:

- Inflicting severe punishment violates human dignity when the purpose is nothing more than the pointless infliction of suffering.
- If a less severe punishment can achieve the same purpose, then it must be used instead.
- Evidence indicates that severe punishment is not useful for correction or treatment, and actually breeds counter-hostility, resulting in greater aggression by a child.
- The beatings had aroused animosity toward the school and frustrated its rehabilitative purpose.
- Corporal punishment is subject to abuse in the hands of the sadistic and unscrupulous.

(Continued)

(Continued)

- Formalized procedures governing the use of corporal punishment at the School were not adequately in place.

The court also determined that the use of tranquilizing drugs for the use of controlling residents' behavior was in violation of the Eighth Amendment. Sparine and Thorazine were occasionally administered for the purpose of controlling juveniles' behavior, not as part of a psychotherapeutic program. The drugs were prescribed by the nurses upon the custodial staff recommendations and based on standing orders by the physician. Juveniles were not examined by medical staff to determine their individual tolerances for the drugs. Experts testified that the tranquilizing drugs can cause collapse of the cardiovascular system, closing of a patient's throat with consequent asphyxiation, a depressant effect on the production of bone marrow, jaundice from an affected liver, drowsiness, hemotological disorders, sore throat, and ocular changes. The court did not ban the use of these drugs when prescribed in necessary and appropriate cases by the institutional physician, but ruled that the manner in which they were used in the school violated the plaintiffs' Eighth and Fourteenth Amendment rights.

Do Juveniles Have a Right to Treatment?

The U.S. Supreme Court has never definitively decided that a youth who is confined under the order of a juvenile court has a constitutionally guaranteed right to treatment. The Appellate Court nevertheless ruled that juveniles *do* have a right to rehabilitative treatment. The justices based their decision on the following arguments:

- The right to rehabilitative treatment for juvenile offenders has roots in the general social reform of the late 19th century.
- State courts have since the beginning emphasized the need for "treatment" in their Juvenile Court Acts.
- Previous rulings indicate that the U.S. Supreme Court has assumed that a state must provide treatment for juveniles.
- In *Gault*, the Court stated that the child was to be "treated" and "rehabilitated" and the procedures were to be "clinical" rather than punitive [387 U.S. 1, 15–16 (1967)].
- In *Kent*, the Court was critical of juvenile courts, based on evidence that juveniles were not getting the care and treatment that had been promised them [383 U.S. at 556 (1966)].
- Federal courts have decided that juvenile inmates have both a constitutional and a statutory right to treatment [*Martarella v. Kelley*, 349 F.Supp. 575 (S.D.N.Y. 1972); *Morales v. Turman*, 384 F. Supp. 53 (E.D. Tex. 1973)].

The Seventh Circuit Court in *Nelson v. Heyne* also ruled that the "right to treatment" includes the right to minimum acceptable standards of care and treatment for juveniles and the right to *individualized* care and treatment (italics in original). The right to treatment was based on the statutory provisions of the state of Indiana regarding youth in custody; but the Court emphasized that the federal constitution gives juveniles the right to treatment, so failure of the state to provide treatment would itself be unconstitutional.

SOURCE: *Nelson v. Heyne*, 491 F.2d 352 (7th Cir. 1974).

Discussion Questions

1. Based on what you have read so far about the purposes of juvenile courts and corrections, and of the distinctions between the adult criminal justice system and juvenile justice, does it make sense that the U.S. Supreme Court decided that juveniles have a right to treatment?

2. Is it likely that a court would declare that adult criminal offenders also have a right to treatment in prisons? Why, or why not?

Questions have been raised since the *Nelson v. Heyne* decision about the constitutional basis for the "right to treatment." See *Santana v. Collazo,* 533 F. Supp. 966 (D. Puerto Rico 1982) and any other more recent cases on the right to treatment. Based on your search, are there any court decisions that challenge the *Nelson v. Heyne* decision?

In summary, there is little evidence that offers support for effective correctional and rehabilitative treatment of youthful offenders in juvenile training schools. Despite goals of education, training, and treatment, the first priority of training school staff is to maintain close supervision and security. In correctional institutions, treatment programs and correctional services are secondary to the primary goal of maintaining order and control. Residential facilities that house juvenile offenders who do not pose a public safety or security risk are able to place more emphasis on rehabilitation programs.

Other Residential Programs

The main types of community-based residential programs are group homes, foster care, and day treatment programs. Group homes are small residential facilities in the community that are designed to house about 10 to 15 youths. Group homes serve as an alternative to incarceration; are a short-term community placement for youth on probation or aftercare supervision; and they serve as a "halfway house" for youth needing semisecure placement, less than that of a training school. Foster care programs offer temporary placement for juveniles who must be removed from their own homes. Foster parents provide a temporary home for neglected, abused, or delinquent children and receive a subsidy from local or state governments to cover their expenses. Foster parents are able to provide more consistent and firm supervision than troubled juveniles may have been receiving in their own homes. Short-term placement with foster parents gives more time for probation officers to seek other placement alternatives. It is difficult to find enough persons who are willing to serve as foster parents, especially for delinquent youth. Foster care places considerable stresses on a home, because many delinquent youth have experienced abusive parental relationships and are therefore distrustful and often rebellious toward foster parents. Day treatment programs are

(Continued)

2. Correctional experts have research evidence that correctional institutions change the behavior of both the "keepers" and the "kept"; and that institutions have a "brutalizing effect" on persons in them. Explain how the image and purpose of a "boot camp" or "training school" might promote brutal and severely punitive behavior.

3. It is likely that the boot camp guards did not know Martin Anderson's background, family, or why he was sent to the camp. Do you believe that might make a difference in how they treat residents?

4. Most correctional workers have children and families of their own. Do you believe corrections employees could be trained to treat other people's children the same as they would their own children? How might this change juvenile institutions?

Wilderness Camps

Outdoor education and training programs—the most widely known is "Outward Bound"—have developed as effective institutional alternatives for juvenile offenders. The goals of Outward Bound and similar wilderness programs are to help youth gain self-confidence and self-reliance by placing them in outdoor settings and challenging them with new physical tasks that appear seemingly impossible, especially for most metropolitan juvenile offenders who are unfamiliar with wilderness settings (Greenwood & Zimring, 1985). Wilderness programs attempt to accomplish the goals through backpacking in wilderness areas, high-altitude camping, mountain hiking, rock climbing, and rappelling from platforms, trees, or cliffs. Participants first receive training in basic skills, then participate in an expedition, and are tested in a solo experience. The wilderness experience lasts from 3 to 4 weeks.

VisionQuest is a survival program based in Tucson, Arizona. The program contracts with juvenile courts and takes juveniles who are committed to the program from California, Pennsylvania, and several other states. VisionQuest programs, lasting from 12 to 18 months, include wilderness camps, cross-country travel in a wagon train, or a voyage on a large sailboat. The youth are closely supervised and rigorously challenged emotionally, intellectually, and physically. VisionQuest has drawn some controversy for its confrontational style with juveniles who do not perform up to expectations, slack off, or act out (Greenwood & Zimring, 1985).

Several states have developed wilderness camps as alternatives to placement in a correctional facility. The state of Minnesota has operated a camp for offenders who have failed to comply with probation conditions, but who do not need secure training school placement. Thistledew Camp, located between two lakes in a remote forest area of northern Minnesota, features a unique educational facility intended to serve delinquent youth who have experienced failure in the home, school, and community. Education is provided for youths at all levels, and all classroom teachers are certified in learning disabilities (LD) or emotional/behavioral disorders (EBD) to provide optimum services for students with special needs. About a third of the time at Thistledew Camp is devoted to Challenge, an outdoor wilderness survival program similar to Outward Bound. Challenge is a high-adventure wilderness experience designed to build individual self-confidence, develop leadership abilities, and teach the importance of a group effort. Residents receive training and instruction in the use of equipment and in basic wilderness techniques. Expeditions are conducted throughout the year and geared to the seasons. Treks include canoeing, backpacking, rock climbing, cross-country skiing, and traveling by snowshoe. Expeditions are planned to be rugged and difficult in order to build self-confidence and to teach the importance of teamwork. "Solo camping" is a final phase of Challenge. Camping alone in an isolated area for 3 days and nights, residents experience loneliness, hunger, and cold, and they learn how to handle those situations in a self-reliant manner (Minnesota Department of Corrections, 2009).

Wilderness programs are also used in conjunction with probation supervision. Staffed by probation officers and lay volunteers, wilderness probation involves juveniles in outdoor expeditions to give them a sense of confidence and purpose (Callahan, 1985). Counseling and group therapy are combined with day hikes and a wilderness experience. The programs provide an opportunity for juveniles on probation to confront difficulties in their lives and to attain some personal satisfaction. Wilderness programs have been effective in producing some positive changes in juvenile offenders, but research shows mixed results as to their effectiveness in reducing recidivism. Lipsey, Wilson, and Cothern (2000) found that wilderness and challenge programs alone were not effective in reducing recidivism among serious juvenile offenders, but programs that combine education, skills development, and counseling did show more positive results.

POLICY AND PRACTICE 11.1 — THE "MASSACHUSETTS EXPERIMENT": CLOSING THE TRAINING SCHOOLS

A dramatic event occurred in juvenile corrections in the early 1970s with the closing of the Massachusetts training schools. Jerome Miller had been hired as Commissioner of the Division of Youth Services (DYS) to bring some positive administrative changes. The training schools had been criticized for abusive and inadequate treatment programs, and legislative hearings revealed major breakdowns in management and operations. Miller first attempted to humanize the correctional facilities and transform them into therapeutic communities. When his efforts at change were met with staff resistance and sabotage of the new, more humane policies, he concluded that the only way he could bring about the desired changes would be simply to shut down the training schools. The residents were not just released onto the streets or to their own homes, but were transferred to privately operated community residential group homes. He was severely criticized by judicial and correctional officials, who warned that his actions would result in a dramatic increase in juvenile crime in the state. The increase in crime and recidivism of the former

(Continued)

(Continued)

juvenile residents of the closed-down schools did not occur at the rates predicted by the critics. For the years following the training school closures and to the present, Massachusetts has a very low rate of juvenile crime compared with other states.

Two studies evaluated the results of closing the training schools. Researchers from Harvard University reported on results after the training school closures. Coates, Miller, and Ohlin (1978) compared a sample of youths who had been placed in community-based programs after the schools were closed with a matched group of juveniles who were released from the training schools a few years before they were closed. They found that within 1 year after their release, the youth who had been moved from training schools to community programs had slightly higher rearrest rates (74% vs. 66%). Their research, however, revealed significant differences in the quality of community programs in the state. They found reduced recidivism rates in regions of the state where former training school youth had been placed in community programs that provided the diversity of services that Jerome Miller and his associates had originally envisioned (Coates et al., 1978, p. 177). The costs to the Massachusetts DYS for the new system of smaller community residential programs were about the same as the costs for operating the large training schools. Overall costs were reduced, however, by placing the majority of youths who did not need secure custody in less costly community programs. A second study by researchers from the National Council on Crime and Delinquency (NCCD) evaluated the outcome of the move from training schools to community programs in Massachusetts and found it to be successful. Compared to other states that still relied on traditional training schools, Massachusetts had recidivism rates that were similar to or slightly lower, but at a significant reduction in costs (Krisberg, Austin, & Steele, 1991; Krisberg & Austin, 1993, p. 161).

Other states have followed the example of Massachusetts and have decreased their use of training schools by closing down some schools or reducing the institutional populations by referring juveniles to alternative residential programs such as privately operated group homes. Maryland, Minnesota, Missouri, Pennsylvania, and Utah have taken similar steps toward correctional reform by closing a training school. The Massachusetts reforms have also influenced juvenile justice reforms throughout the United States in states as diverse as Delaware, Florida, Kentucky, Louisiana, New Jersey, Oklahoma, and Texas. Other states, including Alabama, Arizona, Arkansas, Colorado, Georgia, Indiana, Michigan, Nebraska, Rhode Island, South Carolina, Tennessee, and Washington, have adopted policy positions favoring community-based placements in lieu of more training schools (Krisberg & Austin, 1993).

SOURCE: Coates, Miller, & Ohlin, 1978; Krisberg, Austin, & Steele, 1991; Krisberg & Austin, 1993.

Discussion Questions

1. Given what you have read about juvenile correctional institutions and training schools, is it surprising that the Massachusetts experiment did not result in more juvenile crime?

2. Is your state among those that have reduced the use of training schools and large correctional institutions? To compare states, go to the Web site of the residential facility census: http://ojjdp.ncjrs .gov/publications/PubAbstract.asp?pubi=244623

3. Comparison of states and regions in the juvenile corrections populations must be done with caution. Suggest how factors such as population density, urbanization, crime rates, social–political leaning, or others may influence juvenile corrections populations.

Effectiveness of Juvenile Corrections

There is no unanimous agreement on how to assess correctional outcome. Recidivism has been the traditional measure of effectiveness in corrections. Recidivism may refer to a new arrest, a new conviction, or return to prison, however, so evaluative research must clearly specify the exact criteria being used to measure success or failure. Violations of probation conditions ("technical violations") are also indicators of failure, but are less likely to result in revocation of probation. The practice of assessing effectiveness of corrections based on arrests or other measures of recidivism has clear limitations (Latessa & Allen, 2003, p. 471). Corrections researchers believe that success or failure should be viewed on a continuum using multiple indicators rather than a dichotomous win–lose criterion. Petersilia (1993) has recommended that community corrections should be assessed according to several performance indicators that are based on clearly stated goals, methods, and activities. Five goals of community corrections that should be included in an assessment of outcome are the quality and extent to which the probation agency and officer have been able to: (1) assess offender's suitability for placement; (2) enforce court-ordered sanctions; (3) protect the community; (4) assist offenders to change; and (5) restore crime victims (Petersilia, 1993, pp. 78–79). Evaluating the effectiveness of community corrections according to these five goals takes into account the multiple roles and responsibilities of probation officers: investigation, supervision, and monitoring of court orders, including restitution payments to victims. Multiple performance indicators are included to assess the performance of corrections professionals and the responses of offenders to correctional services and supervision. Number of days employed, vocational education, school attendance, and the number of drug- and alcohol-free days are included as performance indicators in addition to the number of arrests and technical violations (Petersilia, 1993, pp. 78–79).

Measures of the effectiveness of juvenile corrections should also assess the quality of programs, including those conducted in institutions, in public and private residential facilities, and those providing supervision and treatment in the community (Latessa & Allen, 2003). While assessment of program effectiveness is important, corrections researchers acknowledge that recidivism remains the most common measure of the effectiveness of corrections programs. A meta-analysis of studies of institutional and community corrections interventions for serious juvenile offenders concluded that the most effective types of treatment were interpersonal skills training, individual counseling, and behavioral programs (Lipsey et al., 2000). Lipsey et al. found that community-based programs showed greater reductions in recidivism than institutional programs. Offenders in nonsecure community supervision programs do commit some new crimes, but the fact that they do as well or better than youths sent to training schools and released to aftercare supervision suggests that community supervision presents no more risk to public safety and recidivism than incarceration. Research on "get-tough" measures such as Scared Straight programs, boot camps, and intensive supervision has indicated that harsher measures, without additional educational or skills training components, do not reduce recidivism (Whitehead & Lab, 2006).

Cullen, Eck, and Lowenkamp (2002) have proposed a new paradigm for effective probation and parole supervision called "environmental corrections" that is based on environmental criminology, a theory that links crime causation and crime reduction to the presence or absence of opportunities to commit crime. Cullen and his associates believe that probation and parole officers would be more effective if they worked closely with offenders, the family, community members, and the police in order to reduce offenders' opportunities and temptations to commit crime. In addition to maintaining the usual responsibilities of assessment and investigation, probation and parole officers would use a problem-solving approach in supervising offenders to help them avoid the opportunities and temptations that lead to offending. Cullen and his associates acknowledge that considerable efforts will be required to put it into practice. A new problem-solving approach for probation and parole officers engaged in "environmental corrections" will add to their responsibilities, but may improve community supervision and be more cost effective.

Current Issues and Future Trends in Juvenile Corrections

Disproportionate Minority Confinement

Minority youth accounted for 7 in 10 (65%) of juveniles held in custody for a violent offense in 1999 (Sickmund, 2004). Blacks (39%) and Hispanics (18%) outnumbered white youth (38%) among the juvenile offenders held in residential placement in 1999. The percentage of minority youth committed to public facilities nationwide (66%) was nearly twice their proportion of the juvenile population (34%). In six states and the District of Columbia, the minority proportion of the total population of juvenile offenders in residential placement was greater than 75%. Custody rates present a dramatic picture of disproportionate minority confinement. For every 100,000 black juveniles in the United States, 1,004 were in a residential placement in 1999, compared with 485 Hispanics and 212 white youth per 100,000 in the general population (Sickmund, 2004, p. 10).

Disproportionate minority confinement (DMC) may be explained by three factors: (1) overrepresentation, (2) disparity, and (3) discrimination (Sickmund, 2004). Overrepresentation means that a larger proportion of a group is in the justice system than their proportion in the general population. Disparity means that the chance of being arrested, detained, or adjudicated differs for different groups of youth. Discrimination means that justice officials treat one group of juveniles differently because of their gender, race, or ethnicity. If racial and ethnic discrimination exists, then minorities are more likely to be arrested by police, referred to court intake, petitioned for formal processing, adjudicated delinquent, and placed in a residential facility. Differential decision making throughout the juvenile justice system by police, probation, and court officials may account for minority overrepresentation. Disparity and overrepresentation may, on the other hand, be the result of minority youth committing disproportionately more crimes than white youth, or being involved in more serious crimes that come to the attention of police and are more likely to be processed through the justice system. Thus, minority overrepresentation in the justice system and in confinement may be explained by behavioral and legal factors, rather than by discrimination (Sickmund, 2004).

Minority youths are disproportionately represented at every stage of the juvenile justice process (Pope & Feyerherm, 1995). Police arrests involve a disproportionate number of minority youth, especially for more serious violent crimes (Snyder, 2004); and a disproportionate number of minority youth are represented in juvenile court cases (Puzzanchera, 2003). Results of self-report measures show that delinquent behavior is spread equally among youth of all social classes and racial/ethnic groups, and white middle-class youth in fact report more drug violations than lower-class and minority youths (Elliott, Huizinga, & Ageton, 1985). Data from victimization surveys have indicated, however, that the violent offending rate for black juveniles was 4 times higher than for white juveniles during the years 1992–1998 (Lynch, 2002; Sickmund, 2004); but there is evidence that victims report a higher rate of violent offenses committed by African Americans compared to white and Hispanic youth (Rubin, 2001).

Research evidence confirms that minority youths receive more severe juvenile court dispositions than do white youths, even after controlling for legal variables. In California, African American youth make up 8.7% of the youth population but 37% of youths in confinement. Police arrest black youths at a rate 2.2 times greater than their share of the population, and judges sentence them to juvenile institutions at rates 4.6 times greater than white youths (Krisberg & Austin, 1993, pp. 123–125). Among youths referred for violent crimes, California juvenile courts detained almost two thirds (64.7%) of black youth compared with fewer than half (47.1%) of white juveniles; and sentenced to juvenile institutions 11.4% of black youths compared with 9.4% of Latino youth, and only 3.4% of white youths (Krisberg & Austin, 1993, p. 125). Race clearly seems to play at least an indirect role in juvenile court decision making, and African Americans are disproportionately represented throughout the system, particularly in detention centers and state training schools. Analyses of juvenile court dispositions in Florida showed a consistent pattern of unequal treatment. Bishop (1996) found that nonwhite youths were more likely than comparable white youths to be recommended for petition to court, to be held in detention prior to the court hearing, to be formally processed in juvenile court, and to receive the most restrictive court dispositions. More recent studies have found mixed results for differential treatment of minority youths in the juvenile justice system. In a study of the arrests of juveniles for violent crimes, Pope and Snyder (2003) found no differences in the overall likelihood of arrest of white and nonwhite juveniles, after controlling for legal factors and the specific crime, such as characteristics of the victim and extent of injury.

Racially disproportionate rates of arrest and confinement may not be simply a benign result of juvenile justice officials' decision making based on youths who presumably need more intervention and social control. Barry Feld (1999a) has argued that the juvenile court was designed and intended to discriminate between white middle-class children and the children of poor and immigrant parents, and it should come as no surprise that arrests and confinement are racially disproportionate.

> If young people's real needs differ because of social circumstances, such as poverty or a single-parent household that correlate strongly with race, then the ideology of "individualized treatment" necessarily will have a racially disparate impact. Racial disproportionality in a system designed to differentiate on the basis of social structural, economic, or personal circumstances should come as no surprise. But in a society formally committed to racial equality, punitive sentences based on social and personal attributes that produce a disparate racial impact implicate the legitimacy, fairness, and justice of the process. (Feld, 1999a, p. 265)

David Cole (1999) has argued that while our criminal justice system is based theoretically on equality before the law, the practices and administration of justice are in fact "predicated on the exploitation of inequality." He contends that we have not simply ignored the effects of inequality in the justice process, or tried but failed to achieve equality in administering justice. Rather, he contends that

> our criminal justice system affirmatively depends on inequality. Absent race and class disparities, the privileged among us could not enjoy as much constitutional protection of our liberties as we do; and without those disparities, we could not afford the policy of mass incarceration that we have pursued over the past two decades. (p. 5; emphasis in original)

Cole cites the example of how the "war on drugs" shifted attention from the users of drugs to the dealers and sellers. In the 1960s, the use of marijuana spread from being a ghetto problem where it was used by the lower class, to widespread use on college campuses. Laws and practices then changed to focus more on the dealers and sellers than on users. The same might be said for the spread of cocaine use since the 1990s, in which many users are middle- and upper-class persons, but a significant number of dealers and sellers are lower-class minorities. Cole (1999) noted that police and prosecutors began to leave users alone, and instead targeted dealers and sellers. He contends that when the criminal law begins to affect the children of the white majority, our response is not to get tough, but rather to get lenient. Americans maintain a harsh tough-on-crime attitude as long as the burden of punishment falls disproportionately on minority populations. "The white majority could not possibly maintain its current attitude toward crime and punishment were the burden of punishment felt by the same white majority that prescribes it" (p. 153).

Drug abuse is a problem that has serious consequences, including health problems, school failure and dropout, unemployment, family problems, and criminal sanctions. The question is not whether the war on drugs was the most effective approach for control and prevention of drugs. The issue is the unfair and unequal application of the laws regarding the possession, use, and selling of illegal drugs. The enforcement of drug laws by police and the courts have contributed to the disproportionate confinement of minority offenders.

POLICY AND PRACTICE 11.2 FEDERAL GUIDELINES TO REDUCE DMC

In an ongoing effort to encourage and offer guidance to states to address problems of disproportionate minority confinement (DMC), the Office of Juvenile Justice and Delinquency Prevention published an update on the federal mandate (Hsia, Bridges, & McHale, 2004). Based on a review of the extent of DMC throughout the 50 states, the authors noted that several factors within the juvenile justice system contribute to DMC:

- Racial stereotyping and cultural insensitivity
- Lack of alternatives to detention and incarceration
- Misuse of discretionary authority in implementing laws and policies
- Lack of culturally and linguistically appropriate services

The Update concludes with OJJDP's "Action Steps to Reduce Disproportionate Minority Contact" that are intended to help juvenile justice administrators in each state identify and reduce the problem of DMC:

- Complete a full DMC progress review and report on state progress in addressing it.
- Develop delinquency prevention programs that focus on reducing offender risk and improving public safety; provide training and assistance to communities for their development.
- Provide guidance and technical assistance to improve state juvenile justice data systems.
- Develop Web-based data entry to monitor progress in DMC reduction efforts.
- Emphasize the importance of instituting and sustaining juvenile justice system change.
- Encourage states to develop procedures to assess and respond effectively to DMC issues.
- Implement a DMC national evaluation initiative under OJJDP's State Evaluation Support program.
- Invest in the evaluation and replication of promising strategies to reduce DMC; provide information on effective practices and lessons learned in the field.
- Provide leadership in improving data collection and analysis from the states.
- Work with the states to develop data that will better inform their policy and program development.

SOURCE: Adapted from Hsia, Bridges, & McHale. (2004). *Disproportionate minority confinement 2002 update.* Washington, DC: Office of Juvenile Justice & Delinquency Prevention.

Discussion Questions

1. Recall that DMC is the result of justice officials treating a group of juvenile offenders differently because of their gender, race, or ethnicity. Are you aware of cases in your city, county, or state where that may have occurred?

(Continued)

(Continued)

2. Most state departments of corrections have a Web site that includes the proportion of residents by racial background. Check the Web site for your state or other states and note the proportion of minority offenders in correctional facilities. A Web search can also provide information on population demographics for each state. Note any interesting or surprising findings.

Most justice officials insist that race is *not* a factor in their decisions to arrest, prosecute, or sentence to a correctional facility. Based on this report by OJJDP, how might DMC occur despite officials' commitments to fairness and "color blindness"?

Changes and Future Trends

Dramatic changes have taken place in juvenile corrections in the past few decades. Juvenile corrections policies have changed from an emphasis on deinstitutionalization and "least restrictive" alternatives, to a "get-tough" approach that emphasizes accountability and social control. Juvenile justice officials recognized two decades ago that committing delinquents together in isolated training schools away from the community was not an effective long-range answer to juvenile crime. Thus began a trend toward deinstitutionalization and greater use of community alternatives. That trend was reversed in the 1990s and continues today in the new century. Policymakers have been pressured by public demands to "do something" about youth involvement in drugs, gangs, and violent crime. The usual response has been to "get tough" on crime and criminals, which usually means a return to incarceration of offenders. Statistics indicate that after a decade of deinstitutionalization efforts, the number of juveniles being incarcerated has increased. From 1985 to 1989 the average daily population and total census count of juveniles in public facilities increased 14%; and the juvenile custody rate per 100,000 increased 19% during that period (Allen-Hagen, 1991, p. 2). We noted previously in this chapter that the Juvenile Residential Facility Census (JRFC) in 2002 reported a total of 102,388 juveniles who were held in 2,964 facilities (Sickmund, 2006). This is a slight decline from the previous biannual facility census; the most recent facility census reports another 7% decline in the population of juvenile offenders in custody since 2002 (Livsey, Sickmund, & Sladky, 2009). Crowding is still a problem in some facilities, but improvements are being made. The most recent census—from 2004—reports a smaller number of residents in a larger number of juvenile facilities, up 9% to 3,257 facilities (Livsey et al., 2009). The number of adjudicated youths sent to juvenile corrections facilities, however, does not include the number who are waived to criminal court, tried as adults, and sent to adult institutions.

The commitment to rehabilitation of offenders began to shift by the 1970s, in part due to a widely publicized report by Robert Martinson (1974; see also Lipton, Martinson, & Wilks, 1975) claiming that rehabilitation programs had not had an effect on recidivism. Martinson's conclusion that "nothing works" in corrections had a great national impact, despite the fact that Ted Palmer (1975) wrote a detailed rebuttal questioning Martinson's findings, and Martinson (1979) himself retracted some of his earlier premature and exaggerated conclusions. The demise of the rehabilitative ideal actually had less to do with whether correctional programs were effective in changing offenders, and more to do with a shift in the viewpoints of the public and politicians regarding crime and criminals. Cullen and Gilbert (1982) suggested that crime control policies reflect lawmakers' ideological assumptions about the causes of crime and the most effective strategies to reduce crime. Garland (2001) has contended that cultural patterns structure how the public and politicians feel about offenders. The politics of the 1980s produced a greater division between the jobless and those employed, between blacks and whites, and between the affluent suburbs and the struggling inner cities; and social problems such as violence, street crime, and drug abuse became worse. Accompanying these political and social changes was the view that punishing individuals for criminal and delinquent behavior was more appropriate than rehabilitation and change strategies. Contrary to the views of positivist criminologists, that crime was caused by individual and social problems over which an individual had little control, law violators were now seen as evil individuals who deserved to be punished. Crime was seen not as a sign of need or deprivation, but was viewed as a rational choice by persons who lacked discipline and self-control, who needed to be deterred and deserved to be punished harshly (Garland, 2001, p. 102). Intolerance of crime and criminals has pervaded society and legislative chambers, and the proposed solutions are harsh discipline and punishment.

There are signs that rehabilitation is making a comeback (Cullen, 2005). Reasons for a return to the rehabilitative ideal (Allen, 1981) are not necessarily due to a softening of attitudes toward crime and criminals, but to a realization that attempting to control crime through incarceration is costly and produces no significant reduction in crime rates. Although there is considerable disagreement as to whether training schools and prisons are an effective deterrent to crime, many criminal justice experts point to research evidence that greater use of incarceration may increase rather than decrease crime rates (Garland, 2001). Cullen and his associates have conducted studies on public opinions about rehabilitation, and have found that Americans still strongly support the view that efforts should be made to rehabilitate offenders (Cullen, Fisher, & Applegate, 2000; Cullen, 2005). The field of juvenile corrections may well see a resurgence of rehabilitative strategies in this new century, particularly with new developments based on best practices and what works.

CASE IN POINT 11.3

Juvenile Institutions in the Movies

We noted earlier (Chapters 4 and 5) that crime is a popular form of entertainment in America, and many Hollywood movies focus on crime and criminals. Some popular films (often based on true stories) illustrate the causes and correlates of delinquency, and other films illustrate the consequences of delinquency. The screenplay writers seek to entertain, but also force us as viewers to critically examine how we view crime and criminals, as well as the actions of police, courts, and correctional institutions. We encourage you to view these films and consider how the characters in each story illustrate some of the challenges and dilemmas of using correctional institutions as punishment and correction of offenders.

In the Custody of Strangers. Director: Robert Greenwald; Writer: Jennifer Miller. Release date: May 26, 1982. This film is about an angry small town teenager who is at odds with his father. Danny gets in serious trouble when he goes on a drunken joyride and runs into a police car. The father thinks that a night in jail is just what his kid needs to straighten him up; but events happen in jail that result in Danny spending far longer behind bars after an assault charge. The parents realize the mistake of leaving their son in jail and question the system's treatment of their son. Danny returns to his family, but the home is dramatically changed by his time in jail.

Sleepers. Director: Barry Levinson; Writers: Lorenzo Carcaterra (book) and Barry Levinson (screenplay). Release date: October 12, 1996. This film is about four boys growing up in Hell's Kitchen of New York City in the mid-1960s who play a prank that leads to an old man getting hurt when they steal his vending cart. The boys are sentenced to the Wilkinson Home for Boys in upstate New York, and experience beatings, humiliation, and sexual abuse at the hands of the guards. Thirteen years later, through a chance meeting, they get their revenge against one of the guards and eventually against the Wilkinson Home. The movie depicts how correctional institutions sometimes engender brutality and violence; and how the correctional and judicial processes often confront legal and ethical questions.

SOURCE: The Internet Movie Data Base. Retrieved February 9, 2009, from http://www.imdb.com/.

Discussion Questions

1. After viewing one or both of these films, comment on whether and how the justice and corrections processes may have counterproductive results.

2. According to what you have read in this and previous chapters and other sources, are the stories in these movies realistic events that might occur in many cases? Explain.

3. Based on what you have read in this chapter, what are some policies and safeguards to prevent abuse and brutality from occurring in residential facilities and correctional institutions?

SUMMARY

- The field of juvenile corrections has a long history in America, beginning with the Houses of Refuge in the 19th century, then with correctional reforms and emphases on rehabilitation in the 1970s, to a growing support for punishment and formal control of juvenile offenders in correctional facilities and training schools.
- In 2002, a total of 102,388 juveniles were held in 2,964 facilities, with most juveniles (70,243 or 69%) being held in public facilities; more than one third (1,069 or 36%) of the facilities (mostly public) were at or over capacity.
- The most recent juvenile facility census (from 2004) reports an increase in the number of juvenile facilities and fewer facilities that were operating over their rated capacity.
- Juvenile correctional facilities and training schools are often oppressive institutions where inhumane and brutal conditions exist, and verbal and physical assaults from staff and other juvenile residents are common.
- Minority youth are disproportionately represented in juvenile corrections programs, and federal legislation and mandates have been directed toward examining the sources and reducing disproportionate minority confinement.
- The emphasis in juvenile corrections the past two decades has been on individual accountability and punishment; but there are signs that rehabilitation is making a comeback.

KEY TERMS

Community corrections	Measures of effectiveness
Institutional corrections	"Technical violations"
Group homes	"Environmental corrections"
Foster care	Overrepresentation
Day treatment	Disparity
Recidivism	Discrimination

DISCUSSION QUESTIONS

1. Based on the available research, what do you see as the strengths and limitations of juvenile institutions and residential placement? What types of juvenile offenders are most appropriate for those facilities and placements?

2. Suggest reasons why correctional facilities and training schools tend to become inhumane and oppressive institutions; and why the angry, hostile attitudes of residents are often met with punitive responses by correctional staff.

3. Imagine you have been appointed to your State Youth Commission, and the governor has asked for recommendations for the "best practices" that are most effective in juvenile correctional facilities and residential programs. List the five most important points you would offer.

WEB RESOURCES

Juvenile Offenders and Victims: 2006 National Report: http://ojjdp.ncjrs.gov/ojstatbb/nr2006/downloads/NR2006.pdf

Census of Juveniles in Residential Placement/EZAccess: http://www.ojjdp.ncjrs.gov/ojstatbb/Cjrp/

Innovative Information on Juvenile Residential Facilities: http://www.ncjrs.gov/pdffiles1/ojjdp/fs200011.pdf

Juvenile Residential Facility Census, 2002: http://www.ncjrs.gov/pdffiles1/ojjdp/211080.pdf

Introduction to the Survey of Youth in Residential Placement, 2008: http://www.ncjrs.gov/pdffiles1/ojjdp/218390.pdf

Juvenile Residential Facility Census, 2004: Selected Findings (2009): http://ojjdp.ncjrs.gov/publications/PubAbstract.asp?pubi=244623

Juvenile Probation and Community Corrections

Juvenile Probation

The concept of **probation** was originally developed through the efforts of John Augustus, a Boston boot maker who persuaded a judge in 1841 to release an offender to him for supervision in the community rather than sentence him to prison. Augustus worked with hundreds of offenders and set the stage for probation as we know it today. As the first probation officer, John Augustus developed many of the probation strategies that continue to be used in probation today: investigation and screening, supervision, educational and employment services, and providing guidance and assistance. Probation has been called "the workhorse of the juvenile justice system" (Torbet, 1996) and is the most common juvenile court disposition and the predominant form of

is lacking, the youth may be placed with a legal guardian, foster parents, or in a group home. In either case, the placement is less punitive than commitment to a juvenile institution. The time period for probation supervision is generally for an indefinite period of time, but it usually does not exceed 2 years. Each probation case is usually reviewed periodically to ensure that progress is being made, treatment goals are being met, and to ensure that the juvenile is not kept on probation unnecessarily. If a juvenile commits another offense and is rearrested, or does not comply with the conditions of probation, the probation officer is expected to take the case before the judge for probation violation. The judge may choose to revise the probation conditions or order the youth to a residential program or to a correctional facility or training school. The choice of sanctions for probation violation depends on each youth's risk level, prior offense record, the probation officer's assessment of needs and willingness to cooperate with correctional goals, and the available resources and placements in the jurisdiction.

Probation Officer Responsibilities

Probation officers have three primary responsibilities: intake, investigation, and supervision. We discussed the intake function in Chapter 8 ("Juvenile Detention and Court Intake") and the investigation function in Chapter 10 ("The Juvenile Court Process"). The third major function of a probation officer is to provide **supervision of offenders** in the community and to monitor the court-ordered probation conditions. Following the judge's probation order, the probation officer meets with the youth and parents to explain the rules and conditions of probation, answer any questions about the term of probation and the court's expectations, and to ensure that they understand the importance of complying with the probation conditions. Special probation conditions require additional explanation, especially if the court has included an order to make **restitution** payments to victims or community service restitution, to avoid drinking or drug use, or to participate in drug-treatment programs (see Policy and Practice 12.1). Juvenile probation officers face a special challenge in supervising delinquents, because they often receive little assistance and support from the parents. Many juvenile offenders have a poor relationship with their parents and show little respect for their parents' authority. Families of delinquents are often characterized by parental negligence or abuse, inconsistent discipline, poor communication, and poor parenting skills. Probation supervision is more difficult without solid parental and family support. Under rare but ideal conditions, parents can play an important role in helping a youth comply with probation conditions, in closely supervising their child, and by communicating regularly with the probation officer. Parental support is especially important in closely monitoring the child's school attendance and behavior, peer associations, and in complying with curfew requirements. Probation officers must perform a dual role of encouraging, helping, and assisting the young offender to make a positive adjustment; but also acting as an authority figure who will report probation violations to the court.

POLICY AND PRACTICE 12.1   PROBATION CONDITIONS AND RULES

Juvenile courts include a number of conditions and rules of probation that must be followed by the juvenile, and the parent(s) or legal guardian is expected to cooperate with the court and help to enforce these rules. Probation officers are responsible for monitoring the probation conditions and to report to the court when the juvenile is not in compliance and has violated any of the conditions. The following standard conditions are generally included as part of the juvenile court disposition for probation.

- Obey all city, county, state, and federal laws.
- Not leave the county without verbal permission of the probation officer and/or judge; not leave the state without written permission of the probation officer and/or judge, and only in the company of a parent or legal guardian.
- Report to your probation officer weekly or as directed.
- Be home no later than 7:00 p.m. (or _____) on weekdays; and no later than 10:00 p.m. (or _____) on weekends unless accompanied by your parent or legal guardian.
- Attend school regularly and obey all school rules and regulations. [For older juveniles: maintain gainful employment, as approved by the probation officer and/or judge.]

The juvenile court judge may add additional requirements based on the special costs and circumstances of the offense and based on the juvenile's assessed needs for correctional services and treatment. These may include the following:

- Pay restitution in the amount of _____ by _____ .
- Pay court costs of $ _____ and fines of $ _____ by _____ .
- Participate in Restitution Program at _____ , beginning _____ .
- Provide _____ hours/days of community service with _____ , beginning _____ .
- Attend counseling at _____ , beginning _____ .
- Attend day treatment, day reporting, or evening reporting at _____ , beginning _____ . This disposition is ordered for the following reasons and based on the evidence: _____ _____

The juvenile court judge may add additional requirements of the parent(s) or legal guardian, based on the special costs and circumstances of the offense and based on the juvenile's assessed needs for correctional services and treatment. These may include the following:

- Attend treatment, counseling, or probation appointments with your child.
- Pay restitution in the amount of _____ by _____ .
- Report any and all violations of your child's court orders to the probation officer.
- Attend parental responsibility training at _____ beginning _____ .

(Continued)

(Continued)

- Pay child support in the amount of $ _____ per week/month to _____ during the time your child is in placement or under probation supervision.
- Other: _____
- These orders are made for the following reasons: _____
_____

SOURCE: Adapted from National Council of Juvenile & Family Court Judges. (2005). *Juvenile delinquency guidelines: Improving court practice in juvenile delinquency cases.* Appendix E, pp. 21–22. Retrieved February 3, 2009, from http://www.ncjfcj.org/content/blogcategory/87/114/.

Discussion Questions

1. Probation is often described by critics or the public as "too lenient" or "meaningless" as a court sanction. Based on the probation conditions and rules listed above, how would you respond to those critics?

2. "Punishment" as it relates to corrections is generally defined as a form of restriction of one's personal freedom. Which of the probation conditions and rules do you believe are most restrictive to probationers' personal freedom and liberty?

3. Court decisions have ruled that probation conditions must not be unreasonably punitive and must relate to the goals and purposes of correctional supervision and treatment, including reducing the risk of reoffending. Which of the probation conditions and rules do you believe most clearly support the goals and purposes of probation?

Probation Officer Roles

In carrying out the supervision responsibility, probation officers fulfill three major roles and functions: casework management, treatment, and surveillance. Casework management involves maintaining current files on each juvenile in a caseload averaging 40 or more cases (Torbet, 1996). In addition to the police offense reports and social history report, the case file includes periodic contact reports of every personal visit and telephone call regarding the juvenile. Contacts are made with each juvenile varying from once a week to once a month or less, depending upon the intensity level of supervision needed. Documentation in the juvenile's file is important. Cases are often managed by more than one caseworker, or may be transferred to another officer who is less familiar with the case. If the probation officer files a court petition for revocation of probation, he or she may be called to testify as to the violations of probation conditions, including the exact dates, circumstances, and details of the violations. Paperwork and file management are sources of frustration and complaints among probation officers, but are an important part of the job responsibilities (Lawrence, 1984).

The treatment function of juvenile probation officers focuses on their role as caseworker or counselor. One of the most difficult challenges faced by probation officers is the large number of juveniles from dysfunctional families. Parents have lost the control and the respect of their child. The parent–child relationship has deteriorated to the point that the youth has become incorrigible, refusing to comply with the parents' demands. Many of the parents have never learned to use effective communication and management strategies. Because a poor parent–child relationship is one of the major problems faced by probation officers in working with delinquents, some educational background in family counseling, social work, or general counseling skills has traditionally been one of the job requirements for juvenile probation. Training seminars in family intervention and guidance are often provided for juvenile probation officers, and probation conferences often include at least one session on the subject. Since the minimum educational requirement for probation officers is a 4-year college degree, they are not expected to provide professional counseling services nor are they qualified to do so. One of their responsibilities is therefore to identify problems that require more professional treatment and then refer the child and family to mental health services for family counseling and guidance. The National Advisory Commission on Criminal Justice Standards and Goals (1973) recommended that probation agencies should "redefine the role of probation officer from caseworker to community resource manager" (p. 320). As a resource manager, the officer's responsibility is to assess the juvenile's needs and then make appropriate referrals to other social agencies that can best provide the needed services. Implementation of the resource manager model of probation depends, however, on the community resources and agencies available to assist in the treatment function. Probation clients in jurisdictions with fewer available resources receive only the extent of counseling and guidance that the probation officers themselves are able to provide.

CASE IN POINT 12.1

From Juvenile Court to a Successful Career—With Help From a Probation Officer

Sally Henderson graduated from college and pursued her dream of becoming a television broadcaster. As a young girl on probation for assault with a knife, however, that dream seemed nearly impossible. Walking through her West Side Chicago neighborhood each morning on her way to school, 12-year-old Sally had faced verbal and physical threats from gang members on the way to catch the bus to a school for gifted students on Chicago's North Side. After her younger sister was robbed, Henderson and her family decided she needed some protection. First she carried a rock in a sock in her book bag; but soon she felt she needed more to defend herself, and she started carrying a "little blade" in her pocket, which she clutched on her way to and from school. She "never intended to have to use it," she said as she reflected back on the incident that got her into juvenile court.

Sally was regularly harassed and bullied by a group of girls in a popular clique at the school. They called her names, and pushed and bumped into her when they passed her in the school hallways. When Sally's mother complained to the principal he just brushed it off, saying "girls will be girls." One day the group of girls boarded Sally's school bus and jumped her. Instinctively, she grabbed her little blade and

(Continued)

(Continued)

cut one of the girls in the hand. She was arrested, taken to the police station, and charged with aggravated battery with a weapon. She was suspended from school for 2 weeks, and when she returned her teacher told her that she would never be a news reporter now that she had been arrested.

Sally went to juvenile court and was sentenced to 6 months probation for the knifing incident, her first and only offense. Her first probation officer did little more than ask a few questions, write down some notes, and leave. She was reassigned to a new probation officer, Karen Jordan, and credits this 6-month period of supervision with turning her life around. Jordan met with her regularly and took her out to eat just to talk and to meet other people. Jordan remained her friend and mentor for years after her probation term ended, and took her to a career conference where they met a local television broadcaster, and Henderson was inspired to pursue her dream of a career as a television reporter.

After Henderson completed high school, Jordan told her about Project Lifeline, a program developed by several probation officers to offer college scholarships to juvenile court wards. Jordan pushed Sally to apply for the scholarship and helped her write and type up the letter. Following an interview, Henderson received a college scholarship that enabled her to go to Parkland Junior College in Champaign, and then she transferred to Illinois State University (ISU) in Normal. Henderson pursued her dream of becoming a television broadcaster at ISU. In her senior year she was a producer, editor, writer, and reporter on a television show that she hosted on ISU's cable channel. She graduated in 1999 with a degree in communications and went to work as an intern at the NBC affiliate station in Bloomington, Illinois.

Sally Henderson reflects back positively on her juvenile court and probation experience. In Sally's words, what had begun as "a nightmare" that could have ruined her life turned out to be "a blessing" that turned her life around. She doubts that she would be where she is today without the help, encouragement, and guidance of her probation officer, Karen Jordan.

SOURCE: Adapted from Justice Policy Institute. (2000). Second chances: Giving kids a chance to make a better choice. *OJJDP Juvenile Justice Bulletin.* Washington, DC: U.S. Department of Justice.

Discussion Questions

1. There are thousands of juveniles in cities throughout America who get in trouble just by responding to the negative environment and threats around them. They are punished for making bad decisions and hurting people. What other responses and strategies would you suggest for responding to and preventing juvenile delinquency?

2. Do you think Sally Henderson's assault with a knife and juvenile court and probation experience is likely to result the same way for most other juveniles? Why or why not?

3. What juvenile **probation officer roles** are illustrated by Karen Jordan in this case?

4. What factors—personal, social, agency emphasis, community resources, or others—might limit other probation officers' ability to do as much for their clients?

The **surveillance** function requires the probation officer to closely monitor juveniles to make certain that they are complying with the probation conditions (see Policy and Practice 12.1). This may be accomplished through questions directed at the juvenile during office visits, through telephone calls, or by personal visits to the juvenile's home or school. Probation agencies may require drug testing for juveniles suspected of illegal drug use. A probation officer's surveillance function is much like that of a police officer's, and probation officers also have the authority to take probationers into custody for violating conditions of probation. Juvenile probation officers work closely with police, and depend on police officers to arrest and take into custody any juveniles on probation who commit a new crime. Violation of probation conditions is considered a **technical violation,** and probation officers have more latitude in whether to file for revocation of probation than when a youth is rearrested by police for a new crime. In either case, probation revocation is not automatic. The juvenile is entitled to a probation revocation hearing under due process guidelines established by the U.S. Supreme Court in the 1972 case of *Morrissey v. Brewer* (408 U.S. 471, 92 S. Ct. 2593). If the judge finds that there is sufficient evidence that probation conditions have been violated, he or she may revoke probation and commit the juvenile to a state training school, or may choose a range of less punitive alternatives, including more intensive probation supervision with more restrictive conditions, or temporary placement in a semisecure group home placement.

Probation Officer Role Conflict

Probation officers are charged with helping offenders to change, but as officers of the court they are also expected to monitor compliance with court orders. The two roles represent treatment versus surveillance; acting as a counselor or social worker one moment, and a law enforcement officer the next. Probation officers experience **role conflict** in attempting to fulfill both functions at the same time (Lawrence, 1984; Latessa & Allen, 2003). The opposing roles of treatment versus surveillance put probation officers in a dilemma: attempting to be a counselor or advocate for a juvenile while simultaneously enforcing probation rules and threatening revocation as a consequence for violations. The officer cannot choose one role over the other. Attention to both responsibilities is necessary. The objectives of probation are to help probationers adjust to problems at home, school, and in the community, but officers are also responsible for monitoring probationers' compliance with probation rules and reporting probation violations to the court. Considerable research has been conducted on the dilemmas and difficulties presented by probation officer role conflict (Latessa & Allen, 2003, pp. 258–263). The nature of the job's requirements means that some role conflict will always be present, but education and training can minimize the adverse effects of role conflict on probation officers and other community corrections personnel.

CASE IN POINT 12.2

From Juvenile Probation to the U.S. Senate

Senator Alan Simpson, a former U.S. Senator from California, is best known for his work as a lawmaker—not as a law breaker. Simpson grew up in Cody, Wyoming, and like most boys liked to shoot and hunt with rifles. He and his friends occasionally went "over the edge" and committed crimes as part of their shooting sport, however, such as stealing .22 caliber rifle shells from the local hardware store. When he was 17, Simpson and four friends drove down a rural road and shot holes through mailboxes with a .22 caliber rifle. They also shot up a road grader, and one of the wayward shots killed a cow. When the postmaster began asking around about the damaged mailboxes, neighbors' descriptions of the shots, noise from firecrackers, and a car they had seen led to Simpson's home. Alan Simpson confessed, and he and his four friends pled guilty in the Cheyenne federal court to destroying federal property. The judge sentenced them to 2 years probation and ordered them to make restitution for the mailboxes, the road grader, and the dead cow.

J. B. Mosley was assigned as the boys' probation officer, and for the next 2 years he visited Simpson and his friends regularly, seeing them at home, in the pool hall, at school, and on the basketball court. Simpson remembers Mosley as a guy who cared about him and showed it in several ways. Mosley kept tabs on Simpson's progress, both in his school work and his success on the basketball team. Simpson says "he paid attention to me. . . . He didn't preach . . . he listened." The people in town all knew what Simpson and his friends had done, and didn't let them forget it. Their reputation as the mailbox shooters who went to federal court followed them through high school. With help and guidance from J. B. Mosley, they all made it through probation and went on to successful lives.

Simpson was the only one of the group to get into trouble again as an adult, when at age 21 he got into a shoving match with a drunken friend in Laramie, Wyoming. A police officer mistook the shoving for a fight, hit Simpson with a billy club, and Simpson lashed back at the officer. He later admitted that was "a real big mistake!" He spent the night in jail, was charged with breaching the peace, and released with a $300 fine. His parents were again devastated, shocked, and disappointed at his behavior. The incident made Simpson realize that his attitude was "stupefying, arrogant, and cocky" and no way to live. From then on, he straightened out, earned a bachelor's degree, served in the army, and earned a law degree. He worked in his dad's law firm for 18 years, served for 13 years in the Wyoming legislature, and was elected to the U.S. Senate, where he served for 18 years.

Reflecting back on his mistakes and the help and guidance he received from his parents and from probation officer Mosley, Senator Alan Simpson believes that everybody should get a second chance. As a lawyer he often worked with juvenile cases. His approach was tough love and getting the juveniles' attention through tough talk, telling them to take advantage of their second chance and to shape up. He credits his probation officer and parents who cared about him but held him accountable for helping him turn his life around. The former Senator continues to have confidence that most kids who get into trouble will—and do—grow and mature beyond their youthful indiscretions.

SOURCE: Adapted from Justice Policy Institute. (2000). Second chances: Giving kids a chance to make a better choice. *OJJDP Juvenile Justice Bulletin.* Washington, DC: U.S. Department of Justice.

Discussion Questions

1. The juvenile court is often criticized for not "cracking down" on juvenile crime, and giving delinquents too many second chances. What does this case suggest about the advantages of a "second chance"?

2. Having a record of arrest, court conviction, and probation is often enough to eliminate a person's chances of getting into law enforcement, probation work, law school, and other professions. Offer arguments for, and against, these policies.

3. Is the Senator Simpson case exceptional, or one that might apply to most juveniles in trouble? What are some "extralegal" (social, family, personal, or regional) factors that might have played out in Simpson's favor in this case?

Do you believe that most juvenile delinquents should get a second chance, regardless of race, ethnicity, family or social background, or region of the country? If so, what changes or policies might have to be implemented for this to happen?

Intermediate Sanctions

The juvenile court judge traditionally was limited to the sentencing options of either probation or residential placement. Many offenders require more supervision than regular probation, but do not require 24-hour care and supervision for several months in a residential placement or secure correctional facility. The concept of intermediate sanctions was developed to provide supervision and correctional services that are literally "between prison and probation" (Morris & Tonry, 1990). A variety of intermediate sanctions have been developed to provide more public safety than regular probation, while being less intrusive and expensive than residential placements. These alternatives to incarceration include intensive probation supervision, day reporting centers, electronic monitoring, and restitution programs. They are commonly used by probation agencies as a part of and in addition to probation supervision. There is evidence that intermediate sanctions are more successful than regular probation supervision, and have advantages over institutional commitment in that they are less expensive and avoid severing ties between the juvenile's family and the community (Latessa & Allen, 2003).

Intensive Supervision Probation (ISP)

Probation has been criticized for being too lenient and for providing only minimal supervision. There is no question that many juveniles need more supervision than what can be provided by a single probation officer with a large caseload. Intensive supervision programs have been adopted by many probation agencies as an alternative to sending high-risk juveniles to a correctional institution (Byrne, 1986). A small number of cases (about 15 to 25) are assigned to a probation officer who is expected to make daily contacts to monitor closely their daily activities. The recidivism rates of juveniles on intensive supervision probation are often higher than those on regular probation, due in part to the higher-risk juveniles in the programs and to the officer's close surveillance, which detects probation violations that may go unnoticed on regular probation supervision. Even if intensive supervision is no more effective in reducing recidivism of high-risk juvenile offenders, the lower cost (about one third that of confinement) makes it a desirable alternative over incarceration (Latessa, 1986).

Day Reporting Centers

Day reporting centers have been implemented as an alternative means of assisting probation officers to keep up with the task of monitoring probation clients through personal visits. It is not possible for most probation officers with a caseload of 50 or more cases to see each of their clients regularly. Day reporting centers were developed to monitor a larger number of probationers with a smaller number of officers. Offenders in the program are court ordered to report in person to a reporting center, to provide a schedule of planned activities, and to participate in designated activities. Offenders must also call the centers by phone throughout the day, and can also expect random phone calls from the center staff during the day and at home following curfew (Gowdy, 1993). In addition to monitoring probationers' activities, day reporting centers offer a variety of services, including job skills training and placement, drug abuse education, and counseling. Research evidence indicates that day reporting centers have been effective in providing closer monitoring of probation clients without significantly increasing the cost of probation services (Latessa & Allen, 2003, pp. 339–343).

Electronic Monitoring and House Arrest

Juveniles may be placed on probation under special conditions requiring that they remain in their home at all times except for school, employment, or medical reasons. House arrest may be coupled with frequent random phone calls or personal visits, or with electronic monitoring. In this technological innovation, probationers are fitted with a nonremovable monitoring device attached to their ankle that signals a probation department computerized monitoring station if the offender leaves the house (Charles, 1986). The monitoring device is connected to the telephone in the house and makes random phone calls to verify the probationer's presence. Electronic monitoring has the advantage of operating as an effective alternative to incarceration in a detention center at less than half the cost. Joseph Vaughn (1989) conducted a survey of eight juvenile electronic monitoring programs and found that most were successful in reducing the number of days that juveniles spent in detention; and the youth were able to participate in school and work activities during the time they were not confined to their homes. Vaughn found, however, that the treatment benefits of electronic monitoring programs still remain in question. Recent evaluations of electronic monitoring have found little evidence that it has a positive impact on offender recidivism (Latessa & Allen, 2003, p. 351).

Restitution Programs

One of the goals of community corrections is to hold offenders accountable and to get them to recognize the harm they have done. Restitution programs represent a way for juvenile offenders to literally "pay for" their crimes while on probation. Four goals of restitution programs have been identified: (1) holding juveniles accountable; (2) providing reparation to victims; (3) treating and rehabilitating juveniles; and (4) punishing juveniles (Schneider, 1985a).

Restitution can be in the form of either monetary or service restitution and to either the victim or the community. Under monetary restitution, the probationer may be ordered to reimburse the victim of the crime for property damages or the medical costs of personal injury. Under the second form, a juvenile may be required to provide some service directly to the victim or to the community. Victim restitution is done with the consent of the victim, and service restitution is usually done under the supervision of a probation officer. Juvenile restitution programs exist in more than 400 jurisdictions throughout the nation, and by 1985 most states had legislation authorizing such programs as part of probation (Schneider & Warner, 1989). Restitution directs attention to the forgotten persons in the justice process, the victims, and provides monetary compensation or service to them. It is rehabilitative in that the juvenile has an opportunity to compensate the victim for injury or damages, and encourages him or her to be accountable for wrongful actions and become a productive member of society. Evaluations of restitution programs indicate that they are quite effective as a treatment alternative. Schneider (1986) evaluated programs in four states and found that program participants had lower recidivism rates than control groups of youths placed on regular probation. The differences were not dramatic (a difference of only 10% in recidivism rates in some comparisons), but the restitution programs did seem to result in more positive attitudes among many juveniles (Schneider, 1986). Restitution programs have been recognized as one of the programs that represent the best practices for juvenile court and probation, as they focus on offender accountability and offer an opportunity for juvenile offenders to make reparations to the victim and the community (Kurlychek, Torbet, & Bozynski, 1999).

Aftercare or Parole Supervision

Supervision of juveniles in the community following release from an institutional facility is referred to as aftercare (comparable to "parole supervision" in some jurisdictions). Intensive aftercare programs provide social control and treatment services for juveniles returning to the community from out-of-home placements, and are important for making the transition from the institution to the community. Aftercare can serve to protect public safety by monitoring the juvenile's reintegration into the community. Aftercare services help the juvenile to overcome negative influences and risk factors by enhancing the skills needed to become a productive and law-abiding member of society. Successful aftercare programs begin developing an offender's aftercare plan early in the residential placement, create links to the youth's family and school throughout treatment, and provide high levels of both social control and treatment services (Gies, 2003).

The Office of Juvenile Justice and Delinquency Prevention (OJJDP) initiated an Intensive Community-Based Aftercare Program (IAP) in 1987 that had three emphases:

- Prerelease and preparatory planning during incarceration
- Structured transition that required the participation of institutional and aftercare staff prior to and following community reentry
- Long-term, reintegrative activities that ensure adequate service delivery and the necessary level of social control (Altschuler & Armstrong, 1996)

Research on the IAP model has indicated that when aftercare supervision is predominantly or exclusively surveillance and social control (e.g., drug testing and electronic monitoring), and treatment services are lacking or inadequate, then neither a reduction in recidivism nor improvement in social, cognitive, or behavioral functioning are likely to occur (Altschuler, Armstrong, & MacKenzie, 1999). Development of successful aftercare programs faces a number of challenges, including not enough qualified staff; cost sharing and contracting between public and private agencies; developing organizational capacity to deliver consistent and compatible services between the institution and the community; and applying those services to problems in the family, peer group, school, work, and drug involvement (Altschuler et al., 1999, p. 4). Altschuler and Brash (2004) noted that young incarcerated offenders face two difficult challenges: the developmental transition from childhood to adulthood; and the transition from life in a correctional facility to living in the community. They emphasized that successful aftercare programs should include family management and parent effectiveness training, educational and vocational training that lead to work opportunities, programs that provide links to positive peer groups, and substance abuse treatment. A review of the research on aftercare programs indicates that they show promise of assisting with successful reentry and reintegration of juvenile offenders returning from institutions to community programs, and that they can combine interventions for individual behavior change with surveillance methods to protect the community (Gies, 2003).

POLICY AND PRACTICE 12.2   HOLDING JUVENILES ACCOUNTABLE: A "BEST PRACTICE"

The federal Office of Juvenile Justice and Delinquency Prevention (OJJDP) promotes and supports practices that have been shown through research to be most effective in reducing juvenile offending. Holding juveniles accountable for their crime through court sanctions and consequences is an important first step in preventing, controlling, and reducing further law violations. The Juvenile Accountability Incentive Block Grants Program was developed by the OJJDP to help States and local jurisdictions develop programs that hold juveniles accountable for their behavior. The program began by identifying research findings on effective programs for delinquency prevention. According to Lipsey (1992), effective programs do the following:

- Concentrate on changing behavior and improving positive social skills.
- Focus on problem solving with both juveniles and their families.
- Have multiple modes of intervention.
- Are highly structured and intensive. (Lipsey, 1992, as cited in Kurlychek, Torbet, & Bozinsky, 1999)

The following have also been recommended:

- Require juveniles to recognize and understand thought processes that rationalize negative behaviors.
- Promote healthy bonds with and respect for persons in a juvenile's life who are positive role models.
- Have consistent, clear, and graduated consequences for misbehavior, and recognition for positive behavior.
- Provide a variety of structured programming activities including education, vocational training, and skill development.
- Provide guidance and training in family problem solving.
- Integrate delinquent and at-risk youth into prosocial groups to prevent the development of delinquent peer groups.

To meet the goals of best practices under the juvenile accountability program, juvenile courts and probation departments are expected to complete the following tasks and responsibilities:

- Identify the problem to be addressed or the current gaps in court sanctions or probation services.
- Identify possible approaches to address the need to keep juveniles accountable.
- Review existing research studies to determine which approaches are effective.
- Adapt programs known to be successful in other communities to fit local needs.
- Make a commitment to implement effective programs and assure they are carried out as planned.
- Monitor program components and delivery, and evaluate the program process and impact.
- Compare recidivism data with those for clients and graduates of other programs handling similar offenders.

What is perhaps most unique and noteworthy about this program is that *accountability begins with juvenile court judges and probation officers.* The emphasis in "Policy and Practice 12.1" (above) is what juveniles must do; the conditions and rules of probation that they must follow and obey. Here, the authors describe the federal government emphasis on holding juveniles accountable, but they emphasize that accountability must begin with juvenile court judges and probation officers. Judges must lead by example by stressing accountability and compliance of all dispositions ordered by the court. Probation officers are responsible for developing and carrying out specialized supervision programs, assuring that restitution is collected, and monitoring community service projects. Just as the system holds juveniles accountable for their actions, the court and probation agencies must be accountable for providing the services promised to juvenile offenders to help meet the desired outcomes. The authors suggest that probation departments can benefit from collaborating with universities to assist in meeting demands for staff training and education and for monitoring and evaluating community corrections programs.

(Continued)

(Continued)

Some exemplary programs that illustrate best practices for juvenile accountability include a prosecuting attorney's office in Washington State that implemented a "fast track" diversion program; a center for dispute resolution and victim offender mediation in the juvenile probation department in Austin, Texas; a juvenile restitution program operated by a Utah juvenile court that holds offenders accountable for restoring harms done to the victim and community; school-based probation programs in Pennsylvania in which probation officers work in schools rather than in a traditional courthouse setting; the Orange County, California, early intervention program that works with young, high-risk juvenile offenders and their families; and the Operation Night Light program in Boston in which police and probation officers work together to ensure offenders are complying with probation conditions.

SOURCE: Adapted from Kurlychek, M., Torbet, P., & Bozynski , M. (1999). Focus on accountability: Best practices for juvenile court and probation. *JAIBG Bulletin*. Washington, DC: U.S. Department of Justice. Retrieved November 18, 2008, from http://www.ncjrs.gov/pdffiles1/177611.pdf.

Discussion Questions

1. Review again the steps in holding juveniles accountable. Now compare them with most of the same steps our parents, teachers, mentors, coaches, music directors, group leaders, or employers have had to do with us—to make us accountable and responsible. Note the similarities to your own experience.

2. Juvenile offenders and at-risk youth have faced all of the same difficulties of adolescence that are a universal experience of growing up. Suggest the ways in which many youth may have had more difficulties through childhood and adolescence due to family problems, lack of parental support, lack of role models, and lack of structure that promotes responsibility.

3. Think of yourself, your siblings, and peers who have avoided problems with delinquency and crime. What personal and social supports can you identify that have helped you to be where you are today?

4. Identify programs in your local or county schools, community organizations, churches, and similar groups that help youth to become responsible young adults.

Effectiveness of Juvenile Corrections

There is no unanimous agreement on how to assess correctional outcome. *Recidivism* has been the traditional measure of effectiveness in corrections. Recidivism may refer to a new arrest, a new conviction, or a return to prison, however, so evaluative research must clearly specify the exact criteria being used to measure success or failure (Snyder & Sickmund, 2006, p. 234). Violations of probation conditions ("technical violations") are also indicators of failure, but are less likely to result in revocation of probation. The practice of assessing effectiveness of corrections based on arrests or other measures of recidivism has clear limitations (Latessa & Allen, 2003). Corrections researchers believe that success or failure should be viewed on a continuum using multiple indicators rather than as a dichotomous win–lose criterion. Petersilia (1993) has recommended that community corrections should be assessed according to several performance indicators that are based on clearly stated goals, methods, and activities. Five goals of community corrections that should be included in an assessment of outcome are the quality and extent to which the probation agency and officer have been able to: (1) assess offender's suitability for placement; (2) enforce court-ordered sanctions; (3) protect the community; (4) assist offenders to change; and (5) restore crime victims (pp. 78–79). Evaluating the effectiveness of community corrections according to these five goals takes into account the multiple roles and responsibilities of probation officers, among them investigation, supervision, and monitoring of court orders, including restitution payments to victims. Multiple performance indicators are used to assess the performance of corrections professionals and the responses of offenders to correctional services and supervision. Number of days employed, vocational education, school attendance, and the number of drug- and alcohol-free days serve as performance indicators in addition to the number of arrests and technical violations (pp. 78–79).

Measures of the effectiveness of juvenile corrections should also assess the quality of programs, including those conducted in institutions, in public and private residential facilities, and those providing supervision and treatment in the community (Latessa & Allen, 2003). While assessment of program effectiveness is important, corrections researchers acknowledge that recidivism remains the most common measure of the effectiveness of corrections programs. A meta-analysis of studies of institutional and community corrections interventions for serious juvenile offenders concluded that the most effective types of treatment were interpersonal skills training, individual counseling, and behavioral programs (Lipsey, Wilson, & Cothern, 2000). Lipsey and his associates found that community-based programs showed greater reductions in recidivism than institutional programs. Offenders in nonsecure community supervision programs do commit some new crimes, but the fact that they do as well or better than youths sent to training schools and released to aftercare supervision suggests that community supervision presents no more risk to public safety and recidivism than incarceration. Research on "get-tough" measures such as Scared Straight programs, boot camps, and intensive supervision has indicated that harsher measures, without additional educational or skills training components, do not reduce recidivism (Whitehead & Lab, 2006).

Cullen, Eck, and Lowenkamp (2002) have proposed a new paradigm for effective probation and parole supervision called environmental corrections, which is based on environmental criminology, a theory that links crime causation and crime reduction to the presence or absence of opportunities to commit crime. Cullen and his associates believe that probation and parole officers would be more effective if they worked closely with offenders, the family, community members, and the police in order to reduce offenders' opportunities and temptations to commit crime. In addi tion to maintaining the usual responsibilities of assessment and investigation, probation and parole officers would use a problem-solving approach in supervising offenders to help them avoid the opportunities and temptations that lead to offending. Cullen and his associates (2002) acknowledge that considerable efforts will be required to put it into practice. A new problem-solving approach for probation and parole officers engaged in environmental corrections will add to their responsibilities, but may improve community supervision and be more cost effective.

SUMMARY

- Probation was first introduced in 1841 for adult offenders, and was soon available for juvenile offenders after the development of juvenile courts in the early 1900s.
- In 2002, adjudicated delinquents ordered to probation (385,400 cases) accounted for 62% of all delinquency cases placed on probation. The number of adjudicated cases that resulted in court-ordered probation rose 103% between 1985 and 2002 (from 189,600 to 385,400).
- Probation officers' responsibilities include both control and rehabilitation, resulting in "role conflict" for many officers.
- Aftercare or parole supervision is essential for successful reentry back into the community of juveniles returning from institutional commitment.
- Evaluating the effectiveness of corrections by recidivism alone has limitations. Performance assessment based on the quality and extent to which probation officers and agencies are able to accomplish the five goals of community corrections offers a more complete outcome assessment.

KEY TERMS

Probation	Technical violations
Casework management	Role conflict
Treatment	Day reporting centers
Resource manager	Aftercare
Probation officer roles	Probation effectiveness
Surveillance	Environmental corrections

DISCUSSION QUESTIONS

1. Probation is a juvenile disposition (sentence) that is an "alternative to incarceration" or to residential placement. Explain how the probation officer's investigation role can help ensure that juvenile offenders placed on probation are (a) *not* a risk to public safety, and (b) receive supervision and services to help them not reoffend and to do well on probation.

2. As a new probation officer, you are assigned a caseload of 30 juvenile offenders, ranging from first-time offenders with single occurrences of property offenses or drug violations to second- and third-time offenders with prior arrests and a history of probation violations. What probation officer roles are you likely to use with various types of offenders, and under what circumstances?

3. Explain "role conflict" of probation officers. Knowing that every officer does have to perform several roles, some of which conflict, suggest ways that officers can deal with role conflict—both when dealing with offenders and as it relates to personal job satisfaction.

4. All professionals, including probation officers, want to do well on their jobs. How do we assess "job performance" of probation officers? When good surveillance detects offender failure, is that a sign of job failure? Explain.

WEB RESOURCES

Juvenile Probation: "Workhorse of the Juvenile Justice System": http://www.ncjrs.gov/pdffiles/workhors.pdf

Juvenile offenders and victims—2006 national report: http://ojjdp.ncjrs.gov/ojstatbb/nr2006/downloads/NR2006.pdf

Juvenile Court Statistics of Juveniles on Probation: http://www.ojjdp.ncjrs.gov/ojstatbb/ezajcs/

Overview of Aftercare Services: http://www.ncjrs.gov/pdffiles1/ojjdp/201800.pdf

"Second Chances: Giving Kids a Chance. . . .": http://www.ncjrs.gov/pdffiles1/ojjdp/181680.pdf

Restorative
Justice

--- ❖

The traditional juvenile justice process has focused to various degrees either on correcting or punishing the offender, or on protecting the community. The victim of juvenile crime has been virtually ignored and omitted from the justice process. A movement referred to as "balanced restorative justice" endeavors to place equal emphasis on the offender, the community, and the victim. The goals include holding the offender accountable for the crime committed and repairing the harm done to the victim and the community. **Restorative justice** aims to involve the victim and community members more in the justice process, and to restore the offender as a responsible member of the community. This new paradigm of justice represents a significant departure from the traditional **retributive justice** process, and depends on the commitment and voluntary involvement of the offender, victim, and community. In this chapter we will examine the history and development of restorative justice, examples of its application in the justice process, and some potential problems and questions that have been raised about restorative justice.

POLICY AND PRACTICE 13.1 | **RESTORATIVE JUSTICE PRACTICES AT WORK**

- In Minnesota, Montana, Pennsylvania, Australia, and New Zealand, family and community members acquainted with a juvenile offender or crime victim gather to determine the best response to the offense. Family group conferences are held in schools, churches, or other community facilities and are facilitated by a trained community justice coordinator to ensure that offenders hear community disapproval of their behavior. Participants develop an agreement for repairing the damage to the victim and community and a plan for reintegrating the offender.
- In Dakota County, Minnesota (a Minneapolis suburb), retailers and citizens whose businesses and homes have been damaged by burglary or vandalism call a crime repair hotline to request a work crew of probationers to repair the damage.
- In Deschutes County, Oregon, offender work crews cut and deliver firewood to senior citizens and work with a local contractor to build a homeless shelter.
- In Montana, college students and young adults in the Montana Conservation Corps supervise juvenile offenders working on environmental restoration, trail building, and other community service projects.
- In more than 150 cities and towns in the United States and Canada, victims and offenders meet with volunteer mediators to develop restitution agreements. Victims express their fears and feelings about crime at these meetings and gain information about the offender and the offense.

SOURCE: Bazemore, G., & Day, S. E. (1996). Restoring the balance: Juvenile and community justice. *Juvenile Justice, 3*(1), pp. 3–14.

History and Development of Restorative Justice

There have been increasing demands for programs and policies in criminal justice that give more attention to the needs of the victim and the community. The concerns and emphases that have formed the concept of restorative justice have roots in ancient systems of justice that viewed crimes as an injury more to the victim than to the government. An ancient Sumerian code (c. 2050 B.C.) and the Code of Hammurabi (c. 1700 B.C.), for example, required restitution to the victim or family even in the case of violent offenses (Van Ness, 1990). Restorative justice practices in the United States have developed over the past 30 years. Restorative justice has roots in a variety of theoretical backgrounds, including the philosophy of punishment, feminist criminology, peacemaking criminology, victims' rights, victim–offender reconciliation, conflict resolution, and mediation. It has been clear for some time that the traditional retributive model that is the foundation of the formal system of justice in America is deficient in not including the victim and community in the justice process; it does not accomplish a balance of offender accountability and restoration.

Restorative justice views crime and the justice process as distinct and different from traditional retributive justice. Restorative justice views crime as a violation of interpersonal relationships, in the sense that victims and the community have been harmed and are in need of restoration (Zehr & Mika, 1998). In contrast to traditional justice where police, the courts, and corrections agencies play a major role, victims, offenders, and the affected communities are the key stakeholders in restorative justice. Offenders are obligated under restorative justice to make things right as much as possible; and the community's obligations are to victims and to offenders and for the general welfare of community members. In place of the formal justice process, restorative justice seeks to heal the harm and make right the wrongs resulting from law violations. The victim, the offender, and the community are all involved in the restorative justice process. The most significant difference between the traditional retributive justice process and restorative justice is the greater role played by the victim and community members. According to Zehr and Mika (1998), "the justice process belongs to the community. . . . Community members are actively involved in doing justice" and "the justice process draws from community resources and, in turn, contributes to the building and strengthening of community" (p. 53). Unlike traditional retributive justice, restorative justice places more emphasis on the community and the victim (for safety, protection, and harms due to criminal acts) and makes the victim and community "partners" with formal justice system agencies in responding to law violations. Similar to traditional justice, the offender is held accountable for crime. In contrast to retributive justice, the restorative justice process requires the offender to make things right with the community and the victim, and replaces punitive sanctions with a process designed to restore the offender, the community, and the victim. Table 13.1 summarizes the main points and distinctions between the current, traditional retributive justice process and restorative justice.

We have noted previously how the juvenile court has changed over the years from an emphasis on rehabilitation to a more punitive approach (in Chapter 10). The juvenile court moved away from its original goal of providing treatment in the "best interests of the child" to what some have called a "criminalized" court that focused on treating juveniles more like adults (Feld, 1999b). The "get-tough" approach toward juveniles has not been effective in deterring juvenile offenders, or in offering effective change strategies to reduce juvenile offending. The traditional retributive justice approach clearly has limits for effectively responding to juvenile crime. Advocates of restorative justice argue that the new balanced approach is an appropriate alternative to the traditional retributive juvenile justice sanctions (Bazemore & Umbreit, 1995). Retributive justice views crime as the violation of laws administered and enforced by government authorities, and focuses on determining guilt and delivering punishment through an adversarial process. In contrast, restorative justice is concerned with the broader relationships between the offender, the victim, and the community (Zehr & Mika, 1998). It is the restorative justice response that sets it apart most distinctively from retributive justice. Juvenile offending is more than simply lawbreaking; it represents injury and harm to victims and the community. The restorative justice response is focused on offender accountability and on resolving the harm done through conflict resolution, mediation, and similar restorative processes. Restorative justice is viewed as a "balanced" approach because it articulates three goals for juvenile justice:

| Table 13.1 | Traditional Retributive Justice Versus Restorative Justice |

Retributive Justice	Restorative Justice
Crime is an act against the state, a violation of the law.	Crime is an act against another person and the community.
The criminal justice system controls crime.	Crime control lies primarily in the community.
Offender accountability is defined as being punished.	Offender accountability is defined as taking responsibility and taking action to repair harm.
Crime is an individual act with individual responsibility.	Crime has both individual and social dimensions of responsibility.
Punishment is effective; threats of being punished deter crime; punishment changes behavior.	Punishment alone does not change behavior; it is disruptive to community harmony and good relationships.
Victims are secondary in the justice process.	Victims are central to the justice process and for resolving a crime.
The offender is defined by deficits, risks, and weaknesses.	The offender is defined by the capacity to make reparation for the crime.
Focus is on establishing blame, guilt, and on the past crime.	Focus is on problem solving, on obligations, and on what must be done in the future.
Emphasis is on adversarial relationship in the formal justice process.	Emphasis is on dialogue and negotiation among offender, victim, and justice professionals.
Imposition of pain to punish, deter, and prevent future crimes.	Restitution as a means of restoring victim, offender, and community; goal of reconciliation and restoration.
Community is not directly involved, but is represented by the state.	Community is actively involved as a facilitator and participant in restorative process.

SOURCE: Adapted from Bazemore & Umbreit, 1995.

- *Accountability:* Offenders are obligated to take responsibility for their actions, for harm to victims, and are expected to make amends by restoring losses.
- *Competency:* The most appropriate change strategies ensure that juvenile offenders gain educational, vocational, social, and civic competencies that enhance their ability to function as responsible young adults.
- *Public Safety:* Tougher laws and incarceration are limited as public safety strategies. A balanced problem-oriented focus includes work, education, and service in offender supervision, thus improving relations with schools, employers, and the community (Bazemore & Day, 1996, p. 7)

Figure 13.1 The Balanced Approach

Restorative Justice

Community Safety

Accountability

Competency
Development

Clients / Customers	Goals	Values
Victims	Accountability	When an individual commits an offence, the offender incurs an obligation to individual victims and the community.
Youth	Competency development	Offenders who enter the juvenile justice system should be more capable when they leave than when they entered.
Community	Community safety	Juvenile justice has a responsibility to protect the public from juveniles in the system.

SOURCE: Pranis, K. (1998). *Guide for implementing the balanced and restorative justice model.* Washington, DC: Office of Juvenile Justice and Delinquency Prevention.

Applications and Forms of Restorative Justice

Juvenile probation departments throughout the United States, Canada, and other countries have taken a "balanced approach" to probation supervision, utilizing a logical consequences model whereby juveniles are held accountable for antisocial behavior. Maloney, Romig, and Armstrong (1988) noted that the purpose of the balanced approach to juvenile probation is to protect the community from delinquency, to make offenders accountable for delinquent acts, and to ensure that juvenile offenders leave the system with more skills to live productively and responsibly in society. Juvenile probation agencies that have adopted the balanced approach place equal attention and focus on the community, the victim, and the juvenile offender (Maloney et al., 1988). Probation officers like the balanced approach with its emphasis on the logical consequences model, because it helps to alleviate much of the role conflict experienced by officers trying to fulfill both treatment and surveillance functions. Adopting a logical consequences approach in probation supervision reminds juveniles to take probation seriously and encourages more of them to be less resistant and more open to a cooperative working relationship with their probation officer. The principles for juvenile probation under a balanced and restorative justice approach include:

- *Community Protection.* The public has a right to a safe and secure community
- *Accountability.* The juvenile must be held accountable when an offense occurs
- *Competency.* Juvenile offenders under probation supervision should also receive skills and preparation to live productively and responsibly in the community
- *Individualization.* Probation investigations should include offender assessments along with the circumstances and factors related to the delinquent behavior, so that responses are individualized and relate to the contributing factors in each case
- *Balance.* Justice is best served when the community, victim, and juvenile offender receive balanced attention toward the goal of observable outcomes from the probation process (see Maloney et al., 1988, p. 10)

CASE IN POINT 13.1

Restorative Practices and Policing

Paul Schnell is a St. Paul, Minnesota, police officer who has applied restorative justice practices in his police work. He discovered that approaching youthful misbehavior and juvenile offending through the traditional law enforcement methods did not always work with many youth. He arrested a lot of kids—many of them several times, over and over. He noted that using his authority as a law enforcement officer did not seem to make much impact on many of them. Officer Schnell learned about restorative justice several years ago, and began applying it in his policing duties, both with victims and with juvenile offenders. He gave an example of how restorative practices in policing can be more effective.

Two juveniles in one neighborhood were causing problems for many of the residents. During a 60-day period, the St. Paul police department had received about 40 calls for service in that area alone, all relating to behavior by those two juveniles. The calls were not about crimes for which police could make an

(Continued)

(Continued)

arrest and a case in court; but included noise, property damage, things destroyed, and broken windows. The police didn't have witnesses to clearly pin it on those juveniles, but people in the neighborhood knew that the two kids were involved, and they were frustrated. Officer Schnell and other officers tried to talk to the two young boys, did the traditional police warnings and lecture, but that didn't work. Talking to their parents also made little difference.

Finally, Officer Schnell set up a restorative justice conference and invited people in the neighborhood, the boys, and their parents to attend. The conference began with a tense, emotional atmosphere, as the neighbors expressed their frustration and wanted a stop to the noise and the property damage. The neighborhood residents didn't focus on how bad the boys were, but on how they wanted a peaceful and safe neighborhood for everyone. Officer Schnell was surprised how the restorative conference turned into a positive and productive meeting. The neighbors, the juveniles, and their parents all spoke and listened to each other. The boys seemed to understand how their behavior had affected so many of their neighbors. The discussion was about reaching some agreement on the rules they wanted and the kind of neighborhood they wanted. The juveniles and their parents were invited to be a part of that for the first time.

In the following 6 months, the police had only one call, and that was the result of one of the boys needing a mental health placement. It had nothing to do with behavior that affected the neighborhood. Officer Schnell and his colleagues in the St. Paul Police Department were impressed with the results of this one restorative practice initiative. What they had unsuccessfully tried to accomplish through traditional policing practices 40 times in the past 60 days was accomplished during a 2-hour restorative justice conference in one night.

SOURCE: Adapted from Schnell, P. (2003). Restorative practices and policing. Restorative Practices E-Forum. Retrieved April 15, 2003 from http://www.iirp.org/Pages/pschnell.html.

Discussion Questions

1. Suggest some reasons why traditional policing practices (interrogation, use of authority, and warnings) may not work for many juvenile offenders.

2. Give examples of how and why victims and "complainants" have very little involvement in settling disputes and resolving harms in traditional policing practices.

3. Using the example in this case, how were the neighborhood victims more involved in settling the case? Why do you believe they seemed more satisfied with the restorative conference practice?

Most persons think that the authority and power of police officers is sufficient to maintain order and law-abiding behavior. Why is that not always true for some juvenile offenders? Suggest reasons why neighbors and other citizens may have more influence in some circumstances than police officers.

Through restitution and community service, offenders are required to make amends to victims and the community. Community protection is increased through closer surveillance and by directing juvenile offenders' time and energy into more productive activities during nonschool hours. The goal of competency development recognizes the need to help juvenile offenders develop skills, get work experience, interact with conventional adults, earn money, and take part in productive activities. Advocates of the balanced approach emphasize the importance of community organizations working together with juvenile justice professionals and offenders.

Restorative justice conferencing models that are applicable to juvenile offenders are victim–offender mediation, family group conferencing, and circle sentencing (Bazemore & Umbreit, 2001).

Victim–offender mediation programs have existed in the United States, Canada, and Europe for 20 years. There are about 320 programs in the United States and Canada, and more than 700 in Europe; hundreds of cases are referred to them each year by the local courts (Bazemore & Umbreit, 2001, p. 2). The victim–offender mediation process offers victims an opportunity to meet offenders in a safe and structured setting to participate with a trained mediator in a discussion of the crime. The victim is able to express to the offender the effects of the crime, which may include a physical, emotional, and financial impact. The victim can receive answers to questions about the crime and the offender, such as: "Why me?" "Was I targeted?" The victim can play a role in helping to develop a restitution plan for the offender to pay back any financial debt for losses or harm incurred. Studies on victim–offender mediation indicate that victims were less fearful and more satisfied with the process; offenders who met with victims were more likely to complete their restitution requirements successfully, and had lower recidivism rates (Bazemore & Umbreit, 2001, p. 3).

Family group conferencing is based on a sanctioning and dispute resolution process that dates back more than a century to a tradition practiced by the Maori peoples of New Zealand. Conferencing has been used in Australia as a police diversion program, and is being used in U.S. cities in Minnesota, Montana, Pennsylvania, and Vermont, and in several parts of Canada (Bazemore & Umbreit, 2001). Family group conferencing has been applied in several types of offenses, including theft, arson, minor assaults, drug offenses, and vandalism. Conferencing involves the persons most affected by a juvenile crime: the victim, the offender, and the family, friends, and supporters of both. They are brought together by a trained facilitator to discuss how they and others have been harmed by the offense, and they decide the resolution of the offense and how the harm might be repaired by the juvenile offender. Preliminary evaluations of conferencing programs indicate high levels of victim satisfaction with the conference process, as well as high rates of offender compliance with agreements reached during conferences (Bazemore & Umbreit, 2001, p. 6).

Circle sentencing is a version of the traditional sanctioning and healing practices that were used by the aboriginal peoples in Canada and Native Americans in the United States. Sentencing circles, which are also called "peacemaking circles," were rediscovered and first implemented again in 1991 in the Yukon Territory and other Canadian provinces. The process was introduced to the United States through a circle sentencing project that was initiated in Minnesota in 1996 (Bazemore & Umbreit, 2001). This restorative justice process is so named because those who are involved in and affected by the crime meet together in a circle to share and discuss how they were affected by the offense. One by one and in turn around the circle, the crime victims, offenders, family and friends of both, as well as justice and social service workers and interested community representatives, speak candidly and honestly about the offense and the harms done. The participants then deliberate to arrive at a consensus for a sentencing plan that addresses the concerns of all the concerned parties. Very little research has been conducted on the effectiveness of circle sentencing, but a study in Canada indicated that recidivism was less likely among offenders who had participated in circles than those processed traditionally (Bazemore & Umbreit, 2001, p. 7).

CASE IN POINT 13.2

Juveniles Face a Restorative Justice Conference

Jason and Michael had grim faces as they looked at those attending the restorative justice conference and struggled to answer the facilitator's questions. When asked how they were involved in the incident, Jason explained how they were walking through the shopping center parking lot on their way home, and noticed some speakers in a car parked there. As Michael stood outside as lookout, Jason admitted he crawled into the car and began pulling out wires. The owner of the car (Rhonda) came out of her office and yelled at them to stop. Jason dropped the speaker, and he and Michael ran away. Later that day, Jason answered a knock on the door, and a sheriff's deputy asked to speak with him and his mother. After a few questions, Jason and Michael were handcuffed and taken to the juvenile detention center.

Jason was asked what he was thinking at the time of the incident. He replied, "Nothing, just that I saw the speakers and wanted them." He struggled when asked who had been affected by his actions, telling the group that *he* had been affected, by being taken down to "juvenile." The facilitator asked "what about the owner of the car?" Jason then acknowledged that, "yes, she was affected," because he "messed up her speakers." Jason also looked at his mother and admitted that she too was affected. Michael also gave his account of what happened and admitted that he wasn't thinking at the time and now knows that he made a big mistake. Michael also expressed regrets about the bad example he made for his younger brother.

Rhonda then described the incident, explaining that she saw the one boy in her car holding the speaker, and yelled at him to stop and then he dropped it and ran. She was asked what she wanted to received from this conference, and she said that she wanted to know why the boys had attempted to steal her speakers. She also wanted the boys to understand how she felt and asked them how they would feel if someone took their possessions.

The facilitator moved around the circle and asked the boys' mothers how the incident had affected them. Jason's mother said that at first she was shocked and found it hard to believe that her would son would be involved in something like this. Michael's mother told the group how disappointed she was that her son had participated in the incident. She had always tried to raise her boys to know the difference between right and wrong, and it would take a while to restore her trust in Michael.

After each participant had an opportunity to speak, the facilitator asked for input on how this incident should be resolved and what should be expected of the boys. The boys each apologized to Rhonda for trying to steal the speakers and for the damage done. Rhonda said that she believed they were remorseful and had learned from their mistake. The speakers had been replaced and there was no permanent damage; so she suggested that rather than pay restitution to her that the boys be required to perform community service work. The conference participants offered suggestions on what type of work would be appropriate and how many hours would be fair. The boys were asked whether they would agree to community service work, and if they had suggestions as to the location. The participants finally agreed that Jason and Michael would perform 20 hours of service at a community center to earn money to pay their court fees. The facilitator wrote up the contract, and all of the participants signed it, thus putting a formal end to the incident.

As the conference participants left, Jason and Michael shook hands with everyone, including Rhonda. They were being held accountable for their behavior, but knew that people cared about them and had worked to help them learn from their mistake. Rhonda felt that she could now put the incident behind her. The boys' parents had a chance to express their feelings about their sons' behavior, had received support from the group, and they helped make this a learning experience for their sons so that it was unlikely to happen again.

SOURCE: Adapted from McGarrell, E. F. (2001). Restorative justice conferences as an early response to young offenders. *OJJDP Juvenile Justice Bulletin.* Washington, DC: U.S. Department of Justice.

Discussion Questions

1. Suggest how the results of this theft incident might have been different—for the juveniles, parents, and the victim—if the boys had been processed in a traditional judicial procedure after they brief stay in juvenile detention.

2. The boys would likely have been asked the same questions by attorneys and a juvenile court judge. Why do you think it may be different to have to answer questions posed by a conference facilitator, parents, and the victim?

Do you think the community service the boys agreed to was a fair "sentence" for their delinquent behavior? Explain why, or why not.

Restorative justice conferences have been effective as an early response to young offenders. An experimental study in Indiana compared matched groups of 232 young offenders assigned to restorative conferences with 236 young offenders in a control group (McGarrell, 2001). Results of the Indianapolis restorative justice study showed that the program was very effective in meeting the objectives of restorative conferencing. The participants in the experimental group who experienced restorative conferencing reported more satisfaction in the process than those in the control group (who

Photo 13.1   A mediation session.

did not participate in conferencing). Participants, including victims, juvenile offenders, and their parents, all reported more satisfaction regarding the effectiveness, fairness, degree of involvement, and respect shown by participants than those in the control group (McGarrell, 2001, p. 7). Participants in the conferencing process were also more likely than those in the control group to report that the program had helped to solve problems. Youth participating in restorative justice conferences demonstrated a significantly higher completion rate (83%) than youth in the control group, who were assigned to other diversion programs (58%). Youth in the restorative conference group included fewer recidivists than the control group by a margin of 13.5%, a statistically significant difference that represents a 40% reduction in rates of rearrest (McGarrell, 2001, p. 8). The results of the Indianapolis study indicate that restorative justice conferences are a promising early intervention for young, first-time juvenile offenders.

Problems and Challenges Faced by Restorative Justice

Advocates of restorative justice emphasize that it represents a new way of administering justice, and is a significant departure from the adversarial approach of the traditional justice process. Viewing and approaching judicial practices from a considerably different perspective will be a challenge for most justice professionals and will not happen easily or without resistance. The juvenile justice process has developed over more than one hundred years. We have noted in previous chapters the roles of the juvenile court judge, prosecuting and defense attorneys, and probation officers, and how the juvenile court process has changed in favor of more formality and due process requirements through various appellate court decisions and statutory changes. Juvenile court officials are specially educated, trained, and experienced in fulfilling their judicial and court services roles and responsibilities. Despite some shortcomings, the existing justice process has a clear and well-defined structure to respond to juvenile offending. The community and the victim are represented by the prosecuting attorney; the juvenile offender may be represented by a defense attorney; the judge acts as a referee to ensure a fair process under recognized due process guidelines, and renders a judgment under the legal code, which in turn has been set in place by duly elected lawmakers. The present judicial process, despite its weaknesses, is a fair and deliberate process, precisely because of its formality and structure. The restorative justice process promises a better system that places emphasis on more victim and community involvement. Therein rest the strengths but also the potential weaknesses of restorative justice. Several critical questions have been directed at restorative justice that must be addressed before it can offer an alternative to the traditional retributive justice process. These are summarized in Policy and Practice 13.2.

POLICY AND PRACTICE 13.2 | **PROBLEMS AND CHALLENGES FOR RESTORATIVE JUSTICE**

Restorative justice faces several problems and challenges that it must meet before it can become a consistent juvenile justice policy and put into practice as a viable alternative to the traditional juvenile justice process. These include:

- The wide range of restorative practices under different names
- The lack of clear definitions of the different restorative practices
- The need for voluntary participation of victims, community members, and offenders
- The reluctance of victims to face their offenders voluntarily
- The reluctance of community members to make the time and commitment to participate
- Offenders' hesitation to admit guilt and face the victim and community members
- Process does not serve all offenders and offenses
- Offenders prefer known court sanctions over unknown community sanctions
- Justice professionals are educated, trained, and experienced in the current justice process
- Restorative justice requires a new way of thinking and working for all juvenile justice professionals
- Conference facilitators and mediators must be trained
- Current juvenile court personnel need to be trained in restorative practices
- It leads to net-widening
- It ignores constitutional due process rights of offenders
- It cannot meet promises to restore harms against all victims and the community
- It cannot resolve educational, family, and social problems that are a source of delinquency.

SOURCE: See Arrigo & Schehr, 1998; Harris, 1998; Feld, 1999b.

The problems and challenges for restorative justice may be summarized in five categories. *First*, restorative justice encompasses a variety of different practices that are not always clearly or uniformly defined. Harris (1998) has noted the need for more clear definitions of the various practices included under restorative justice. A review of the literature on restorative justice shows a wide range of materials with headings that include community justice, peace-making criminology, feminist criminology, conflict resolution, mediation, victim–offender reconciliation programs (VORP), alternative dispute resolution, family group conferencing, and sentencing circles (Galaway & Hudson, 1990; Harris, 1998). The various practices are related in terms of overall goals and objectives, but they also differ in origin, development, and application. Feld (1999b) has noted that many restorative justice practices are similar to those that have been a part of informal juvenile justice for years, and has questioned whether they really differ from other diversionary practices already available in the juvenile justice system.

Second, restorative justice depends on voluntary participation of victims, community members, and offenders. Restorative practices such as family group conferencing and mediation are based on the principle that parties agreeing on a resolution must do so voluntarily and not through force and coercion. This is, after all, what distinguishes restorative justice from traditional justice. Neither victims nor offenders are likely to agree to the outcome if their participation is involuntary. Restorative justice is based on the assumption that community members will voluntarily and willingly become involved to help heal the hurts and meet the needs of all the community's members, including victims and offenders. Communities vary in the extent of crime problems but also in the resources available for dealing with those problems (Harris, 1998); the communities most in need of restorative justice programs that encourage residents to become involved in the problem-solving process are often the communities that are the most dysfunctional (Bazemore & Umbreit, 2001). A related concern is how the "community" is defined, and who is allowed to represent the community (Kurki, 2000). Residents who are willing and available to participate voluntarily may have a personal agenda of wielding power and authority that is not consistent with the principles of restorative justice.

In addition to being an essential foundation for restorative justice, a demand for voluntarism also limits application of restorative justice to situations or cases in which victims or community representatives are willing to participate. There are many reasons why victims and community members may be reluctant to get involved in restorative justice options. The fear of facing an offender who has threatened or harmed someone; reluctance to take what is perceived as a lenient, nonpunitive approach and a desire to punish; a belief in traditional sanctions as a deterrent to crime; and a preference for offenders to get a traditional court sentence and be monitored by a probation agency. These and other factors can keep people from supporting and voluntarily participating in restorative justice procedures (Harris, 1998, p. 63).

Restorative justice is also limited to cases in which those identified as offenders voluntarily agree to participate. Offenders' voluntarily participation means they are willing to acknowledge their guilt. Under restorative justice principles, offenders must be willing to admit that their actions in question were wrong, and they must be willing to examine the reasons for their misbehavior and harmful actions. This requirement of restorative justice eliminates for consideration any crimes in which the accused persons do not define their acts as wrong. Harris (1998) has noted that this requirement also excludes offenders who may lack the full capacity to consent. Children and youth with developmental or emotional disabilities lack the capacity to consent, and therefore would be excluded from participating in restorative conferencing and mediation. Some critics of restorative justice have added another "twist" to the necessity for offenders to admit guilt and take responsibility for their actions in order to participate in restorative justice. In a critical analysis of victim–offender mediation, Arrigo and Schehr (1998) note that adolescent offenders readily learn to offer socially acceptable responses to mediators and victims. They are smart enough to "play the system" and can manipulate the mediation session (p. 653). Proponents of restorative justice acknowledge these limitations, but also note that in cases where offenders are correctly identified and charged with a crime, the first step toward reparation and change is admission of wrong-doing and a determination to make things right.

Third, given that restorative justice is proposed as an alternative to the traditional justice process, and is outside the formal system, how are restorative practices to be implemented and administered in a process that involves the offender, victim, community members, and justice professionals? The promise of restorative justice—a "new way of thinking about and administering justice"—is very ambitious and will be a challenge to accomplish. Proponents have recognized this challenge and have sought to spread the message through a number of channels. Kay Pranis (1998), writing for the Balanced and Restorative Justice Project, has identified an extensive list of what is required for restorative justice to be realized, in a *Guide for Implementing the Balanced and Restorative Justice Model.* The document provides examples to assist juvenile justice professionals at all levels in examining how their roles can change to facilitate greater victim involvement, community partnerships, and positive development for offenders. Juvenile justice professionals—including police officers, probation officers, and judges—are expected to take on more responsibilities to include victims and the community in the justice process. The new roles and daily practices for juvenile justice professionals that are described in the *Guide* are recommended as a part of "comprehensive systemic change in juvenile justice" (Pranis, 1998, p. 7). Proponents of restorative justice are convinced that it has promise for improving justice and reducing crime through more victim and community involvement and offender accountability. They also have the support of the U.S. Department of Justice, through the Office of Juvenile Justice and Delinquency Prevention. Proponents are aware of the challenges of implementing restorative justice as an alternative to the traditional justice process, and are promoting it through education, training, research, and a growing body of literature. Restorative justice practitioners are found in police departments, juvenile probation agencies, and state departments of corrections (Kay Pranis was restorative justice coordinator for the Minnesota Department of Corrections). Centers for the promotion and study of restorative justice have been developed in universities, such as those in Minnesota (Mark Umbreit) and Florida (Gordon Bazemore). The newest division of the Academy of Criminal Justice Sciences (professional organization of criminal justice educators, researchers, and practitioners) is the Restorative Justice Division (see Web Resources at the end of the chapter). Acceptance and implementation of restorative justice practices on a broad scale in most jurisdictions throughout the nation still must resolve numerous challenges and questions.

A *fourth* question facing restorative justice is whether the practices lead to net-widening. Feld (1999b) has questioned whether restorative practices may lead to net-widening as youthful offenders are brought into the process through informal coercion in the absence of objective criteria for decision making. Bazemore and Umbreit (2001) acknowledge that a critical issue facing restorative justice is to determine "who controls the agenda" and makes decisions regarding cases processed through traditional justice processes and those "diverted" to restorative processes. If decision makers in the formal juvenile justice system are unwilling to share discretion and authority with communities, it is likely to result in "net-widening"—that is, expanding the number and types of youth subject to supervision of the juvenile justice system (Bazemore & Umbreit, 2001, p. 16).

A *fifth* question is whether restorative justice practices are in fact "restorative" for the offender, the victim, and the community. Feld (1999b) has questioned whether restorative justice is in fact a "just process" and is "restorative." He notes that there is a "disconnect" when an offender is brought to the justice process for violation of a specific law as defined in the state juvenile or penal code but then is subjected to a restorative justice process and is held responsible for "harms done" to the victim and the community. Feld notes that restorative justice depends upon the formal law for its basis for intervention, but instead defines the law violation as "harm." The law defines crimes according to seriousness, and includes culpability as a necessary factor in determining guilt and appropriate sanctions. Proponents of restorative justice are not clear and specific in defining *harm,* and they do not offer specific, appropriate actions for "undoing the harm" and "making right" the harms to victims and the community (Feld, 1999b, p. 38).

A related question is whether restorative justice is a "just" process for offenders and victims. Offenders who are willing to admit to wrong-doing and "harm" are confronted by a facilitator or mediator, a victim, and community volunteers in an informal conferencing process. The informal, nonjudicial restorative justice practices have no due process guarantees, and are done outside the structured sanctioning process that is a common part of the traditional system. Basic justice procedures require due process standards. Since restorative justice is described as "outside" the formal justice process, are provisions made for legal counsel and representation, and for a fair and just decision-making process (Feld, 1999b, p. 36)? What provisions are made to protect youths from "impositions" made by the community or its volunteer representatives in lieu of the sentence or "disposition" imposed by the state or by a judge? What protections exist for youth in a mediation session that may result in a coercive, nonvoluntary alternative to a court disposition? The lack of specificity raises questions as to fairness and basic due process.

In the traditional juvenile court process, lawyers and the judge are expected to preside over a fair and just process. It is unclear whether the deliberations and mediation process of restorative justice place equal importance on justice and fairness as much as the offender's willingness to voluntarily admit to "harms done." Other questions inherent to basic justice and due process are whether juveniles have a right to appeal the decision of a restorative justice conference or mediation session. Do they understand a right of appeal? Is a record made of the mediation conference to ensure a fair and just decision? When challenged by these legal and due process questions, restorative justice faces the same difficulties that have confronted the rehabilitative juvenile court over the past 40 years (Feld, 1999b, p. 38).

There are parallels between restorative justice and the rehabilitative juvenile court. The original intent of the juvenile court was to facilitate offender change in a social welfare model. It is not clear, however, what the specific procedures are by which restorative justice programs can accomplish the goals of restoring victims, changing offenders, and compensating for the harm done to the community. There are a variety of proposed practices that depend upon voluntary participation, but no specific structural frameworks for this. Similar to the dilemma faced by the rehabilitative juvenile court, the identifying problem for which a youth is referred is a crime; but the "rehabilitative" solution may be related to the family, the school, social conditions, or health and medical problems (Feld, 1999b). Restorative justice may be overly optimistic that it can reduce the juvenile offending that often occurs in the context of complex social problems (Kurki, 2000). It is not clear how restorative justice provides a better solution than the juvenile justice process.

Proponents of restorative justice acknowledge that it does *not* offer complete solutions to all of the complex issues facing juvenile justice policymakers, and that "the goals and values of restorative justice are idealistic and utopian" (Bazemore & Umbreit, 1995, p. 312). Throughout the restorative justice literature are hypothetical references to what must happen for restorative practices to be effectively implemented. For example, we are reminded by proponents that restorative practices can supplement or replace traditional retributive practices "*if* . . . (community members and victims voluntarily participate)" and "*when* . . . (justice professionals are willing and trained to adopt restorative principles)." Restorative justice proponents admit they are proposing a new way of administering justice that is dependent on justice officials' willingness to view the process from different perspectives, and on the voluntary participation of victims and community members (Maloney et al., 1988; Bazemore & Umbreit, 1995; Pranis, 1998).

The goal and promise of restorative justice to involve victims and the community in the process is worthy of pursuing, particularly if that leads to community problem solving in reducing juvenile crime and delinquency. Ensuring a fair and just process for holding offenders accountable and also offering support for their reintegration as productive members of the community will be a challenge, however. Those of us who have been practitioners and advocates of juvenile justice for decades look with some enthusiasm to restorative justice as a promising alternative to traditional retributive justice. Yet we are quickly reminded that victims and community volunteers are no less prone to administering punitive, retributive sanctions than those in the formal justice process. We agree with the concerns expressed by Harris (1998), who fears that the "family model" can be overextended to control behavior that is not harmful to others, that vague and undefined "community values" may drive restorative sanctions, that racial stereotyping and fears may affect community responses, and that a select few community volunteers and mediators may define "harms" and the proper restorative sanction in a manner that is less just and consistent than the existing formal structure of justice. Restorative justice may be a viable alternative to traditional retributive justice for some juvenile court cases, but it must be able to address these problems and challenges. It has yet to be accepted and implemented by juvenile justice professionals on a wide scale, but may be a part of the future of juvenile justice, to which we turn next in the final chapter.

SUMMARY

- Restorative justice is a new approach that is promoted as an alternative to traditional retributive justice, but is based on justice principles originally practiced more than 2,000 years ago.
- The goals include holding the offender accountable for the crime committed and repairing the harm done to the victim and the community.
- Restorative justice aims to involve the victim and community members in the justice process, and to restore the offender as a responsible member of the community.
- The restorative justice process requires the offender to make things right for the community and the victim, and replaces punitive sanctions with a process designed to restore the offender, the community, and the victim.

- Restorative justice is a "balanced approach," making offenders accountable and competent, and providing for public safety for victims and the community.
- Restorative justice models that are applicable to juvenile offenders are victim–offender mediation, family group conferencing, and circle sentencing.
- Restorative justice faces several problems and challenges that must be overcome for it to be a viable alternative to traditional retributive justice.

KEY TERMS

Restorative justice

Retributive justice

Victim–offender reconciliation

Conflict resolution

Mediation

Balanced approach

Offender accountability

Offender competency

Public safety

Restitution

Community service

Victim–offender mediation

Family group conferencing

Circle sentencing

DISCUSSION QUESTIONS

1. Review the list of distinct differences between restorative justice and traditional retributive justice (see Table 13.1). List five (5) that you believe seem most important in distinguishing restorative justice from traditional justice.

2. Imagine you are a victim of a property crime, and explain whether and why you would prefer to have your case processed by either restorative justice or the traditional justice process.

3. Offer reasons and arguments why many juvenile offenders might prefer to go into a juvenile court than a victim–mediation session or restorative conferencing process.

4. Given that judges, lawyers, and probation officers have much authority and power in the justice process, does it make sense to you that restorative justice as an alternative could be as effective as the regular court process? Explain how and why a mediator, victim, and group of community volunteers might have an equal impact on a juvenile offender.

5. Suggest three or more requirements that must happen in order for restorative justice practices to become an effective and fair alternative to traditional justice in any community, according to the proponents and critics of restorative justice.

WEB RESOURCES

The Center for Restorative Justice & Peacemaking, University of Minnesota: http://rjp.umn.edu/resources.html

Restorative Justice Online: http://www.restorativejustice.org/

Restorative Justice in Canada: http://www.csc-scc.gc.ca/text/rj/index-eng.shtml

Centre for Restorative justice, Simon Fraser University (Canada): http://www.sfu.ca/crj/about.html

Restorative Justice in Australia: http://www.aic.gov.au/rjustice/australia.html

14

The Future of Juvenile Justice

❖

J uvenile justice has changed dramatically over the past century, from a "child-saving" movement, to a treatment-oriented system, and more recently to a "get-tough" emphasis that aims to hold juvenile offenders more accountable like adult criminals. This concluding chapter begins with a summary of developments and policy changes in juvenile justice over the past 40 years that are likely to shape the future. We examine social, cultural, and political factors affecting the future of juvenile justice; issues that must be addressed in the future; areas that are likely to see more change; and we conclude with a discussion of broader strategies and a comprehensive framework for delinquency prevention and juvenile justice in the 21st century.

The Past as Prologue to the Future

Juvenile crime is a local community problem, but the federal government has played an important role in crime control and delinquency prevention the past several decades. It became increasingly apparent that many local communities lacked the resources to deal adequately with the challenges of juvenile crime. The federal government has in the past 40 years provided research funding, technical assistance, policy recommendations, and resources for implementing delinquency prevention strategies.

The Federal Government and Juvenile Justice

One of the first major federal government initiatives in juvenile delinquency assessment and prevention was the President's Commission on Law Enforcement and Administration of Justice (1967b), which produced a series of reports, including the *Task Force Report: Juvenile Delinquency and Youth Crime.* The report contributed to our understanding of delinquency, informed legislators and government officials of the nature and sources of juvenile crime, recommended a number of legislative and statutory changes to juvenile court processes, and urged policymakers to allocate funding and resources for delinquency prevention programs. The major recommendations of the Task Force were:

- Decriminalization of status offenses
- Diversion of youth from court procedures into public and private treatment programs
- Due process rights for juveniles
- Deinstitutionalization of youth from large training schools to group homes or nonresidential treatment programs
- Diversification of services
- Decentralization of control agencies and services (President's Commission on Law Enforcement and Administration of Justice, 1967a, 1967b; Ohlin, 1998, p. 145)

The second major presidential crime commission, the National Advisory Commission on Criminal Justice Standards and Goals (1976), supported the recommendations of the 1967 President's Commission, and spelled them out in more detail with a series of specific standards and goals relating to juvenile justice and delinquency prevention. The recommendations of these two presidential commissions received broad support among juvenile justice experts, practitioners, and researchers. Most states and larger jurisdictions have made progress in responding to the recommendations with legislative and policy changes, and have implemented programs and agency practices reflecting the goals and standards. Implementation of the recommendations has not been uniform or universal throughout the United States, however, and the results have been difficult to evaluate (Ohlin, 1998; Krisberg, 2005).

The federal Juvenile Justice and Delinquency Prevention Act of 1974 (JJDPA) increased efforts to **decriminalize status offenders,** and the results have been a significant reduction of juveniles being held in adult jails (Krisberg, 2005; Snyder & Sickmund, 2006, p. 236). **Diversion** programs were implemented in cities throughout the United States, and the result has been that many youth who would have been processed through the formal juvenile court have been referred to alternative community programs. The **due process** emphasis has been supported through a number of U.S. Supreme Court decisions, and continues to be a major emphasis of juvenile justice advocates who are calling for equal justice for juvenile offenders comparable to that in the criminal court (Feld, 1999a). Efforts to **deinstitutionalize** produced mixed results, the most dramatic being Massachusetts's closing of most of its state juvenile training schools in the early 1970s (discussed in Chapter 11). Other states have attempted to follow that example and have worked to reduce the number of juvenile commitments to training schools, recognizing that institutions are an expensive and ineffective alternative (Snyder & Sickmund, 2006, p. 198). Referrals and purchase of services from the private sector have increased diversification and decentralization of services in many states. Private juvenile treatment programs often provide better services in residential settings that are more humane and less institutional. They represent a significant portion of the annual budgets of county and state juvenile corrections programs, however and many private programs refuse to accept the more serious and chronic juvenile offenders (Ohlin, 1998). Despite some questions and hesitation to implement early federal commission recommendations fully, we believe that those policies and practices will continue to play a role in the future of juvenile justice.

The Shift to "Law-and-Order" and "Get-Tough" Policies

In the 1980s and 1990s we saw a dramatic shift away from many of the policies advocated by the national crime commissions. A number of factors accounted for the shift in juvenile justice policies. *First,* from 1984 to 1994 the United States experienced an increase in juvenile delinquency that many referred to as a "juvenile crime wave." Some criminologists predicted an ongoing trend of serious and violent juvenile crime, spurred by a group of "superpredators" (DiIulio, 1996; Fox, 1996). Increased news media coverage on serious and violent juvenile crime focused more attention on these youth and gave the impression that they were more numerous than at any time in U.S. history. The increase in juvenile crime and the perception that traditional juvenile justice policies were not working led to law-and-order, "get-tough" policies. Statutory revisions to state juvenile codes included reducing the maximum juvenile court age; expanding the number of youths eligible for transfer to adult court; shifting transfer power from the judge to the prosecutor; increasing the number of serious offenses subject to mandatory sentences of incarceration; and opening juvenile court records for use in criminal court sentencing (Sanborn & Salerno, 2005, p. 506). Given the public intolerance for juvenile violence, lawmakers are likely to continue the trend of a tough response to serious and chronic offending.

A *second* reason for the shift in juvenile justice policy was due in part to a widely publicized report by Robert Martinson (1974; Lipton, Martinson, & Wilks, 1975) in which he argued that rehabilitation programs had not had an effect on recidivism. Martinson's conclusions that "nothing works" in corrections had a great national impact, despite the fact that Ted Palmer (1975) wrote a detailed rebuttal questioning Martinson's findings, and Martinson (1979) himself retracted some of his earlier premature and exaggerated conclusions. The disproportionate national attention questioning correctional rehabilitation nevertheless had a significant and lasting impact on lawmakers, who were also finding that more public support and votes rested on a law-and-order position on crime while there was less support for a rehabilitation emphasis.

There are signs that rehabilitation is making a comeback (Cullen, 2005). Reasons for a return to the rehabilitative ideal (see Allen, 1981) are not necessarily due to a softening of attitudes toward crime and criminals, but to a realization that attempting to control crime through incarceration is costly and produces no significant reduction in

Photo 14.1   Gangs and gun violence are a challenge for juvenile justice and delinquency prevention.

crime rates. Although there is considerable disagreement as to whether training schools and prisons are effective deterrents to crime, many criminal justice experts point to research evidence that greater use of incarceration may increase rather than decrease crime rates (Garland, 2001). Cullen and his associates have conducted studies on public opinions about rehabilitation, and have found that Americans still strongly support the view that efforts should be made to rehabilitate offenders (Cullen, Fisher, & Applegate, 2000; Cullen, 2005). There is evidence of significant public and legislative support for rehabilitation of juvenile offenders, who are still generally seen as more amenable to treatment than adult offenders. The exceptions are the serious and chronic juvenile offenders who are likely to face waiver to criminal court or extended juvenile jurisdiction prosecution (as discussed in Chapters 9 and 10). The majority of juvenile offenders do receive some rehabilitative interventions on juvenile probation and in community corrections programs.

A *third* reason for the shift in juvenile justice policy is a change in how we view both those who violate the law and the reasons for criminal and delinquent behavior. The demise of the rehabilitative ideal actually had less to do with whether correctional programs were effective in changing offenders, and more to do with a shift in the viewpoints of the public and politicians regarding crime and criminals. Cullen and Gilbert (1982) suggested that crime control policies reflect lawmakers' ideological assumptions about the causes of crime and the most effective strategies to reduce crime. Garland (2001) has contended that cultural patterns structure how the public and politicians feel about offenders. The politics of the 1980s produced a greater division between the jobless and those employed, between blacks and whites, and between the affluent suburbs and the struggling inner cities; and social problems such as violence, street crime, and drug abuse became worse. Accompanying these political and social changes was the view that punishing individuals for criminal and delinquent behavior was more appropriate than rehabilitation and change strategies. Contrary to the views of positivist criminologists—that crime was caused by individual and social problems over which an individual had little control—law violators were now seen as bad individuals who deserved to be punished. Crime was seen not as a sign of need or deprivation, but was viewed as a rational choice by persons who lacked discipline and self-control, who needed to be deterred and deserved to be punished harshly (Garland, 2001, p. 102). Garland noted that the term that best describes this new conservative crime control policy is "zero tolerance." Intolerance of crime and criminals has pervaded society and legislative chambers, communities and school hallways, and the proposed solutions are harsh discipline and punishment.

POLICY AND PRACTICE 14.1 NATIONAL JUVENILE JUSTICE ACTION PLAN

Recommended policies and strategies for the future of juvenile justice were spelled out in 1967 with the President's Commission on Law Enforcement and Administration of Justice, and again in 1997 with the National Juvenile Justice Action Plan. Attorney General Janet Reno convened a meeting of the Coordinating Council on Juvenile Justice and Delinquency Prevention, which included juvenile justice practitioners and representatives from the U.S. Departments of Justice, Health and Human Services, Housing and Urban Development, Labor, Treasury, and Education, and the Office of National Drug Control Policy. The Coordinating Council called on citizens to work together to advance the Action Plan's eight key objectives to reduce youth violence:

- Provide immediate intervention and appropriate sanctions and treatment for delinquent juveniles.
- Prosecute certain serious, violent, and chronic juvenile offenders in criminal court.
- Reduce youth involvement with guns, drugs, and gangs.
- Provide opportunities for children and youth.
- Break the cycle of violence by addressing youth victimization, abuse, and neglect.
- Strengthen and mobilize communities.
- Support the development of innovative approaches to research and evaluation.
- Implement an aggressive public outreach campaign on effective strategies to combat juvenile violence. (Ingersoll, 1997, p. 12)

To help meet these objectives the Office of Juvenile Justice and Delinquency Prevention (OJJDP) has provided funding, information, and education programming to juvenile justice practitioners in selected sites throughout the United States. Programs to reduce juvenile gun violence were funded in California, Louisiana,

(Continued)

(Continued)

and New York, and a teleconference on programs to reduce youth gun violence was viewed by over 8,000 people at 271 downlink sites. The OJJDP funded 10 substance use prevention initiatives at various sites and held a national teleconference on preventing drug abuse among youth that was viewed by about 10,000 people at 300 downlink sites. Five jurisdictions with chronic gang problems (Mesa and Tucson, Arizona; Riverside, California; Bloomington, Illinois; and San Antonio, Texas) have received OJJDP funds to develop programs to prevent gang violence; and the National Youth Gang Center received funding to promote effective gang prevention strategies, collect and analyze statistical data on gangs, analyze gang legislation, and review literature and research on gangs. OJJDP's national satellite teleconference on gang prevention strategies was viewed by about 17,000 people at 635 downlink sites.

The *Action Plan* called for communities throughout the nation to provide positive opportunities for youth. Research has demonstrated that mentoring, afterschool activities, conflict resolution programs, remedial education, and vocational training can prevent young people from becoming delinquents. The OJJDP has disseminated a variety of research-based documents that provide guidelines and examples of effective prevention and intervention programs. The Department of Justice has funded several afterschool programs, Juvenile Mentoring Programs (JUMP), and conflict resolution programs, and has collaborated with the Department of Education to fund the National School Safety Center to focus on school problems including truancy, suspensions and expulsions, behavioral disruptions, and bullying that often lead to more serious delinquent and violent behavior in schools. Through the Juvenile Justice Clearinghouse, the OJJDP annually distributes more than two million copies of Reports, Summaries, Bulletins, Fact Sheets, and other publications providing research findings and program information. These are available in libraries, or may be received by mail, FAX, or the Internet.

SOURCE: Ingersoll, S. (1997). The national juvenile justice action plan: A comprehensive response to a critical challenge. *Juvenile Justice, 3*(2), 11–20. Retrieved January 19, 2009, from http://www.ncjrs.gov/pdffiles/165925.pdf.

Lawmakers are constantly faced with difficult choices between trying to improve public education, social and medical services, law enforcement, and public safety with limited resources and revenues and without raising taxes. In the age of what Garland (2001) refers to as the "culture of control," crime is viewed as a product of bad choices by bad individuals and not a result of unequal educational and employment opportunities for low-income persons who are disproportionately ethnic and racial minorities. Faced with increasing public demands to "do something" about youth involvement in drugs, gangs, and violent crime, the usual response of policymakers has been to "get tough" on crime and criminals. "Getting tough" usually means a return to incarceration of offenders. Statistics indicate that after a decade of deinstitutionalization efforts, the number of juveniles being incarcerated has increased. From 1985 to 1989 the average daily population and total census count of juveniles in public facilities increased 14%, and the juvenile custody rate per 100,000 increased 19% during that period (Allen-Hagen, 1991, p. 2). According to the Juvenile Residential Facility Census (JRFC) in 2002, a total of 102,388 juveniles were held in 2,964 facilities (Sickmund, 2006, p. 2).

The number of delinquent offenders in residential facilities decreased 7% from 2000 to 2002, but the national rate of custody was 326 per 100,000 juveniles in the general population, with a wide variation among the states ranging from 85 to 688 per 100,000 juveniles in the state populations (Sickmund, 2006, p. 4). The number of juvenile facilities and residents declined again in 2004, with a total of 94,875 juveniles held in 2,809 public and private facilities. Crowding is a problem in many facilities, with a total of 860 (31%) of facilities (mostly public) reporting being at or over capacity, affecting 34,500 (33%) of the residents in 2004 (Livsey, Sickmund, & Sladky, 2009, p. 7). The increasing number of adjudicated youths sent to juvenile corrections facilities does not even include the increasing number who are waived to criminal court, tried as adults, and often sent to adult institutions. Juvenile corrections policies from the 1990s to the present are being dominated by a more conservative, control-oriented philosophy.

Factors Affecting the Future of Juvenile Justice

Throughout its history and development, the juvenile court has been shaped by numerous social and political factors. Most of those same factors will continue to have a significant impact on the future of the juvenile justice system. An overview of the social, cultural, and political factors that will continue to affect the court and the juvenile justice system will aid our vision of the future. The juvenile court was developed in the context of social science and the social welfare responses to individual, family, and social problems. Criminological explanations and theories of juvenile delinquency were based primarily on positivism and the recognition that most delinquency originated from structural, social, and individual factors that were beyond the control of the juvenile. The positivist model of delinquency promoted juvenile court responses based on the "rehabilitative ideal." The primary educational qualifications for juvenile probation officers and caseworkers in metropolitan juvenile courts throughout the United States were college degrees in psychology, sociology, and social work. Social histories and background information included in predisposition reports emphasized juveniles' family circumstances and child development, socioeconomic factors, school background, and social environment. Legislative and political changes in the past 20 years now emphasize personal accountability and punishment of juvenile offenders, based on a rational choice model. This trend reflects a general "culture of control" in the United States that has increased punitive responses to both juvenile and adult offenders in recent decades (Garland, 2001).

Social Factors Versus Individual Responsibility

Research evidence based on a wealth of excellent criminological research shows that the causes and explanations of delinquent behavior are virtually unchanged in the past 50 years. The social and economic causes of delinquency have *not* changed; the responses to delinquency have changed. The majority of juvenile offenders today are characterized by the same social conditions as those in the past century, including poverty, unemployment, unequal opportunities to quality education, and different treatment based on race, ethnicity, and social class. Today legislators, prosecutors, and judges portray youthful offenders as responsible and autonomous individuals rather than as dependent and vulnerable children, and view their behavior as deliberate rather than as determined. The portrayal of children and youth as mature and responsible when they commit crimes is used by many lawmakers to justify holding them accountable as adults for offenses committed and punishing them as criminals.

Neither the rehabilitative ideal nor the social control approach has been effective in significantly reducing juvenile crime in America, but for different reasons. First, the juvenile court ideal of attempting to combine social control and social welfare in one single institution has proven to be an impossible goal (Feld, 1999a). The juvenile court over the past 100 years has been able to adjudicate and order graduated sanctions for juvenile offenders within the limited probation and community resources available. The juvenile court, however, can accomplish few if any changes in parents, families, schools, social service agencies, and the political and social structure that includes poverty, unemployment, and inequalities that limit young people's chances for growth and development. Second, justice policies of social control too often perpetuate the inequalities already present in society that disproportionately affect racial minorities and lower social class youth and families.

Poverty and Juvenile Crime

Poverty is the biggest single risk factor for the welfare of young people. Children represent a disproportionate share of the poor in the United States. In 2007 the family poverty rate was 9.8% or 7.6 million families. For children under age 18 the poverty rate was 18% (an increase from 17.4% in 2006), representing a total of more than 13 million children living in poverty (U.S. Census Bureau, 2008). The poverty rates vary significantly by race and Hispanic origin. A total of 21.5% of Hispanics and 24.5% of blacks were living in poverty, compared with 8.2% of non-Hispanic whites (U.S. Census Bureau, 2008). According to the National Center for Children in Poverty (2008) at Columbia University, of the total of 73 million children in the United States, 28.8 million (39%) live in low-income families and 13.2 million (18%) live in poor families. Poverty can affect children's ability to learn and may contribute to social, emotional, and behavioral problems. The detrimental effects of poverty are greatest for children who experience poverty when they are young and those who experience deep and persistent poverty (National Center for Children in Poverty, 2008). The rate of child poverty in the United States (more than 20%) is more than double that of Canada (9.3%) and 4 to 8 times that of Western European industrial and democratic countries (Feld, 1999a, p. 334).

Wheeler (1971) studied the relationship of child neglect and delinquency to poverty, and noted that a majority of neglect and delinquency cases can be attributed to economic stress. Sociological research has generally treated poverty as a dependent variable or a secondary influence on family social functioning. Wheeler argued that we must treat poverty as an independent variable or determinant factor in other social problems, including child neglect, abuse, and delinquency. Loeber and Farrington (2001) maintain that risk factors such as family problems and poverty predict greater involvement in delinquency. Findings from studies of childhood exposure to family poverty have been very consistent. Children raised in poor, disadvantaged families are at greater risk for offending than children who are raised in relatively affluent families. In a critical analysis of poverty in America, Gans (1995) suggested that affluent people stereotype the poor as undeserving. In describing American policy as a "war against the poor," Gans contended that the poor are labeled and stigmatized as persons with questionable morals and values. His thesis is that the terms and labels that designate poor people as undeserving may be obstacles preventing their escape from poverty. Cultural and political views of poverty in America are intertwined with racial and social justice. Politicians and the public tend to view youth crime, violence, and child poverty in the same context as race and social class (Gans, 1995; Feld, 1999a). Both crime and poverty are characterized as the *private* problems of minority families and children, rather than as matters of *public* concern for the entire community (Feld, 1999a, p. 336). Because poverty is a major factor in the quality of child development and is an important risk factor in delinquency, any public policies directed at reducing youth crime must consider ways to enhance the economic status of families with children (National Commission on Children, 1991; Feld, 1999a). Juvenile court and justice policies have developed with a focus on children and families at risk, but the court faces greater challenges as the social conditions of young people continue to deteriorate. Poverty poses overwhelming challenges and adversely affects children's health, development, educational attainment, and socioeconomic potential. These social and economic factors become more evident as children reach adolescence (National Research Council, 1993; Feld, 1999a).

Social Factors and the Future of Juvenile Justice

Poverty, social class, and racial biases shape public attitudes and juvenile justice policies. The disproportionate confinement of ethnic and racial minorities is a problem in juvenile corrections (noted previously in Chapter 11). Although research has not established a pattern of intentional bias against minority youth, the fact remains that minority youth are more likely to be arrested, taken into custody, processed in juvenile court, and committed to correctional facilities than are white youth. Children of families in poverty, living in high-crime neighborhoods, and struggling to overcome the challenges of lower socioeconomic conditions are at greater risk of delinquency and involvement with the juvenile justice system. The juvenile court has come to be viewed as the court for primarily lower-class children from poor families, with parents who are unable to control and properly supervise their children. The public and policymakers tend to view juvenile crime as a problem of poor judgment and irresponsibility, rather than as a product of social and economic factors. Social class and racial biases are illustrated by the tendency of Americans to distinguish between their own children and "other people's children" (Feld, 1999a, p. 337; see also Grubb & Lazerson, 1982, p. 85). Viewing poverty, low educational attainment, and unemployment as personal failures and individual irresponsibility explains the change in policy toward punishment and social control. How we view crime determines how we choose to prevent crime. Fear of crime and public perceptions of young offenders presented by sensational media depictions have a great influence on juvenile justice policies (Ohlin,

1998). For some people, poverty, lower school achievement, and youth crime demonstrate the need to improve the conditions for minority children and to pursue social justice. For others, these recurring social problems demonstrate that government efforts to reduce poverty and improve education just do not work for all people, and provide evidence with which to "blame the victims" and confirm why government should initiate no further social action (Ohlin, 1998; Feld, 1999a).

POLICY AND PRACTICE 14.2	NEGLECT IN JUVENILE JUSTICE LEAVES CHILDREN BEHIND

Thirty years ago Charles Colson and Joseph Califano, Jr., were opposing each other in a legal battle. As Assistant to then-President Richard Nixon, Charles Colson was defending the former president during the Watergate scandal. Joseph Califano was legal counsel for the *Washington Post* in a lawsuit against Nixon and the Committee to Reelect the President. Today these men have joined together in their concern for troubled youth. They have charged that local, state, and federal officials are neglecting children and youth caught up in the juvenile justice system. Colson and Califano commented on findings of The National Center on Addiction and Substance Abuse (CASA) of Columbia University and noted several problems that were not being adequately addressed:

- *Alcohol and drug abuse.* Nearly half (44%) of juveniles arrested were under the influence of alcohol or drugs, but only about 4% receive any treatment.
- *Mental health problems.* Most (75%) of juveniles locked up in detention centers and correctional facilities are likely to have a mental health problem, but no mental health treatment is available.
- *Learning disabilities.* Most (up to 80%) of incarcerated juveniles have learning disabilities, but few ever receive any special education.
- *Disproportionate minority confinement (DMC).* Black youths are twice as likely to be arrested, adjudicated, and committed to correctional programs as white youths, but delinquency prevention programs are not implemented equally in communities and schools where they are most needed.
- *Increase in female delinquency.* Arrest rates among females have increased 50% in the past decade, but most prevention and correctional programs are directed toward male offenders.
- *Juvenile correctional facilities.* Nearly half (40%) of juvenile facilities are overcrowded, and residents are subjected to inhumane conditions. Federal courts have found several state correctional juvenile systems in violation of the Eighth Amendment against cruel and unusual punishment.

America faces many challenges, including education reform, the economy, unemployment, healthcare, and the rising costs of crime control. Colson and Califano strongly believe that the federal educational reform program known as No Child Left Behind should apply equally to the juvenile justice system, and they have recommended:

- Creation of a *model juvenile justice code* to improve practices and accountability in handling juvenile offenders
- Referral of more juveniles to *diversion programs* such as drug courts

- *Substance abuse training* for all juvenile justice officials to recognize and deal with substance-involved juveniles
- *Healthcare, education, and job training* for juveniles in the justice system
- Development of *faith-based programs* such as Prison Fellowship to provide spiritual support and positive change for troubled youth
- Expansion of *federal grant programs* to help states that are willing to reform their juvenile justice system
- More accurate and complete *state and national data* to help assess and monitor the progress in meeting the needs of children and youth in the justice system

Califano and Colson have called for major changes throughout the juvenile justice system. The reforms they recommended will be expensive, but improving juvenile justice will reduce the enormous costs of incarcerating a growing number of adult offenders in most states and the federal system. Major justice system reforms would pay off in terms of reduced crime, greater public safety, and significant economic benefits.

SOURCE: Califano, J. A., Jr., & Colson, C. W. (2005). Criminal neglect. *USA Today* (January), pp. 34–35. Retrieved May 9, 2009, from http://www.casacolumbia.org/absolutenm/templates/OpEds.aspx?articleid=377&zoneid=29.

Discussion Questions

1. It is evident that the failure of juvenile justice to reduce juvenile offending is *not* because we do not know how. What are some reasons we have failed to adequately address the points noted by Colson and Califano?

2. Review the list of proposals to overhaul the juvenile justice system, and discuss at least three that you believe are the best starting points for improving juvenile justice.

What effective juvenile justice programs are being used in your county or state? Check for information on the Internet, printed information, or from practitioners and administrators in your county or state.

Policy Issues for Juvenile Justice in the 21st Century

The juvenile justice system must face a number of issues and questions, including the future of the juvenile court, the jurisdictional definition of *juvenile* and the age of responsibility, the role and responsibilities of juvenile justice personnel, greater demands on correctional workers in an age of limited resources, the use of technology in monitoring offenders, and community and public support for crime prevention strategies.

The Future of Juvenile Court

Most states have revised their juvenile codes and redefined the purpose of the juvenile court, de-emphasizing rehabilitation and placing more importance on public protection and safety (Torbet et al., 1996). Feld (1999a) has argued that judicial and legislative changes have "criminalized" the juvenile court. There are fewer differences between the juvenile and the adult/criminal courts, and he contends that the current juvenile court provides neither therapy nor justice and cannot be rehabilitated (Feld, 1999a). Feld has therefore argued for abolition of the juvenile court as we know it. A more formal criminal court hearing would ensure that juvenile offenders receive the same due process safeguards and constitutional rights as adults in criminal court. Juveniles would be treated differently only at the sentencing phase, when they would receive a "youth discount" in consideration of their lower level of maturity and culpability (Feld, 1999a, p. 317). In addition to a youth discount in sentencing, Feld recommends that youths who are sentenced to an institution be placed in separate correctional facilities for youthful offenders (p. 326).

Abolition of the juvenile court is unlikely in the near future, but juvenile justice experts welcome the ongoing reforms and agree that more changes are needed. Supporters of the current juvenile court acknowledge that juveniles receive "unequal" and "dual" processing in court: not the same quality of due process as adults, and for the purpose of both punishment and rehabilitation (Sanborn & Salerno, 2005). Supporters emphasize that not everything about juvenile justice is negative or unfair, especially when juvenile courts do pursue the "best interests" of the youthful offender and make positive efforts to provide beneficial interventions and programs aimed at offender change. The juvenile court in most cases does take into account the child's needs and risks, and aims to arrive at a disposition that will best facilitate offender change and public safety. Juvenile justice still does focus on both the youthful offender and the offense (Sanborn & Salerno, 2005).

The National Council of Juvenile and Family Court Judges (2005) has responded to the need to analyze the practices and results of the juvenile process and to identify areas for improvement (discussed in Chapter 10). With support from the federal Office of Juvenile Justice and Delinquency Prevention (OJJDP), this national organization of juvenile and family court judges has developed resource guidelines that are directed at improving court practices in juvenile delinquency cases. The guidelines are intended to assist juvenile courts in assessing current practices, identify areas in need of improvement, and help in planning and working toward positive change. Assessment of juvenile court initiatives toward these goals may help determine the extent to which the courts are able to improve on the handling of juvenile delinquency cases, and improve on public and private agency responses to at-risk youth.

Juveniles and the Age of Responsibility

States vary in statutory definitions of the ages for juvenile court jurisdiction (Snyder & Sickmund, 2006, p. 103), ranging from a minimum age of 10 to a maximum age of 16 or 17. Recent trends are for treating younger offenders as adults in cases of serious offenses. The inconsistencies in laws defining juvenile jurisdiction reflect different assumptions about adolescent maturity and the age of responsibility as well as sentencing policies of deterrence and punishment rather than rehabilitation. The juvenile age inconsistency question goes beyond juvenile court jurisdiction. Minors can be executed at age 18 for murder, 3 years before they can legally purchase and use tobacco products, alcohol, or acquire handguns (Zimring, 2005, p. 64). Juveniles aged 15 and 16 who commit serious crimes may be held accountable and tried in criminal court with adults. Criminal behavior is supposedly a sign of maturity and therefore legal culpability. The age question poses an interesting and challenging paradox in the United States. Violent criminal behavior brings adult consequences, but the same juvenile under 18 years of age is presumed to be immature and irresponsible in other matters so is not allowed to sign contracts, enlist in the military, or legally purchase tobacco and alcohol products (Zimring, 2005, p. 64).

POLICY AND PRACTICE 14.3 | **JUVENILE JUSTICE POLICY AND THE AGE OF MATURITY**

The juvenile court was first implemented in 1899 based on the understanding that juveniles were different from adults and should be tried separately from adults. Over the past century we have inclined to treat many juvenile offenders like adult criminals, based not on their greater maturity but on the seriousness of their crimes. We now have scientific evidence to support the decisions of the early founders of the juvenile court a century ago, and that provide direction for juvenile justice policy changes in the 21st century.

A basic principle of American justice is "penal proportionality," a doctrine that holds that fair criminal punishment is based not only on the harm caused by the crime, but also on the blameworthiness of the offender. A central question, therefore, is whether a juvenile's immaturity mitigates his or her blameworthiness and should reduce his or her punishment. Immaturity does *not* excuse a juvenile from responsibility for crime, but should mitigate the level of culpability or responsibility and therefore the severity of punishment.

The idea that developmental immaturity mitigates youths' criminal culpability is founded on both legal principles (noted in the previous paragraph) and social science research findings. Scientific evidence on the psychosocial maturity of adolescents is especially relevant to understanding legal culpability. Adolescents are distinguished from adults in four ways: (1) susceptibility to peer influences, (2) attitudes about risk, (3) ability to adopt a future orientation, and (4) the capacity for self-management. Research has documented that on all four of these points adolescents are less mature than adults. "Peer pressure," risk-taking behaviors, living in the "here and now" with little regard for the future, and poor decision making and self-management are adolescent characteristics that are generally accepted as common knowledge. As applied to criminal law and punishment, adolescents' immaturity compared to adults has important implications. The legal standard for judging culpability is whether "reasonable people" would be unlikely to commit the same act under similar circumstances. In applying the standard to criminal acts by adolescents, the correct basis for applying the principle should be the behavior of other adolescents—not adults—under similar circumstances. Given youths' impulsivity, susceptibility to peer pressure, and failure to consider long-term consequences, they should *not* be judged by the same criteria and standards as adults. Adolescence is *not* a defense against guilt and punishment, but an argument for a diminished level of culpability and a reduction in the severity of punishment.

(Continued)

(Continued)

Policy Implications of Scientific Findings on Age and Maturity. Lawmakers and juvenile justice professionals who understand and acknowledge the scientific findings on age and maturity will begin to apply them in revised legislation, statutes, juvenile court dispositions, and correctional supervision. Anyone who doubts the likelihood of these scientific findings making a difference in juvenile justice in the 21st century should consider the fact that they have *already* been applied by the U.S. Supreme Court in a major case. In making its decision on the constitutionality of the juvenile death penalty in *Roper v. Simmons,* 543 U.S. 541 (2005), the Court drew upon the findings of Elizabeth Scott and Laurence Steinberg, which we have summarized here.

SOURCE: Scott, E. S., & Steinberg, L. (2003). Less guilty by reason of adolescence: Developmental immaturity, diminished responsibility, and the juvenile death penalty. *American Psychologist, 58,* 1009–1018; Scott, E. S., & Steinberg, L. (2008). Adolescent development and the regulation of youth crime. *Future of Children, 18*(2), 15–33; Steinberg, L., & Haskins, R. (2008). Policy brief: Keeping adolescents out of prison. *Future of Children, 18*(2), 1–7. Retrieved January 22, 2009, from http://www.futureofchildren.org/pubs-inf02825/pubs-info_show.htm?doc_id=708717.

Discussion Questions

1. From your own personal experience or observations of siblings, peers, or your own children, give examples of how children and adolescents are less mature than adults on the four points noted above.

2. Do immaturity and limited culpability mean that adolescents "get off" and are not held accountable for juvenile crimes? What do they mean? Give suggestions and examples for how youth found guilty of crimes might receive a youth discount when being sentenced to either institutional or residential placement or to community supervision probation.

The 2005 U.S. Supreme Court case of *Roper v. Simmons* (U.S. 125 S.Ct. 1183) took a step toward defining the age of responsibility when a majority of the Court limited the sentence of death to convicted murderers 18 years of age and older. As we noted in Chapter 2 on the history and development of juvenile justice, this recent Supreme Court case will have some impact on juvenile justice trends in sentencing juveniles. The majority opinion cited scientific findings on brain research and differences in maturity between adolescents and adults. The close 5–4 decision was not without controversy and is unlikely to put to rest the differences of opinion on the age of responsibility and culpability of juveniles aged 16 or 17 who commit violent crimes. The Supreme Court decision in *Roper* is nevertheless one indication that states can and must address the age inconsistency question. The growing body of scientific research and knowledge about adolescent brain structure and chemistry compared with adults supports the need to address the question (American Bar Association, 2004). Scientific evidence can help temper the current wave of demands for accountability for violent juvenile offenders, and may reduce the tendencies toward retributive justice based on strong emotions that are evoked by violent victimization. Research results from the field of developmental psychology show that there is ample evidence and support for reduced culpability of juveniles based on their lower level of maturity (Bishop, 2004). It is appropriate to continue to treat youth under 18 as too immature and irresponsible to purchase alcohol or tobacco products, to serve in the military, or to sign contracts. It is inconsistent to treat them as mature and responsible adults for commission of violent crimes. Murder and violent crimes are not exclusively adult activities, and it is illogical to reason that a youth who kills is more mature than a youth who steals (Bishop, 2004). Persons who are under 18 years of age are referred to as *minors* and *juveniles* for a reason: They are less than adult. A challenge for lawmakers in the 21st century is to acknowledge and address the inconsistency in laws and policies for dealing with juvenile offenders.

The Role of Juvenile Justice Personnel

The 21st century will bring greater demands on juvenile court officers and correctional workers in an age of limited resources. Juvenile corrections officers are confronted with a number of challenges that will require changes in qualifications and training, and we are likely to see changes in the juvenile offender population, crowding, litigation, and greater use of technology (Mays & Winfree, 2000). These challenges will require a reexamination of **probation and correctional officer training and qualifications**. Changes in legislation and juvenile statutes require regular training for juvenile court workers. Federal legislation has mandated the deinstitutionalization of status offenders, but intake probation officers in most jurisdictions continue to receive referrals of status offenders for curfew violations, school truancy, and runaway. These "children in need of protective services or supervision" ("CHINS" or "CHIPS") must be processed for some form of informal adjustment or supervision. Adding to the diversity and complexity of the juvenile probation population are the chronic, habitual, and serious juvenile offenders, many of whom are "state-raised youths" (Mays & Winfree, 2000). *Changes in the juvenile offender population* are being addressed with demands for more "evidence-based practices," such as tools for risk and needs assessment of offenders. More objective and reliable classification of offenders provides more accurate recommendations for court dispositions, and better management of juvenile clients on probation supervision and in correctional facilities. Administration and analyses of risk-need assessments require regular and ongoing education and training (see Mears & Kelly, 1999; Young, Moline, Farrell, & Bierie, 2006).

The **problem of crowding** affects workers in both community corrections and residential facilities. Probation officers are seeing more court cases, requiring extensive time for investigation and report writing. Metropolitan juvenile court offices have specialized intake, investigative, and supervision units, but they have growing caseload sizes as probation agencies are faced with limited resources for hiring additional personnel. Smaller jurisdictions are experiencing the same problems, and juvenile court workers are responsible for the entire process from intake to supervision. Caseload sizes will increase for most juvenile court officers, exceeding 100 cases with larger metro courts seeing caseloads of 200 or more (Mays & Winfree, 2000). One exception to the growing caseload size is the practice of assigning some officers to intensive supervision probation (ISP) with a smaller number (20–25) of offenders charged with violence, sexual assaults, drug trafficking, and those with emotional or mental problems (Mays

& Winfree, 2000; Clear, Cole, & Reisig, 2006). Residential and correctional facilities are experiencing the stresses of too many inmates in too little space. Added to the problem of crowding is the diversity of juvenile residents, ranging in both age and in the level of risks and needs. Corrections workers must maintain appropriate separation of residents for safety and security, and provide some types of meaningful programming.

The problem of litigation is likely to increase in the future as correctional facilities face population increases, crowding, and poor conditions. Federal courts began to target state departments of corrections more than 20 years ago for crowded and inhumane conditions that constituted a violation of the Eighth Amendment against cruel and unusual punishment (Clear et al., 2006). Litigation involving juvenile inmates has also addressed the conditions of confinement, and courts have ruled that the conditions in some juvenile facilities do constitute cruel and unusual punishment. A second legal issue is the question of protecting children from harm and maintaining safe conditions for them while in the state's care and custody. Federal courts have ruled that states do have an obligation to take reasonable steps to protect children in their care from assaults by other inmates, and are liable for nonaccidental injuries sustained as a result of inattention and inaction (del Carmen, Parker, & Reddington, 1998). States are faced with the dilemma of immense costs associated with litigation, and the growing cost of building and operating correctional facilities. Litigation is directly linked to crowded facilities that increase the stress levels of residents and workers who are struggling to maintain control of a growing and diverse population of offenders. Trying to maintain adequate staffing levels and reduce personnel costs often results in underqualified and undertrained workers who may increase the risk of abusive behavior toward a diverse and growing institutional population.

The use of technology in monitoring offenders will continue to expand and develop in the future, as the helping philosophy may grow dimmer or disappear entirely (Mays & Winfree, 2000). Over the past couple decades we have seen a change from the rehabilitative ideal in corrections to a control emphasis whereby probation officers focus on accountability and monitoring offender behavior (Lawrence, 1991a). Probation officers are routinely involved in administering urinalyses to probation clients with a history of substance abuse. Electronic surveillance has become a common form of technology for most community corrections agencies as an aid to control and monitor offenders. The use of technology has changed the roles and responsibilities of officers and can be expected to grow more abundant in the future. Developments in the use of the Global Positioning System (GPS) may well be applied to monitoring offenders in the future (Mays & Winfree, 2000). Advances in technology offer advantages in offender supervision, and will enable probation officers to monitor and track more offenders more efficiently (Scott, 1996). Using portable laptop computers in their offices and in their automobiles will enable officers to gain access to offender case files and to record chronological and contact reports as they are completed. Greater use of technology also raises questions about the direction of juvenile corrections. Technology aids in monitoring offenders, and enhances the control or punishment function of probation. It will *not*, however, eliminate the challenges of changing offender behavior, and may actually reduce the amount of personal contact and interpersonal communication between workers and clients that is considered essential for long-term offender change.

Responding to More Demands With Fewer Resources

Juvenile court and corrections workers will have to find ways to meet the growing demands with fewer resources in the future. There is likely to be a growing tendency for the juvenile justice system to develop and implement policy responses based on the worst crimes and on the most publicized cases that are in fact "behavioral anomalies" (Mays & Winfree, 2000, p. 363). School shootings involving multiple fatalities are a case in point. Although victims of school shooting incidents involve no more than 1% of juvenile homicide cases per year, the media attention focused on the judicial process in these few cases puts the court under public scrutiny (Lawrence & Mueller, 2003). The media, however, do reflect a public concern with serious and violent juvenile offenders. From a practical standpoint, it makes sense for the juvenile justice process to focus on the most serious and violent crimes. In the face of limited resources, it is necessary to identify this small group from among all the other serious offenders (Walker, 1998, p. 70). A policy of directing limited resources to maximize benefits is supported by research and practice in Orange County, California, where juvenile probation administrators found that a majority of crimes were committed by only a small percentage (8%) of the most chronic, habitual offenders (Schumacher & Kurz, 1999). They documented the characteristics of this small group of chronic juvenile offenders and found that they could be reliably identified after the first contact with the juvenile justice system. An evaluation of the probation department's "8% solution" has shown that the number of chronic juvenile recidivists can be reduced through a coordinated program of early intervention and treatment of high-risk youth and families (Office of Juvenile Justice and Delinquency Prevention, 2001).

Delinquency Prevention and Juvenile Justice for the 21st Century

Juvenile justice has a long history during which a variety of correctional interventions have been tried, ranging from punishment to different methods of treatment interventions. Considerable debate has ensued around the question of whether correctional programs have been effective in changing offenders (Martinson, 1974). Murray and Cox (1979) argued that juvenile institutions have a "suppression effect" and have been a more effective deterrent to delinquency than community-based corrections programs. Others have raised questions about that conclusion, however, with evidence indicating that community-based treatment is as effective as juvenile residential programs, without the detrimental effects of institutionalization (Lundman, 1986; Whitehead & Lab, 2006). The juvenile justice process has several limitations as a primary source of delinquency prevention, for a number of reasons: (a) The justice system is always a "reactive" response, not "proactive" or preventive. The juvenile court can intervene only after a juvenile's delinquent involvement is serious or persistent enough to warrant police arrest and referral. Delinquency prevention is more effective

Photo 14.2 Involving youth in prosocial activities is important for delinquency prevention, such as these youth painting a wall mural over gang graffiti.

at an early age, before the onset of more serious behavior (Hawkins & Lishner, 1987). (b) Correctional agencies may actually promote rather than prevent delinquency, by bringing offenders together and isolating them from the community. Juvenile correctional institutions have been called "schools for crime," where young offenders' delinquent tendencies often became worse (Tannenbaum, 1938). Criminologists have suggested that group interventions such as positive peer culture and guided group interaction used in juvenile institutions may actually maintain and enhance delinquent behavior of the youth (Elliott, Huizinga, & Ageton, 1985, p. 149; Gottfredson, 1987, p. 710). The factors that generate and influence delinquent behavior usually lie within the community, the family, and the school—factors that are for the most part beyond the power of correctional agencies to change. Delinquency prevention requires a coordinated and consolidated effort of the entire community (Sherman et al., 1997). A proactive approach to delinquency prevention must include community-wide efforts to address unequal educational opportunities, unemployment, poverty, and racism. This requires the combined efforts of lawmakers with the support of citizens. Delinquency prevention requires long-range, comprehensive programs that combine the coordinated efforts of multiple agencies. Such programs will be expensive and require financial commitments that many voters and legislators will be reluctant to accept. The threat of punitive sanctions has little deterrent effect on desperate youth who foresee little future for themselves. A comprehensive strategy of delinquency prevention must offer more opportunities for at-risk youth to experience positive alternatives and to succeed in productive social and economic roles.

A Public Health Approach to Delinquency Prevention

Despite the fact that there are many serious mental and physical health consequences of crime and violence, crime has been addressed solely by the criminal justice system and not as a concern for the public health system. The juvenile justice system, through law enforcement, the courts, and corrections agencies, responds to crime after it has occurred; but it cannot stem the increase in violence by and against youth. Former U.S. Surgeon General Koop and his colleague Lundberg (1992) argued that a **public health approach** could be effective for preventing youth violence. The public health approach addresses critical health concerns by placing emphasis on primary prevention; that is, prevention taking place before the onset of disease or injury. The main features of the public health model are: (a) community-based methods for problem identification; (b) data collection to track incidents, trends, and relevant risk factors; intervention design and evaluation; and (c) outreach, education, and information dissemination (Hamburg, 1998, p. 40). The public health approach to delinquency prevention differs from a law-and-order approach in that it views violence as a threat to community health rather than community order, and follows scientific principles in primary prevention strategies as opposed to a reactive approach to the problem. Welsh (2005) emphasizes that this new approach should be seen not as a challenge to law and order, but rather as a complementary effort to create a more balanced and comprehensive strategy for preventing and reducing juvenile crime and violence.

POLICY AND PRACTICE 14.4 | **DELINQUENCY PREVENTION AND INTERVENTION PROGRAMS FOR THE 21ST CENTURY**

Many high-quality studies have identified programs that prevent or reduce delinquency. Five points that summarize what works to prevent juvenile crime include:

- For youth in community settings, family-based programs that work with the juvenile and the family have proven effective.
- For youth in institutional settings, treatments that base therapy on learning what goals youth have for their life and then helping them achieve those goals are effective.

(Continued)

(Continued)

- Programs that are excessively harsh or punitive have either no effects or are counter-productive.
- Incarceration is expensive and yields few if any benefits other than short-term incapacitation.
- Even the best evidence-based programs must be fully and faithfully implemented if they are to produce the effects that the evidence shows they can.

Peter Greenwood has summarized a number of "proven" or "promising" delinquency prevention and intervention programs that have been identified by evaluation researchers. Some of the outstanding programs are summarized here under the categories of Prevention Programs, Community-Based Interventions, and Institutional Settings.

Prevention Programs

- *Nurse Home Visitation Programs:* Trains and supervises registered nurses as home visitors, to provide child-care training and social skills development for mothers. Results show reduced child abuse and neglect, lower arrest rates for the children and the mothers.
- *Bullying Prevention Program:* Involves teachers and parents in setting and enforcing clear rules against bullying. Bullying problems have declined 50% in treated schools.
- *Life Skills Training:* A classroom-based approach to substance abuse prevention; has reduced alcohol, cigarette, and marijuana use among participants.
- *Project STATUS:* A school-based program to improve junior and senior high school climate and reduce delinquency and dropout; has resulted in less delinquency, drug use, and negative peer pressure and greater academic success and social bonding.
- *School Transitional Environmental Program (STEP):* Aims to improve school climate, peer and teacher support, and reduce student academic and emotional difficulties. Evaluations show decreased absenteeism and dropout, more academic success, and more positive feelings about school.

Community-Based Interventions

- For youth on probation or aftercare/parole who are returning to the community after a residential placement.
- *Functional Family Therapy (FFT):* For youth facing problems with delinquency, substance abuse, or violence. Aims to improve the functioning of the family unit by improving family problem-solving skills and emotional connections, and strengthen parents' ability to provide structure and guidance and set limits for their children.
- *Multisystemic Therapy (MST):* Designed to help parents deal effectively with their youth's behavior problems, including engaging with deviant peers and poor school performance.
- *Intensive Protective Supervision (IPS):* Targets nonserious status offenders. Counselors make frequent home visits, provide support for parents, develop individualized service plans, and arrange for professional or therapeutic services as needed.

Institutional Settings

- Three program strategies improve institutional program effectiveness:

  o Focus on dynamic or changeable risk factors—low skills, substance abuse, defiant behavior, delinquent peer relationships
  o Tailor programs to clients' needs using evidence-based methods
  o Focus interventions on high-risk youth

- The Correctional Program Inventory (CPI) is a program assessment instrument to evaluate the quality of program services and delivery.
- Good correctional programs are effective only if they are implemented and maintained as originally designed.
- Programs that support mental health issues are more successful than those that focus on punishment; and those administered by mental health professionals are more effective than those delivered by regular correctional staff.
- Programs that focus on specific skills issues such as behavior management, interpersonal skills training, family counseling, group counseling, or individual counseling have all demonstrated positive effects in institutional settings.
- Programs that work well with institutionalized youth are cognitive–behavioral therapy, aggression replacement training, and family integrated transition.
- Family integrated transitions (FIT) focus on tackling dynamic risk factors—substance abuse, mental health issues, and community reentry from residential placement.
- Policymakers and juvenile justice administrators would do well to follow these prescriptions for "best practices" for delinquency prevention and intervention in the 21st century.

SOURCE: Greenwood, P. (2008). Prevention and intervention programs for juvenile offenders. *Future of Children, 18*(2), 185–210; Steinberg, L., & Haskins, R. (2008). Policy brief: Keeping adolescents out of prison. *Future of Children, 18*(2), 1–7. Retrieved January 22, 2009, from http://www.futureofchildren.org/pubs-inf02825/pubs-info_show.htm?doc_id=708717.

Discussion Questions

1. Based on what you have read and learned about the causes of delinquency and the challenges of correcting juvenile offenders, list and discuss five of the above programs and how they may be effective in preventing delinquency or reducing recidivism.

2. As you review the above programs, are the knowledge, skills, and qualifications to administer them primarily criminal justice? Counseling and psychology? Social work? Or other disciplines?

What does your answer suggest about the preparation and education required for juvenile probation officers and corrections counselors who want to be qualified to deliver and administer the most effective prevention and intervention programs?

Redefining Juvenile Justice Objectives

Juvenile justice administrators and researchers have called for a revitalized juvenile justice system in the 21st century. With a focus on chronic and serious juvenile offenders, there has been a call to make it clear to young people that they will be held accountable if they break the law. It is clear that a system of graduated sanctions must be developed so that agencies can make immediate responses to juvenile crime with appropriate sanctions. Recognizing that much delinquent behavior is associated with problems in families, schools, and the community, effective interventions and treatment programs must be developed. The balanced and restorative justice model (discussed in Chapter 13) provides the framework for redefining juvenile justice objectives (Bazemore & Umbreit, 1995). The model is being adopted in juvenile justice agencies throughout the United States as a means for balancing the needs of victims, the community, and the juvenile. An effective juvenile justice system must meet three objectives: (1) hold the juvenile offender accountable; (2) enable the juvenile to become a capable, productive, and responsible citizen; and (3) ensure the safety of the community (Bilchik, 1998, p. 90). In order to meet these objectives, the juvenile justice system must have the support and cooperation of community agencies, including health (and mental health) providers, schools, and social services, working together with law

SOURCE: ©Will & Deni McIntyre/Corbis.

Photo 14.3　A comprehensive strategy for delinquency prevention emphasizes a cooperative effort of parents, schools, counselors, and community agencies working with the juvenile justice system.

enforcement and the juvenile court (Bilchik, 1998). This interagency cooperation must include more frequent and open communication and information sharing. To develop a more effective juvenile justice system it is essential to place equal emphasis on the goals of victim assistance, offender accountability, and public safety.

A Comprehensive Approach to Juvenile Justice

A comprehensive strategy to help communities prevent delinquency and establish a more effective juvenile justice system was developed by two administrators of the Office of Juvenile Justice and Delinquency Prevention (OJJDP; Wilson & Howell, 1993; Howell, 2003). They summarized the available research and received input from researchers and practitioners on the policies and practices that appear to be most effective in reducing and preventing juvenile offending. Because the comprehensive strategy was based on research on the causes and correlates of delinquent behavior, it focused more on prevention than on law-and-order responses. Social institutions such as schools and youth-serving organizations, faith-based groups, recreational services, and cultural organizations in the community were important components of effective prevention strategies (Howell, 2003; Krisberg, 2005). Research has indicated that there is a relatively small number of chronic, serious, and violent juvenile offenders. The comprehensive strategy is to identify these offenders through assessment, use graduated sanctions to control them, and provide a range of services for early intervention, prevention, and treatment programming with juvenile justice responses (Bilchik, 1998; Howell, 2003; Krisberg, 2005). Implementing the comprehensive strategy for an effective juvenile justice system will require statutory changes to include prevention, intervention, and treatment in the purpose clauses of state juvenile codes. Effective implementation of the strategy will require coordination and oversight by a state-level agency that focuses on juvenile justice matters; local and regional advisory boards and offices to develop and manage service-delivery programs; and funding mechanisms by which the state gives financial incentives to local juvenile justice programs to reduce the number of commitments to state juvenile facilities (Bilchik, 1998; Howell, 2003). The comprehensive strategy was for a time the official policy view of the U.S. Department of Justice, and was implemented in nearly 50 communities (Krisberg, 2005). Although the strategy has not been a focal point for the OJJDP in the past decade, if properly implemented and adequately funded, expected benefits include (a) increased juvenile justice system responsiveness; (b) increased juvenile accountability; (c) decreased costs of juvenile corrections; and (d) increased program effectiveness (Bilchik, 1998, pp. 96–97). We believe that a comprehensive strategy is essential, and is the only approach that shows promise for effectively preventing and reducing juvenile crime while reducing the growing costs of controlling and punishing juvenile offenders. There are no easy or simple solutions to preventing and responding to the complexities and problems posed by juvenile crime and violence. The question is not whether we have the knowledge and ability to respond to the problem, but whether we have the will and determination to commit adequate funds and resources to implement the best evidence-based practices.

SUMMARY

- The historical foundation of juvenile justice and developments through the past 100 years will continue to have an influence on juvenile justice policies in the future.
- Social factors including poverty, racial and ethnic biases, and a "culture of control" will affect the future of juvenile justice.
- Policies and strategies for juvenile justice in the 21st century must address poverty and the sense of hopelessness among many youth, and must limit the easy access to handguns among youth.
- The public health model and the comprehensive approach to delinquency prevention represent promising strategies for the future of juvenile justice.

KEY TERMS

Decriminalization of status offenders

Diversion

Due process rights

Deinstitutionalization

Diversification of services

Decentralization of services

"Law and order"

"Get-tough"

Social factors

Individual responsibility

Poverty and crime

Officer qualifications

Correctional crowding

Correctional litigation

Correctional technology

Correctional demands

Correctional resources

Delinquency prevention

Public health approach

Comprehensive approach

DISCUSSION QUESTIONS

1. Based on your understanding of the history and past developments in juvenile justice, list and briefly explain five issues that are likely to be important for the future of juvenile justice.

2. Based on what you have read, what social, cultural, and political factors do you believe will continue to have the greatest impact on juvenile offending? What is the relationship between poverty and delinquency? What policies would you recommend for dealing with poverty and other social, cultural, and political factors to reduce juvenile offending?

3. The question of whether to punish juveniles who commit violent crime draws a variety of strong opinions from most Americans. Based on your reading of the inconsistencies in juvenile age and responsibilities, U.S. Supreme Court arguments, and scientific evidence on brain development of juveniles, how is this inconsistency likely to be resolved in the 21st century?

4. Based on the proposed changes that are likely to face juvenile justice workers in the future, what do you believe are some of the qualifications and skills that will be most important for successfully working in this field in the future?

5. What do you believe are three advantages of the public health model or the comprehensive strategy for meeting the challenges of juvenile crime and violence in the future?

WEB RESOURCES

Office of Juvenile Justice and Delinquency Prevention (OJJDP) programs and initiatives: http://ojjdp.ncjrs.org/

Guide for Impl ementing the Comprehensive Strategy, OJJDP: http://www.ncjrs.gov/pdffiles/guide.pdf

National Juvenile Justice Action Plan, OJJDP: http://www.ncjrs.gov/pdffiles/165925.pdf

Public Health strategy to reduce gun violence, OJJDP: http://www.ncjrs.gov/pdffiles1/yfs9903.pdf

The Future of Children—Policies and programs for children: http://www.futureofchildren.org/index.htm

References

Addington, L. A., Ruddy, S. A., Miller, A. K., DeVoe, J. F., & Chandler, K. A. (2002). *Are America's schools safe? Students speak out: 1999 school crime supplement.* Washington, DC: National Center for Education Statistics.

Adler, F. (1975). *Sisters in crime.* New York: McGraw-Hill.

Ageton, S. S., & Elliott, D. S. (1974). The effects of legal processing on delinquent orientations. *Social Problems, 22,* 87–100.

Agnew, R. (1991). The interactive effects of peer variables on delinquency. *Criminology, 29,* 47–72.

Agnew, R. (1992). Foundation for a general strain theory of crime and delinquency. *Criminology, 30,* 47–87.

Agnew, R. (2001). *Juvenile delinquency: Causes and control.* Los Angeles: Roxbury.

Agnew, R., & White, H. R. (1992). An empirical test of general strain theory. *Criminology, 30,* 475–499.

Aichhorn, A. (1936). *Wayward youth.* New York: Viking.

Akers, R. L. (1985). *Deviant behavior: A social learning approach* (3rd ed.). Belmont, CA: Wadsworth.

Akers, R. L. (1990). Rational choice, deterrence, and social learning theory in criminology. *Journal of Criminal Law and Criminology, 81,* 653–676.

Alexander, K., & Alexander, M. D. (2005). *American public school law* (6th ed.). St. Paul, MN: West.

Allen, F. A. (1981). *The decline of the rehabilitative ideal.* New Haven, CT: Yale University Press.

Allen-Hagen, B. (1991). *Children in custody 1989.* Washington, DC: Office of Juvenile Justice and Delinquency Prevention.

Altschuler, D., & Armstrong, T. (1984). Intervening with serious juvenile offenders: A summary of a study on community-based programs. In R. Mathias (Ed.), *Violent juvenile offenders: An anthology.* San Francisco: National Council on Crime and Delinquency.

Altschuler, D., & Armstrong, T. (1996). Aftercare not afterthought: Testing the IAP model. *Juvenile Justice, 3*(1), 15–25.

Altschuler, D., Armstrong, T., & MacKenzie, D. L. (1999). Reintegration, supervised release, and intensive aftercare. *OJJDP Juvenile Justice Bulletin.* Washington, DC: U.S. Department of Justice.

Altschuler, D. M., & Brash, R. (2004). Adolescent and teenage offenders confronting the challenges and opportunities of reentry. *Youth Violence and Juvenile Justice, 2*(1), 72–87.

Altschuler, D. M., & Brounstein, P. J. (1991). Patterns of drug use, drug trafficking, and other delinquency among inner-city adolescent males in Washington, D.C. *Criminology, 19,* 589–622.

American Academy of Child & Adolescent Psychiatry. (2002). *Facts for families: Children and TV violence.* Washington, DC: American Academy of Child & Adolescent Psychiatry. Retrieved July 16, 2008, from http://www.aacap.org/cs/root/facts_for_families/children_and_tv_violence

American Bar Association. (1995). *A call for justice: An assessment of access to counsel and quality of representation in delinquency proceedings.* Washington, DC: ABA Juvenile Justice Center.

American Bar Association. (2004). *Adolescence, brain development, and legal culpability.* Washington, DC: American Bar Association/Juvenile Justice Center. Retrieved April 30, 2009, from http://www.abanet.org/crimjust/juvjus/Adolescence.pdf

American Bar Association Center on Children and the Law. (2004). *National court improvement progress report.* Chicago: American Bar Association. Retrieved on February 3, 2007, from http://www.abanet.org/abanet/child/home.cfm

American Bar Association–Institute of Judicial Administration. (1980). *Juvenile justice standards relating to dispositions.* Cambridge, MA: Ballinger.

American Bar Association–Institute of Judicial Administration. (1982). *Juvenile standards relating to non-criminal misbehavior.* Cambridge, MA: Ballinger.

Armstrong, G. (1977). Females under the law—Protected but unequal. *Crime & Delinquency, 23,* 109–120.

Arrigo, B. A., & Schehr, R. C. (1998). Restoring justice for juveniles: A critical analysis of victim-offender mediation. *Justice Quarterly, 15,* 629–666.

Arum, R., & Beattie, I. R. (1999). High school experience and the risk of adult incarceration. *Criminology, 37,* 515–540.

Atkinson, A. J. (2001). School resource officers: Making schools safer and more effective. *Police Chief, 68*(3), 55–57, 60–62.

Auerhahn, K. (2006). Conceptual and methodological issues in the prediction of dangerous behavior. *Crime and Public Policy, 5*(4), 771–778.

Baker, M. L., Sigmon, J. N., & Nugent, M. E. (2001). Truancy reduction: Keeping students in school. *OJJDP Juvenile justice bulletin.* Washington, DC: U.S. Department of Justice.

Bandura, A. (1977). *Social learning theory.* Englewood Cliffs, NJ: Prentice Hall.

Bannister, A. J., Carter, D. L., & Schafer, J. (2001). A national police survey on juvenile curfews. *Journal of Criminal Justice, 29,* 233–240.

Barnes, G. M., Welte, J. W., & Hoffman, J. H. (2002). Relationship of alcohol use to delinquency and illicit drug use in adolescents: Gender, age, and racial/ethnic differences. *Journal of Drug Issues, 32*(1), 153–178.

Bartollas, C., Miller, S. J., & Dinitz, S. (1976). *Juvenile victimization: The institutional paradox.* Beverly Hills, CA: Sage.

Battin, S., Hill, K. G., Abbott, R., Catalano, R. F., & Hawkins, J. D. (1998). The contribution of gang membership to delinquency beyond delinquent friends. *Criminology, 36*(1), 93–115.

Bavolek, S. J. (2000). The nurturing parenting programs. *OJJDP Juvenile Justice Bulletin.* Washington, DC: U.S. Department of Justice. Retrieved February 17, 2009, from http://www.ncjrs.gov/pdffiles1/ojjdp/172848.pdf

Bazemore, G., & Day, S. E. (1996). Restoring the balance: Juvenile and community justice. *Juvenile Justice, 3*(1), 3–14.

Bazemore, G., & Umbreit, M. (1995). Rethinking the sanctioning function in juvenile court: Retributive or restorative responses to youth crime. *Crime & Delinquency, 41*(3), 296–316.

Bazemore, G., & Umbreit, M. (2001). A comparison of four restorative conferencing models. *OJJDP Juvenile Justice Bulletin.* Washington, DC: Office of Juvenile Justice and Delinquency Prevention.

Becker, H. S. (1963). *The outsiders.* New York: Free Press.

Beger, R. R. (2003). The "worst of both worlds": School security and the disappearing Fourth Amendment rights of students. *Criminal Justice Review, 28*(2), 336–354.

Bell, A. J., Rosen, L. A., & Dynlacht, D. (1994). Truancy intervention. *Journal of Research and Development in Education, 27,* 203–211.

Benekos, P. J., & Merlo, A. V. (2005). Juvenile offenders and the death penalty: How far have standards of decency evolved? *Youth Violence and Juvenile Justice, 3*(4), 316–333.

Benigni, M. D. (2004). Need for school resource officers. *FBI Law Enforcement Bulletin, 73*(5), 22–24.

Bennett, W. J., DiIulio, J. J., & Walters, J. P. (1996). *Body count: Moral poverty . . . and how to win America's war against crime and drugs.* New York: Simon & Schuster.

Bergsmann, I. R. (1989). The forgotten few: Juvenile female offenders. *Federal Probation, 5,* 73–78.

Bernard, T. J. (1992). *The cycle of juvenile justice.* New York: Oxford University Press.

Bilchik, S. (1998). A juvenile justice system for the 21st century. *Crime & Delinquency, 44*(1), 89–101.

Bishop, D. M. (1996). Race effects in juvenile justice decision-making: Findings of a statewide analysis. *Journal of Criminal Law and Criminology, 86,* 392–413.

Bishop, D. M. (2004). Reaction essay: Injustice and irrationality in contemporary youth policy. *Criminology & Public Policy, 4*(3), 633–644.

Bishop, D. M., & Frazier, C. E. (2000). Consequences of transfer. In J. Fagan & F. E. Zimring (Eds.), *The changing borders of juvenile justice: Transfer of adolescents to the criminal court* (pp. 227–276). Chicago: University of Chicago Press.

Bishop, D. M., Frazier, C. E., & Henretta, J. C. (1989). Prosecutorial waiver: Case study of a questionable reform. *Crime & Delinquency, 35,* 179–201.

Bishop, D. M., Frazier, C. E., Lanza-Kaduce, L., & Winner, L. (1996). The transfer of juveniles to criminal court: Does it make a difference? *Crime & Delinquency, 42*(2), 171–191.

Blauvelt, P. D. (1990, Fall). School security: "Who you gonna call?" *School Safety,* pp. 4–8.

Blumberg, A. (1979). *Criminal justice: Issues and ironies* (2nd ed.). New York: New Viewpoints.

Bortner, M. (1986). Traditional rhetoric, organizational realities: Remand of juveniles to adult court. *Crime & Delinquency, 32*(1), 53–73.

Browning, K., Huizinga, D., Loeber, R., & Thornberry, T. P. (1999). Causes and correlates of delinquency program. *OJJDP Fact Sheet.* Washington, DC: U.S. Department of Justice. Retrieved February 19, 2009, from http://www.ncjrs.gov/pdffiles1/fs99100.pdf

Bureau of Justice Statistics. (1988). *Report to the nation on crime and justice* (2nd ed.). Washington, DC: U.S. Department of Justice.

Burgess, R. J., Jr., & Akers, R. L. (1966). A differential association-reinforcement theory of criminal behavior. *Social Problems, 14,* 128–147.

Byrne, J. (1986). The control controversy: A preliminary examination of intensive probation supervision programs in the United States. *Federal Probation, 50,* 4–16.

Califano, J. A., Jr., & Colson, C. W. (2005, January). Criminal neglect. *USA Today Magazine,* pp. 34–35. Retrieved January 21, 2009, from http://www.casacolumbia.org/absolutenm/templates/OpEds.aspx?articleid=377&zoneid=29

Callahan, R. (1985). Wilderness probation: A decade later. *Juvenile & Family Court Journal, 36,* 31–35.

Campbell, A. (1990). Female participation in gangs. In C. R. Huff (Ed.), *Gangs in America* (pp. 163–182). Newbury Park, CA: Sage.

Cantelon, S., & LeBoeuf, D. (1997). Keeping young people in school: Community programs that work. *OJJDP Juvenile Justice Bulletin.* Washington, DC: U.S. Department of Justice.

Canter, R. (1982). Sex differences in self-report delinquency. *Criminology, 20,* 373–393.

Carnevale Associates. (2005). *New DARE program: Communications manual.* Darnestown, MD: Carnevale Associates. Retrieved May 18, 2009, from http://www.ncjrs.gov/app/publications/abstract.aspx?ID=233018

Carter, D. L. (1995). Community policing and D.A.R.E.: A practitioner's perspective. *BJA Bulletin.* Washington, DC: Bureau of Justice Assistance. Retrieved April 25, 2009, from http://www.ncjrs.gov/pdffiles/comdare.pdf

Centers for Disease Control. (2008a). Youth Risk Behavior Surveillance: United States, 2007. *Morbidity and Mortality Weekly Report, 57*(SS-4). Atlanta: Department of Health and Human Services. Retrieved January 30, 2009, from http://www.cdc.gov/HealthyYouth/yrbs/pdf/yrbss07_mmwr.pdf

Centers for Disease Control. (2008b). Youth violence prevention. Atlanta: Department of Health and Human Services. Retrieved May 18, 2009 from http://www.cdc.gov/ViolencePrevention/pub/PreventingYV.html

Cernkovich, S., & Giordano, P. (1979). A comparative analysis of male and female delinquency. *Sociological Quarterly, 20,* 131–145.

Cernkovich, S., & Giordano, P. (1987). Family relationships and delinquency. *Criminology, 25,* 295–321.

Charles, M. (1986). The development of a juvenile electronic monitoring program. *Federal Probation, 53,* 3–12.

Chesney-Lind, M. (1977). Judicial paternalism and the female status offender. *Crime & Delinquency, 23,* 121–130.

Chesney-Lind, M. (1989). Girls' crime and woman's place: Toward a feminist model of female delinquency. *Crime & Delinquency, 35*(1), 5–29.

Chesney-Lind, M. (1995). Girls, delinquency, and juvenile justice: Toward a feminist theory of young women's crime. In B. R. Price, & N. Sokoloff (Eds.), *The criminal justice system and women* (pp. 71–88). New York: McGraw-Hill.

Chesney-Lind, M., & Shelden, R. G. (1998). *Girls, delinquency, and juvenile justice* (2nd ed.). Belmont, CA: West/Wadsworth.

Clear, T. R., Cole, G. F., & Reisig, M. D. (2006). *American corrections* (7th ed.). Belmont, CA: Thomson Wadsworth.

Cloward, R., & Ohlin, L. (1960). *Delinquency and opportunity.* New York: Free Press.

Coates, R. B. (1990). Victim–offender reconciliation programs in North America: An assessment. In B. Galaway & J. Hudson (Eds.), *Criminal justice, restitution and reconciliation* (pp. 125–134). Monsey, NY: Criminal Justice Press.

Coates, R. B., Miller, A. D., & Ohlin, L. E. (1978). *Diversity in a youth correctional system: Handling delinquents in Massachusetts.* Cambridge, MA: Ballinger.

Cohen, L., & Felson, M. (1979). Social change and crime rate trends: A routine activities approach. *American Sociological Review, 44,* 588–608.

Cole, D. (1999). *No equal justice: Race and class in the American criminal justice system.* New York: New Press.

Colvin, M., & Pauly, J. (1983). A critique of criminology: Toward an integrated structural–Marxist theory of delinquency prevention. *American Journal of Sociology, 89,* 513–551.

Committee on the Rights of the Child. (2007). *Children's rights in juvenile justice.* Geneva: Office of the United Nations High Commissioner for Human Rights. Retrieved May 19, 2009 from http://www2.ohchr.org/english/bodies/crc/comments.htm

Conger, J. J., & Miller, W. C. (1966). *Personality, social class, and delinquency.* New York: Wiley.

Conley, D. J. (1994). Adding color to a black and white picture: Using qualitative data to explain disproportionality in the juvenile justice system. *Journal of Research in Crime and Delinquency, 31*(2), 135–148.

Cordner, G. W. (2005). Community policing: Elements and effects. In R. G. Dunham & G. P. Alpert (Eds.), *Critical issues in policing* (pp. 401–418). Long Grove, IL: Waveland.

Cornish, D. B., & Clarke, R. V. (Eds.). (1986). *The reasoning criminal: Rational choice perspectives on offending.* New York: Springer-Verlag.

Cothern, L. (2000). *Juveniles and the death penalty.* Washington, DC: Office of Juvenile Justice and Delinquency Prevention. Retrieved May 18, 2009, from http://ojjdp.ncjrs.org/publications/PubAbstract.asp?pubi=184748&ti=&si=&sei=&kw=&PreviousPage=PubResults&strSortby=&p=&strPubSearch=

Cullen, F. T. (2005). The twelve people who saved rehabilitation: How the science of criminology made a difference. *Criminology, 43*(1), 1–42.

Cullen, F. T., Eck, J. E., & Lowenkamp, C. T. (2002). Environmental corrections—A new paradigm for effective probation and parole supervision. *Federal Probation, 66*(2), 28–37.

Cullen, F. T., Fisher, B. S., & Applegate, B. K. (2000). Public opinion about punishment and corrections. In M. Tonry (Ed.), *Crime and justice: A review of research* (Vol. 27, pp. 1–79). Chicago: University of Chicago Press.

Cullen, F. T., & Gilbert, K. (1982). *Reaffirming rehabilitation.* Cincinnati, OH: Anderson.

Curry, G. D., Ball, R. A., & Fox, R. J. (1994). Gang crime and law enforcement recordkeeping. *National Institute of Justice Research in Brief.* Washington, DC: U.S. Department of Justice.

Curry, G. D., & Spergel, I. A. (1988). Gang homicide, delinquency, and community. *Criminology, 26,* 381–405.

Curtis, G. C. (1963). Violence breeds violence—perhaps? *American Journal of Psychiatry, 12,* 386–387.

Czajkoski, E. (1973). Exposing the quasi-judicial role of the probation officer. *Federal Probation, 37*(2), 9–13.

Davies, G., & Dedel, K. (2006). Violence risk screening in community corrections. *Criminology & Public Policy, 5*(4), 743–769.

Davis, S. M. (1980). *Rights of juveniles: The juvenile justice system* (2nd ed.). New York: Clark Boardman.

Death Penalty Information Center. (2007). *U.S. Supreme Court: Roper v. Simmons, No. 03-633.* Retrieved April 30,, 2009, from http://www.deathpenaltyinfo.org/article.php?scid=38&did=885

Decker, S. (1985). A systematic analysis of diversion: Net widening and beyond. *Journal of Criminal Justice, 13,* 206–216.

del Carmen, R. V. (1985). Legal issues and liabilities in community corrections. In L. F. Travis, III (Ed.), *Probation, parole, and community corrections: A reader* (pp. 47–70). Prospect Heights, IL: Waveland.

del Carmen, R. V., Parker, M., & Reddington, F. P. (1998). *Briefs of leading cases in juvenile justice.* Cincinnati, OH: Anderson.

Demuth, S., & Brown, S. L. (2004). Family structure, family processes, and adolescent delinquency:

The significance of parental absence versus parental gender. *Journal of Research in Crime and Delinquency, 41*(1), 58–81.

DeVoe, J. F., Peter, K., Kaufman, P., Ruddy, S. A., Miller, A. K., Planty, M., Snyder, T. D., & Rand, M. R. (2003). *Indicators of school and safety: 2003.* Washington, DC: U.S. Departments and Education and Justice.

DiIulio, J. D. (1996). How to stop the coming crime wave. *Manhattan Institute Civil Bulletin, 2,* 1–4.

Dinkes, R., Cataldi, E. F., Lin-Kelly, W., & Snyder, T. D. (2007). *Indicators of school crime and safety: 2007.* Washington, DC: U.S. Departments of Education and Justice. Retrieved February 21, 2009, from http://www.ojp.usdoj.gov/bjs/pub/pdf/iscs07.pdf

Dorfman, L., & Schiraldi, V. (2001). *Off balance: Youth, race and crime in the news. Building blocks for youth.* Retrieved May 18, 2009, from http://www.buildingblocksforyouth.org/media/

Dorn, M. (2004). How to start an SRO program: School resource officers serve as important liaisons between police departments and local schools. *Police, 28*(10), 16–18, 22–24.

Dorne, C., & Gewerth, K. (1995). *American juvenile justice: Cases, legislation and comments.* Bethesda, MD: Austin & Winfield.

Drennon-Gala, D. (1995). *Delinquency and high school dropouts.* New York: University Press of America.

Dryfoos, J. G. (1990). *Adolescents at risk.* New York: Oxford University Press.

Dunham, R. G., & Alpert, G. P. (1987). Keeping juvenile delinquents in school: A prediction model. *Adolescence, 22,* 45–57.

Ekstrom, R. B., Goertz, M. E., Pollack, J. M., & Rock, D. A. (1986). Who drops out of high school and why? Findings from a national study. *Teachers College Record, 87,* 356–373.

Elliott, D. S. (1994). Serious violent offenders: Onset, developmental course, and termination. *Criminology, 32*(1), 1–21.

Elliott, D. S., Ageton, S. S., & Canter, R. J. (1979). An integrated theoretical perspective on delinquent behavior. *Journal of Research in Crime and Delinquency, 16,* 3–27.

Elliott, D. S., Huizinga, D., & Ageton, S. E. (1985). *Explaining delinquency and drug use.* Beverly Hills, CA: Sage.

Elliott, D. S., & Voss, H. H. (1974). *Delinquency and dropout.* Lexington, MA: Lexington Books.

Ennett, S. T., Tobler, N. S., Ringwalt, C. L., & Flewelling, R. L. (1994). How effective is drug abuse resistance education? A meta-analysis of project DARE outcome evaluations. *American Journal of Public Health, 84,* 1394–1401.

Esbensen, F. (2000). Preventing adolescent gang involvement. *OJJDP Juvenile Justice Bulletin.* Washington, DC: U.S. Department of Justice.

Esbensen, F., & Huizinga, D. (1993). Gangs, drugs, and delinquency in a survey of urban youth. *Criminology, 31*(4), 565–589.

Esbensen, F., Huizinga, D., & Weiher, A. W. (1995). Gang and non-gang youth: Differences in explanatory factors. In M. W. Klein, C. L. Maxson, & J. Miller (Eds.), *The modern gang reader* (pp. 192–201). Los Angeles: Roxbury.

Esbensen, F., & Osgood, D. W. (1999). Gang resistance education and training (G.R.E.A.T.): Results from the national evaluation. *Journal of Research in Crime and Delinquency, 36*(2), 194–225.

Esbensen, F., & Winfree, L. T. (1998). Race and gender differences between gang and non-gang youth: Results from a multisite survey. *Justice Quarterly, 15*(3), 505–526.

Executive Office for Weed and Seed. (2004). *Frequently asked questions about Weed and Seed DEFY (Drug Education for Youth).* Washington, DC: U.S. Department of Justice. Retrieved February 21, 2009, from http://www.ojp.usdoj.gov/ccdo/pub/pdf/faqdefy.pdf

Fagan, J. (1989). The social organization of drug use and drug dealing among urban gangs. *Criminology, 27,* 633–669.

Fagan, J. (1990). Social processes of delinquency and drug use among urban gangs. In C. R. Huff (Ed.), *Gangs in America* (pp. 183–219). Newbury Park, CA: Sage.

Fagan, J. (1996). The comparative advantage of juvenile versus criminal court sanctions on recidivism among adolescent felony offenders. *Law and Policy, 18,* 77–113.

Fagan, J., & Guggenheim, M. (1996). Preventive detention and the judicial prediction of dangerousness for juveniles: A natural experiment. *Journal of Criminal Law and Criminology, 86,* 415–488.

Fagan, J., Hansen, K. V., & Jang, M. (1983). Profiles of chronically violent delinquents: Empirical test of an integrated theory. In J. Kleugel (Ed.), *Evaluating juvenile justice* (pp. 91–119). Beverly Hills, CA: Sage.

Farrington, D., Gallagher, B., Morley, L., St. Ledger, R., & West, D. (1986). Unemployment, school leaving, and crime. *British Journal of Criminology, 26,* 335–356.

Farrington, D. P. (1993). Understanding and preventing bullying. In M. Tonry (Ed.), *Crime and justice: A review of research* (Vol. 17, pp. 381–458). Chicago: University of Chicago Press.

Faust, F. L., & Brantingham, P. J. (1979). *Juvenile justice philosophy: Readings, cases and comments* (2nd ed.). St. Paul, MN: West.

Federal Bureau of Investigation. (2008). *Crime in the United States, 2007.* Washington, DC: U.S. Department of Justice. Retrieved January 30, 2009, from http://www.fbi.gov/ucr/cius2007/

Feld, B. C. (1977). *Neutralizing inmate violence: The juvenile offender in institutions.* Cambridge, MA: Ballinger.

Feld, B. C. (1988). *In re Gault* revisited: A cross-state comparison of the right to counsel in juvenile court. *Crime & Delinquency, 34,* 393–424.

Feld, B. C. (1989). The right to counsel in juvenile court: An empirical study of when lawyers appear and the difference they make. *Journal of Criminal Law & Criminology, 79,* 1185–1346.

Feld, B. C. (1993). Criminalizing the American juvenile court. In M. Tonry (Ed.), *Crime & justice: An annual review of research* (Vol. 17, pp. 197–280). Chicago: University of Chicago Press.

Feld, B. C. (1995). Violent youth and public policy: A case study of juvenile justice law reform. *Minnesota Law Review, 79,* 965–1128.

Feld, B. C. (1999a). *Bad kids: Race and the transformation of the juvenile court.* New York: Oxford University Press.

Feld, B. C. (1999b). Rehabilitation, retribution and restorative justice: Alternative conceptions of juvenile justice. In G. Bazemore & L. Walgrave (Eds.), *Restorative juvenile justice: Repairing the harm of youth crime* (pp. 17–44). Monsey, NY: Criminal Justice Press.

Feld, B. (2000). Legislative exclusion of offenses from juvenile court jurisdiction: A history and critique. In F. Fagan & F. E. Zimring (Eds.), *The changing borders of juvenile justice: Transfer of adolescents to the criminal court* (pp. 83–144). Chicago: University of Chicago Press.

Feld, B. (2003). The politics of race and juvenile justice: The "due process revolution" and the conservative reaction. *Justice Quarterly, 20,* 765–800.

Feld, B. (2004). Editorial introduction: Juvenile transfer. *Criminology & Public Policy, 4*(3), 599–603.

Felson, M. (1986). Linking criminal choices, routine activities, informal control, and criminal outcomes. In D. B. Cornish & R. B. Clarke (Eds.), *The reasoning criminal* (pp. 119–128). New York: Springer-Verlag.

Felson, M. (1994). *Crime and everyday life.* Thousand Oaks, CA: Pine Forge Press.

Ferdinand, T. N. (1991). History overtakes the juvenile justice system. *Crime & Delinquency, 37*(2), 204–224.

Ferguson, A. A. (2000). *Bad boys: Public schools in the making of black masculinity.* Ann Arbor: University of Michigan Press.

Fishbein, D. (1990). Biological perspectives in criminology. *Criminology, 28,* 27–72.

Ford, J. A. (2008). Nonmedical prescription drug use and delinquency: An analysis with a national sample. *Journal of Drug Issues, 38*(2), 493–516. Retrieved February 19, 2009, from http://www.ncjrs.gov/app/Search/Abstracts.aspx?id=246076

Foster, J. D., Dinitz, S., & Reckless, W. C. (1972). Perceptions of stigma following public intervention for delinquent behavior. *Social Problems, 20,* 202–209.

Fox, J. A. (1996). *Trends in juvenile violence: A report to the United States Attorney General on current and future rates of juvenile offending.* Washington, DC: Bureau of Justice Statistics.

Friedman, W., Lurigio, A. J., Greenleaf, R., & Albertson, S. (2004). Encounters between police officers and youths: The social costs of disrespect. *Journal of Crime & Justice, 27*(2), 1–25.

Fritsch, E. J., Caeti, T. J., & Taylor, R. W. (1999). Gang suppression through saturation patrol, aggressive curfew, and truancy enforcement: A quasi-experimental test of the Dallas anti-gang initiative. *Crime & Delinquency, 45*(1), 122–139.

Galaway, B., & Hudson, J. (Eds.). (1990). *Criminal justice, restitution, and reconciliation.* Monsey, NY: Criminal Justice Press.

Gans, H. J. (1995). *The war against the poor: The underclass and antipoverty policy.* New York: Basic Books.

Garland, D. (2001). *The culture of control: Crime and social order in contemporary society.* Chicago: University of Chicago Press.

Garrett, C. (1985). Effects of residential treatment on adjudicated delinquents: A meta-analysis. *Journal of Research in Crime and Delinquency, 22,* 287–308.

Garry, E. M. (1996). Truancy: First step to a lifetime of problems. *OJJDP Juvenile Justice Bulletin.* Washington, DC: U.S. Department of Justice.

Gelles, R., & Straus, M. (1988). *Intimate violence.* New York: Simon & Schuster.

Gibbs, J. P. (1966). Conceptions of deviant behavior: The old and the new. *Pacific Sociological Review, 9,* 9–14.

Gies, S. V. (2003). After care services. *OJJDP Juvenile Justice Bulletin.* Washington, DC: U.S. Department of Justice.

Giordano, P. C., Cernkovich, S. A., & Pugh, M. D. (1986). Friendship and delinquency. *American Journal of Sociology 91,* 1170–1202.

Girod, R. J. (1999). Operation Linebacker: Using status offenses to reduce crime in communities. *FBI Law Enforcement Bulletin, 68*(7), 7–9. Retrieved April 25, 2009, from http://www.fbi.gov/publications/leb/1999/jul99leb.pdf

Girouard, C. (2001). School resource officer training program. *OJJDP Fact Sheet.* Washington, DC: U.S. Department of Justice.

Glueck, S., & Glueck, E. (1950). *Unraveling juvenile delinquency.* Cambridge, MA: Harvard University Press.

Goddard, H. (1920). *Efficiency and levels of intelligence.* Princeton, NJ: Princeton University Press.

Goldstein, H. (1977). *Policing a free society.* Cambridge, MA: Ballinger Publishing.

Gordon, R. A. (1987). SES versus IQ in the race–IQ–delinquency model. *International Journal of Sociology and Social Policy, 7,* 30–96.

Gottfredson, D. C. (2001). *Schools and delinquency.* Cambridge, UK: Cambridge University Press.

Gottfredson, G. D. (1987). Peer group intervention to reduce the risk of delinquent behavior: A selective review and a new evaluation. *Criminology, 25,* 671–714.

Gottfredson, M. R., & Hirschi, T. (1990). *A general theory of crime.* Stanford, CA: Stanford University Press.

Gove, W. R., & Crutchfield, R. D. (1982). The family and juvenile delinquency. *Sociological Quarterly, 23,* 301–319.

Gowdy, V. B. (1993). *Intermediate sanctions.* Washington, DC: U.S. Department of Justice.

Gray, E. (1988). The link between child abuse and juvenile delinquency: What we know and recommendations for policy and research. In G. T. Hotaling, D. Finkelhor, J. T. Kirkpatrick, & M. A. Straus (Eds.), *Family abuse and its consequences* (pp. 109–123). Newbury Park, CA: Sage.

Gray, J. P. (2003). The peer court experience. *Perspectives, 27*(4), 31–33.

Greenwood, P. (2008). Prevention and intervention programs for juvenile offenders. *Future of Children, 18*(2), 185–210. Retrieved January 22, 2009, from http://www.futureofchildren.org/information2826/information_show.htm?doc_id=710236

Greenwood, P., & Zimring, F. (1985). *One more chance: The pursuit of promising intervention strategies for chronic juvenile offenders.* Santa Monica, CA: RAND.

Griffin, P., Torbet, P., & Szymanski, L. (1998). *Trying juveniles as adults in criminal court: An analysis of state transfer provisions.* Washington, DC: U.S. Department of Justice.

Grisso, T. (1981). *Juveniles' waiver of rights: Legal and psychological competence.* New York: Plenum.

Grubb, W. N., & Lazerson, M. (1982). *Broken promises: How Americans fail their children.* New York: Basic Books.

Guevara, L., Spohn, C., & Herz, D. (2004). Race, legal representation, and juvenile justice: Issues and concerns. *Crime & Delinquency, 50*(2), 292–314.

Hagan, J., Gillis, A. R., & Simpson, J. (1985). The class structure of gender and delinquency: Toward a power–control theory of common delinquent behavior. *American Journal of Sociology, 90*(6), 1151–1178.

Hagan, J., Simpson, J., & Gillis, A. R. (1987). Class in the household: A power–control theory of gender and delinquency. *American Journal of Sociology, 92*(4), 788–816.

Hamburg, M. A. (1998). Youth violence is a public health concern. In D. S. Elliott, B. A. Hamburg, & K. R. Williams (Eds.), *Violence in American schools* (pp. 31–54). Cambridge, UK: Cambridge University Press.

Hamparian, D. M., Estep, L., Muntean, S., Priestino, R., Swisher, R., Wallace, P., & White, J. (1982). *Major issues in juvenile justice information and training youth in adult courts—Between two worlds.* Washington, DC: U.S. Department of Justice.

Hamparian, D. M., Schuster, R., Dinitz, S., & Conrad, J. (1978). *The violent few: A study of dangerous juvenile offenders.* Lexington, MA: Lexington Books.

Harmon, M. A. (1993). Reducing the risk of drug involvement among early adolescents: An evaluation of Drug Abuse Resistance Education (DARE). *Evaluation Review, 17,* 221–239.

Harris, M. K. (1998). Reflections of a skeptical dreamer: Some dilemmas in restorative justice theory and practice. *Contemporary Justice Review, 1*(1), 57–69.

Hawkins, J. D., & Catalano, R. (1992). *Communities that care.* Seattle, WA: Developmental Research Programs.

Hawkins, J. D., & Lishner, D. M. (1987). Schooling and delinquency. In E. H. Johnson (Eds.), *Handbook on crime and delinquency prevention* (pp. 179–221). New York: Greenwood.

Haynie, D., Simons-Morton, B., Beck, K. H., Shattuck, T., & Crump, A. D. (1999). Associations between parent awareness, monitoring, enforcement and adolescent involvement with alcohol. *Health Education Research, 14*(6), 765–775.

Heaviside, S., Cassandra, R., Williams, C., Farris, E., Burns, S., & McArthur, E. (1998). *Violence and discipline problems in U.S. public schools: 1996–97.* Washington, DC: U.S. Department of Education.

Helfer, R. E., & Kempe, C. H. (Eds.). (1976). *Child abuse and neglect: The family and the community.* Cambridge, MA: Ballinger.

Hemmens, C., & Bennett, K. (1999). Juvenile curfews and the courts: Judicial response to a not-so-new crime control strategy. *Crime & Delinquency, 45*(1), 99–121.

Hepburn, J. R. (1977). The impact of police intervention upon juvenile delinquents. *Criminology, 15,* 235–262.

Heron, M. P., & Smith, B. L. (2007). Deaths: Leading causes for 2003. *National Vital Statistics Reports, 55*(10), 1–96. Retrieved July 23, 2008, from http://www.cdc.gov/nchs/products/pubs/pubd/hestats/leadingdeaths03/leadingdeaths03.htm

Hill, K. G., Howell, J. C., Hawkins, J. D., & Battin-Pearson, S. R. (1999). Childhood risk factors for adolescent gang membership: Results from the Seattle Social Development Project. *Journal of Research in Crime and Delinquency, 36*(3), 300–322.

Hindelang, M. J. (1973). Causes of delinquency: A partial replication and extension. *Social Problems, 21,* 471–487.

Hinton, W. J., Sheperis, C., & Sims, P. (2003). Family-based approaches to juvenile delinquency: A review of the literature. *Family Journal: Counseling and Therapy for Couples and Families, 11*(2), 167–173. Retrieved February 17, 2009, from http://www.ncjrs.gov/App/Publications/abstract.aspx?ID=207022

Hirschi, T. (1969). *Causes of delinquency.* Berkeley: University of California Press.

Hirschi, T. (1986). On the compatibility of rational choice and social control theories of crime. In D. B. Cornish & R. V. Clarke (Eds.), *The reasoning criminal* (pp. 105–118). New York: Springer-Verlag.

Hirschi, T., & Hindelang, M. (1977). Intelligence and delinquency: A revisionist review. *American Sociological Review, 42,* 471–486.

Hoffer, A. (1975). The relation of crime to nutrition. *Humanist in Canada, 8,* 3–9.

Holden, G. A., & Kapler, R. A. (1995). Deinstitutionalizing status offenders: A record of progress. *Juvenile Justice (OJJDP), 2,* 3–10.

Horowitz, R. (1990). Sociological perspectives on gangs: Conflicting definitions and concepts. In C. R. Huff (Ed.), *Gangs in America* (pp. 37–54). Newbury Park, CA: Sage.

Howell, J. C. (2003). *Preventing and reducing juvenile delinquency: A comprehensive framework.* Thousand Oaks, CA: Sage.

Hsia, H. M., Bridges, G. S., & McHale, R. (2004). *Disproportionate minority confinement 2002 update.* Washington, DC: Office of Juvenile Justice & Delinquency Prevention.

Huff, C. R. (1989). Youth gangs and public policy. *Crime & Delinquency, 35*(4), 524–537.

Huff, C. R. (1990). *Gangs in America.* Newbury Park, CA: Sage.

Huizinga, D. (2005). *Effects of neighborhood and family structure on violent victimization and violent delinquency.* Washington, DC: Office of Juvenile Justice and Delinquency Prevention. Retrieved February 19, 2009, from http://www.ncjrs.gov/pdffiles1/ojjdp/grants/216000.pdf

Huizinga, D., Esbensen, F., & Weiher, A. W. (1991). Are there multiple paths to delinquency? *Journal of Criminal Law & Criminology, 82*(1), 83–118.

Huizinga, D., Loeber, R., & Thornberry, T. (1995). *Urban delinquency and substance abuse: Initial findings.* Washington, DC: Office of Juvenile Justice and Delinquency Prevention.

Huizinga, D., Loeber, R., Thornberry, T., & Cothern, L. (2000). Co-occurrence of delinquency and other problem behaviors. *OJJDP Juvenile Justice Bulletin.* Washington, DC: U.S. Department of Justice.

Huizinga, D., Menard, S., & Elliott, D. (1989). Delinquency and drug use: Temporal and developmental patterns. *Justice Quarterly, 6,* 419–455.

Hurst, Y. G., & Frank, J. (2000). How kids view cops: The nature of juvenile attitudes toward the police. *Journal of Criminal Justice, 28*(3), 189–202.

Ingersoll, S. (1997). The national juvenile justice action plan: A comprehensive response to a critical challenge. *Juvenile Justice, 3*(2), 11–20. Retrieved January 19, 2009, from http://www.ncjrs.gov/pdffiles/165925.pdf

Jarjoura, G. R. (1993). Does dropping out of school enhance delinquent involvement? Results from a large-scale national probability sample. *Criminology, 31,* 149–171.

Jarjoura, G. R. (1996). The conditional effect of social class on the dropout–delinquency relationship. *Journal of Research in Crime and Delinquency, 33*(2), 232–255.

Jensen, E. L., & Metsger, L. K. (1994). A test of the deterrent effect of legislative waiver on violent juvenile crime. *Crime & Delinquency, 40,* 96–104.

Jensen, G. F. (1973). Inner containment and delinquency. *Criminology, 64,* 464–470.

Johnson, I. M. (1999). School violence: The effectiveness of a school resource officer program in a southern city. *Journal of Criminal Justice, 27*(2), 173–192.

Johnson, R. E. (1979). *Juvenile delinquency and its origins.* Cambridge, UK: Cambridge University Press.

Johnson, R. E., Marcos, A. C., & Bahr, S. J. (1987). The role of peers in the complex etiology of adolescent drug use. *Criminology, 25,* 323–340.

Johnston, L. D., O'Malley, P. M., Bachman, J. G., & Schulenberg, J. E. (2008). *Various stimulant drugs show continuing gradual declines among teens in 2008, most illicit drugs hold steady* [Press release]. University of Michigan News Service: Ann Arbor, MI. Retrieved January 30, 2009, from http://www.monitoringthefuture.org/data/08data.html#2008data-drugs

Josephson, W. L. (1987). Television violence and children's aggression. *Journal of Personality and Social Psychology, 53,* 882–890.

Justice Policy Institute. (2000). Second chances: Giving kids a chance to make a better choice. *OJJDP Juvenile Justice Bulletin.* Washington, DC: U.S. Department of Justice. Retrieved January 8, 2009, from http://www.ncjrs.gov/pdffiles1/ojjdp/181680.pdf

Juvonen, J., & Graham, S. (Eds.). (2001). *Peer harassment in school: The plight of the vulnerable and victimized.* New York: Guilford.

Kempe, C. H., Kempe, R. S., Silverman, F. N., Steele, B. F., Droegemueller, W., & Silver, H. K. (1962). The battered-child syndrome. *Journal of the American Medical Association, 181,* 17–24.

Kempe, R. S., & Kempe, C. H. (1978). *Child abuse.* Cambridge, MA: Harvard University Press.

Kirkegaard-Sorensen, L., & Mednick, S. A. (1977). A prospective study of predictors of criminality: Intelligence. In S. A. Mednick & K. A. Christiansen (Eds.), *Biosocial basis of criminal behavior* (pp. 260–275). New York: Gardner.

Klinteberg, B. A., Magnusson, D., & Schalling, D. (1989). Hyperactive behavior in childhood and adult impulsivity: A longitudinal study of male subjects. *Personality and Individual Differences, 10*(1), 43–49.

Kobrin, S., & Klein, M. W. (1982). *National evaluation of the deinstitutionalization of status offender programs: Executive summary.* Washington, DC: U.S. Department of Justice.

Kohlberg, L. (1964). Development of moral character and moral ideology. In M. L. Hoffman & L. Hoffman (Eds.) *Review of child development research, Vol. I* (pp. 47–70). New York: Russell Sage Foundation.

Konopka, G. (1966). *The adolescent girl in conflict.* Englewood Cliffs, NJ: Prentice Hall.

Koop, C. E., & Lundberg, G. D. (1992). Violence in America: A public health emergency. *Journal of the American Medical Association, 267,* 3075–3076.

Kozol, J. (1991). *Savage inequalities.* New York: HarperCollins.

Krisberg, B. (2005). *Juvenile justice: Redeeming our children.* Thousand Oaks, CA: Sage.

Krisberg, B., & Austin, J. (1993). *Reinventing juvenile justice.* Newbury Park, CA: Sage.

Krisberg, B., Austin, J., & Steele, P. (1991). *Unlocking juvenile corrections.* San Francisco: National Council on Crime and Delinquency.

Krohn, M., Thornberry, T., Collins-Hall, L., & Lizotte, A. (1995). School dropout, delinquent behavior, and drug use. In H. Kaplan (Ed.), *Drugs, crime and other deviant adaptations: Longitudinal studies* (pp. 163–183). New York: Plenum.

Kumpfer, K. L., & Alvarado, R. (1998). Effective family strengthening interventions. *OJJDP Juvenile Justice Bulletin.* Washington, DC: U.S. Department of Justice.

Kupchik, A. (2004). Direct file of youth to criminal court: Understanding the practical and theoretical implications. *Criminology & Public Policy, 4*(3), 645–650.

Kurki, L. (2000). Restorative and community justice in the United States. In M. Tonry (Ed.), *Crime and justice: A review of research* (Vol. 27, pp. 235–303). Chicago: University of Chicago Press.

Kurlychek, M. C., & Johnson, B. D. (2004). The juvenile penalty: A comparison of juvenile and young adult sentencing outcomes in criminal court. *Criminology, 42*(2), 485–515.

Kurlychek, M. C., Torbet, P., & Bozynski, M. (1999). Focus on accountability: Best practices for juvenile court and probation. *JAIBG Bulletin.* Washington, DC: U.S. Department of Justice. Retrieved November 18, 2008, from http://www.ncjrs.gov/pdffiles1/177611.pdf

Lab, S., & Whitehead, J. (1988). Analysis of juvenile correctional treatment. *Crime & Delinquency, 34,* 60–83.

LaLonde, M. (1995, Fall). The Canadian experience: School policing perspective. *School Safety,* pp. 20–21.

Lane, J., Lanza-Kaduce, L., Frazier, C. E., & Bishop, D. M. (2002). Adult versus juvenile sanctions: Voices of incarcerated youths. *Crime & Delinquency, 48*(3), 431–455.

Lanza-Kaduce, L., Lane, J., Bishop, D. M., & Frazier, C. E. (2005). Juvenile offenders and adult felony recidivism: The impact of transfer. *Journal of Crime and Justice, 28,* 59–77.

Latessa, E. J. (1986). The cost effectiveness of intensive supervision. *Federal Probation, 50,* 70–74.

Latessa, E. J., & Allen, H. E. (2003). *Corrections in the community* (3rd ed.). Cincinnati, OH: Anderson.

Laub, J. H., & Sampson, R. J. (1988). Unraveling families and delinquency: A reanalysis of the Gluecks' data. *Criminology, 26,* 355–379.

Lauritsen, J. (2003). How families and communities influence youth victimization. *OJJDP Juvenile Justice Bulletin.* Washington, DC: U.S. Department of Justice. Retrieved February 20, 2009, from http://www.ncjrs.gov/pdffiles1/ojjdp/201629.pdf

Law Enforcement Assistance Administration. (1976). *Two hundred years of American criminal justice: An LEAA bicentennial study.* Washington, DC: U.S. Department of Justice.

Lawrence, R. (1983). The role of legal counsel in juveniles' understanding of their rights. *Juvenile & Family Court Journal, 34*(4), 49–58.

Lawrence, R. (1984). Professionals or judicial civil servants? An examination of the probation officer's role. *Federal Probation, 43*(4), 14–21.

Lawrence, R. (1985). School performance, containment theory, and delinquent behavior. *Youth and Society, 17,* 69–95.

Lawrence, R. (1991a). Reexamining community corrections models. *Crime & Delinquency, 37*(3), 449–464.

Lawrence, R. (1991b). School performance, peers and delinquency: Implications for juvenile justice. *Juvenile & Family Court Journal, 42*(3), 59–69.

Lawrence, R. (1995). Classrooms vs. prison cells: Funding policies for education and corrections. *Journal of Crime & Justice, 18,* 113–126.

Lawrence, R. (2007). *School crime and juvenile justice* (2nd ed.). New York: Oxford University Press.

Lawrence, R., & Mueller, D. (2003). School shootings and the man-bites-dog criterion of newsworthiness. *Youth Violence and Juvenile Justice, 1*(4), 330–345.

Lemert, E. M. (1951). *Social pathology.* New York: McGraw-Hill.

Lieber, M. J., Nalla, M. K., & Farnsworth, M. (1998). Explaining juveniles' attitudes toward the police. *Justice Quarterly, 15*(1), 151–174.

Linden, E., & Hackler, J. C. (1973). Affective ties and delinquency. *Pacific Sociological Review, 16,* 27–46.

Lindner, C. (2008). Probation intake: Gatekeeper to the family court. *Federal Probation, 72* (1), 48–53. Retrieved February 25, 2009, from http://www.uscourts.gov/fedprob/June_2008/1 3_probation_intake.html

Lipsey, M. W. (1992). Juvenile delinquency treatment: A meta-analytic inquiry into the variability of effects. In T. Cook, H. Cooper, & D. S. Cordray (Eds.), *Meta-analysis for explanation.* New York: Russell Sage.

Lipsey, M. W., Wilson, D. B., & Cothern, L. (2000). Effective intervention for serious juvenile offenders. *OJJDP Juvenile Justice Bulletin.* Washington, DC: U.S. Department of Justice.

Lipsitt, P. D., Buka, S. L., & Lipsitt, L. P. (1990). Early intelligence scores and subsequent delinquency: A prospective study. *American Journal of Family Therapy, 18,* 197–208.

Lipton, D., Martinson, R., & Wilks, J. (1975). *The effectiveness of correctional treatment: A survey of treatment evaluation studies.* New York: Praeger.

Liska, A. E., & Reed, M. D. (1985). Ties to conventional institutions and delinquency: Estimating reciprocal effects. *American Sociological Review, 50,* 547–560.

Livsey, S., Sickmund, M., & Sladky, A. (2009). Juvenile residential facility census, 2004: Selected findings. *Juvenile offenders and victims: National Report Series Bulletin.* Washington, DC: U.S. Department of Justice. Retrieved January 7, 2009, from http://www.ncjrs .gov/pdffiles1/ojjdp/222721.pdf

Loeber, R., & Farrington, D. P. (Eds.). (2001). *Child delinquents: Development, intervention, and service needs.* Thousand Oaks, CA: Sage.

Loeber, R., & Stouthamer-Loeber, M. (1986). Family factors as correlates and predictors of juvenile conduct problems and delinquency. In M. Tonry & N. Morris (Eds.), *Crime and justice: An annual review of research* (Vol. 7, pp. 29–149). Chicago: University of Chicago Press.

Lombroso, C. (1920). *The female offender.* New York: Appleton.

Lundman, R. J. (1986). Beyond probation: Assessing the generalizability of the delinquency suppression effect measures reported by Murray and Cox. *Crime & Delinquency, 32,* 134–147.

Lundman, R. J., Sykes, R. F., & Clark, J. P. (1990). Police control of juveniles: A replication. In R. A. Weisheit & R. G. Culbertson (Eds.), *Juvenile delinquency: A justice perspective* (2nd ed., pp. 107–115). Prospect Heights, IL: Waveland.

Lynch, J. P. (2002). Trends in juvenile violent offending: An analysis of victim survey data. *OJJDP Juvenile Justice Bulletin.* Washington, DC: U.S. Department of Justice.

Mack, J. W. (1909). The juvenile court. *Harvard Law Review, 23,* 104–122.

MacKenzie, D. L. (1994). Results of a multisite study of boot camp prisons. *Federal Probation, 58*(2), 60–66.

MacKenzie, D. L., Wilson, D. B., Armstrong, G. S., & Gover, A. R. (2001). The impact of boot camps and traditional institutions on juvenile residents: Perceptions, adjustment and change. *Journal of Research in Crime and Delinquency, 38*(3), 279–313.

Maguin, E., & Loeber, R. (1996). Academic performance and delinquency. In M. Tonry (Ed.), *Crime and justice: An annual review of research* (Vol. 20, pp. 145–262). Chicago: University of Chicago Press.

Males, M. (2000). *Kids and guns: How politicians, experts, and the media fabricate fear of youth.* Monroe, ME: Common Courage Press.

Malmgren, K., Abbott, R. D., & Hawkins, J. D. (1999). Learning disabilities and delinquency: Rethinking the link. *Journal of Learning Disabilities, 32,* 194–200.

Maloney, D., Romig, D., & Armstrong, T. (1988). The balanced approach to juvenile probation. *Juvenile and Family Court Journal, 39,* 1–49.

Martinson, R. (1974). What works? Questions and answers about prison reform. *Public Interest, 35,* 22–54.

Martinson, R. (1979). New findings, new views: A note of caution regarding sentencing reform. *Hofstra Law Review, 7,* 243–258.

Matsueda, R. L., & Heimer, K. (1987). Race, family structure, and delinquency: A test of differential association and social control theories. *American Sociological Review, 52,* 826–840.

Maxson, C. L., Whitlock, M. L., & Klein, M. W. (1998). Vulnerability to street gang membership: Implications for practice. *Social Service Review, 72,* 70–91.

May, D. C., Fessel, S. D., & Means, S. (2004). Predictors of principals' perceptions of school resource officer effectiveness in Kentucky. *American Journal of Criminal Justice, 29*(1), 75–93.

Mays, G. L., & Winfree, L. T. (2000). *Juvenile justice.* Boston: McGraw-Hill.

McCardle, L., & Fishbein, D. (1989). The self-reported effects of PCP on human aggression. *Addictive Behaviors, 4,* 465–472.

McCarthy, B. (1987). Preventive detention and pretrial custody in the juvenile court. *Journal of Criminal Justice, 15,* 185–200.

McCluskey, C. P., Bynum, T. S., & Patchin, J. W. (2004). Reducing chronic absenteeism: An assessment of an early truancy initiative. *Crime & Delinquency, 50*(2), 214–234.

McCord, J. (1982). A longitudinal view of the relationship between paternal absence and crime. In J. Gunn & D. P. Farrington (Eds.), *Abnormal offenders, delinquency, and the criminal justice system* (pp. 113–128). Chichester, UK: Wiley.

McCurley, C., & Snyder, H. N. (2008). Co-occurrence of substance use behaviors in youth. *OJJDP Juvenile Justice Bulletin.* Washington, DC: U.S. Department of Justice. Retrieved January 30, 2009, from http://www.ncjrs.gov/pdffiles1/ojjdp/219239.pdf

McDowell, E., Loftin, C., & Wiersema, B. (2000). The impact of youth curfew laws on juvenile crime rates. *Crime & Delinquency, 46,* 76–91.

McGarrell, E. F. (2001). Restorative justice conferences as an early response to young offenders. *OJJDP Juvenile Justice Bulletin.* Washington, DC: U.S. Department of Justice.

Mears, D. P. (2003). A critique of waiver research: Critical next steps in assessing the impacts of laws for transferring juveniles to the criminal justice system. *Youth Violence and Juvenile Justice, 1*(2), 156–172.

Mears, D. P., & Kelly, W. R. (1999). Assessments and intake processes in juvenile justice processing: Emerging policy considerations. *Crime & Delinquency, 45*(4), 508–529.

Menard, S., & Morse, B. J. (1984). A structuralist critique of the IQ-delinquency hypothesis: Theory and evidence. *American Journal of Sociology, 89,* 1347–1378.

Mennel, R. M. (1972). Origins of the juvenile court: Changing perspectives on the legal rights of juvenile delinquents. *Crime & Delinquency, 18,* 68–78.

Mennel, R. M. (1973). *Thorns and thistles.* Hanover, NH: University Press of New England.

Merton, R. K. (1957). *Social theory and social structure.* New York: Free Press.

Miller, A. K., & Chandler, K. (2003). *Violence in U.S. public schools: 2000 School Survey on Crime and Safety.* Washington, DC: U.S. Department of Education.

Miller, W. (1958). Lower class culture as a generating milieu of gang delinquency. *Journal of Social Issues, 14,* 5–19.

Minnesota Department of Corrections. (2009). *Thistledew Camp.* St. Paul: Minnesota Department of Corrections. Retrieved February 3, 2009, from http://www.doc.state.mn.us/facilities/togo.htm

Moffitt, T. E. (1990). Juvenile delinquency and attention deficit disorder: Boys' developmental trajectories from age 3 to age 15. *Child Development, 61,* 893–910.

Moffitt, T. E. (1993). Adolescence-limited and life-course-persistent antisocial behavior: A developmental taxonomy. *Psychological Review, 100*(4), 674–701.

Moffitt, T. E., Gabrielli, W. F., Mednick, S. A., & Schulsinger, F. (1981). Socioeconomic status, IQ, and delinquency. *Journal of Abnormal Psychology, 90*(2), 152–156.

Monahan, J. (1981). *Predicting violent behavior: An assessment of clinical techniques.* Beverly Hills, CA: Sage.

Moon, M. M., Sundt, J. L., Cullen, F. T., & Wright, J. P. (2000). Is child saving dead? Public support for juvenile rehabilitation. *Crime & Delinquency, 46*(1), 38–60.

Moore, M. H. (1992). Problem-solving and community policing. In M. Tonry & N. Morris (Eds.), *Crime and justice: An annual review of research: Vol. 15. Modern policing* (pp. 99–158). Chicago: University of Chicago Press.

Morash, M. (1984). Establishment of a juvenile police record. *Criminology, 22,* 97–111.

Morash, M. (1986). Gender, peer group experiences, and seriousness of delinquency. *Journal of Research in Crime and Delinquency, 25,* 43–61.

Morash, M., & Chesney-Lind, M. (1991). A reformulation and partial test of the power control theory of delinquency. *Justice Quarterly, 8,* 347–377.

Morris, N., & Tonry, M. (1990). *Between prison and probation.* New York: Oxford University Press.

Mueller, D., & Giacomazzi, A. (2003). Reeling in disengaged students: An assessment of a countywide juvenile court attendance program. *Juvenile & Family Court Journal, 54*(2), 25–39.

Murray, C., & Cox, L. (1979). *Beyond probation.* Beverly Hills, CA: Sage.

Myers, D. L. (2003a). Adult crime, adult time: Punishing violent youth in the adult criminal justice system. *Youth Violence and Juvenile Justice, 1*(2), 173–197.

Myers, D. L. (2003b). The recidivism of violent youths in juvenile and adult court: A consideration of selection bias. *Youth Violence and Juvenile Justice, 1,* 79–101.

Myers, S. M. (2002). *Police encounters with juvenile suspects: Explaining the use of authority and provision of support.* Washington, DC: National Institute of Justice.

National Advisory Commission on Criminal Justice Standards and Goals. (1973). *Corrections.* Washington, DC: U.S. Department of Justice.

National Advisory Commission on Criminal Justice Standards and Goals. (1976). *Report of the Task Force on Juvenile Justice and Delinquency Prevention.* Washington, DC: U.S. Department of Justice.

National Center for Children in Poverty. (2008). Ten important questions about *child poverty and family economic hardship.* New York: Columbia University. Retrieved February 5, 2009, from http://www.nccp.org/faq.html

National Clearinghouse on Child Abuse and Neglect Information. (1998). *Child maltreatment 1996: Reports from the states to the National Child Abuse and Neglect Data System.* Washington, DC: Government Printing Office.

National Commission on Children. (1991). *Beyond rhetoric: A new American agenda for children and families.* Washington, DC: Government Printing Office.

National Council of Juvenile and Family Court Judges. (2005). *Juvenile delinquency guidelines: Improving court practice in juvenile delinquency cases.* Reno, NV: National Council of Juvenile & Family Court Judges. Retrieved February 3, 2009, from http://www.ncjfcj.org/content/blog category/87/114/

National Institute of Justice. (2003). *Arrestee drug abuse monitoring: 2000 annual report.* Washington, DC: U.S. Department of Justice. Retrieved January 30, 2009, from http://www .ojp.usdoj.gov/nij/topics/drugs/adam.htm

National Research Council. (1993). *Losing generations: Adolescents in high-risk settings.* Washington, DC: National Academy Press.

National School Safety Center. (2008). *School-associated violent deaths.* Westlake Village, CA: National School Safety Center. Retrieved April 25, 2009, from http://www.schoolsafety.us/pub files/savd.pdf

Needleman, H., Gunnoe, C., Leviton, A., Reed, R., Peresie, H., Maher, C., & Barrett, P. (1979). Deficits in psychologic and classroom performance of children with elevated dentine lead levels. *New England Journal of Medicine, 300,* 689–695.

Needleman, H., Riess, J., Tobin, M., Biescecker, G., & Greenhouse, J. (1996). Bone lead levels and delinquent behavior. *Journal of the American Medical Association, 275,* 363–369.

Needleman, H., Schell, A., Bellenger, D., Leviton, A., & Allred, E. (1990). The long-term effects of exposure to low doses of lead in children. *New England Journal of Medicine, 322,* 83–88.

Nelson, M. (2008). Federal probe lingers in Florida boot camp death. *USAToday.com.* Retrieved May 18, 2009, from http://www.usatoday.com/ news/nation/2008-10-132468108240_x.htm

Office of Community Oriented Policing Services. (2003). *Promising strategies from the field: Community policing in smaller jurisdictions.* Washington, DC: U.S. Department of Justice. Retrieved February 22, 2009, from http://www.ncjrs.gov/App/Publications/abstract.aspx?ID=202694

Office of Community Oriented Policing Services. (2008). *Community policing defined.* Washington, DC: U.S. Department of Justice. Retrieved February 22, 2009, from http://www.cops.usdoj.gov/default.asp?item=36

Office of Juvenile Justice and Delinquency Prevention. (2001). The 8% solution. *OJJDP Fact Sheet.* Washington, DC: U.S. Department of Justice. Retrieved May 16, 2007, from http://www.ncjrs.gov/pdffiles1/ojjdp/fs200139.pdf

Offord, D. R., Sullivan, K., Allen, N., & Abrams, N. (1979). Delinquency and hyperactivity. *Journal of Nervous and Mental Disease, 167*(12), 734–741.

Ohlin, L. E. (1998). The future of juvenile justice policy and research. *Crime & Delinquency, 44*(1), 143–153.

Olweus, D. (1980). Familial and temperamental determinants of aggressive behaviour in adolescent boys: A causal analysis. *Developmental Psychology, 16,* 644–660.

Olweus, D. (1991). Bully/victim problems among schoolchildren: Basic facts and effects of a school based intervention program. In D. J. Pepler & K. H. Rubin (Eds.), *The development and treatment of childhood aggression* (pp. 411–448). Hillsdale, NJ: Lawrence Erlbaum.

Orpinas, P., Murray, N., & Kelder, S. (1999). Parental influences on students' aggressive behaviors and weapon carrying. *Health Education & Behavior, 26*(6), 768–781.

Packer, H. L. (1975). *The limits of the criminal sanction.* Stanford, CA: Stanford University Press.

Palmer, T. (1975). Martinson revisited. *Journal of Research in Crime and Delinquency, 12,* 133–152.

Pasternack, R., & Lyon, R. (1982). Clinical and empirical identification of learning disabled juvenile delinquents. *Journal of Correctional Education, 33*(2), 7–13.

Patchin, J. W., & Hinduja, S. (2006). Bullies move beyond the schoolyard: A preliminary look at cyberbullying. *Youth Violence & Juvenile Justice, 4*(2), 148–169.

Paternoster, R., & Mazerolle, P. (1994). General strain theory and delinquency: A replication and extension. *Journal of Research in Crime and Delinquency, 31,* 235–263.

Patterson, G. R., & Stouthamer-Loeber, M. (1984). The correlation of family management practices and delinquency. *Child Development, 55,* 1299–1307.

Perin, M. (2008). Return to D.A.R.E.: Armed with scientific credibility, the new D.A.R.E. program makes a comeback. *Law Enforcement Technology, 35*(10), 22, 24, 28. Retrieved April 30, 2009, from http://www.ncjrs.gov/App/Publications/abstract.aspx?ID=247525

Petersilia, J. (1993). Measuring the performance of community corrections. In BJS-Princeton Project (Eds.), *Performance measures for the criminal justice system* (pp. 61–84). Washington, DC: Bureau of Justice Statistics. Retrieved February 3, 2009, from http://www.ojp.usdoj.gov/bjs/pub/pdf/pmcjs.pdf

Piaget, J. (1932). *The moral judgment of the child.* London: Kegan Paul.

Piliavin, I., & Briar, S. (1964). Police encounters with juveniles. *American Journal of Sociology, 70,* 206–214.

Piquero, A., Farrington, D., Welsh, B., Tremblay, R., & Jennings, W. (2008). *Effects of early family/parent training programs on antisocial behavior and delinquency.* Washington, DC: U.S. Department of Justice. Retrieved February 19, 2009, from http://www.ncjrs.gov/pdffiles1/nij/grants/224989.pdf

Pisciotta, A. W. (1982). Saving the children: The promise and practice of *parens patriae,* 1838–98. *Crime & Delinquency, 28*(3), 410–425.

Platt, A. (1974). The triumph of benevolence: The origins of the juvenile justice system in the United States. In R. Quinney (Ed.), *Criminal justice in America: A critical understanding* (pp. 50–69). Boston: Little, Brown.

Platt, A. (1977). *The child savers: The invention of delinquency.* Chicago: University of Chicago Press.

Podboy, J. W., & Mallory, W. A. (1978). The diagnosis of specific learning disabilities in a juvenile delinquent population. *Federal Probation, 42,* 26–33.

Podkopacz, M. R., & Feld, B. C. (1996). The end of the line: An empirical study of judicial waiver. *Journal of Criminal Law and Criminology, 86,* 449–492.

Podkopacz, M. R., & Feld, B. C. (2001). The back-door to prison: Waiver reform, blended sentencing, and the law of unintended consequences. *Journal of Criminal Law and Criminology, 91,* 997–1071.

Pollak, O. (1950). *The criminality of women.* Philadelphia: University of Pennsylvania Press.

Pope, C. E., & Feyerherm, W. (1995). *Minorities in the juvenile justice system: Research summary.* Washington, DC: U.S. Department of Justice.

Pope, C. E., & Snyder, H. N. (2003). Race as a factor in juvenile arrests. *OJJDP Juvenile Justice Bulletin.* Washington, DC: U.S. Department of Justice.

Post, C. H. (1981). The link between learning disabilities and juvenile delinquency: Cause, effect and "present solutions." *Juvenile & Family Court Journal, 31,* 58–68.

Pranis, K. (1998). *Guide for implementing the balanced and restorative justice model.* Washington, DC: Office of Juvenile Justice and Delinquency Prevention.

President's Commission on Law Enforcement and Administration of Justice. (1967a). *The challenge of crime in a free society.* Washington, DC: Government Printing Office.

President's Commission on Law Enforcement and Administration of Justice. (1967b). *Task force report: Juvenile delinquency and youth crime.* Washington, DC: Government Printing Office.

Puzzanchera, C. M. (2003). Delinquency cases waived to criminal court, 1990–1999. *OJJDP Fact Sheet.* Washington, DC: U.S. Department of Justice.

Puzzanchera, C. M., & Sickmund, M. (2008). *Juvenile court statistics 2005.* Pittsburgh, PA: National Center for Juvenile Justice. Retrieved December 31, 2008, from http://www.ncjjserve http.org/NCJJWebsite/pdf/jcsreports/jcs2005.pdf

Quinney, R. (1974). *Criminal justice in America: A critical understanding.* Boston: Little, Brown.

Rankin, J. H. (1980). School factors and delinquency: Interactions by age and sex. *Sociology and Social Research, 64*(3), 420–434.

Rankin, J. H., & Kern, R. (1994). Parental attachments and delinquency. *Criminology, 32,* 495–515.

Reckless, W. C. (1961). A new theory of delinquency and crime. *Federal Probation, 25,* 42–46.

Reckless, W. C., Dinitz, S., & Kay, B. (1956). Self concept as an insulator against delinquency. *American Sociological Review, 21,* 744–746.

Redding, R. E. (2008). Juvenile transfer laws: An effective deterrent to delinquency? *OJJDP Juvenile Justice Bulletin.* Washington, DC: U.S. Department of Justice.

Redding, R. E., & Fuller, E. J. (2004). What do juvenile offenders know about being tried as adults? Implications for deterrence. *Juvenile and Family Court Journal, 55*(3), 35–45.

Redl, F., & Wineman, D. (1951). *Children who hate.* New York: Free Press.

Reiman, J. (1990). *The rich get richer and the poor get prison: Ideology, class, and criminal justice* (3rd ed.). New York: Macmillan.

Reynolds, K. M., Seydlitz, R., & Jenkins, P. (2000). Do juvenile curfew laws work? A time-series analysis of the New Orleans law. *Justice Quarterly, 17,* 205–230.

Romer, D., Jamieson, K. H., & deCoteau, N. J. (1998). The treatment of persons of color in local television news: Ethnic blame discourse or realistic group conflict? *Communication Research, 25*(3), 286–305.

Rosen, L. (1985). Family and delinquency: Structure or function. *Criminology, 23,* 553–573.

Rosenbaum, D. P., Flewelling, R. L., Bailey, S. L., Ringwalt, C. L., & Wilkinson, D. L. (1994). Cops in the classroom: A longitudinal evaluation of Drug Abuse Resistance Education (DARE). *Journal of Research in Crime and Delinquency, 31,* 3–31.

Rosenbaum, J. E. (1976). *Making inequality: The hidden curriculum of the high school.* New York: Wiley.

Rosenbaum, J. L., & Lasley, J. R. (1990). School, community context, and delinquency: Rethinking the gender gap. *Justice Quarterly, 7*(3), 493–513.

Roush, D. W. (1996). *Desktop guide to good juvenile detention practice.* Washington, DC: Office of Juvenile Justice and Delinquency Prevention.

Roush, D. W. (2004). Juvenile detention: Issues for the 21st century. In A. R. Roberts (Ed.) *Juvenile justice sourcebook* (pp. 217–246). New York: Oxford University Press.

Rowe, D. C., & Osgood, D. W. (1984). Heredity and sociological theories of delinquency: A reconsideration. *American Sociological Review, 49,* 526–540.

Rubin, H. T. (1985). *Juvenile justice: Policy, practice, and law* (2nd ed.). New York: Random House.

Rubin, H. T. (2001). A community imperative: Curbing minority overrepresentation in the juvenile justice system. *Juvenile Justice Update, 7*(2), 1–2, 14–16.

Rudman, C., Hartstone, E., Fagan, J., & Moore, M. (1986). Violent youth in adult court: Process and punishment. *Crime & Delinquency, 32*(1), 75–96.

Rumberger, R. W. (1983). Dropping out of high school: The influence of race, sex, and family background. *American Educational Research Journal, 20,* 199–220.

Rumberger, R. W. (1987). High school dropouts: A review of issues and evidence. *Review of Educational Research, 57,* 101–122.

Sampson, R. J., & Laub, J. H. (1997). A life-course theory of cumulative disadvantage and the stability of delinquency. In T. P. Thornberry (Ed.), *Developmental theories of crime and delinquency* (pp. 133–161). New Brunswick, NJ: Transaction Publishers.

Sanborn, J. B., Jr. (1996). Factors perceived to affect delinquent dispositions in juvenile court: Putting the sentencing decision into context. *Crime & Delinquency, 42*(1), 99–113.

Sanborn, J. B., Jr. (2003). Hard choices or obvious ones: Developing policy for excluding youth from juvenile court. *Youth Violence and Juvenile Justice, 1*(2), 198–214.

Sanborn, J. B., Jr., & Salerno, A. W. (2005). *The juvenile justice system: Law and process.* Los Angeles: Roxbury Publishing.

Schafer, W. E., Olexa, C., & Polk, K. (1972). Programmed for social class: Tracking in high school. In K. Polk & W. E. Schafer (Eds.), *Schools and delinquency* (pp. 33–54). Englewood Cliffs, NJ: Prentice Hall.

Schafer, W. E., & Polk, K. (1972). School conditions contributing to delinquency. In K. Polk & W. E. Schafer (Eds.), *Schools and delinquency* (pp. 181–238). Englewood Cliffs, NJ: Prentice Hall.

Schauss, A. (1981). *Diet, crime, and delinquency.* Berkeley, CA: Parker House.

Schneider, A. L. (1985a). *Guide to juvenile restitution.* Washington, DC: U.S. Department of Justice.

Schneider, A. L. (1985b). *The impact of deinstitutionalization on recidivism and secure confinement of status offenders.* Washington, DC: U.S. Department of Justice.

Schneider, A. L. (1986). Restitution and recidivism rates of juvenile offenders: Results from four experimental studies. *Criminology, 24,* 533–552.

Schneider, A. L. (2003). Community policing in action: A practitioner's view of organizational change. Washington, DC: Office of Community Oriented Policing Services. Retrieved February 23, 2009, from http://www.cops.usdoj.gov/files/RIC/Publications/communitypolicinginaction.pdf

Schneider, A. L., & Schram, D. D. (1986). The Washington state juvenile justice reform: A review of findings. *Criminal Justice Policy Review, 2,* 211–235.

Schneider, A. L., & Warner, J. (1989). *National trends in juvenile restitution programming.* Washington, DC: U.S. Department of Justice.

Schoenthaler, S., & Doraz, W. (1983). Types of offenses which can be reduced in an institutional setting using nutritional intervention. *International Journal of Biosocial Research, 4,* 74–84.

Schoenthaler, S., Doraz, W., & Wakefield, J. (1986). The impact of a low food additive and sucrose diet on academic performance in 803 New York City public schools. *International Journal of Biosocial Research, 8,* 185–195.

Schumacher, M., & Kurz, G. A. (1999). *The 8% solution: Preventing serious, repeat juvenile crime.* Thousand Oaks, CA: Sage.

Scott, E. S., & Steinberg, L. (2003). Less guilty by reason of adolescence: Developmental immaturity, diminished responsibility, and the juvenile death penalty. *American Psychologist, 58*(12), 1009–1018.

Scott, E. S., & Steinberg, L. (2008). Adolescent development and the regulation of youth crime. *Future of Children, 18*(2), 15–33. Retrieved May 19, 2009, from http://www.futureofchildren.org/usr_doc/18_2_02_Scott.pdf

Scott, L. (1996). Probation: Heading in new directions. In R. Muraskin & D. Sheppard (Eds.), *Visions for changes: Crime and justice in the twenty-first century* (pp. 172–183). Upper Saddle River, NJ: Prentice Hall.

Shaw, C. R., & McKay, H. D. (1942). *Juvenile delinquency and urban areas.* Chicago: University of Chicago Press.

Sheridan, W. H. (1969). *Legislative guide for drafting family and juvenile court acts.* Washington, DC: U.S. Children's Bureau.

Sherman, L. W. (1997). Policing for crime prevention. In L. W. Sherman, D. Gottfredson, D. MacKenzie, J. Eck, P. Reuter, & S. Bushway (Eds.), *Preventing crime: What works, what doesn't, what's promising* (pp. 8-1–8-58). Washington, DC: U.S. Department of Justice.

Sherman, L. W., Gottfredson, D., MacKenzie, D., Eck, J., Reuter, P., & Bushway, S. (Eds.). (1997). *Preventing crime: What works, what doesn't, what's promising.* Washington, DC: U.S. Department of Justice.

Sickmund, M. (2004). Juveniles in corrections. *Juvenile offenders and victims: National Report Series.* Washington, DC: U.S. Department of Justice. Retrieved January 30, 2009, from http://www.ncjrs.gov/pdffiles1/ojjdp/202885.pdf

Sickmund, M. (2006). Juvenile residential facility census, 2002: Selected findings. *Juvenile Offenders and Victims National Report Series Bulletin.* Washington, DC: U.S. Department of Justice. Retrieved December 5, 2008, from http://www.ncjrs.gov/pdffiles1/ojjdp/211080.pdf

Sickmund, M., Sladky, A., & Kang, W. (2008). *Easy access to juvenile court statistics: 1985–2005.* Pittsburgh, PA: National Center for Juvenile Justice. Retrieved December 31, 2008, from http://ojjdp.ncjrs.gov/ojstatbb/ezajcs/

Sickmund, M., Snyder, H. N., & Poe-Yamagata, E. (1997). *Juvenile offenders and victims: 1997 update on violence.* Washington, DC: Office of Juvenile Justice and Delinquency Prevention.

Simon, R. J. (1975). *Women and crime.* Lexington, MA: D. C. Heath.

Simons, R. L. (1978). The meaning of the IQ–delinquency relationship. *American Sociological Review, 43,* 268–270.

Simons, R. L., Wu, C., Conger, R. D., & Lorenz, F. O. (1994). Two routes to delinquency: Differences between early and late starters in the impact of parenting and deviant peers. *Criminology, 32*(2), 247–272.

Singer, S. I., & McDowell, D. (1988). Criminalizing delinquency: The deterrent effects of the New York juvenile offender law. *Law and Society Review, 22,* 521–535.

Skinner, B. F. (1953). *Science and human behavior.* New York: Macmillan.

Smith, B. (1998). Children in custody: 20-year trends in juvenile detention, correctional, and shelter facilities. *Crime & Delinquency, 44*(4), 526–543.

Snell, T. L. (2006). Capital punishment, 2005. *Bureau of Justice Statistics Bulletin.* Washington, DC: U.S. Department of Justice.

Snyder, H. N. (2004). Juvenile arrests 2002. *OJJDP Juvenile Justice Bulletin.* Washington, DC: U.S. Department of Justice.

Snyder, H. N. (2007). Juvenile arrests 2005. *OJJDP Juvenile Justice Bulletin.* Washington, DC: U.S. Department of Justice.

Snyder, H. N., & Sickmund, M. (2006). *Juvenile offenders and victims: 2006 national report.* Washington, DC: Office of Juvenile Justice and Delinquency Prevention.

Snyder, H. N., Sickmund, M., & Poe-Yamagata, E. (2000). *Juvenile transfers to criminal court in the 1990's: Lessons learned from four studies.* Washington, DC: Office of Juvenile Justice and Delinquency Prevention.

Sorenson, S. B., Manz, J. G. P., & Berk, R. A. (1998). News media coverage and the epidemiology of homicide. *American Journal of Public Health, 88,* 1510–1514.

Spergel, I., Chance, R., Ehrensaft, K., Regulus, T., Kane, C., Laseter, R., Alexander, A., & Oh, S. (1994). *Gang suppression and intervention: Community models—Research summary.* Washington, DC: Office of Juvenile Justice and Delinquency Prevention.

Spergel, I., Curry, D., Chance, R., Kane, C., Ross, R., Alexander, A., Simmons, E., & Oh, S. (1994). *Gang suppression and intervention: Problem and response: Research summary.* Washington, DC: Office of Juvenile Justice and Delinquency Prevention.

Sridharan, S., Greenfield, L., & Blakley, B. (2004). A study of prosecutorial certification practice in Virginia. *Criminology and Public Policy, 4*(3), 605–632.

Stahl, A. L. (2008). Drug offense cases in juvenile courts, 1985–2004. *OJJDP Fact Sheet.* Washington, DC: U.S. Department of Justice. Retrieved January 30, 2009, from http://www.ncjrs.gov/pdffiles1/ojjdp/fs200803.pdf

Stahl, A., Finnegan, T., & Kang, W. (2007). *Easy access to juvenile court statistics: 1985–2004.* Pittsburgh, PA: National Center for Juvenile Justice. Retrieved July 30, 2007, from http://ojjdp.ncjrs.gov/ojstatbb/ezajcs/

Steffensmeier, D. J., & Steffensmeier, R. H. (1980). Trends in female delinquency. *Criminology, 18*(1), 62–85.

Steinberg, L. (2000, April). Youth violence: Do parents and families make a difference? *National Institute of Justice Journal,* pp. 30–38.

Steinberg, L., Brown, B. B., & Dornbusch, S. M. (1996). *Beyond the classroom: Why school reform has failed and what parents need to do.* New York: Touchstone/Simon & Schuster.

Steinberg, L., & Haskins, R. (2008). Policy brief: Keeping adolescents out of prison. *Future of Children, 18*(2), 1–7; Retrieved May 19, 2009, from http://www.futureofchildren.org/usr_doc/FOC_Brief_Summer08.pdf

Steiner, B., & Wright, E. (2006). Assessing the relative effects of state direct file waiver laws on violent juvenile crime: Deterrent on irrelevance? *Journal of Criminal Law and Criminology, 96,* 1451–1477.

Straus, M. A., Gelles, R. J., & Steinmetz, S. K. (1980). *Behind closed doors: Violence in the American family.* Garden City, NY: Anchor/Doubleday.

Streib, V. L. (2005). *The juvenile death penalty today: Death sentences and executions for juvenile crimes, January 1973–February 28, 2005.* Retrieved December 3, 2007, from http://www.law.onu.edu/faculty_staff/faculty_profiles/coursematerials/streib/juvdeath.pdf

Substance Abuse and Mental Health Services Administration. (2002). *Results from the 2001 National Household Survey on Drug Abuse: Volume I. Summary of national findings.* Rockville, MD: National Clearinghouse for Alcohol and Drug Information.

Surette, R. (1998). *Media, crime, and criminal justice: Images and realities* (2nd ed.). Pacific Grove, CA: Brooks/Cole.

Sutherland, E. H., & Cressey, D. R. (1970). *Principles of criminology.* New York: J. B. Lippincott.

Tannenbaum, F. (1938). *Crime and the community.* New York: Columbia University Press.

Taylor, C. S. (1996). Growing up behind bars: Confinement, youth development, and crime. In Vera Institute of Justice (Ed.), *The unintended consequences of incarceration* (pp. 41–65). New York: Vera Institute of Justice. Retrieved November 7, 2008, from http://www.vera.org/publication_pdf/uci.pdf

Taylor, T. J., Turner, K. B., Esbensen, F., & Winfree, T. L. (2001). Coppin' an attitude: Attitudinal differences among juveniles toward police. *Journal of Criminal Justice, 29*(4), 295–305.

Thomas, W. I. (1923). *The unadjusted girl.* New York: Harper.

Thornberry, T. P. (1987). Toward an interactional theory of delinquency. *Criminology, 25,* 863–891.

Thornberry, T. P. (Ed.). (1997). *Developmental theories of crime and delinquency.* New Brunswick, NJ: Transaction Publishers.

Thornberry, T. P., & Hall, G. P. (2005). *The joint impact of family and community structure on violent delinquency.* Washington, DC: Office of Juvenile Justice and Delinquency Prevention. Retrieved February 19, 2009, from http://www.ncjrs.gov/pdffiles1/ojjdp/grants/215999.pdf

Thornberry, T. P., Krohn, M. D., Lizotte, A. J., & Chard-Wierschem, D. (1993). The role of juvenile gangs in facilitating delinquent behavior. *Journal of Research in Crime and Delinquency, 30*(1), 55–87.

Thornberry, T. P., Moore, M., & Christenson, R. L. (1985). The effect of dropping out of high school on subsequent criminal behavior. *Criminology, 23,* 3–18.

Thornberry, T. P., Smith, C. A., Rivera, C., Huizinga, D., & Stouthamer-Loeber, M. (1999). Family disruption and delinquency. *OJJDP Juvenile Justice Bulletin.* Washington, DC: U.S. Department of Justice.

Torbet, P. (1996). Juvenile probation: The workhorse of the juvenile justice system. *OJJDP Juvenile Justice Bulletin.* Washington, DC: U.S. Department of Justice.

Torbet, P., Gable, R., Hurst, H., Montgomery, I., Szymanski, L., & Thomas, D. (1996). *State responses to serious and violent juvenile crime: Research report.* Washington, DC: Office of Juvenile Justice and Delinquency Prevention.

Torbet, P., Griffin, P., Hurst, H., IV, & MacKenzie, L. R. (2000). *Juveniles facing criminal sanctions: Three states that changed the rules.* Washington,

DC: Office of Juvenile Justice and Delinquency Prevention.

Towberman, D. B. (1992). National survey of juvenile needs assessment. *Crime & Delinquency, 38*(2), 230–238.

Trojanowicz, R., & Bucquerox, B. (1990). *Community policing.* Cincinnati, OH: Anderson.

U.S. Census Bureau. (2008). Household income rises, poverty rate unchanged, number of uninsured down. *U.S. Census Bureau News.* Washington, DC: U.S. Census Bureau. Retrieved February 5, 2009, from http://www.census.gov/Press-Release/www/releases/archives/income_wealth/012528.html

U.S. Department of Health and Human Services. (2007). *Child maltreatment 2005.* Washington, DC: Superintendent of Documents. Retrieved April 30, 2009, from http://www.ncjrs.gov/App/Publications/abstract.aspx?ID=240753

VanderWaal, C. J., McBride, D. C., Terry-McElrath, Y. M., & VanBuren, H. (2001). *Breaking the drug-crime cycle: A guide for practitioners and policymakers.* Washington, DC: U.S. Department of Justice. Retrieved February 21, 2009, from http://www.ncjrs.gov/pdffiles1/nij/186156.pdf

Van Ness, D. W. (1990). Restorative justice. In B. Galaway & J. Hudson (Eds.), *Criminal justice, restitution, and reconciliation* (pp. 7–14). Monsey, NY: Criminal Justice Press.

Vaughn, J. B. (1989). A survey of juvenile electronic monitoring and home confinement programs. *Juvenile and Family Court Journal, 40,* 1–36.

Vaughn, M. S., & del Carmen, R. V. (1997). The fourth amendment as a tool of actuarial justice: The 'special needs' exception to the warrant and probable cause requirements. *Crime & Delinquency, 43,* 78–103.

Walker, S. (1998). *Sense and nonsense about crime and drugs* (4th ed.). Belmont, CA: West/Wadsworth.

Walsh, A. (1987). Cognitive functioning and delinquency: Property versus violent offenses. *International Journal of Offender Therapy & Comparative Criminology, 31,* 285–289.

Walters, G. D. (1992). A meta-analysis of the gene–crime relationship. *Criminology, 30,* 595–613.

Warr, M. (2000). Public perceptions of and reactions to crime. In J. Sheley (Ed.), *Criminology: A contemporary handbook* (3rd ed., pp. 13–31). Belmont, CA: Wadsworth.

Weiss, A., & Chermak, S. M. (1998). The news value of African-American victims: An examination of the media's presentation of homicide. *Journal of crime and Justice 21*(2), 71–88.

Wells, L. E., & Rankin, J. H. (1988). Direct parental controls and delinquency. *Criminology, 26,* 263–285.

Wells, L. E., & Rankin, J. H. (1991). Families and delinquency: A meta-analysis of the impact of broken homes. *Social Problems, 38,* 71–93.

Welsh, B. C. (2005). Public health and the prevention of juvenile criminal violence. *Youth Violence and Juvenile Justice, 3*(1), 23–40.

West, D. J., & Farrington, D. P. (1973). *Who becomes delinquent?* London: Heinemann.

Wheeler, G. R. (1971). Children of the court: A profile of poverty. *Crime & Delinquency, 17*(2), 152–159.

White, M. D., Fyfe, J. J., Campbell, S. P., & Goldkamp, J. S. (2001). The school–police partnership: Identifying at-risk youth through a truant recovery program. *Evaluation Review, 25*(5), 507–532.

Whitehead, J., & Lab, S. (1989). Meta-analysis of juvenile correctional treatment. *Journal of Research in Crime and Delinquency, 26,* 276–295.

Whitehead, J., & Lab, S. (2006). *Juvenile justice: An introduction.* Cincinnati, OH: Anderson/LexisNexis.

Widom, C. S. (1989a). Child abuse, neglect, and violent criminal behavior. *Criminology, 27,* 251–270.

Widom, C. S. (1989b). Does violence beget violence? A critical examination of the literature. *Psychological Bulletin, 106,* 3–28.

Wilkinson, J. H. (1996). Constitutionalization of school discipline: An unnecessary and counterproductive solution. *Michigan Law & Policy Review, 1,* 309–313.

Wilson, J. Q. (1968). *Varieties of police behavior.* Cambridge, MA: Harvard University Press.

Wilson, J. Q., & Herrnstein, R. J. (1985). *Crime and human nature.* New York: Simon & Schuster.

Wilson, J. W., & Howell, J. C. (1993). *A comprehensive strategy for serious, violent, and chronic juvenile offenders.* Washington, DC: U.S. Department of Justice.

Wolfgang, M. F., Figlio, R. M., & Sellin, T. (1972). *Delinquency in a birth cohort.* Chicago: University of Chicago Press.

Wooden, K. (1976). *Weeping in the playtime of others: America's incarcerated children.* New York: McGraw-Hill.

Wordes, M., Bynum, T. S., & Corley, C. J. (1994). Locking up youth: The impact of race on detention decisions. *Journal of Research in Crime and Delinquency, 31*(2), 149–165.

Wright, K. N., & Wright, K. E. (1994). *Family life, delinquency, and crime: A policymaker's guide.* Washington, DC: Office of Juvenile Justice and Delinquency Prevention.

Young, D., Moline, K., Farrell, J., & Bierie, D. (2006). Disseminating new assessment technologies in a juvenile justice agency. *Crime & Delinquency, 52*(1), 135–158.

Zahn, M., Brumbaugh, S., Steffensmeier, D., Feld, B., Morash, M., Chesney-Lind, M., Miller, J., Payne, A., Gottfredson, D., & Kruttschnitt, C. (2008). *Girls study group: Understanding and responding to girls' delinquency.* Washington, DC: Office of Juvenile Justice and Delinquency Prevention.

Retrieved July 11, 2008, from http://www.ncjrs .gov/pdffiles1/ojjdp/218905.pdf

Zehr, H., & Mika, H. (1998). Fundamental concepts of restorative justice. *Contemporary Justice Review, 1*(1), 47–55.

Zimmerman, J., Rich, W., Keilitz, I., & Broder, P. (1981). Some observations on the link between learning disabilities and juvenile delinquency. *Journal of Criminal Justice, 9,* 9–17.

Zimring, F. E. (1998). *American youth violence.* New York: Oxford University Press.

Zimring, F. E. (2000). Penal proportionality for the young offender: Notes on immaturity, capacity, and diminished responsibility. In T. Grisso & R. G. Schwartz (Eds.), *Youth on trial: A developmental perspective on juvenile justice* (pp. 271–290). Chicago: University of Chicago Press.

Zimring, F. E. (2005). *American juvenile justice.* New York: Oxford University Press.

Zingraff, M. T., & Belyea, M. J. (1986). Child abuse and violent crime. In K. C. Haas & G. P. Alpert (Eds.), *The dilemmas of punishment* (pp. 49–63). Prospect Heights, IL: Waveland.

Index

Supporting researchers for more than 40 years

Research methods have always been at the core of SAGE's publishing program. Founder Sara Miller McCune published SAGE's first methods book, *Public Policy Evaluation*, in 1970. Soon after, she launched the *Quantitative Applications in the Social Sciences* series—affectionately known as the "little green books."

Always at the forefront of developing and supporting new approaches in methods, SAGE published early groundbreaking texts and journals in the fields of qualitative methods and evaluation.

Today, more than 40 years and two million little green books later, SAGE continues to push the boundaries with a growing list of more than 1,200 research methods books, journals, and reference works across the social, behavioral, and health sciences. Its imprints—Pine Forge Press, home of innovative textbooks in sociology, and Corwin, publisher of PreK–12 resources for teachers and administrators—broaden SAGE's range of offerings in methods. SAGE further extended its impact in 2008 when it acquired CQ Press and its best-selling and highly respected political science research methods list.

From qualitative, quantitative, and mixed methods to evaluation, SAGE is the essential resource for academics and practitioners looking for the latest methods by leading scholars.

For more information, visit **www.sagepub.com**.